WHAT STALIN KNEW

WHAT STALIN KNEW THE ENIGMA OF BARBAROSSA

David E. Murphy

Yale University Press   New Haven & London

Designed by James J. Johnson and set in New Aster type by Keystone Typesetting, Inc.
Printed in the United States of America

ISBN 0-300-10780-3 (cloth : alk. paper)

In the early 1920s, Stalin and a few colleagues were relaxing in Morozovka Park, lying in the grass. One asked: "What's the best thing in the world?" "Books," replied one. "There is no greater pleasure than a woman, your woman," said another. Then Stalin said, "The sweetest thing is to devise a plan, then, being on the alert, waiting in ambush for a goo-oo-ood long time, finding out where the person is hiding. Then catch the person and take revenge!"

—MIKLOS KUN, *Stalin: An Unknown Portrait*

Contents

Acknowledgments

This book is the result of a suggestion by Jonathan Brent, editorial director of Yale University Press, who first brought to my attention the extensive collection of archival documents on Soviet intelligence being assembled by Aleksandr N. Yakovlev and members of his International Democracy Foundation in Moscow. Brent felt it would be a valuable contribution to an understanding of the events leading up to the German invasion of the USSR on June 22, 1941, if I, as a career intelligence officer, were to examine how the Soviet intelligence services functioned at that time and how Stalin reacted to the information they provided on the German threat. From the outset, Jonathan Brent and his staff at Yale University Press were unstinting in their support of my efforts. Special thanks to my copy editor, Roslyn Schloss, whose herculean work transformed this text.

My research has greatly benefited from the advice and assistance of friends and colleagues in the United States who brought to my attention publications on this subject. Robert Tarleton made available to me material from his own extensive library, as did Harriet Scott, who continues to follow Russian military affairs. My old friend William J. Spahr, Zhukov's biographer, was always ready to respond to my questions. Another friend, Hayden B. Peake, now curator of the CIA Historical Collection, encouraged me in my work, as did CIA historians Kevin C. Ruffner, Donald P. Steury, and Michael Warner. Serge Karpovich, a former colleague and longtime friend, was most helpful in housing me in Moscow, introducing me to friends and relatives there, and untangling particularly difficult Russian sentences encountered in translation.

I owe special thanks to Gennady Inozemtsev for his hospitality and that of his family in Moscow and his help in guiding me through the complexities of Russian bureaucracy and the Russian Internet. Very important was his contact on my behalf with Lidiya Ivanovna Morozova, General Proskurov's daughter, who shared her memories of her father. Sergei A. Kondrashev, my coauthor on *Battleground Berlin: CIA versus KGB in the Cold War,* also deserves mention for his efforts on my behalf in dealing with the Russian Foreign Intelligence Service (SVR) and for his hospitality in Moscow.

Finally, and most significantly, without the help of my wife, Star, this book would never have been finished. Her encouragement was constant, as were her proofreading and patient transformation of my rough chapters into acceptable computer form.

Sources

My principal resource in the research carried out in writing this book was the two-volume collection of documents *1941 god* (The Year 1941) published in Moscow in 1998 by the Mezhdunarodny Fond "Demokratiya" (International Democracy Foundation) in the series Rossiya—XX Vek. According to the principal editor, academician Aleksandr N. Yakovlev, the collection was prepared in response to a 1995 directive from Boris N. Yeltsin, then president of the Russian Federation. The Russian documents were assembled from the Foreign Policy Archive of the Russian Federation (AVP RF), Archive of the President of the Russian Federation (AP RF), Central Archive of the Foreign Intelligence Service (TsA SVR), Russian State Military Archive (RGVA), Russian State Economics Archive (RGAEh), Russian Center for the Preservation and Study of Documents of Recent History (RtsKhIDNI), Center for the Preservation of Current Documentation (TsKhSD), Central Archive of the Defense Ministry of the Russian Federation (TsA MO RF), and Central Archive of the Federal Security Service (TsA FSB). The collection also contains German documents bearing on this period from various archives in the Federal Republic of Germany.

I used two collections of documents in addition to the principal collection by A. N. Yakovlev. One, *Organy Gosudarstvennoy Bezopasnosti SSSR v Velikoy Otechestvennoy Voine* (Organs of State Security USSR in the Great Fatherland War), was published in two volumes in early 1995 by the Federal Service of Counterintelligence (FSK), later renamed the Federal

Security Service (FSB). It contains documents reflecting reporting by both the FSK and the Foreign Intelligence Service (SVR) for the period up to June 1941. It is particularly valuable because it contains detailed biographic summaries on each of the persons named in the documents. The second, *Sekrety Gitlera Na Stole U Stalina* (Hitler's Secrets on Stalin's Desk), was jointly published later in 1995 by the FSB and the SVR. It deals with documents covering just the period of March through June 22, 1941. There is some duplication in entries in both books of documents from the TsA SVR and TsA FSB. Some documents from both publications are also to be found in *1941 god.*

The goal of these publications is to demonstrate that in the prewar period the internal security and foreign intelligence services of state security provided the Soviet leadership with ample warning of an impending German attack, yet their reporting was disregarded. The ostensible reasons for this are argued in both books in slightly different ways. In addition, they both present their versions of the events and circumstances that led up to the German invasion of the Soviet Union, contending that France and England, supported by the United States, planned from the early 1930s to direct Germany's growing military might against the USSR in a campaign to eliminate "Bolshevism." As a result, the West and the Soviet Union failed to form an anti-Hitler coalition and Stalin was forced to conclude a nonaggression treaty with Germany. I do not agree with this position but it enjoys wide support in official circles in Russia today. It is still used by some to exonerate Stalin for his behavior in the months leading up to the German invasion and to explain the failure of intelligence reporting to sway Stalin from his conviction that if only Hitler were not provoked by Soviet defensive measures, he would not invade until the USSR was better prepared.

Unlike these two collections, Yakovlev's *1941 god* places the blame squarely on Stalin. Some complain that in his selection of documents Yakovlev emphasized ones predicting a German invasion rather than those indicating German forces would be used in attacking England. This criticism is not completely accurate but it is true that the Yakovlev collection does not discuss the contributing archives' criteria for submitting documents or the standard the compilers observed in their selection process. We do know, however, that *1941 god* is the only Russian publication that contains officially released military intelligence reports and summaries, complete with the appropriate references from the Central Archive of the Defense Ministry (TsA MO RF).

No official history of the GRU, the military intelligence, has yet been published. In 2001 Olma Press in Moscow published a two-volume collection by Aleksandr I. Kolpakidi and Dmitry P. Prokhorov entitled *Imperia GRU,* which assembles information on the history, organization, and personalities of the military intelligence without, though, providing archival references. In 2002 the St. Petersburg publishing house Neva, in conjunction with Olma Press, published *GRU: Dela i Liudi* in the series Rossia v Litsakh. This work by Vyacheslav M. Lure and Valery Ya. Kochik, while also nonofficial, contains the names of over 1,000 military intelligence officers and, wonder of wonders, includes an index. There are, however, no archival references supporting its data.

The other references to intelligence reports and various documents in my book were taken from the Russian and foreign books and periodicals cited in the end notes. Virtually all these sources suffer from the same lack of archival documentation. It is thus nearly impossible to prove or disprove statements in these sources, which are cited by some and condemned as false by others. A good example is the series of articles by Ovidy Gorchakov entitled "Nakanune ili Tragedia Kassandry: Povest v Dokumentakh" in issues 6 and 7 of the periodical *Gorizont* (1988). Gorchakov presents a series of reports from NKGB agents on various foreign embassies. I checked these reports with a recently retired major general of state security, who claimed there was no record of the agents' code names, expressed doubts about Gorchakov's veracity, and added that in any case, because of losses suffered in the purges, the NKGB would have been incapable of handling agents on that scale. Possibly, but a review of chapter 8, "Organs of State Security in the Prewar Period (1939–June 1941)" in *Istoria Sovietskikh Organov Gosudarstvennoy Bezopasnosti* (History of Soviet Organs of State Security), a top-secret document published in 1997 under the editorship of then KGB chairman Viktor M. Chebrikov for use as a textbook in KGB schools, shows that the NKGB's Second (Counterintelligence) Directorate was indeed capable of running very sophisticated agent and technical operations against foreign personnel and installations in Moscow. A recent article describes a very complex technical operation against the residence of the senior German military attaché involving tunneling from a neighboring house. Completed in April 1941, this operation provided excellent insights into German embassy attitudes and actions during the last two months before the invasion.

My only direct archival access was at the Russian State Military Archive (RGVA), where I was able to review the military personnel file of

Ivan I. Proskurov. The testimonials from military superiors and political officers revealed Proskurov to have been a dedicated pilot and devoted Communist. As for the Central Archive of the Defense Ministry (TsA MO RF), I was unable to gain access to it, nor was I able to obtain answers to an extensive series of questions I had prepared on military intelligence issues discussed in unclassified publications.

I knew access to the Central Archive of the SVR, successor to the First Chief Directorate (foreign intelligence of the KGB), would be impossible so I prepared a similar set of questions, again based on items from the SVR archive and published in *1941 god*. For these I also included the official archival references and submitted them to the SVR Public Affairs Bureau in October 2002. In May 2003 I was advised that the SVR would not release even those documents that had appeared in *1941 god*. To all intents and purposes they had been reclassified. Furthermore, the SVR would not release archival documents relating to questions on events or incidents derived from unclassified articles or from the SVR's own unclassified publications.

The first issue of the *Bulletin* of the Cold War International History Project (1992), contains this sentence: "For Cold War historians, frustrated for decades by the secrecy enshrouding the Soviet archives, the long wait appears to be ending." Over ten years later, this researcher found that for his topic, the intelligence available to Stalin on German intentions in 1940–41, there was absolutely no access to the prewar archives of the Soviet intelligence and security services. It was evident that this lack of access reflected deliberate policy decisions by the present Russian leadership to ensure that these services, and these services alone, would be able to use their archival material in interpreting the past.

Introduction

Stalin's Absolute Control, Misconceptions, and Disastrous Decisions

On June 17, 1941, Stalin received a report signed by Pavel M. Fitin, chief of NKGB Foreign Intelligence, asserting that "all preparations by Germany for an armed attack on the Soviet Union have been completed, and the blow can be expected at any time." The source was an intelligence officer in Hermann Göring's Air Ministry. In the margin of the report, Stalin scrawled this note to Fitin's chief, the people's commissar for state security, Vsevolod N. Merkulov: "Comrade Merkulov, you can send your 'source' from the headquarters of German aviation to his fucking mother. This is not a 'source' but a *dezinformator.*" Five days after Stalin expressed these sentiments, the German onslaught broke, bringing with it a war that would result in the deaths of twenty million Soviet citizens.

The scale of this catastrophe was such that the Russian people have still not been able to come to grips with that period. Their need for closure is so great that agonizing debates continue in Russia up to this day, focusing primarily on Stalin's role. Before examining Stalin's actions in the years leading up to the war, however, it is essential to understand that Stalin was in total control. Unchallenged by any serious opposition, he had become the center of all decision making, the source of foreign and domestic policies, the supreme "Boss" who would tolerate no dissent. Stalin, already first secretary of the Central Committee, VKP(b), became chairman of the Council of People's Commissars on May 5, 1941. Many Western observers assumed that the new position was necessary to enable Stalin to play a stronger role in negotiations with Germany. In reality the change created only the impression of a consolidation of power. As first secretary of the party, Stalin alone already dominated the Politburo and the Central Committee.

Stalin's power derived only in part from his formal position and in larger part from the universal fear that without warning, at Stalin's behest, citizens might find themselves in the clutches of Beria and his inquisitors. Everyone, from people's commissars to senior generals to the lowest-level functionaries knew that either execution or a lengthy term in the GULAG could befall them at any time. Exploiting their fear, Stalin was able to advance his anomalous views on foreign policy, military strategy, weapons development, and so forth, usually unopposed by professionals. His insistence on adopting his crony Marshal Grigory I. Kulik's suggestion that the 107 mm field piece, used in the 1917–19 Russian civil war, should be adapted for use in tanks as of early 1941 is but one example. His refusal to permit Soviet air defense forces to halt massive German air reconnaissance on the eve of the invasion is another.

This climate of abject fear, reinforced by the complete secrecy in which Stalin and his minions worked, kept even the best Soviet generals and managers off balance as the confrontation with Germany drew near. In his dealings with those around him and with foreign emissaries, Stalin was the ultimate conspirator, a master at playing the role of either the genial leader or the tough negotiator. Stalin adhered to Leninist formulations and to party jargon in dealing with his own people or the Executive Committee of the Comintern. Some Western historians have said that Stalin was not a revolutionary but a statesman whose goal was to advance his country's national interests. They overlook the fact that while Stalin could moderate his revolutionary rhetoric, he remained a believer in the Communist cause who would use revolutionary tactics to achieve his objectives whenever circumstances were appropriate.

As early as 1937 the terror against party officials suspected of opposition to Stalin extended to the Red Army. Purportedly needed to avoid creation of a fifth column in the event of war, Stalin's actions not only resulted in the loss of senior commanders such as Marshal Mikhail N. Tukhachevsky but also depleted the ranks of the officer corps at all levels. Thousands of officers with combat experience and higher education were executed, sent to the GULAG, or discharged from the service. These actions did not end in 1938–39 but continued right up to the early days of the German invasion. The arrests and executions in this later phase were directed in great measure at officials of the aviation industry and the Red Army air forces' technical specialists, who were made scapegoats for the failure of the Stalinist system to develop an effective air arm.

The other group under attack in May–June 1941 were veterans of the Spanish civil war. Former advisers to the republican government, they were brought back to Moscow ostensibly to replace officers purged earlier and many of them had advanced to senior rank in the Red Army, yet they displayed an independence of spirit that Stalin could not tolerate. These highly decorated veterans were tortured and executed without trial at Stalin's insistence, depriving the Soviet forces of the only cadres with actual experience in fighting the Germans.

Stalin's decision to conclude the nonaggression pact with Germany, with its secret protocols, enabled the USSR to expand its western borders at the expense of a defeated Poland and to lay the groundwork for incorporation of the Baltic States into the USSR and the acquisition of territory in Romania. But this expansion came at a high cost. Instead of being improved, the Soviet Union's defensive posture was severely undermined. The Soviets acquired virulently hostile populations who provided the German intelligence services with ready recruits for sabotage operations on the eve of the invasion. From the military point of view, these operations played havoc with Soviet communications and transportation. The field fortifications along the former border, vital to the Red Army's forward force posture, were dismantled and a new fortified line along the new frontier was never completed. In the wrangling over this issue, Stalin insisted on keeping the first echelons close to the new border despite the lack of defensive structures, a fatal misjudgment. He refused to consider the defensive strategy urged on him by men like Marshal Shaposhnikov, who strongly believed Soviet defenses should take advantage of the fortifications along the pre-1939 border, thereby providing defense in depth. Stalin would not, it was said, concede any part of these new lands to an invader because of his pride in his conquest of the new territories in the West. His chief military advisers were unable to change his mind. Was pride Stalin's only reason for rejecting this "defense in depth" strategy?

There are other possible explanations, not only for his rejection of defense in depth but for the decision to enter into the nonaggression pact. One factor was Stalin's firm conviction, evidenced by the 1938 Sudeten crisis, that neither France nor England, as capitalist states, would ever cooperate with Communist Russia in maintaining peace in Central and

Eastern Europe. Stalin was convinced they would rather connive to ensure that Hitler would turn eastward, leaving Western Europe untouched, even going so far as to join Hitler in an attack on the USSR. Again, Stalin was wrong in his assessment, and once England had declared war on Germany and Churchill had joined the Chamberlain government, there was little possibility of such fears being realized. Stalin knew only that Churchill had staunchly opposed communism as a system beginning in the 1920s, and he expected that Churchill would willingly accept a German invasion of the USSR. He appeared to have little awareness of the tenacity with which Churchill, describing Hitler as a major threat to British interests, tried to persuade successive Conservative governments to improve England's defenses during the 1930s. Stalin's lack of awareness of the complexities of Western politics and his naive acceptance of Marxist dogma explains much about his erratic foreign affairs performance in the years leading up to the German invasion.

The theory that Stalin's plans for a preventive attack on Germany explain his passivity in the face of the German buildup remains alive in current Russian studies. Linked to this theory is the charge that because Soviet intelligence could not discover the exact date of the German attack, Stalin was unable to know precisely when to launch his preemptive strike.

The documents examined in this book establish beyond any reasonable doubt that the Soviet services were highly alert to this threat. (For a chronology of agent reporting, see appendix 4.) Both foreign intelligence and counterintelligence elements exploited the full range of sources, human and technical, available to them. Admittedly, they did not have penetrations of Hitler's personal staff or the highest levels of the German high command. Neither, insofar as we know, did they have in the immediate prewar period the level of signals intelligence achieved by the British. Still, their coverage of German military preparations for the June 1941 invasion was impressive by any standard. Nor can we accept the argument advanced by several publications that it was primarily German deception that made it difficult for the Soviet services to analyze available information, screen out the deception material, and provide the results to the Soviet politico-military leadership. Of course, those defending the intelligence services have argued that they had no analytical capability at the time. That is certainly not true of Soviet military intelligence, which had an analytical unit and carried the main burden of interpreting the activities of German forces in the Soviet border area. As for the Foreign Intelligence Service of State Security (NKVD/NKGB), the practice of deception, or "active measures," had been a major part of its doctrine and operations since its founding. Surely, it should not have been beyond the capabilities of this service to discern the main outlines of the German deception campaign.

It would not be the first time, of course, that intelligence services felt obliged to serve up intelligence estimates that conformed to the plans and policies of political leaders. Nor is the failure by political leaders to take action based on warnings from intelligence unprecedented. These perennial problems affect many societies but tend to be more prevalent in democracies, where popular attitudes can inhibit a leader's freedom of action. The unwillingness of Conservative governments in England during the 1930s to appreciate the danger of the German threat is one example. Closer to hand are the failures of the Bush administration in America with respect to Iraq. While the intelligence community produced intelligence on weapons of mass destruction that turned out to be wrong, previous administrations apparently ignored a variety of indicators of al-Qu'aida's intention to conduct a major attack on U.S. domestic targets.

One cannot, however, equate the Soviet situation in 1941 with that of other governments in other times. For one thing, the dimensions of the threat were considerably greater. Fresh from their victories in France in June 1940, the Germans amassed along the Soviet border with occupied Poland large forces of combat-hardened veterans. They possessed weapons and the combined arms tactics to exploit them that threatened not only the Red Army units facing them but the very survival of the Soviet regime itself. Also, the extent of intelligence available to the Soviet leadership on the specifics of this threat was precise and detailed, yet Stalin rejected it and refused to permit his military to take necessary actions to respond lest they "provoke" the Germans. The results in terms of human losses were catastrophic, exceeding those suffered by any other nation during the Second World War.

On June 21, 1941, the troops of Germany and its allies were poised at the Soviet border in full combat readiness. They faced Soviet troops not fully deployed and by no means combat ready. In Soviet and foreign historiography, their lack of preparedness is normally attributed to Stalin's procrastination. The motives for this procrastination are still the subject of quarrels both in the former USSR and abroad. Some historians contend that he had rational reasons. He strongly believed, for one, that Hitler, who had just succeeded in dominating Western Europe, was much too clever to believe he could conquer Russia, where others before him had failed.

Indeed, Stalin's actions in June 1941 demonstrate that he had been convinced by Hitler and German deception that German troops had been deployed to occupied Poland solely to evade British bombing and observation. He was also persuaded that Hitler still intended to invade the British Isles, an action that would certainly delay any attack on the Soviet Union but might, if German forces were hurled back in defeat, open the way for Stalin to Western Europe. These all turned out to be delusional concepts.

Others might argue that Stalin's procrastination, his insistence that his military take no actions that might provoke Hitler or his generals to invade the USSR, derived from his awareness that the Red Army was not ready to face the Wehrmacht. But it was Stalin himself and the system he created that brought about this situation. His purges of the officer corps, animated by the threat he feared the military posed to his power, his refusal to act against persistent Luftwaffe aerial reconnaissance, the delays in completing construction of fortified areas, the inability of the economy (including the collective farms) to provide the Red Army with essential transport, all stemmed from a system in which one man, ever fearful of threats to his personal power, was able to subordinate the needs of the nation to his irrational delusions. The result was historical catastrophe.

Though bearing ultimate responsibility, Stalin could not have acted alone any more than he could have singlehandedly carried out the purges. Stalin had many willing accomplices in the party, the state, the military, and the intelligence and security services. In the climate of fear and subservience he had created, massive errors of commission and omission were inevitable, particularly on the part of the intelligence services. Awareness of German preparations to invade so pervaded Moscow that even Stalin's most sycophantic collaborators in these services found it difficult to choke off the constant flow of intelligence reporting.

Without doubt, sufficient intelligence was available to Stalin on German preparations to invade the USSR. Had it been properly evaluated and disseminated, defensive measures could have been undertaken that might have either dissuaded Hitler or blunted the attack when it came.

Abbreviations and Acronyms

AMTORG: Soviet trade company in New York City

AVP RF: Soviet Foreign Policy Archive of the Russian Federation

CC: Central Committee of the Communist Party

Cheka: Extraordinary Commission for Combating Counterrevolution and Sabotage. Founded 1918. Precursor of other state security organizations: GPU, OGPU, NKVD, NKGB, MGB, and KGB

ENIGMA: German encryption machine

FSB: Federal Security Service

GKO: State Defense Committee, 1941–45

GPU: State Political Directorate, 1923–34

GRU: Chief Intelligence Directorate (Military Intelligence)

GTU: Chief Transport Directorate, NKVD

GUGB: Chief Directorate for State Security, NKVD

GULAG: Chief Directorate of Prison Camps

GUPV: Chief Directorate of Border Troops

JIC: British Joint Intelligence Committee

MGB: Ministry of State Security

MI-5: British Counterintelligence Organization

MI-6: British Secret Intelligence Service

Narkom: Acronym for People's Commissar

NKGB: People's Commissariat for State Security

NKID: People's Commissariat for Foreign Affairs

NKO: People's Commissariat for Defense

NKPS: People's Commissariat of Transport Routes

NKVD: People's Commissariat for Internal Affairs

OKW: High Command of the German Armed Forces

OUN: Organization of Ukrainian Nationalists

PVO: National Air Defense

RF: Russian Federation

RGVA: Russian State Military Archive

RKKA: Workers and Peasants Red Army

RU: Military Intelligence Directorate

RU GS KA: Intelligence Directorate, General Staff, Red Army

SIS: British Secret Intelligence Service (MI-6)

SMD: Special Military District

SNK: Council of People's Commissars

Stavka: Highest organ of strategic leadership of the Soviet armed forces during World War II

SVR: Russian Foreign Intelligence Service

ULTRA: Code word for British decryption of German codes

VENONA: Declassified messages obtained by Anglo-American decryption of Soviet codes

VKP(b): All-Union Communist Party (Bolsheviks)

VNOS: Soviet air observation, warning, and communications service

WHAT STALIN KNEW

CHAPTER **1**

Stalin versus Hitler

Background

The year 1945 saw the end of the most destructive war in the history of mankind. Among the nations that suffered the greatest human and physical losses were Germany and Soviet Russia. It was a decision made final in August 1939 by the German and Soviet leaders that rendered this catastrophic war inevitable. Why was that decision made? How did the German leader, Adolf Hitler, and his Soviet counterpart, Josef Stalin, view the world at that time?

Both Germany and Soviet Russia were losers in World War I. After a relatively brief but important period of diplomatic, military, and economic cooperation during the 1920s, the two nations followed different paths of development in the 1930s. Stalin achieved total control of the ruling Communist Party and embarked on a wholesale transformation of the rural economy, eliminating a rising group of independent peasants and forcing others onto collective farms. This policy eventually enabled the state to control agricultural output, but it also produced massive famine in which millions died. Concurrently, Stalin began a gigantic industrialization program that greatly expanded existing industries (most of which had been expropriated following the 1917 revolution) and created vast new industrial centers. The pace and intensity of this effort were unprecedented but made necessary, in Stalin's view, by the "capitalist encirclement" of Soviet Russia.

Stalin saw criticism of any aspect of his agricultural and industrial policies as an attack on his leadership of the party, and he responded by instituting widespread purges of those he termed "the opposition." The arrest, imprisonment, or execution of many thousands of the nation's most talented people would in time be felt throughout the party, government, and economy, but most severely in the armed forces. Apart from the problems caused by the loss of experienced cadres, the purges resulted in an atmosphere of fear and suspicion that paralyzed many of the survivors, making them incapable or unwilling to work effectively or creatively.

Abroad, Stalin saw his socialist regime surrounded by capitalist states that had been hostile to Soviet Russia since the Revolution of 1917. To the west were Great Britain, France, and their client states such as Czechoslovakia, Romania, and Poland, all of which were in some degree anti-Soviet. Japanese aggression, notably in Manchuria and North China, figured as the main threat in the Far East. When Hitler and his National Socialist Party came to power via the ballot box in Germany, Stalin understood his election as a natural evolution from democratic capitalism to fascism that would hasten the development of a revolutionary situation. He therefore forbade the German Communists, a formidable, well-organized party, to make common cause with the German Socialist Party, then the largest party of the left, against the Nazis and their storm troopers. The result of this decision was the destruction of both parties and the consolidation of Hitler's power as Führer.

While Stalin was preoccupied with his purges, Hitler set about eliminating the restraints on Germany imposed by the Treaty of Versailles. In October 1933 Germany seceded from the League of Nations. In January 1935, following a plebiscite, it reincorporated the Saar, a German province that had been placed under a League of Nations mandate after World War I. On March 16, 1935, in defiance of the treaty, Hitler reintroduced compulsory military service and created an air force. A year later he remilitarized the Rhineland. The former Allies protested but took no other action.

In June 1935 Germany signed a naval agreement with Great Britain that greatly relaxed the Versailles Treaty's limitations on German naval tonnage and permitted Germany to build a submarine fleet, forbidden under Versailles. The agreement came as a shock to many, including Winston S. Churchill, as with it the British government appeared to lend support to Hitler's violations of the treaty. Admittedly, strict enforcement of its provisions had never been popular in the United Kingdom, where sympathy for Germany as the underdog was not inconsiderable. Furthermore, if enforcement risked war, it is unlikely that the British public would have stood for it. Memories of the trench slaughter of the 1914–18 war were fresh in the minds of most families, and the British economy was still suffering from the effects of the Great Depression. The naval treaty was seen by some British politicians as an effort, therefore, to demonstrate to Hitler that Great Britain was willing to work with him to ensure stability in Europe. In this, of course, they completely misjudged their man. On June 23, 1939, Hitler renounced both the 1936 naval agreement and a subsequent version.

Despite the apparent similarities in their government structures, Fascist Italy and Germany were not that close until October 1935, when the Italian army invaded Ethiopia. The League of Nations labeled Italy an aggressor and imposed economic sanctions, but to no avail. Ethiopian resistance was overcome in May 1936 and the King of Italy was crowned Emperor of Ethiopia. The prestige of the League of Nations suffered, as did that of France and England. Meanwhile, Germany was the only European power that refrained from acting against Italy. The two "have not" powers drew closer after this experience. Military cooperation between the two grew as they joined in supporting General Francisco Franco's revolt against the Spanish Republic, which began in July 1936.

This revolt had its origins in the long-standing tension between urban workers and landless peasants on the one hand and extremely conservative landowners and industrialists on the other. The latter groups and the Catholic hierarchy upheld the monarchy, while the urban and rural poor supported those working to establish a republic. Victory in the municipal elections of April 1931 was interpreted as a vote for a republic, and King Alfonso went into exile. The new republic could not satisfy the demands of the poor for social justice and at the same time persuade the upper middle class that their rights would be respected. Frustrated, the poor engaged in industrial strikes, seized land, and attacked Church property, prompting a brutal army crackdown and, in turn, the creation of a Popular Front formed of liberal republicans and socialists. In the elections of February 1936, the Popular Front gained control of the parliament. During the months that followed, Spanish society split into two factions. The left grew increasingly radical and opposition to the republic from the right was centered in the Falange Party, a Spanish version of fascism. By July, large elements of the army, particularly the officer corps, felt they had to save Spain from communism.

It was this feeling that invited them to launch a rebellion under General

German Aggression, 1936–39

As part of its policy to rectify the terms of the 1919 Versailles Treaty, Hitler's Germany remilitarized the Rhineland in 1936 and annexed Austria in March 1938. In September 1938 it absorbed the Sudeten area of Czechoslovakia, and in March 1939 the Bohemian and Moravian areas of that country became a German protectorate. Slovakia became independent although in reality it was a German client state. Also in March 1939 the Memel area of Lithuania was made part of East Prussia.

Francisco Franco, who turned to Germany and Italy for help. They both sent units of their regular forces lightly camouflaged as "volunteers." The republic also turned to England, France, and the United States for assistance but these countries demurred, choosing instead a policy of nonintervention, although some of their citizens participated as individuals. Soviet Russia sent weapons and its own volunteers to support the republican cause but tried to mask the extent of its aid (see chapter 2 for details on the activities of Soviet volunteers in Spain). It also coordinated the operations of international brigades recruited from foreign communist parties.[1] When the Spanish civil war ended in early 1939 with a Franco victory, it was seen by many as a victory "over communism," adding to the prestige of the Tripartite Anti-Comintern Pact, which Italy had joined in November 1937.

While the Spanish conflict ground on, Hitler had been taking other actions to expand German territory. In March 1938, when a Nazi, Arthur Seyss-Inquart, was named Austrian chancellor, the Austrian frontier was opened to the German army. There were no protests by France or Great Britain. On March 13 Hitler announced the return of Austria to the Reich. What happened in fact was the isolation of Czechoslovakia, Hitler's next victim.[2]

In Czechoslovakia, Hitler's tactics were similar to those he used in Austria. The Sudeten German minority, occupying territory along Czechoslovakia's western border with Germany, was included in the state following the Versailles Treaty. This area was also the location of Czechoslovakia's new line of very modern fortifications, vital to that nation's defense against Germany. Throughout the summer of 1938, the Sudeten German National Socialists continued to make impossible demands on the Czechs, followed by Hitler's threats of military action. At this point Prime Minister Neville Chamberlain of Britain took over. On September 15 he visited Hitler in Germany at Obersalzberg, and again on September 20–24 at Godesberg, offering to intercede with the Czechs. Hitler would not budge, but he did say that "this will be the last territorial claim I shall have to make in Europe." On September 26 he issued a forty-eight-hour ultimatum. France and Great Britain began to mobilize. Mussolini now intervened to agree with Chamberlain's proposal for a four-power conference, which was held in Munich. Neither Soviet Russia nor the Czechs themselves were invited. Britain and France accepted Hitler's demands and on October 1 German troops entered the Sudeten area. Chamberlain returned to London claiming he had achieved "peace in our time." On March 15, 1939, as the Spanish

Republic disintegrated, Hitler's army entered Prague. On March 16 Hitler proclaimed the "Protectorate of Bohemia and Moravia." Slovakia declared its independence; in reality it was a German client state.[3]

These events surely convinced Hitler that if he could be assured of Soviet neutrality in a Polish-German conflict, the odds were good that neither France nor Great Britain would intervene to help Poland. Stalin, on the other hand, must have certainly known, after his rebuff in the Czech crisis at the hands of the British and French, that he could expect little help from them were he to oppose a German invasion of Poland. Consequently, he would drive the best bargain he could with Hitler. He would look on his negotiations with the British and French during the summer merely as a negotiating device to obtain more from Hitler. Stalin never imagined that in reaching an agreement with Hitler he would be deceived by the Führer on a scale that rivaled that of the infamous Trojan horse.

CHAPTER 2

The Outspoken General
Ivan Iosifovich Proskurov

How could Stalin have trusted Hitler? Here follows the history by which Stalin, supplied by his own country's intelligence services with absolutely solid information on Hitler's intentions, blindly disregarded the intelligence in favor of Hitler's lies.

The interwoven careers of three intelligence officers dramatize this history and will enable the reader to determine what Stalin knew and how he came to know it. The first of these was Ivan I. Proskurov, a talented military pilot and air force commander who had fought in Spain. The second was Pavel M. Fitin, who was assigned to the NKVD's Foreign Intelligence Service by the party and rose rapidly to become its chief in May 1939. The last was Filipp I. Golikov, who had served in the Red Army since the postrevolutionary Russian civil war, primarily on political assignments. In July 1940, Stalin appointed Golikov head of the Soviet Military Intelligence Service as Proskurov's replacement.

Proskurov had no previous intelligence experience, but he was ideally suited for the task given to him. A brave combatant and imaginative commander, he was highly intelligent and had an excellent memory. Instinctively honest, he refused to shade the truth in preparing intelligence reports. He was also a modest, unassuming man devoted to his country, wife, and children. Unusual for that time and place, he always showed great concern for the welfare of his subordinates, protecting those who feared repression (the purges) whenever he could. On the other hand, in

the USSR under Stalin, where subservience to the "Boss" and the concealment of unpleasant truths were the rule, Proskurov's qualities, especially
his independence of mind, were not ones that would endear him to Stalin.
Indeed, his outspokenness often enraged Stalin, who knew he couldn't
control him.

Proskurov was born on February 18, 1907, in the village of Malaya
Tokmachka in what is now Zaporozhskaya Oblast of Ukraine.[1] His father
was a railroad worker and Ivan attended the Aleksandrovsky Railroad
Academy in Zaporozhe and the Kharkov Institute of Mechanization and
Electrification of Agriculture during the unsettled years of World War I,
the February and October revolutions of 1917, the brief Ukrainian independence period from 1918 to 1920, and the civil war. From 1924 to 1926
he worked at the Zaporozhe Cable Factory, where he belonged to the Kom-
somol. From 1926 to 1927 he was chairman of the district council of labor
unions, joining the Communist Party in 1927. In 1931 he joined the Red
Army air forces.

Some of Proskurov's biographers characterize his entry into the Soviet
air forces as simply a party assignment (*partnabor*). Proskurov himself
reportedly agreed, saying that he did not become a pilot "from birth, but
rather by chance—I was even a bit afraid of the idea of flying." But "at
the district committee they talked me into attending flight school."[2] The
school was the Higher School for Pilots at Stalingrad, which he completed
in March 1933. He was fortunate in this assignment as it allowed him to
escape the severe famine conditions brought on in his native Ukraine by
Stalin's decision to impose collectivization on the peasantry, an action
from which Soviet agriculture never recovered. Pilots in training, however,
enjoyed a reasonably nutritious diet.

Proskurov was assigned to the aviation brigade of the prestigious Zhu-
kosvky Air Academy in Moscow as a flight instructor. A year later he was
sent to the commanders' course at the Stalin School for Naval Aviators at
Eisk, on the Sea of Azov in Krasnodarsky Kray, where he finished first
in his class. In May 1934 a special commission appointed him aircraft
commander in the Ninetieth Heavy Bombardment Squadron. Next he
was assigned to the Eighty-ninth Heavy Bombardment Squadron of the
Twenty-third Aviation Brigade as instructor in instrument navigation; his
superiors characterized him as a "highly disciplined officer." His unit's
party organization named him a delegate to a party congress and he was
promoted to senior lieutenant. The next year, 1935, Proskurov became a
member of the Soviet exhibition team attending an air show in Romania.

In 1936 he made a record flight to Khabarovsk in the Soviet Far East to deliver engineers and spare parts to the famous Soviet pilot Valery P. Chkalov who had damaged his plane in an accident. Proskurov and his navigator made it to Khabarovsk in fifty-four hours and thirteen minutes, including refueling stops, a record for which Defense Commissar Kliment Ye. Voroshilov awarded them certificates and engraved gold watches. It was while Proskurov and his navigator were on a well-deserved leave that they heard of the invasion of republican Spain by General Franco and his troops. They both immediately volunteered to help the Loyalist forces.[3]

In Proskurov's personnel file, the only reference to his service in the Spanish civil war is a brief memorandum stating that "Sr. Lt. Proskurov was on a special assignment abroad (Sept. 1936–June 1937) carrying out a special task of the government for strengthening the defensive might of the USSR."[4] This opaque treatment isn't surprising. The entire Spanish operation, from recruitment of advisers to weapons acquisition, was undertaken and controlled by the Red Army's Military Intelligence Directorate (RU). The highly experienced former RU chief Jan K. Berzin ran the show in Spain, while Semen P. Uritsky, RU chief in Moscow, bore responsibility for keeping the defense commissar informed.[5] There seemed to be a good reason for this arrangement. None of the nations involved in assisting the two sides in the conflict (that is, Germany, Italy, and the Soviet Union) wished to enter the fray openly. Pretending they were not involved was a face-saving bow to international diplomatic niceties insofar as the Germans and Italians were concerned. In the absence of declarations of war, they had committed elements of their armed forces and made no special effort to conceal this fact.

Not so the conspiratorial Soviet regime. Soviet personnel from Berzin down to the lowest-ranking artillery adviser followed procedures intended to conceal their true names and nationalities. The cases of Proskurov and his navigator are instructive. Both were documented as representatives of the Moscow Automobile Factory, planning to visit the French Renault plant in Paris. Proskurov's documents bore the Czech name "Soldatchik." They flew on commercial flights from Moscow to Paris, where they met RU guides who took them through France across the Spanish border to the area of Albacete. When they arrived, they were assigned to the First International Bombardment Squadron.

In February 1937 changes took place in the Soviet air effort. Boris Sveshnikov was replaced as senior air adviser by Yakov V. Smushkevich, and Proskurov replaced Ernst G. Shakht as commanding officer of the

First Bombardment Squadron.[6] Among the squadron's engagements was an effort in the spring of 1937 to disrupt operations of the Italian expeditionary force participating in an offensive against Madrid from the north. The squadron attacked from the east and largely destroyed an Italian troop and supply train near the major rail center of Siguenza. Proskurov's men then turned their attention to an adjoining highway jammed with trucks carrying Italian troops moving south toward Madrid. The squadron's machine guns ripped into the truck columns, set vehicles ablaze, and sent troops fleeing into the adjacent fields. Proskurov appeared indifferent to personal danger and fatigue, as he did, too, when his squadron, along with other elements of the republican air force, flew continuous sorties against the rebels. His courage and endurance, combined with his careful attention to variations in attack plans, showed him to be an extraordinarily able air commander.[7]

The last combat action in which Proskurov's bombers took part undoubtedly brought him to Stalin's attention. On May 29, 1937, the republican air force was ordered to bomb Palma on the island of Mallorca. Two Soviet-made and piloted bombers broke off and attacked the German battleship *Deutschland* at neighboring Ibiza. Thirty-one German sailors were killed and seventy-four wounded. An angry Hitler retaliated by ordering the bombardment of the republican port of Almeria. In a telegram sent from RU headquarters in Moscow, top Soviet advisers were reminded that the Boss "considers it unacceptable to have planes bomb Italian and German ships, and this must be prohibited."[8] Some sources have credited Proskurov with participation in the raid.[9] It seems doubtful that an officer with his record would have disobeyed orders on his own or have made a navigational error of this magnitude (Ibiza is at least 115 kilometers from Palma). It is not, therefore, impossible that Proskurov had tacit approval to attack the *Deutschland* but that when Stalin saw Hitler's reaction, he backed off and gave orders forbidding further actions of this kind. Whatever the explanation, Proskurov returned to the Soviet Union shortly after the event, and on June 21, 1937, he was promoted to major and made a Hero of the Soviet Union. It was presumably the happiest day of what turned out to be a very short and painful life.

In July 1937 Proskurov took command of the Fifty-fourth Bombardment Brigade. On February 22, 1938, he was promoted ahead of schedule to the senior rank of brigade commander (*kombrig*), and in May he assumed command of the Second Special-Purpose Air Army, remaining in that position until April 1939. During this time he acquired the reputation of a demanding officer who spoke out for what he believed was right. His courage was not restricted to the battlefield. Gavril M. Prokofev, his former navigator, recalls Proskurov's attendance at a meeting of a commission considering the design for a four-engine aircraft with retractable landing gear. V. K. Kokkinadi, a prominent military test pilot, asked: "Why do we need such an expensive and complicated aircraft? The Il-4 and TB-3 are enough; with them we can easily fly from Moscow to Berlin." After his comments there was silence while all present waited for Stalin's views. Normal protocol consisted of "never expressing yourself until you've heard Stalin's view and then agreeing with him," but Proskurov spoke out bluntly: "You, Kokkinadi, fly alone, for a record. We fly in squadrons and must maneuver." Stalin, who might have been expected to be angry, rose, went to the globe, and asked, "Comrade Kokkinadi, what if you have to fly to Berlin via the Baltic, Finland?" Kokkinadi admitted that the older aircraft couldn't. The matter was decided. As future events suggest, it is doubtful that Stalin forgot Proskurov's show of independence.[10]

Proskurov was made chief of the RU on April 14, 1939. On May 21, 1937, Stalin had declared that "the Intelligence Directorate and its apparatus have fallen into the hands of the Germans," signaling the virtual decapitation of the RU in the purges and the loss of valuable cadres. It was probably to restore confidence in the service and improve morale that a Hero of the Soviet Union with combat experience in the Spanish civil war was chosen. The story is told that two months earlier, in February 1939, Defense Commissar Voroshilov had asked a gathering of RU officers if they would accept Aleksandr G. Orlov, the acting chief, as their permanent head. The officers demurred, noting that, while Orlov was a good analyst who spoke several languages, he was no operations chief. What RU needed was a fresh face.[11]

Accompanied by his wife and two daughters, Proskurov arrived in Moscow as chief of the RU and deputy defense commissar. His rank entitled him to an apartment in the famous House on the Embankment, for many years the residence of the privileged in Soviet society.[12] His medals entitled him to a raise, which he refused to accept for doing what he considered his duty. He was also given a two-story dacha in the prestigious area of Arkhangelskoye, west of Moscow. Proskurov never used this dacha; instead he turned it over to his colleagues in military intelligence for their children to use as a summer camp. His younger daughter, then seven, attended it.

Usually Proskurov vacationed at Sochi on the Black Sea and on summer Sundays visited with colleagues at their dachas on the outskirts of Moscow. His favorite pastimes were his visits in his new Renault to the elaborate dacha of Admiral Nikolai G. Kuznetsov, the people's commissar of the navy, whom he knew from their service in the Spanish civil war; many of the veteran volunteers would gather at the dacha to reminisce.[13] Proskurov was also a close friend of Mikhail V. Vodopianov, one of the earliest Heroes of the Soviet Union and famous as an explorer of the polar region.

By virtue of his position as a deputy defense commissar, on June 9, 1939, Proskurov was made a member of the Main Military Council (Glavny Voenny Soviet). This council, chaired by Defense Commissar Kliment Voroshilov, was created in March 1938. Composed of senior military officers and party leaders (including Stalin himself), it served as a forum for discussion of major issues of military policy. Orders on such topics promulgated by the defense commissar were first discussed and approved by the council. In the period from June 1939 until his dismissal in July 1940, Proskurov regularly attended council meetings at which Stalin was also present. As we follow Proskurov's career it is important to recognize that he was involved in important policy decisions and must have been well known to Stalin.[14]

Why was Proskurov chosen for this major position? Some have pointed to his acquaintance with Jan Berzin, whom he met in Spain when Berzin was chief soviet adviser there. Others have noted his youth and his rapid rise in rank and position. On his return from Spain he spent a few weeks in Paris, and his frequent absences suggest he was carrying out clandestine tasks of some sort, although no available information sheds light on that speculation. Stalin may simply have been determined to insert someone into the position who had no previous ties to RU personalities. This was, indeed, the pattern he followed in filling the vacancies in the armed forces caused by his purges.[15]

It is true, of course, that reports reaching Stalin from the Soviet Military Intelligence Service were couched in Marxist-Leninist jargon, but they still tended to reflect the realities of the noncommunist world faced by the USSR. In addition, the Red Army inherited a military tradition from the tsarist past that in practice demanded intellectual discipline and obedience to one's immediate superiors. It was nearly impossible for senior officers of the Red Army to find a balance between the atmosphere in which they lived their lives and the insatiable demands of Josef Stalin for complete subservience. This balancing act was even more difficult for members of the Military Intelligence Service. On the one hand, they dealt with foreign matters, spoke foreign languages, and lived long periods of their lives abroad. The best of them were trained to be totally objective in their reporting. On the other hand, these traits guaranteed that Stalin's normally conspiratorial mind would interpret such behavior as treason.[16]

The integrity and competence of the RU chief, his insistence on fairness in dealing with his subordinates, and his ability to stand up to the pressures exerted on the intelligence process by the Soviet leadership all combined to determine how effective the service would be in meeting the 1939–41 crisis. The chief was responsible for directing the entire effort from the collection to the analysis, production, and dissemination of information. He was also responsible for selecting the personnel needed to staff the system. In the four years preceding Proskurov's arrival, changes in the RU leadership had hardly been conducive to good management. In 1935, after accepting responsibility for a serious security flap in Western Europe, Berzin resigned as chief, although by 1936 he was sent to Spain as senior adviser. He was replaced by Semen P. Uritsky, a person with little intelligence experience, who lasted in the job until June 1937. He was arrested in November 1937 and shot in January 1938. Berzin was brought back from Spain and briefly occupied the chief's slot from June until August of that year. He, too, was arrested in November 1937 and executed in July 1938. The next two chiefs, Semen G. Gendin and Aleksandr G. Orlov, were both acting heads. Proskurov's appointment would test the degree to which Stalin was really interested in an effective military intelligence service.

All intelligence reporting was sent to the Soviet leadership, meaning Stalin. Whether Stalin accepted the reports as accurate is another matter. In 1939, during the events leading up to the nonaggression pact and the Polish invasion, Stalin apparently appreciated the intelligence provided by Proskurov from the marvelous sources of the RU's Warsaw residency.

CHAPTER 3

Proskurov Sets Stalin Straight

To appreciate the value of the intelligence reporting from the Warsaw RU residency under Proskurov in 1939, it is necessary to know something of the residency's history and of the backgrounds and capabilities of its agent sources. Warsaw was an important RU residency (the term describes an operational station of Soviet intelligence abroad) because Poland had been considered a potential Soviet adversary since the Soviet-Polish conflict in 1920. But the intelligence activity that would impact most importantly on the period 1939–41 began with the arrival of Rudolf Herrnstadt in Warsaw in 1933. The Moscow correspondent of the German newspaper *Berliner Tageblatt*, Herrnstadt was forced to leave, along with other German correspondents, in retaliation for the new Nazi government's expulsion of Soviet journalists from Berlin. While working in Moscow, Herrnstadt had been recruited by the RU and, following their instructions, moved to Warsaw to become his newspaper's correspondent there. As soon as he arrived, he plunged into the life of the German community, where he was highly respected for his knowledge of East European affairs. He developed a close relationship with German ambassador Hans-Adolf von Moltke, who frequently sought his advice and through whom he was able to meet, assess, and recruit several individuals who would produce outstanding intelligence reports.

Among them was the redoubtable Ilse Stöbe (code name Alta), a well-known journalist in her own right as well as Herrnstadt's mistress. She later served as the communications link with some of Herrnstadt's best sources, who had been transferred to Berlin and Bucharest. She was arrested by the Gestapo in August 1942 but she never betrayed a single person. Among those she worked with was Gerhard Kegel (code name KhVS), an employee of the Trade Section of the German embassy in Warsaw, who would later be assigned to the Moscow embassy. Another was Rudolf von Scheliha (code name Ariets), first secretary in the German embassy in Warsaw; after the German conquest of Poland, he was assigned to the German Foreign Ministry in Berlin. A member of the German foreign service for many years, he had excellent contacts in German political and military circles. The third and fourth members of this Warsaw group were Kurt and Margarita Völkisch (code names AVS and LTsL). Kurt dealt with press matters in the Warsaw embassy and was later assigned to the embassy in Bucharest. Margarita, his wife, worked there as a secretary. Taken as a whole, this group provided the RU with some of its best intelligence on German plans and activities.

On May 17, 1939, Proskurov sent a report to Stalin with a six-page attachment entitled "The Future Plans of Aggression by Fascist Germany in the Estimation of an Official of the German Foreign Ministry, Kleist." The report was classified "Top Secret" (*Sovershenno Sekretno*) and "Of Special Interest" (*Osobo Interesno*). Provided by the Warsaw residency of Soviet military intelligence, it was based on a briefing given by Dr. Peter Kleist, head of the Eastern Department of Ribbentrop's office, to senior officers of the German embassy in Warsaw during Kleist's visit there on May 2, 1939.[1] Coincidentally, May 2 was the day Stalin informed Maksim M. Litvinov that he would be replaced by Molotov as commissar of foreign affairs. Litvinov was Jewish and had favored an agreement with England and France to curb Nazi aggression. Thus, Stalin's action was a signal to Hitler of the possibility of an agreement between their two countries. This was to be one of the first steps in a minuet that would be danced by Moscow, Berlin, London, and Paris during the next few months over the question of what to do about Poland.

Kleist's comments on Hitler's plans for Poland and his longer-range intentions must have been read by Stalin with great interest. Kleist, after all, was the one person in Ribbentrop's immediate entourage who was continuously involved in German actions in Eastern Europe. He began by stating that "Germany at the present moment is in the first phase of its military consolidation in the east, which, without regard to ideological considerations, must be achieved by whatever means. After the merciless cleansing of the east will come the western phase that must end in the defeat of France and England either by military or by political means. Only after this can one count on the feasibility of the destruction of the Soviet Union. At the present time we are still in the phase of military consolidation in the East. It is Poland's turn next. . . . The preparations already taken by Germany—the creation of the protectorate in Bohemia and Moravia, the creation of a Slovakian state, the annexation of the Memel region— were all directed against Poland." Here Kleist was presumably referring to the March 15, 1939, agreement forced on the Czech government that led to the occupation of Bohemia and Moravia, the creation of Slovakia, and the March 23 occupation of the Memel region.

Kleist went on to say: "Hitler . . . has decided it is necessary to bring Poland to her knees. To a small circle of persons around Hitler, it was known that the last German proposal would be rejected by Poland. Hitler and Ribbentrop were convinced that because of foreign and domestic policy considerations, the Polish government would not accept the German demands. Only for this reason could Germany have been able to insert the point in its proposal on guarantees of the inviolability of frontiers for 25 years. German calculations were correct. On the strength of Poland's refusal, we now have a free hand in dealing with her." At this point in his briefing, Kleist was probably referring to negotiations with Poland's foreign minister, Josef Beck.

Kleist's next words were harsher:

> If Poland does not agree to German proposals and does not capitulate in the weeks ahead, one can scarcely doubt that in July, August she will be the victim of a military attack. . . . Major strategic opposition by the Polish army will be overcome in 8–14 days. The attack on Poland will be carried out simultaneously from Germany's eastern border, from Slovakia, Carpatho-Ukraine, and East Prussia. The offensive must be carried out in the fiercest way and, as the German general staff conceives it, should lead to a stunning success. The remaining centers of opposition that will, without doubt, exist in the entire country will be suppressed in the most merciless fashion. . . . German preparations against Poland have been postponed to July–August. Military measures will be undertaken not long before the offensive. They must be executed thoroughly and completely camouflaged.

Kleist concentrated on the themes for a propaganda offensive against Poland, listing the ploys and slogans that were to be emphasized in the campaign: "Under the slogan 'Poland—State of Reaction and Decay,' we must reveal the poverty of the Polish peasants, the cultural backwardness of the country, the feudal methods of running the economy and existence of a starving Polish population. . . . The goal of this campaign is to affect world public opinion and the Polish population; one must achieve a split within the Polish nation and dissatisfaction with the Polish leadership on the part of the Polish population, exploiting class differences. Preparations for the propaganda attack against Poland will take about two months."

Kleist examined various situations that would provide Germany with a pretext for initiating military action:

> It would be ideal if the conflict with Poland was not seen as brought about by Germany. At the present time, we in Berlin are discussing the question of bringing the Ukraine into the affair. Voloshin [A. Voloshin, head of the autonomous government of Carpatho-Ukraine] and Iu. Revai [a minister in that government] are agreed concerning . . . the broad autonomy of the Carpatho-Ukraine within the framework of the Hungarian states. With this we have again won the trust of the Ukrainian masses in eastern Galicia and strengthened the frayed military might of the Ukraine. No special propaganda is needed to work up Ukrainian leading circles; they will remain faithful to Berlin. We might later give the western Ukraine the signal to revolt. From Slovakia and Transcarpathian Ukraine we could send weapons and arms as well as well-trained Ukrainian fighters. There is such close contact between Lvov and Berlin that there can be no doubt about an uprising in the Ukraine. Thus, creating the seeds of unrest in the Ukraine will give Germany the opportunity to intervene militarily on a large scale. This project, however, creates concern in Germany over one danger—the possible reaction of the Soviet Union. If we think otherwise, the Ukrainian factor will be put into play in the future.

Signing the Nazi-Soviet nonaggression pact precluded this scheme. It demonstrates, however, the degree to which the Germans had made common cause with Ukrainian nationalists, a factor that would become active in the spring and summer of 1941.

Kleist's view of the future was oddly prophetic:

> We adhere to the view that a conflict with Poland can be localized. England and France, as in the past, are not ready to act on Poland's behalf. If we crush Poland's main opposition in a short time, then England may demonstrate with her fleet in the Mediterranean. France will rattle its guns behind the Maginot line—that will end the affair. If, despite expectations, a European war begins in connection with a

German attack on Poland, then we'll know that a German strike against Poland will serve as a pretext for a preventive war against Germany by the Western powers—something agreed on in advance.... If this happens, Hitler will be ready to engage in lengthy discussions. In any case, we will not allow ourselves to be provoked at a time not of our choosing. Choice of the moment for action we reserve to ourselves. At present we have decided not to involve ourselves in a European war as a result of our inadequate readiness and, for us, the unrewarding international situation; however, in three or four months we can be completely ready. The German command is convinced it will be victorious . . . because of our aviation. According to the calculations of our military specialists, all the ports of England can be destroyed within six hours. The destructive action of German aviation has up until now, been demonstrated only once, during the Spanish civil war in the port of Guernica. The success was stupendous—the city was flattened. In this light, the defeat of England and France will not be a difficult affair.... America will not intervene in time and the Soviet Union will stay neutral.

Kleist continued his prophesying:

In order to deliver a blow against Poland, at present Berlin has begun to be intensively involved in the southeast. We must get closer to Romania. Gafencu [the Romanian foreign minister] spread around kind words in Berlin but then in London and Paris engaged in anti-German politics. We will not achieve our goals this way. Direct pressure on Bucharest is needed. . . . We will . . . make Hungary a German protectorate and then move troops up to Romania's borders. Romania will capitulate. We expect to achieve our goals in the Baltic States in a different way. The neutrality of the Baltic States in the event of war is just as important to us as is the neutrality of Belgium or Holland. Some time later, when a favorable moment occurs for us, we can violate it but for now, on the strength of the nonaggression pact concluded earlier [with Poland in 1934], we avoid automatic interference by the Soviet Union.

In conclusion, he said: "Thus, the offensive against Poland is set for July or August. If the Poles provoke a preventive war against us before that time, things will be different. Whether we respond to this provocation with an offensive will depend on the Führer's decision and his evaluation of the international situation. In any case, it would be unpleasant for us if the Poles force us into war at present, when the international situation does not favor us and our preparations for war are not yet in place."

After reading the report, Stalin wrote this instruction in the margin:

"Speak with Proskurov—who is this 'source'?" The word *source* was under-lined twice. Proskurov had an answer to Stalin's question. There were three Soviet agents among the officers of the German embassy in Warsaw: Rudolf von Scheliha, Gerhard Kegel, and Kurt Völkisch, whose wife also worked by photographing documents obtained by other members of the Herrnstadt group. Von Scheliha would have been present at Kleist's brief-ing, and the report was probably his work. Proskurov would have given Stalin reason to believe in the reliability of these sources, and if one com-pares the points raised by Kleist with the actions Stalin went on to take to frustrate some of Hitler's plans, it appears that he took at least parts of the report to heart. Stalin had no intention, of course, of acquiescing in the "destruction of the Soviet Union," but he must have seen that Hitler's de-signs on Poland were serious and he probably agreed that England and France could do little to prevent its defeat. It would be this line of reason-ing that would produce the Nazi-Soviet nonaggression pact, an agreement Stalin felt would delay a possible German invasion. He would have agreed that once the Polish victory had been digested, Hitler would have turned on Britain and France. He could not, however, have anticipated that Ger-many's defeat of their forces in France would have come about as rapidly as Kleist predicted.

Kleist's comments about German plans for the Baltic States, coming after the German occupation of Memel, must have stayed in Stalin's mind. No sooner was the German pact signed and the German assault on Poland under way than the USSR entered into mutual assistance treaties with the Baltic States that provided for the stationing there of Soviet troops. In Stalin's view, this action signaled to Hitler that Lithuania, Latvia, and Es-tonia were and would remain in the Soviet sphere of interest. Ever a stick-ler for the diplomatic niceties, Stalin would wait until the summer of 1940 to hold elections in the Baltic States, followed by their incorporation into the USSR as union republics. As for Kleist's comments about German plans for Romania, Stalin would have to wait until 1940 to recover the provinces of Bessarabia and northern Bukovina.

As the summer of 1939 wore on, both sides were busy sending signals. Hitler, of course, desired that his interest in reaching an accommodation with Stalin be masked in a variety of ways, such as trade talks. Given his long and very public history of anticommunism, he had no desire to make his real goals known. On July 5, 1939, for example, Proskurov sent to Defense Commissar Voroshilov an RU translation of an anonymous letter received by the Soviet diplomatic mission in Berlin. The letter might as well have been an under-the-table diplomatic note, beginning as it did with this statement: "The German government would welcome a proposal from the Soviet government concerning an immediate agreement by both governments on the future fate of Poland and Lithuania."[2] The document went on to propose a return to 1914 borders, "that is, to reoccupy the territory lost to a third power." The reference here was clearly to Poland. The following paragraph stated that "before the beginning of action by both sides, it would be expedient to establish a demarcation line that neither side would violate." It added that, in view of the "relatively large territorial gains by the USSR, Germany would occupy Lithuania."

Although couched in purposely vague terms, this unofficial proposal came close to the terms of the secret protocol that would eventually be agreed on by Germany and the USSR during the discussions of the nonaggression pact. While the pact bound both sides to refrain from aggressive action against each other, either singly or together with other powers, the secret protocol placed Latvia, Estonia, and Finland in the Soviet sphere of interest and Lithuania in Germany's sphere of interest. It was agreed that the border between the spheres of interest of Germany and the USSR in Poland would be along the Narv, Visla, and San rivers.

Stalin kept channels open to both the Germans and the Anglo-French side, intent on obtaining the best deal he could for the Soviet Union. Aware that Hitler had firmly decided to attack Poland and was therefore eager to ensure Soviet neutrality, the Soviets endeavored to obtain agreement from the British and French to begin military talks. It would not be until July 25 that the British cabinet would comply. Even then, it seemed clear to Ivan M. Maisky, the Soviet envoy to London, that the British were in no hurry to get the talks moving. He was right in this assessment. Just before he departed, the head of the British delegation, Admiral Reginald Drax, asked the British foreign minister, Viscount Halifax, how he should proceed if no agreement seemed possible. He was told to "draw out the talks as long as possible" in the hope that any German invasion of Poland would be delayed.[3]

Stalin believed that such discussions, carried out in parallel with trade agreement talks, would create additional pressure on Hitler to accede to his demands in return for a Soviet agreement. He hoped, therefore, that the military talks could begin as soon as possible. The delay continued, however, amid arguments over the mode of transport. There was no regular air service between London and Moscow, while rail travel was deemed unsuitable. Finally, it was agreed the delegations would go by sea. But rather than avail themselves of a fast cruiser, the French and English delegations took a slow cargo and passenger ship, arriving in Leningrad only on August 9. They left that night for Moscow. The Soviets, of course, had already selected the members of their delegation and made other arrangements to ensure that the discussions got under way promptly.[4]

Proskurov became involved in these preparations, procuring a French-language interpreter for Voroshilov. Proskurov remembered meeting a young Russian studying at the Sorbonne from his time in Paris during the Spanish civil war. That person was Aleksandr Nikolayevich Ponomarev, later to become a colonel–general engineer and a leading figure in the Soviet aviation industry. "I understand you speak French better than Russian," Voroshilov said when Proskurov introduced Ponomarev to him. "Tell us in French what you did in Paris." Ponomarev did so, and it was obvious his French was very good indeed. Voroshilov thanked Proskurov for helping him and gave an aide instructions to fit Ponomarev out within thirty-six hours.[5]

Only then did Voroshilov explain that an Anglo-French military delegation was due to arrive the day after next to conduct negotiations leading to a military agreement. According to Voroshilov, "it took two and a half months to talk them [the British and the French] into it. Finally, they agreed, but not of their own free will: the people demanded that a muzzle be put on Hitler. These gentlemen are not in a hurry, even now. Both delegations turned down aircraft and cruiser transportation and embarked on a slow freighter, taking a week to get to Leningrad. And this at a time when every missed day threatens catastrophe." After this introduction, Voroshilov told Ponomarev he was to act as interpreter for the Soviet delegation and each night prepare a transcript of the day's session. Ponomarev was then issued a new, snowy white summer uniform of the type worn by the other officers in the Soviet delegation.

The Soviet delegation was certainly a cut above that of the British or the French. Headed by Defense Commissar Voroshilov, it included the most senior officers of the Soviet military establishment: Boris M. Shaposhnikov, chief of the general staff; Admiral Nikolai G. Kuznetsov of the Soviet navy; Aleksandr D. Loktionov, new head of the Soviet air forces; and I. V. Smorodinov, deputy chief of the general staff. This was an impressive group whose ranks and responsibilities were manifestly greater than those of the Anglo-French delegation members.

It seemed to Ponomarev that Voroshilov was determined to humiliate the Anglo-French side at the first session on 12 August by asking them to provide documents attesting to their authority. When General Joseph

Doumenc of France produced a paper signed by the Premier Edouard Daladier, authorizing him "to negotiate on military matters," Voroshilov responded to the effect that authority to negotiate was not the same as authority to sign a military convention. The head of the British delegation, Sir Reginald Drax, did not improve the atmosphere when he admitted he had no written authority. Matters grew worse on August 13 when Voroshilov asked the Western delegations to describe the forces they would make available for the common defense and their operational plans for deploying those forces. Voroshilov told Ponomarev he expected him to translate their presentations very carefully. Doumenc gave a figure of 110 available divisions but seemed unsure when asked by Voroshilov what the French would do if the Soviet Union, Poland, or Romania were attacked by Germany. When the British turn came, they gave the number of divisions as sixteen. The Soviets found this figure hard to believe and, in questioning it, discovered that British plans called for sending an expeditionary force to France consisting of only five infantry divisions and a single mechanized one. On August 14, it was Shaposhnikov's turn to present the Soviet figures. He asserted that the Soviet Union would commit 120 infantry divisions, 16 cavalry divisions, 5,000 heavy guns, 9,000–10,000 tanks, and, 5,000–5,500 combat aircraft to the common defense!

Shaposhnikov's report was followed by complete silence, after which the British and French delegations turned to questions of aviation. These naturally were of great interest to Ponomarev. Air Marshal Charles Burnett had little to say about the condition of British aviation. There were 3,000 first-line aircraft in the British Isles, with production of 700 new aircraft per month. At the end of World War I, he concluded, England had 22,000 aircraft, the largest air fleet in the world. At this, Loktionov whispered to Ponomarev: "Advertising is for fools!"

Next came General Valin of the French air force, who stated that in 1940 the French would have 300 first-line aircraft, including bombers with speeds of 450–500 kilometers per hour, ranges of 800–10,000 kilometers, and bomb capacity of 1,000–2,500 kilograms. This was pretty general, and Loktionov asked Ponomarev to translate for him in asking for more specifics. Unfortunately, Valin said he could not provide additional information. Loktionov ended the aviation discussion with a detailed picture of Soviet military aviation, after which he responded to questions from both British and French air officers.

The real sticking point came over the next few days on the question of whether the British and French governments had actually secured the agreement of the Poles and Romanians. General T. G. G. Heywood of Britain commented that the Poles and Romanians were sovereign governments; only they could respond. The French and British delegations have to ask their respective governments to review the problem. "Good," said Voroshilov, "I think we should adjourn our discussions until you hear from your governments." He also said, "Responsibility for the failure of our negotiations will naturally fall upon the British and French." This comment brought cries of indignation and the accusation that Ponomarev had translated incorrectly. "No, it was correct," said Voroshilov. "We asked for transit rights for our troops, so they could repel the aggressor. Do we really have to ask for the right to fight our common foe?"

Although the conference was scheduled to resume on Monday, August 21, this was the last of any serious discussions. Voroshilov looked at Ponomarev with a bitter smile and said, "We're pretty bad diplomats." Ponomarev ended his description of the event with this observation, which remains to this day the Soviet version of what happened: "The Soviet delegation did everything for the success of the negotiations. However, the efforts of the representatives of England and France came to this: under cover of these Moscow negotiations concluding a perfidious deal with Fascist Germany and compelling her to move against the east. For the sake of this, they would have gone for any deal with the Fascists."[6]

The French attempted over the weekend to persuade the Poles to agree to the passage of Soviet troops in the event of a German invasion. They failed. The talks did resume on August 21 but they soon adjourned as it appeared that Voroshilov was well aware of the futile French approach to the Poles. The same day, however, Stalin, having received assurance from Hitler that there would be a secret protocol to the nonaggression pact that would likely grant him the concessions he had sought in Poland, the Baltic, Finland, and Romania, wrote to him agreeing to the pact and expressing willingness to receive Foreign Minister Ribbentrop on August 23 in Moscow.

The weekend of August 18–20 had been a busy one for Stalin. He had decided to negotiate a nonaggression pact with Hitler and give up on the Anglo-French military talks. He had never expected much from them anyway, and the inferior quality of the representatives and the limitations of their military resources convinced him he had been right. Besides, he probably knew that some elements in the British government, working through Chamberlain's confidante, Sir Horace Wilson, were still trying to double-cross the Poles and make a deal with Hitler.[7] What were Stalin's thoughts over that fateful weekend? Were they confined to expectations that he would recover those portions of Belorussia and Ukraine that had been under Polish rule, gain German acquiescence in obtaining Bessarabia from Romania, and get Hitler's agreement on Soviet primacy in the Baltic States? Or did he revert to long-held Leninist views that the capitalists/imperialists would ultimately exhaust themselves in wars, thus paving the way for revolutionary socialism in the industrialized countries? According to Churchill, the decision to enter into the nonaggression pact with Germany was made at a Politburo meeting on Saturday, August 19, 1939. In addition to the Politburo, the leaders of the Comintern were also present. In late 1994, a Russian translation of a French version of the speech that Stalin purportedly made at the August 19 meeting was published in Moscow.[8]

Here is an English translation of that Russian text:

The question of war or peace has entered a critical phase for us. If we conclude a treaty of mutual assistance with France and Great Britain, Germany will give up on Poland and begin to find a "modus vivendi" with the Western powers. War will be prevented but in the future events can become dangerous for the USSR. If we accept the proposal of Germany to sign a nonaggression pact with her, she will, of course, attack Poland and the intervention of France and England in the war will become inevitable. Western Europe will be exposed to serious unrest and disorders. Under these conditions we will have many chances to remain on the sidelines in the conflict and we can hope for an advantageous entry into the war.

The experience of the last twenty years shows that in peacetime it is impossible to have a communist movement in Europe strong enough to permit a Bolshevik party to seize power. The dictatorship of that party will become possible only as the result of a major war. We will make our choice and it is clear. We must accept the German proposal and politely send the Anglo-French mission back. The first advantage we can derive from this is the destruction of Poland up to the approaches to Warsaw, including Ukrainian Galicia.

Germany will grant us complete freedom of action in the Baltic countries and will not object to the return of Bessarabia to the USSR. She is ready to concede to us a zone of influence in Romania, Bulgaria, and Hungary. There remains an open question tied to Yugoslavia. . . . At the same time we must foresee the consequences that may arise from the defeat, as well as the victory, of Germany. In the case of her defeat, the Sovietization of Germany becomes inevitable and a communist government will be created. We must not forget that the Sovietization of Germany will be in great danger if it results from the defeat of Germany in a short war. England and France will still be sufficiently strong to capture Berlin and destroy Soviet Germany. And we will be in no condition to come to the aid of our Bolshevik comrades in Germany.

Thus, our task consists of ensuring that Germany can carry on the war as long as possible in order that a tired and exhausted England and France will not be in any condition to defeat a Sovietized Germany. Adhering to a position of neutrality and awaiting its hour, the USSR will provide assistance to present-day Germany, furnishing her with raw materials and food products. It goes without saying, of course, that our aid cannot exceed a certain level in order that we not harm our economy and weaken the might of our army.

At the same time we must carry out an active communist propaganda campaign, particularly in the Anglo-French bloc and principally in France. We must be prepared for a situation whereby in that country in wartime, the party will be forced to give up legal activities and go underground. We know that such work will demand many sacrifices, but our French comrades will not question this. In the first place, their tasks will be the disintegration and demoralization of the army and police. If this preparatory work is carried out satisfactorily, the security of Soviet Germany will be assured and this will make possible the Sovietization of France.

For the realization of these plans it is necessary that the war last as long as possible, and it is in this direction that we must concentrate all the forces that we possess in Western Europe and the Balkans.

Let us now examine a second possibility, the victory of Germany. Some hold to the opinion that this would pose a serious danger for us. There is a grain of truth in this view, but it would be a mistake to believe that this danger is as close and great as many imagine it. If Germany is victorious, it will emerge from the war too exhausted to begin an armed conflict with the USSR for at least ten years.

Her main concern will be to maintain control over defeated France and England with the intention of preventing their rehabilitation. On the other hand, a victorious Germany will have enormous territories at her disposal and for many years she will be busy "exploiting them" and establishing German regimes there. It is obvious that Germany will be too busy in other areas to turn against us. And there is still another thing that will serve our security. In a defeated France the French Communist Party will always be very strong. A communist revolution will inevitably take place, and we can use this situation to come to the aid of France and make her our ally. Later all nations having come under the "protection" of a victorious Germany will become our allies. We will have a broad field of action for the development of a world revolution.

Comrades! It is in the interests of the USSR, motherland of the workers, that a war break out between the Reich and the capitalist Anglo-French bloc. One must do everything to ensure that the war lasts as long as possible in order to exhaust both sides. It is precisely for this reason that we must agree to the pact proposed by Germany and work for the goal of having the war, once declared, last for the longest possible time. We must strengthen propaganda activity in the warring countries in order to be ready for the time when the war ends.

Sometime after August 19, the French news agency Havas, published excerpts from the speech. On November 30, 1939, the official party newspaper, *Pravda*, printed a letter from Stalin on the Havas release:

The editor of *Pravda* has put the following question to Comrade Stalin: What is Comrade Stalin's reaction to the message issued by the Havas agency on "Stalin's speech" allegedly made by him in the Politburo on August 19, at which ideas were supposedly advanced to the effect that "the war must be continued for as long as is needed to exhaust the belligerent countries"?

Comrade Stalin has sent the following answer:

This report issued by the Havas agency, like many more of its messages, is nonsense. I, of course, cannot know in precisely which nightclub these lies were fabricated. But no matter how many lies the gentlemen of the Havas news agency tell, they cannot deny that:

a. it was not Germany that attacked France and Britain but France and Britain that attacked Germany, thereby taking on themselves responsibility for the present war;

b. after hostilities began, Germany made peace proposals to France and Britain, while the Soviet Union openly supported these German peace proposals, for it considered and continues to consider that only as early as possible an end to the war can bring relief . . . to the condition of all countries and all peoples.

c. the ruling circles in Britain and France rejected out of hand both the German peace proposals and the Soviet Union's efforts to end the war as quickly as possible. Such are the facts. What can the nightclub politicians of the Havas agency provide to counter these facts? J. Stalin[9]

How Havas obtained the text of this speech is not known, but the most likely avenue would have been elements of the French Communist Party unwilling to accept the Soviet-Nazi rapprochement and seeking a way to embarrass Stalin. They would have had access to a French translation of the speech since translations were the normal order of business for the Executive Committee of the Communist International. It could be claimed, of course, that the speech was a fabrication. Stalin's reaction in *Pravda* suggests the Havas release deeply irritated him; the article omits the word *Poland* entirely. As for German "peace proposals" supported by the Soviet Union, Stalin's concern in the first several days of September was not peace but the speed of the Wehrmacht's advance, the collapse of Polish resistance, and whether the Red Army could occupy its promised slice of Polish territory in Belorussia and Ukraine before the Germans took it over.

The principal issue arising from the language of the apparent August 19, 1939, speech is not how Havas got it but whether it reflected Stalin's innermost thoughts on "the question of war or peace." I believe it does and my belief is buttressed by the comments Stalin made on September 7, 1939, in the presence of Georgy Dimitrov, Molotov, and Andrei A. Zhdanov and recorded by Dimitrov in his diary. They parallel the statements contained in the August 19 speech. Consider this: "A war is on between two groups of capitalist countries . . . for the redivision of the world, for the domination of the world. We see nothing wrong in their having a good fight and weakening each other. It would be fine if at the hands of Germany the position of the richest capitalist countries (especially England) were shaken." Or this: "The position of Communists in power is different from the position of Communists in the opposition. We are the masters in our own house. Communists . . . in the opposition are in the opposition; there the bourgeoisie is master. We can maneuver, pit one side against the other to set them fighting with each other as fiercely as possible." In the remainder of his comments Stalin laid out the reasons for abandoning the Popular Front, explained why he decided not to continue negotiations with the French and English, and outlined the slogans to guide the working class in their fight against "the bosses of capitalist countries . . . waging war for their own imperialist interests." In September 1939 Stalin could not foresee how quickly Hitler would overrun Western Europe, but he clung to his view that Germany would not attack the USSR in 1941 and never abandoned his hope that Hitler would deal with England first before launching such an attack.[10]

As late as May 5, 1941, there were still echoes, in a speech Stalin gave to the graduates of military academies, of his fascination with Lenin's view of war as the midwife to revolution. In the wake of the speech, the Red

Army's Chief Directorate for Political Propaganda began work on a new Red Army Political Handbook (*Krasnoarmeiski Polituchebnik*). This handbook contained the following statements:

> If, as a result of war, a situation arises in some countries whereby a revolutionary crisis ripens and the power of the bourgeoisie is weakened, the USSR will go to war against capitalism, to the aid of proletarian revolution. Lenin said, "As soon as we are strong enough to crush capitalism, we will immediately grab it by the scruff of the neck."

> If the USSR had gone along with England and France, there is no doubt that the German military machine would have been turned against the Soviet Union.

> The possibility is not excluded that the USSR, in situations that might develop, will take the initiative of offensive military operations.

The new handbook was reviewed by members of the Main Military Council on June 10, 1941, and these paragraphs (from pages 149, 152, and 155) were excised.[11]

On September 17, 1939, the Red Army began the occupation of the western regions of Belorussia and Ukraine. The impact of these and other territorial acquisitions will be examined in the next chapter.

by surprise and it was not until September 17, 1939, that he released a statement blaming the Poles for leaving defenseless "its kindred Ukrainian and Belorussian people" and announcing the Red Army's entry into Poland. Actually, extensive preparations had been made earlier. Therefore Soviet forces, together with special NKVD units, had begun advancing at 5:40 a.m. that day on two fronts formed from the Belorussian and Kiev Special Military Districts. The Belorussian Front under General Mikhail P. Kovalev, composed of four armies, moved rapidly against little resistance. By September 28 it was able to organize elections to a People's Assembly that on November 2 voted to become part of the Belorussian SSR.[1]

Ukrainian areas were occupied by the Ukrainian Front under Semen K. Timoshenko. The Front had a force of the Fifth, Sixth, and Twelfth armies, containing a total of eight infantry corps, three cavalry corps, plus a tank corps and five tank brigades. Each army created a special mobile force from tank and cavalry units in order to reach the demarcation line in the shortest possible time.[2] Stalin was taking no chances: even though he had Hitler's agreement on the territory to be occupied, the Soviet assistant military attaché in Berlin had earlier reported a different plan. This attaché had been shown a Wehrmacht map placing the line east of Lvov and Drogobych, an oil-producing area much coveted by the Germans.[3] It should have been expected, therefore, that when forward elements of the Sixth Army arrived in the Lvov area on September 19, the Germans were already approaching the city from the west. A firefight had ensued, resulting in casualties on both sides and the loss of equipment.[4] Incidentally, the Sixth Army was commanded by Filipp I. Golikov, the "politically correct" corps commander who in 1938 had been the political member of the Military Council of the Belorussian Military District and in 1940 would become the head of Soviet military intelligence.[5] By mid-October, elections to a People's Assembly were held, paralleling the procedure in Belorussia. By October 27 the assembly, sitting in Lvov, voted to become part of the Ukrainian SSR and the union was accepted on November 15, 1939. Glowing reports were received in Moscow describing the happiness of the western Ukrainians at joining the Soviet family. This one from Lev Z. Mekhlis, chief of the Political Directorate of the Red Army, was typical: "The Ukrainian population is meeting our army as true liberators. . . . As a rule, even advance units are being met by entire populations coming out onto the streets. Many weep with joy." The youth of Drogobych said "their hearts were filled with deep love for the great Soviet people, the Red Army, and the Ukrainian Communist Party."[6] These first reactions on the part of western Ukrainians reflected their dislike of the Poles, who had governed them since 1919, and their lack of experience with either the tsarist or the Soviet government. They had, after all, been part of the Austro-Hungarian Empire from the first partition of Poland in 1772 to the end of World War I.

The Soviet security forces had a more realistic view of the difficulties they would encounter when the Belorussian and Ukrainian populations of Poland were brought under Soviet control. On September 1, 1939, soon after the Germans launched their attack on Poland, they began to plan for a massive NKVD presence in the new territories. A week later, NKVD chief Beria issued orders to Ivan S. Serov and Lavrenti F. Tsanava, the heads of the NKVD in the Ukrainian and Belorussian SSRs, to create special Chekist groups composed of operational and political workers from their own staffs and from the border troop districts in their republics. Personnel for these groups, approximately 500 officers, were also to be taken from temporary assignments in the Leningrad NKVD Directorate and from the central NKVD staff. Arrangements were made for assigning these groups to army units in accordance with plans of the defense commissar. Serov was directed to coordinate his activities with Ukrainian Communist Party Secretary Nikita S. Khrushchev and with Ukrainian Front Commander Semen K. Timoshenko. In Belorussia the same pattern was to have been followed. Every day at 6:00 p.m. Serov and Tsanava were to report by telegraph on their progress. The deputy chief of the USSR NKVD for troops, Ivan I. Maslennikov, was to place personnel of the Ukrainian and Belorussian border troop districts at the disposal of the chiefs of the operational Chekist groups; these troops were to be formed into battalions, one per group, to carry out special tasks. Sergei N. Kruglov, NKVD deputy commissar, was directed to form a reserve group of 300 taken from the local organs of the NKVD and to compile a list of the selected persons by September 10. Beria concluded by ordering Vsevolod N. Merkulov, his first deputy, to the Ukrainian SSR to supervise operations there, and Viktor M. Bochkov, chief of NKVD Special Departments, to Belorussia. By the next day, Serov responded, noting that the required personnel were either on hand or en route; the First and Second operational groups were already being provided by agreement with the Kiev Special Military District. Serov added that he was in regular contact with Khrushchev and Timoshenko. From these communications one can see how quickly and efficiently the NKVD functioned to create the administrative structure to support military operations in the new territories.[7]

On September 15, two days before the Red Army made its move, Beria sent a directive to Serov and Tsanava explaining how and what was to be done as Soviet forces entered former Polish territory. When Soviet troops occupied a town, a temporary civil administration including leaders of the NKVD operational groups was to be created. Working in close contact with the military and under the leadership of the temporary civil administrations, NKVD operatives would maintain public order, eliminate sabotage, suppress counterrevolution, and form the nucleus of future NKVD offices for the area. Here are some of their specific tasks:

> Immediately seize all communications facilities—that is, telephone, telegraph, radio stations, post offices—and place trusted persons in charge. Seize all private and government banks and treasury branches, impound all funds, and arrange for their safekeeping.
>
> Extend all possible cooperation to political departments of the Red Army in seizing printing presses, newspaper editorial offices, and newsprint warehouses and start up new newspapers. Also seize all government archives, particularly those of the intelligence and counterintelligence services of the former Polish government.
>
> Arrest the more reactionary representatives of the former government, such as local police officers, members of the gendarmerie, border police, military intelligence officers, etc. Also arrest leaders and active members of counterrevolutionary political parties and organizations. Also occupy the jails, check the backgrounds of prisoners. Release those with records of resistance to the Polish government, establish a new prison system staffed by reliable people and headed by an NKVD operative.

In addition to the above measures, the NKVD component of the administration was to deal with criminal matters and establish a reliable fire department. Its main concern, however, was the detection and elimination of espionage and terror, as well as sabotage, in industry and transport. In organizing this replica of NKVD operations within the existing Soviet Union, Stalin and Beria did not for a moment consider any other model or allow for a period of transition. The inhabitants of the new areas were to be transformed overnight into obedient Soviet citizens. The term *reliable people* referred to those individuals who were already known to be anti-Polish and pro-Soviet, some of whom had served as agents of Soviet intelligence.[8]

Problems in Western Ukraine

On September 19, 1939, Merkulov and Serov got their first taste of the operational problems they would encounter in implementing Beria's orders. They complained that they would need even more operational Chekist groups than they had planned to create. On September 28, in an interim report on NKVD operations, Merkulov noted that Ukrainian nationalists such as the Organization of Ukrainian Nationalists (OUN) exceeded all other persons arrested in accordance with the criteria established by the Beria order. To illustrate, Merkulov reported that of the 1,923 arrests made by operational group 1, over 1,000 were members or activists of nationalist organizations. He also commented on the "enormous quantity of weapons" uncovered.[9]

Merkulov's mention of the OUN should not have surprised Serov or Khrushchev. This group had been in existence in various forms since the collapse of the short-lived Ukrainian National Republic. Proclaimed in January 1919 and incorporating all Ukrainian lands, including western Ukraine, or Galicia, and those in the Carpathian Mountain area and in Bukovina and Bessarabia, this briefly independent entity ceased to exist after the Treaty of Riga in 1921. The Soviet Union retained the eastern and central areas of Ukraine as the Ukrainian SSR. Czechoslovakia obtained the Carpatho-Ukraine, Romania occupied Bessarabia and Bukovina, and western Ukraine, or Galicia, was given to Poland. During the 1920s and 1930s the idea of an independent Ukraine was kept alive in Galicia despite efforts by the Poles and the Soviets to suppress its adherents. The OUN, at that time headed by Colonel Yevhen Konovalets, was considered a serious threat by the Soviet NKVD, which believed he had made contact with the German Abwehr, had even met with Hitler, and was allowed to train his followers at the Nazi Party school in Leipzig. According to Pavel A. Sudoplatov, a veteran NKVD special operations officer, in 1935 he was sent abroad as an illegal to make contact with Konovalets and penetrate the OUN; two years later, he briefed Stalin personally. In May 1938 Sudoplatov assassinated Konovalets, who was replaced in the OUN by his deputy, Colonel Andrei A. Melnyk. His authority was disputed by Stepan A. Bandera, and by the time Poland was defeated the nationalist movement had split into two camps, supporters of Melnyk and those of Bandera, referred to as *Banderivtsi*. Both sides proclaimed that their sole allegiance was to Ukrainian independence and denied they were subservient to German interests.[10]

Evidence of the size of the Ukrainian nationalists' paramilitary grew. In December 1940 a member of one of the paramilitary groups, arrested while trying to cross the border, reported that in Lvov there was a counter-revolutionary insurgent organization of 2,000 armed members. The group also possessed six heavy machine guns and had subordinate units in the towns of Stanislav, Kolomye, Peremyshl, and Tarnopol. By December 1940 the Ukrainian SSR NKVD knew from its agent "Ukrainets" that Lvov was the underground center of the OUN in the western Ukraine. It also knew about the split between Bandera and Melnyk, both of whom were in contact with the Germans.[11] The fears developing in Kiev and Moscow over the strength and intentions of the OUN were not misplaced, as can be seen in the "unified general plan of the insurgency staff of the OUN," a response to Abwehr directives to create an uprising in the Ukraine to disrupt the rear of the Red Army, an uprising in which the OUN would emerge from underground to lead the people "in all Ukrainian lands, in order to achieve the complete breakdown of the 'Muscovite, Soviet prison of peoples.'"[12]

In mid-April 1941, Pavel Ia. Meshik, commissar for state security of the Ukrainian SSR, wrote Khrushchev that his organization had concluded that the Germans would be using the OUN as a fifth column in their planned invasion of the USSR; the group, he said, "represent a serious force inasmuch as they are well armed and continue to increase their weapons stocks through transfers from Germany." The OUN was not content to wait to act until a war had begun; its units were terrorizing chairmen of village councils to the point that even pro-Soviet people were afraid to report them. Meshik recommended actions to deprive the OUN of its base of support, including the death penalty for members of its organizations living illegally in the western Ukraine, confiscation of their property, and exile of members of their families. Because wealthy peasants formed an important part of the OUN structure, they were to be exiled and their lands given to collective farms.[13]

On April 29, Beria sent a directive to the commissars for state security and internal affairs of the Ukrainian SSR on improving measures for stopping terrorist activity by the OUN in the western oblasts of the republic. He reported an increase in incidents (there were thirty-eight in April 1941) and noted that the OUN was even inflicting casualties on members of the NKGB and NKVD. The NKGB, he emphasized, had ultimate responsibility for destroying the OUN.[14] With this order and previous ones in hand, the NKGB of the Ukrainian SSR announced on May 23, 1941, that it had detained and loaded on freight cars for their journey into exile 11,476 persons.[15] On May 31 the Third (Secret-Political) Directorate of the USSR NKGB issued an orientation on anti-Soviet nationalist organizations operating in the former Polish territories. It named the OUN as the most active and described its close ties with the Abwehr and Ukrainian emigration in the west. According to the report, after the Soviet absorption of the western Ukraine, that portion of the OUN under Stepan Bandera transferred its headquarters from Lvov to Cracow, which was also the site of a large Abwehr unit that ran training schools for OUN members in espionage, sabotage, diversion, and the organization of underground activities. After completing this school, selected graduates were sent to the German Special Forces Regiment Brandenburg-800 for additional instruction, after which they were infiltrated into the Soviet Ukraine either singly or in groups. This NKGB orientation also accused the Ukrainian Catholic, or Uniate Church, clergy of supporting the OUN. Because by now the majority of the Ukrainian population of the western oblasts thoroughly detested Soviet rule and yearned for independence, they, along with the clergy, would often risk cooperating with the OUN, an organization they saw as patriotic and proindependence.[16]

On June 15, 1941, NKVD Commissar Serov reported on the result of his operations against the OUN for the period January–June 1941. Although sixty-three political and criminal bands were liquidated, with arrests of 273 of their members as well as 212 persons operating in a support capacity, Serov stated that a significant number of these bands were still active in Lvov, Rovno, and Drogobych oblasts.[17] The same was true of Tarnopol and Volynsk oblasts. That Serov's concern was well founded can be seen in a directive from USSR NKGB head Merkulov issued just hours before the German attack. Obviously dissatisfied with NKGB attempts to rein in the OUN, Merkulov proposed a massive new operation aimed at the arrest and relocation of "counterrevolutionary elements, especially OUN members." The directive concluded with this order: "Telegraph immediately the dates by which you can prepare such an operation." The recipients never had a chance to consider the order because by the time they received it German attacks had started. Concurrently, the OUN activists, were busy causing as much havoc behind Soviet lines as they could.[18]

Belorussia

A September 12, 1939, report from the Belorussian NKVD on conditions in Polish-held territory revealed that the only "partisan" activity they expected was from groups of rural workers who intended to attack landed estates, wealthy farmers, and commercial enterprises. There was no suggestion that anti-Soviet nationalist organizations would arise to cause the same problems faced in western Ukraine.[19] By May 1941, however, the

USSR NKGB was able to describe in some detail the history and activities of significant anti-Soviet groups in the western oblasts of the Belorussian SSR. The largest was Gromada, the word for a rural assembly in the Belorussian language. Ironically, this organization had been created by Polish intelligence in the 1920s as cover for the recruitment of Belorussian agents to send into Soviet Belorussia. To their chagrin, the Poles saw Gromada grow into a huge organization, with as many as 100,000 members among the Belorussian peasantry. Afraid it was losing control, the Polish service disbanded the organization. Others followed, such as the Christian Democrats, using Vilnius as a center from which to propagandize Belorussian peasants in Poland. There were also groups who preached "national socialism," but the organization with the greatest appeal to Belorussians was apparently the Belorussian Committee for Self-Help, or BKS, founded at the end of 1939 after the Soviet takeover. The NKGB report on Belorussian anti-Soviet organizations also included a lengthy section on the Jewish Bund, which existed in Belorussia, Poland, and Russia. According to the NKGB, it contained many members of Trotskyist persuasion. Although unlikely, for obvious reasons, to align themselves with German intelligence, Bund members spoke out against measures taken by the Soviets in Belorussia.[20]

A long special report by the Belorussian NKGB contains a section on sabotage of rail lines to be carried out by several Belorussian agents of the Abwehr at the onset of military operations. On June 17, 1941, a group of five were arrested by Soviet troops while trying to cross the border. Under interrogation they revealed that they had undergone training at Lamsdorf, in the Berlin area. There were fifty agents in their class, one of whom had left on June 16 to perform an act of sabotage in the area of Luninets in Brestskaia Oblast, Belorussian SSR. Of those in custody, each team of two had specific sabotage targets. One was a portion of the rail line between Baranovichi in Brestskaia Oblast and Stolbtsy in Minskaia Oblast; the second was a section of track between Lida in Brestskaia Oblast and Molodechno in Minskaia Oblast. These actions, the agents were told, would cut off movement of Red Army reserves to the front the moment hostilities began between Germany and the Soviet Union. The fifth agent was assigned to perform acts of sabotage in the Luninets area. Although the agents were informed that hostilities would begin in early July, they were to blow up targets of opportunity and return to German territory if war had not begun by August 1. They were armed with pistols, slabs of gun cotton, and explosive devices and had been given 1,800 Soviet rubles for expenses, as well as ground panels with which to signal German aircraft. Theirs were not the only sabotage teams, the agents said. Six others were to be infiltrated at the same time with the same type of missions.[21]

Lest one conclude that these preparations were spurred by the young agents' vivid imaginations, it might be useful to examine an order from German Army Group B instructing sabotage agents to destroy targets in Soviet territory of the Fourth Army either just before or during the army's advance. The sabotage unit assigned to the Fourth Army consisted of one company of Regiment Brandenburg-800, then undergoing training at the Lamsdorf training site; companies of Brandenburg-800 were divided into two units of 220 men each. Some of the Fourth Army targets were to be seized and neutralized by groups of thirty dressed in Red Army uniforms; timing for this operation was to be just before the main offensive. Other targets were to be assigned to units of sixty men wearing civilian clothes over their Wehrmacht uniforms. Still others were to be seized by the remainder of Regiment Brandenburg-800's unit during the advance of the first echelon of the Fourth Army. Liaison officers would be appointed from the Abwehr and the regiment to work with the units of the Fourth Army in the various target areas. Compare this Army Group B order with the statements made by the persons interrogated by the Soviet border troops and it is clear that the use of agents drawn from the local population was an important part of German operational plans for the June 22 invasion.[22]

Moldavia

As part of the definition of "German and Soviet spheres of interest" covered in the secret protocol to the nonaggression pact, Stalin had insisted on receiving Bessarabia, a former Russian province that had been seized by Romania following World War I. Not until late June 1940, however, did the Red Army move in and the process of Sovietization begin. The provincial capital, Kishinev, became the capital of the greatly expanded Moldavian SSR. Here the Soviets encountered difficulties similar to those that had plagued them in the western Ukraine and Belorussia.

A USSR NKGB report dated May 11, 1941, alerted Moldavian authorities to German preparations for diversionary operations against targets in the Bendery area of the Moldavian SSR. On June 19, 1941, the Moldavian NKGB reported that it had taken action on June 13 to arrest several categories of potentially anti-Soviet elements and have their families evacuated. The arrestees were listed by category, and the second-largest group, 1,681, consisted of members of counterrevolutionary groups and participants in nationalist organizations. Forming the slightly larger group (1,719) were the old Soviet standbys: former landowners, factory owners, wealthy merchants, and house owners. They must have had large families because the total number of family members evacuated came to 13,980.[23]

The Baltic States

Stalin was determined not to allow the Germans a foothold in the Baltic States, whose people he knew were decidedly anti-Soviet after twenty years of independence. He could not undo the German annexation of the Lithuanian port of Memel in March 1939, but he knew Hitler had designs on Lithuania. For this reason he insisted that the secret protocol to the nonaggresion pact provide that the Baltic States were to be in the Soviet sphere of influence. The ink on the signatures was hardly dry before Stalin moved to nail down his rights in the Baltic by concluding treaties of mutual assistance with each of the countries, beginning with Estonia on September 28, 1939, and followed by Latvia and Lithuania on October 5 and 10. The treaties gave the Soviets the right to station troops in each country. Beria recognized, of course, that placing Soviet garrisons in countries that had for two decades enjoyed a higher standard of living than the Soviet Union, among people who were accustomed to speaking their minds openly, involved serious problems of morale and political disaffection. On October 19, 1939, he gave new orders to the military counterintelligence Special Departments that would be assigned to these troop units. After making the ritual bow to the danger of foreign intelligence services recruiting Red Army personnel, Beria got down to business. He warned the units to check on their informant nets among the troops, enlarging them as necessary, so as to observe any suspicious activity on the part of the local citizenry. Reports on troop morale or infractions of discipline were to be sent to Moscow every three days. Obviously, Beria was very concerned about the impact on his socialist soldiers of their bourgeois surroundings.[24] Defense Commissar Voroshilov followed up on October 25 with orders to each of the major Soviet units. Commanders were to explain to their troops the reasons for the mutual assistance treaties and the policies of friendship adopted by the USSR toward the Baltic countries. After warning the troops to be on the lookout for provocations, Voroshilov forbade them to have contact with the local population either in groups or individually.[25]

A November 23, 1939, report by a Soviet military attaché in Riga, Latvia, illustrates how difficult this operation was for the Red Army. The Latvian military, responsible for dealing with the Soviets on the problems of their garrisons, was extremely unfriendly and uncooperative. Senior Latvian officers expressed the hope that the Soviet presence would be short-lived. These attitudes affected every aspect of their dealings with the Red Army. Asked to make a Latvian army casern available for use by a Soviet unit, the Latvians stripped the buildings bare, right down to the sinks and toilets. They made it difficult for Soviet garrisons to reach commercial contracts with suppliers of foodstuffs and interfered with mail deliveries. The Soviets complained of being under constant, obvious, if not insolent surveillance.[26]

Similar attitudes toward Soviet garrisons existed in each of the Baltic States. While the Winter War with Finland was under way, there was little Stalin could do. By mid-June 1940, however, the Soviets were ready to embark on the final phase of their program to eliminate the independence of the Baltic States. Accusing them of conspiring together to create an anti-Soviet military alliance, the USSR demanded the resignation of their governments and the acceptance of additional Soviet troops to be stationed near all their principal cities.[27]

On June 19, 1940, Proskurov disseminated an intelligence report describing increases in German troop strength along the East Prussian–Lithuanian border following the entry of additional Soviet troops into the Baltic States. Two days later, Timoshenko, the new Soviet defense commissar, received an excited handwritten note from Colonel General Dimitry G. Pavlov, commander of the Belorussian Special Military District. After asserting that it was impossible to permit the units of the Lithuanian, Latvian, and Estonian armies to remain together, Pavlov recommended that all three armies be disarmed and their weapons taken to the USSR. Alternatively, after a purge of the officer corps and reinforcement by "our commanders," the Lithuanian and Estonian units were to be used in war, possibly against Afghans, Romanians, or Japanese, but not in the Belorussian Special Military District's area. "I consider it necessary to disarm the Latvians completely. Once the matter of the armies is taken care of, we should immediately disarm the civilian population. Failure to turn in weapons should result in death by firing squad," Pavlov added. The Special Military District was prepared to assist in carrying out these measures, he said, but asked that the order for them "be given 36 hours before the beginning of the action." There is no record of any answer from Timoshenko.

While Pavlov's reaction to the problems presented by integrating Baltic troops into the Red Army may have sounded a bit exaggerated at the time, he would see his worst fears come true in June 1941 when Lithuanian units on his left flank mutinied and supported the advancing Germans.[28]

By August 6, 1940, the Supreme Soviet acknowledged the entry of the Baltic States into the USSR and on August 17 Defense Commissar Timoshenko ordered that the existing armies of Lithuania, Latvia, and Estonia be preserved for one year, with politically untrustworthy elements to be weeded out. Then each republic's army would become a corps in the Red Army. This process of Sovietization in the military and in civilian life naturally angered even politically moderate elements in the three states.[29] But Soviet counterintelligence seemed mainly concerned about the danger of espionage arising from the presence of the German Repatriation Commission and other organizations to which Germans awaiting repatriation belonged. By early April, however, it became apparent that these Germans were trying to unify Latvian nationalists, creating groups known as "Defenders of Latvia," who could terrorize those Latvians cooperating with the Soviet Latvian administration. The Germans were also supplying the groups with arms and other equipment for use against Red Army garrisons.[30] On May 3, 1941, the NKGB of the Lithuanian SSR uncovered a German intelligence team operating a radio transmitter in Kaunas and broadcasting to Stettin, Germany, the location of an Abwehr station training agents for sabotage operations in the Baltic. The principal agent at the radio site in Kaunas was a former Lithuanian Army officer. Clearly, though the Lithuanian nationalist underground may have started slowly, its ardor was fanned by the repressive nature of Soviet actions. According to the NKGB, between July 1940 and May 1941 it uncovered and liquidated seventy-five illegal anti-Soviet organizations, all of which had as their mission the instigation of uprisings against the Soviet government as soon as war began between Germany and the USSR. There were many different groupings among the nationalists but in January 1941 they united under the title of the "Lithuanian Activists Front."[31]

By May 16, 1941, the Soviets were desperate. The Central Committee and the Council of People's Commissars issued a decree on "measures for the purging of the Lithuanian, Latvian, and Estonian SSRs of anti-Soviet, criminal, and socially dangerous elements." Noting the "significant quantity of former members of various counterrevolutionary nationalist parties, of former policemen, gendarmes, landowners, manufacturers, high officials of the former government apparatuses of Lithuania, Latvia, and

Estonia, and of other persons carrying out subversive anti-Soviet work and being used by foreign intelligence for espionage tasks," the decree enumerated those categories of persons (and their families) subject to confiscation of property, prison terms, and exile, as well as the procedures to be used and the locations of camps and places of exile. The whole operation was to be executed over three days under the supervision of the people's commissar for state security, Vsevolod N. Merkulov; his deputy, Ivan A. Serov; and the deputy commissar for internal affairs, Viktor S. Abakumov. It is said that even in the brief time before the German invasion, Stalin managed to deport thousands of persons, amounting to 4 percent of the Estonian population and 2 percent of the populations of Lithuania and Latvia.[32]

Still, the Soviets did not succeed in wiping out all vestiges of Lithuanian nationalism. On May 27 the Lithuanian NKGB described a group calling itself the "Lithuanian Legion." Predicting the Germans' imminent invasion of the USSR, it set as its goal to "create an uprising in the rear of the Red Army and engage in diversionary and subversive activity, destroying bridges and rail lines and disrupting communications." An NKGB report of June 10 dealt with a "Guard for the Defense of Lithuania" that sought to unify Lithuanians around the idea of an independent Lithuania. The group instructed its members that the signal for a national uprising would be the moment Germany crossed the frontier of the Lithuanian SSR; its tasks would include "the arrest of commissars and communist activists, seizure of Communist Party centers without destruction of their archives, stopping deportations, rendering rail lines and highways in the rear of Soviet troops unusable, and finally, in the event of assistance by the Lithuanian corps [of the Red Army], disarming Soviet troops and creating panic." Another report on the Guard and on the so-called Diversionists was sent to Moscow by a USSR NKGB operational group working in Lithuania; it described them as prepared to lend armed support to German troops invading the USSR. The Lithuanian NKGB hoped to arrest twenty-four members of these organizations and asked Moscow to send a group of "qualified interrogators." Wonder if they made it before June 22?[33]

Theater Infrastructure and Fortified Areas

It was not only the hostility of the populations of the areas absorbed by the Soviet Union in 1939–40 that would create problems for the Red Army. It was also the absence of a well-developed military infrastructure of the type that had existed along the old frontier. Meeting the needs of a fully

The Partition of Eastern Europe

FINLAND

SWEDEN

Tallinn

Leningrad

ESTONIA
Occupied by
Russia 1940

Pskov

BALTIC SEA

Riga

LATVIA
Occupied by Russia 1940

LITHUANIA
Occupied by Russia 1940

Königsberg

Danzig

EAST
PRUSSIA

Vilnius

Minsk

R. Neman

BELORUSSIA

Poznan

GERMANY

R. Vistula

Kutno

Lodz

German-Soviet
demarcation line
Sept. 8, 1939

U.S.S.R.

Warsaw

Brest-Livotsk

German-Soviet
Nonaggression
Pact
August 23, 1939

P O L A N D

GOVERNMENT
GENERAL

Lublin

Cracow

PROTECTORATE OF
BOHEMIA-MORAVIA

Lvov

SLOVAKIA

NORTHERN
BUKOVINA

M O L D A V I A

HUNGARY

Transylvania to
Hungary 1940

B E S S A R A B I A

R. Dniester

YUGOSLAVIA

0   50 100 150 200 km

0   50   100 mi

ROMANIA

Bucharest

BLACK
SEA

R. Danube

BULGARIA

N

mobilized army meant improving roads, rail lines, and telecommunications and constructing airfields, firing ranges, barracks, repair shops, hospitals, warehouses, fuel storage tanks, and so on. At enormous expense, work on these facilities went on intermittently all during the 1930s in the Kiev and Belorussian Special Military Districts and also in the Far East, reflecting concern with Germany and Japan as potential adversaries. With the territorial expansion of 1939–40, Soviet western borders were moved as much 400 kilometers westward. What was missing was the military infrastructure that had taken many years to create along the old frontier. The capacities of the road nets and railroads had to be increased; the latter needed to convert their tracks to the broader Russian gauge. Although existing structures such as barracks or warehouses could be adapted to military needs, many had to be built from scratch. The most difficult problem, though, was the total absence of the kinds of fortifications, known as the Stalin Line, that had already been constructed along the former state frontier. Here is a description of fortifications along that line:

> The original fortified areas, in Russian *ukreplennye raiony,* were between 50 and 140 kilometers in length, straddled major lines of communications, and tended to have one or both flanks anchored on a natural obstacle. The Kiev Fortified Area, for example, formed an arc west of the city whose ends rested on the Dnepr River. The general arrangement called for a support zone with a depth of ten to twelve kilometers to precede a fortified area's main defense zone; the support zone's scattered outposts and obstacles were supposed to report, harass, and delay an enemy's advance. Behind it, the blockhouses and pill boxes in the main defense zone were scattered across a swath with a depth of three to four kilometers. Within it, a grouping of several fortifications formed a support point; a cluster of three to five support points comprised a battalion defense area assigned to a machine gun battalion. The battalion defense area was positioned so that its fixed weaponry dominated the routes through

---

(Map opposite page) On the basis of the August 23, 1939, nonaggression pact and its secret protocols, the USSR acquired eastern districts of Poland that were incorporated into the Belorussian and Ukrainian SSRs. Romania also ceded Bessarabia to the USSR. It was incorporated into the Moldavian SSR. The acquisition of northern Bukovina and its transfer to the Ukrainian SSR, as well as the incorporation of the Baltic States into the USSR in 1940, were unilateral Soviet actions.

the sector being protected. The two-story blockhouses and single-story pillboxes typically were armed with machine guns mounted in casemates. Embrasures with armored coverings enabled these weapons to be fired to an emplacement's front and sides. Fortifications were equipped with air filtration systems for protection against chemical weapons, water storage tanks, generators, and land line communications. The outfitting process was neither smooth nor uniformly effective; for example, battalion defense areas were often linked by unprotected open wire or tactical field cables because of the failings of the buried cable industry. In addition to weapon emplacements, there were command posts, communications centers, personnel shelters, and depots distributed throughout a fortified area. The fortifications themselves obtained additional protection from anti-tank ditches, wire entanglements, and the minefields that would be laid upon mobilization.[34]

Defensive operations were to provide only a brief interlude that allowed for completion of mobilization and a rapid transition to the offensive, in which the enemy would be decisively defeated, his homeland occupied, and socialism triumphant. This offensive spirit dominated Soviet military thought in the 1930s. It, and the inability of Soviet military leaders to rid themselves of the idea that the opening phases of the next war would follow the leisurely pattern of previous wars, would make it difficult for the Red Army to decide how to defend the new territories.

The issue now faced by Stalin and the general staff was what to do with the existing fortified areas covering the old frontier and how and where to build fortifications in the newly acquired territories in the west. Some, such as Shaposhnikov, urged defense in depth, which meant retention of the old fortifications so as to be able to fall back on them in the face of a German assault. This view was anathema to Stalin, who did not wish to give up a single *vershok* of the new land (a Russian unit of measurement equal to a few centimeters). Indeed, motivated entirely by his desire to demonstrate that Soviet power had advanced westward, Stalin would insist that fortifications in the western oblasts be constructed along the line of the new border. This decision meant that German observers were able to follow the progress of construction and pinpoint weaknesses, but Stalin, until the real blow fell, was never one to be concerned with military details that countered his own views. Consequently, it was decided to shut down the Stalin Line fortifications and remove their weapons for use in the new system.[35]

What actually happened? In the first place, all was not well with the fortified areas of the original Stalin Line. On January 11, 1939, some time before the signing of the Nazi-Soviet Nonaggression Pact and its secret protocol, the NKVD of the Ukrainian SSR informed the Central Committee of the Ukrainian Communist Party of the poor condition of the Kiev Fortified Area: "Of the 257 structures in the area, only five are prepared for combat action. They consist primarily of machine gun emplacements but do not have special equipment such as communications, chemical protection, water, heating, light, etc. . . . At 175 of the 257 structures the natural relief (mounds, hills, dense woods, bushes) limits the horizon of fire. The forward sector of the permanent fortifications is only 15 kilometers from Kiev which would permit enemy artillery to bombard Kiev without approaching the fortified area. . . . Hermetic seals around machine gun embrasures date from the years 1929–1930." The list of deficiencies goes on and on. "The Special Department of the Kiev Special Military District has informed the command of the Kiev SMD of the fact that the Kiev Fortified Area is not combat ready, but despite this nothing has been done," the report concluded. A similar report, on deficiencies at the Tiraspol Fortified Area, was submitted to the Central Committee of the Ukrainian Communist Party the same day. First Secretary Nikita S. Khrushchev inserted this resolution in the report: "Comrade Timoshenko. This is an important question. It must be checked and discussed at the Military Council." Khrushchev's order did not carry much weight with Timoshenko because on January 16, 1939, a third report on fortified area deficiencies was sent to Kiev by the USSR NKVD. This time it was about the Mogilev-Yampolsky Fortified Area. Apart from the usual design and equipment problems, the area was criticized for its personnel shortages at the command level. Here again, the report concluded by noting that the Special Department of the Kiev Special Military District had brought this issue to the attention of the commanding general, S. K. Timoshenko. Nothing was done.[36]

In November 1939, after the acquisition of the new territories, the original fortified areas were abolished, the equipment put in long-term storage, and the personnel reassigned. It seemed doubtful, given their deplorable state in early 1939, that the preservation of the older fortifications would be carried out effectively. Indeed, when retreating Red Army units tried to organize defensive positions in these fortified areas in July 1941, they found them abandoned and overgrown with tall grass and weeds.[37]

It would not be until 1940 that construction would begin on fortified areas along the new western border. Although in March 1941 responsibility for the program would be given to Boris M. Shaposhnikov, former chief of the general staff, it was impossible to complete the plan for

with the Finns, who knew Rybkin as "the legation secretary, Yartsev." On April 14 Rybkin called the Finnish foreign minister, Rudolf Holsti, and they arranged to meet that evening. Rybkin told Hosti that he had recently been given full authority by his government to discuss the improvement of relations with Finland. The government was concerned, he said, that Germany might attack the USSR. One aspect of the attack would include a landing in Finland, followed by a thrust toward Leningrad. Given its policy of neutrality, would Finland resist this German attack or would the German landings be unopposed? In the latter case, the Soviets would not wait for the Germans to attack but would enter Finland and engage the German forces there. If, on the contrary, the Finns planned to resist, the Soviet Union would provide economic and military assistance and guarantee to withdraw its troops after the war. After further discussion, the foreign minister said he would have to have government approval to continue.[3]

Rybkin met with A. K. Cajander, the Finnish prime minister, in June, telling him that if Finland would guarantee that Germany would be permitted no bases there, the Soviets would help Finland defend itself against German attack. When Cajander urged expansion of Finnish-Soviet trade, Rybkin replied that trade would have to wait until political agreements were reached; there must be Finnish guarantees. Rybkin did not elaborate on these guarantees. At this point Cajander asked Tanner, a member of the cabinet's Foreign Affairs Committee, to meet with Rybkin to try to clarify the Soviet proposals, which were still to be kept secret, even from the Soviet minister and his staff. Accordingly, Tanner met Rybkin on June 30 and asked for a specific proposal. When they met again on August 5, Rybkin did not have such a proposal but suggested that it might be best to shift the discussions to Moscow. Surprised, Tanner pointed out that doing this would certainly attract attention, making it difficult to maintain secrecy. The two met again on August 10 but Rybkin still had no proposal. Prime Minister Cajander advised Tanner to tell Rybkin: "Finland will always adhere to the neutrality policy of the northern countries; Finland will . . . permit no violation of Finnish territorial integrity nor consequently the acquisition by any great power of a foothold in Finland for an attack against the Soviet Union." Tanner did as Cajander instructed, and Rybkin again spoke of moving the negotiations to Moscow. Then on August 18 Rybkin read a statement to Tanner in "slightly defective German." In essence, the Soviet Union would be satisfied with a written agreement under which Finland stood prepared to ward off possible attacks and, to that end, to accept Soviet military aid. The Soviet Union would assent to the fortification of the Aaland Islands if it could take part in the arming and maintain surveillance over the use of the fortifications. It was prepared to guarantee Finland's inviolability within the present Finnish boundaries, first and foremost the sea frontiers. In the event of need, the Soviet Union would assist Finland by force of arms. Moscow would "also approve an exceptionally advantageous trade treaty."[4]

During October, Rybkin had additional discussions with Foreign Minister Holsti and received an essentially negative written response from him. According to Tanner, it elicited a shrug from Rybkin, who declared himself "just an inexperienced young secretary." Rybkin's final effort in Helsinki was to talk with the Acting Foreign Minister Vaino Voionmaa (Holsti had resigned from the government on November 16). When Rybkin continud to press for a transfer of the negotiations to Moscow, Voionmaa agreed to use the December 1938 visit of a delegation to dedicate the new Finnish legation building in Moscow as a pretext. Rybkin returned to Moscow; his last act in this drama was to tell the Finns that they "would have the opportunity to meet a high-ranking Soviet government official." The official turned out to be Anastas Mikoyan, commissar for foreign trade. It seemed that the Commissariat for Foreign Affairs knew nothing of the delegation's purpose beyond the dedication of the new legation building. As a result, the Finnish minister to Moscow, A. S. Yrjo-Koskinen, withdrew and did not participate in the discussions that took place in Mikoyan's office. These talks, on December 7, covered the same ground as those held with Rybkin/Yartsev in Helsinki and no agreements were reached.[5]

Thus ended Boris A. Rybkin's adventure in secret diplomacy. When the Winter War began he returned to Moscow, where he was appointed chief of a section of the Fifth (Foreign Intelligence) Department, Chief Directorate for State Security (GUGB), NKVD USSR. In February 1941 he was appointed a department chief of the First Foreign Intelligence Directorate of the newly constituted People's Commissariat for State Security (NKGB). In September 1941 he was posted to Stockholm as resident. His cover this time was counselor and he remained Boris N. Yartsev.[6] Some historians believe that the proposals he advanced were seriously intended by Stalin as a way of improving Leningrad's defenses without imposing unacceptable conditions on the Finns. Knowing Stalin's approach to negotiations of this type, this seems unlikely. Rather, Stalin may well have used the Rybkin Yartsev ploy to study Finland's position and attitudes without revealing his ultimate demands.

Not until March 1939 would the Soviets, acting this time through diplomatic channels, ask the Finns to lease several islands in the Gulf of Finland "as guard posts for the approaches to Leningrad." The Finns refused, citing their neutrality. The new Soviet commissar for foreign affairs, V. M. Molotov, reopened the question on October 7, asking that representatives of Finland and the USSR meet in Moscow to resume negotiations. On October 9 the Finns announced that they would send the Finnish minister to Sweden, J. K. Paasikvi, to Moscow. He would be authorized to discuss only the transfer of islands in the Gulf of Finland in exchange for territorial compensation elsewhere. During this meeting and those that followed, it became clear that Stalin's minimal position went beyond anything that had been discussed in negotiations to date, including those with Rybkin/ Yartsev. Stalin's demands included use of the island of Hanko as a Soviet base, cession of certain islands in the Gulf of Finland, and movement of the border on the Karelian Isthmus northward. These demands were rejected by the Finnish government. Discussion continued sporadically for a time, but on November 13 the Finnish delegation returned to Helsinki.[7]

In his memoirs, Kiril A. Meretskov, appointed commander of the Leningrad Military District in February 1939, recalls visiting Defense Commissar Voroshilov in Moscow and being told by him to assess the district as a possible theater of military operations. This would indicate that Stalin was already considering the use of military force against the Finns. Meretskov found the district's operational plans out of date, and its infrastructure inadequate. He also claimed that there was no intelligence on the Mannerheim Line, the Finnish fortifications of the Karelian Isthmus (a strange conclusion as the emplacements on this line were designed by foreign specialists and resembled elements of French fortifications). Meretskov's recommendation, supported by Andrei A. Zhdanov, first secretary of the Leningrad Oblast Party Committee and Politburo member, was to undertake a major effort to construct new roads, airfields, and fortifications. When it became apparent that the Finns were not ready to accede to the Soviet demands and that war was likely, Chief of the General Staff Boris M. Shaposhnikov predicted the Finns would not be easy to defeat and recommended that a front be created that would drive through the Mannerheim Line as far as Helsinki if necessary. For reasons that are still not fully understood, Stalin rejected his advice and placed the entire operation in the hands of Zhdanov, Meretskov, and the Leningrad Military District. The operational plan devised by Meretskov involved attacks directly against the Mannerheim Line by the district's Seventh Army while the Eighth Army attacked northeast of Lake Ladoga in an effort to envelop the line. Meretskov estimated that Finnish resistance could be overcome in twelve to fifteen days.[8]

On November 26 Finnish artillery was reported to have opened fire on Soviet border troops. Seven shells had apparently been fired, killing three Soviet privates and a noncommissioned officer and wounding seven soldiers and two officers. The Soviet government protested, proposing that the Finns withdraw their forces to a distance of twenty to twenty-five kilometers from the frontier. "The Finns investigated the incidents and found that Finnish border troops heard seven shots and observed the shells explode in the village square of the Soviet village," one historian writes. "The guards concluded that the gun or guns that produced the seven shots were located some one and a half kilometers to the southeast of the place where the shells exploded." No Finnish artillery troops were stationed in this area. If the Finns' report was accurate, the so-called artillery barrage must have been a preplanned Soviet provocation. Whether this is true or not, the Finnish information was given to the Soviets, who responded by accusing the Finnish government of having committed an unfriendly act against the USSR. The accusation freed the Soviet government of its obligations under the nonaggression pact between the two countries. The war could now begin, which it did on November 30 with a surprise Soviet attack.[9]

Meanwhile, other preparations had already been made on the Soviet side. On November 10, 1939, O. W. Kuusinen, former Finnish Communist Party leader in exile in the USSR and a member of the Presidium of the Executive Committee of the Communist International, met with Stalin "regarding Finnish affairs."[10] Evidently on the basis of decisions reached in their talks, Kuusinen wrote on November 13 to Arvo Tuominen, secretary-general of the Finnish Communist Party, then living in exile in Stockholm, directing him to come to Moscow as soon as possible. As Vaino Tanner later described the letter, Kuusinen told Tuominen that "it was necessary to resort to more forceful measures with respect to Finland . . . of the kind the Finnish Communist Party had long hoped for and that Tuominen would find waiting for him a task that would make him very happy."[11] Tuominen, whose attitude toward Moscow had changed while he was in exile, responded on November 17 that he could not come. Before long, he received a verbal order from the Soviet legation in Stockholm to leave at once for Moscow. Since this produced no effect, on November 21 a courier arrived from Moscow with a letter from the Politburo ordering Tuominen to leave the next day on the Moscow plane. The courier explained that a Finnish

The Mannerheim Line

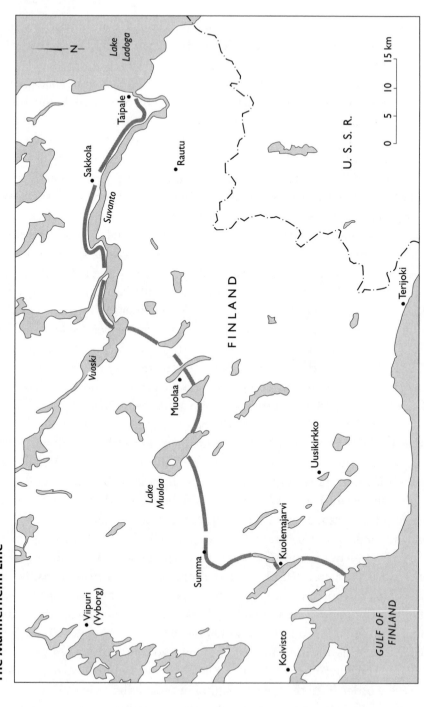

"popular government" would be set up composed of Finnish exiles living in the Soviet Union. Kuusinen would be president and Tuominen prime minister. Tuominen still refused. Nonetheless, according to a Tass communiqué of December 1, 1939, a Finnish Democratic Republic (FDR) was established in Terijoki, a small town just inside the Soviet-Finnish border.[12]

On December 2 Moscow announced a treaty between the FDR and the USSR whereby the FDR granted to the USSR all that the USSR had demanded and then some. The Finnish Social Democrats and other political parties wholly rejected this "puppet Kuusinen government."[13] Why did Stalin create the FDG? Was it merely a device to appease the League of Nations by claiming that the Soviet Union had been asked by the Finnish Democratic Republic to come to its assistance? If so, it didn't work, and on December 14 the USSR was unanimously expelled from the League of Nations. Did Stalin really believe, as Vaino Tanner said, that it was merely a matter of parading to Helsinki, "where . . . the Russian forces would find themselves . . . joyously acclaimed as liberators"?[14]

In accordance with the Meretskov plan, the Seventh Army moved north against stiff Finnish resistance. The entire Finnish frontier security zone was heavily mined, fortified, and defended; the Red Army troops were no match for the warmly clad Finns with their Suomi submachine guns. The main elements of the Seventh Army would not reach the Mannerheim Line until December 12. This fortified area was begun in the 1920s; work then slacked off and was taken up in the late 1930s. By the summer of 1939 thousands of volunteers had participated in the construction work. The name "Mannerheim" is said to have been given to the area by the foreign journalists who were shown it in the autumn of 1939. The line, which covered the entire Karelian Isthmus from Lake Ladoga to the Gulf of Finland, relied to a great extent on the natural obstacles of lakes and rivers. It was up to ninety kilometers in depth. The reinforced concrete emplacements were two stories high, their machine and artillery embrasures, as well as the roofs, covered by armor plate. Taken together with the marshy and heavily forested terrain, the Mannerheim Line was virtually impenetrable by infantry and armored vehicles. This accounted for the Seventh Army's lack of progress whereas the Ninth Army, expected to advance into central Finland, found itself in trackless forests, harassed by Finnish ski troops, with some units, such as the Forty-fourth Rifle Division, totally surrounded. Elements of the division managed to escape toward the Soviet frontier by abandoning their supplies and equipment. Some observers put Soviet losses by early December at 25,000 killed.

The spectacle of "gallant Finland" standing up to the Soviet colossus aroused public opinion in the West, and although efforts to enlist volunteers to fight for Finland came to naught, the image of the Soviet Union throughout the world was badly battered. Even worse, by subjecting his army to these humiliating defeats, Stalin gave ammunition to Hitler and his generals, whose opinion of the Red Army was formed on the experiences of the Winter War.[15]

Something had to be done. Very quickly a Thirteenth Army was created consisting of two rifle corps of two divisions each. On January 7, 1940, the Northwest Front was created under the command of Semen K. Timoshenko, who was brought up from the Kiev Special Military District. Meretskov was given command of the Seventh Army, which, with the new Thirteenth Army, would try again to crack the Mannerheim Line. The troops would spend the next several weeks training. All elements of this new command were strengthened by the addition of new troops and, above all, new commanders. The front chief of staff was I. V. Smorodinov, formerly deputy chief of the general staff; Yevgeny S. Ptukhin, another Spanish civil war veteran, was commander of the front air forces. A new Fifteenth Army was created while the new commanders of the Eighth and Ninth armies were Grigory M. Shtern and Vasily I. Chuikov, seasoned officers.

In an offensive begun on February 11, the Red Army broke through the Mannerheim Line, then moved on a secondary belt of defenses around Vyborg, which it captured. The Finns sued for peace and the Winter War ended on March 13, 1940. The subsequent treaty restored the old frontier established under Peter the Great. Soviet losses, however, were enormous, and the blow to Stalin's prestige and to that of the Red Army was massive.[16]

Stalin knew, of course, that he was responsible for two of the worst prewar assumptions—that the entire military phase could be accomplished by the Leningrad Military District alone and that the creation of the Finnish Democratic Republic would work either to attract Finnish support or to deflect criticism abroad of Soviet actions. He therefore sought a scapegoat, and he found it primarily in the person of I. I. Proskurov, the military intelligence chief. Other, purely military problems that had surfaced during the war also needed attention. To deal with them and to divert attention from his own role in the events and decisions preceding the war, Stalin prepared a major conference to be held under Central Committee auspices to review the lessons of the "military operations against Finland."

In attendance would be army, corps, and division commanders, representatives of the Defense Commissariat and the general staff, and political workers. They would discuss failures in the condition of the armed forces and their equipment, the system for training troops, as well as the state of intelligence.[17]

The conference began on April 14, 1940, only a month and a day after the end of the war, and lasted through April 17. The timing suggests Stalin's sense of urgency. Although he himself would be present, he selected as joint chairmen of the conference Defense Commissar Kliment Ye. Voroshilov and Grigory I. Kulik, his cronies going back to the defense of Tsaritsyn (later Stalingrad and now Volgograd) in the civil war. This way he was able to control the agenda and the selection of speakers. Thus, the question of inadequate intelligence was first raised in a substantive fashion at the morning session on April 16, the next-to-last day of the conference. It was discussed again at that day's evening session and a final time the next morning, with Proskurov present. The conference ended with the creation of a commission to review the conference's findings. Proskurov was among those named to the commission.[18]

The complaints regarding intelligence began at the morning session on April 16 with Ivan I. Kopets, commander of the air units of the Eighth Army in the Finnish conflict and a veteran of the Spanish civil war.[19] According to him, the intelligence material on Finland in the headquarters of the Leningrad Military District dated back to 1917, the most recent to 1930: "We had nothing from agent operations." Kopets was followed by Kiril Meretskov, Seventh Army commander, who said, "We had no real understanding of the Mannerheim Line. There was information but it never got to us. Also, we attacked without preliminary study and detailed intelligence on the enemy." Later, however, Meretskov said: "We accused agent intelligence operations of not having given us detailed reports. Here we should know limits; it is impossible to always blame intelligence. For example, we had an album of the enemy's fortifications; we were able to orient ourselves using it. I kept it on my desk. But agent intelligence is not enough, you must have good combat reconnaissance." (Meretskov cited an example from the recent fighting.) Then he asked Proskurov rhetorically, "Can you tell me who manages combat reconnaissance?"[20]

At the evening session on April 16, Chief of the General Staff Shaposhnikov was called on. He noted that agent intelligence provided very little information on the enemy's operational plan: "We had, as the commander of the Leningrad Military District has said, fragmentary bits on the belts of concrete fortifications on the Karelian Isthmus. These bits were general information but we did not know the depth of the defenses, as described by the commander of the Leningrad Military District. The same is true regarding the deployment of the Finnish forces. Intelligence told us that the Finns in wartime would have up to ten infantry divisions and separate battalions. . . . The Finns actually possessed up to 16 infantry divisions and several separate battalions."[21]

The confrontation between Stalin and Proskurov occurred during the morning session on the last day of the conference. Kulik, defender of Tsaritsyn, was in the chair. Proskurov opened by commenting that intelligence had been mentioned by most of the commanders who had spoken. Stalin interrupted to say, "No, there will be more." Proskurov said he would be happy if that were the case, then went on:

> What did we know about the Finns? We consider that for a general estimate of the forces required to neutralize the enemy, Intelligence had the information needed to start. Intelligence reported this information to the General Staff. This was not something done by the present staff of the Intelligence Directorate, since the basic information related to the years 1937–1938. We knew as of October 1st, 1939 that Finland had constructed on the Karelian isthmus three defensive lines and two switch positions. The first defensive line was intended for covering units, and was located directly on the frontier and anchored on Lake Ladoga and the Gulf of Finland. . . . Its fortifications consisted for the most part of structures of the field type: rifle trenches, machine guns, and artillery. There were also anti-tank structures and a small number, circa 50, of concrete, stone, and earth-and-timber firing emplacements. These were the so-called forward defensive positions. The second defensive line became known to intelligence as of October 1st.

He was interrupted here by Lev Z. Mekhlis, head of the Red Army Political Directorate: "October 1st of what year?" Proskurov answered, "1939," and went on to describe the second and third lines of defense and their concrete bunkers, "which were in a sketch in the album which was always on Meretskov's desk." Meretskov interjected, "But not one corresponding to reality." "Nothing of the sort," responded Proskurov, "the reports of unit commanders and intelligence showed that the majority of these firing points were located where they were indicated on the sketches." That was a lie, Meretskov said, describing the locations of two points. Proskurov again retorted, "Nothing of the sort." Mekhlis broke in to ask, "When was this material given to the General Staff?" "Before October 1, 1939," replied

Proskurov. "By that time it was known that the Finns were engaged in major construction work. During the summer of 1939 in several reports it was said that large quantities of construction materials were being brought in but we did not have exact information on the second line. All the information about the fortifications we had was entered on maps in Leningrad and distributed to troop units. What can be said of human resources? . . . We knew the Finns had 600,000 men of military age. Trained men amounted to 400,000. In addition there was the civil defense corps composed of men and women. As for the machine pistol Suomi, it was reported by intelligence in 1936. And in 1939 we provided additional detail and photographs." A discussion began on the utility of submachine guns for infantry use.[22]

Stalin and Proskurov veered off into the question of why it took until mid-December to disseminate to the troops information on the Finns' fighting tactics. When Proskurov tried to explain that such information had to be taken from archives, selected for pertinence, and then declassified before it could be disseminated, Stalin pretended not to know that material from abroad was all classified and kept from the rank and file. Proskurov repeated that they were not permitted to make foreign periodicals available. At this point Stalin said to him, "You don't have the soul of an intelligence officer; you have the soul of a very naïve man in the best sense of the word. An intelligence officer must be steeped in venom, in bile; he should trust no one. If you were an intelligence officer you would see how those gentlemen in the West criticize one another: here, you're bad with a weapon, there, something else. You would see how they unmask each other, expose one another's secrets. If you would only come to grips with how the other side works, make a selection, and bring it to the attention of the command, but no, your soul is too honest." Not realizing that he was in fact describing himself, Stalin went on: "You can say the report is from a nonexistent newspaper, from a nonexistent government, something like that, or from foreign information, and so forth, and put it out. You have to be able to do this. Just remove the heading, but leave the substance, and give it to people openly. We have newspapers and journals, don't we?" Proskurov tried to explain that unless something was classified the big chiefs wouldn't read it. Stalin repeated his idea but Proskurov pointed out that it required personnel. When Stalin said, "If it's necessary we'll increase the number," Proskurov replied: "I have reported five times to the Defense Commissar on the need for expansion, but I've been cut, and now we have an organization that is barely able to disseminate secret literature." As he continued to push his idea of using foreign literature on an unclassified basis, Stalin commented that the Red Army newspaper, *Krasnaia Zvezda* (Red Star), wasn't worth a damn, which brought Mekhlis into a discussion about problems with the editor. Proskurov tried to bring the discussion back to intelligence by describing how commanders at various levels used intelligence reports. He complained that some commanders kept them in their safes unread for three or more months. In response to Stalin's remark that "one has to know how to present a dish, if you want it eaten," Proskurov said, "If the material comes to you, it should be read. It's beautifully printed, with illustrations, with pictures." The two continued a detailed exchange about what information should be published and how it should be received by those to whom it was distributed.[23]

Stalin held up a book. "Does it show the locations of German troops here?" Proskurov: "Yes, exactly." Stalin: "This shouldn't have been printed at all." Proskurov: "Not even as classified material?" Stalin: "We must not describe such things; we must not print them at all. We should publish military knowledge, techniques, tactics, strategies, the make-up of divisions and battalions so that people can have some idea of a division, units, artillery, techniques, what new units there are." From this last dialogue, it becomes apparent that Stalin did not understand the nature and purpose of intelligence and that he didn't know much about the military either. On the one hand he berated Proskurov for inadequate intelligence during the Finnish war and on the other hand he stated that printing reports on the deployment of foreign troops was wrong. Or did these statements reflect Stalin's deep-seated fear of offending Hitler by reporting on the location of his troops? We don't know. But it is clear that he was out to get Proskurov and absolve himself of any blame.[24]

Meretskov added his complaint that because the reports were secret he couldn't take them home and he was too busy to read them in the office. Stalin asked, "Who thought this up?" Proskurov answered, "It was Order No. 015 of the Defense Commissar." When someone from the audience called out, "The books should be in the headquarters," Proskurov replied: "How can you explain, Comrade Voronov [Nikolai N. Voronov, chief of artillery], that of 50 reports sent to the Artillery Directorate, only seven were read by two persons? These articles were unclassified." Proskurov ended the discussion by noting that the headquarters of the First Red Banner Army kept reports for three months without distributing them to its units because it expected the Intelligence Directorate to do so directly. "Does this mean," asked Proskurov, "that the Directorate should know the location of every unit? This is absurd!" Everyone at the conference must have winced because they all knew the mania for secrecy that permeated the military and civilian leadership.[25]

Proskurov moved on to the question Meretskov raised earlier of who was responsible for directing combat reconnaissance, saying that he had received hundreds of letters on the subject. In the early days of combat, he pointed out, the personnel of combat reconnaissance units were badly trained, despite a June 1939 meeting of the Main Military Council with Stalin. The council decided then to place responsibility for combat reconnaissance in the Operations Directorate of the general staff and in the staffs of districts, armies, and army groups, this to be accomplished by August 1, 1939. Obviously, Proskurov went on, "this has not been done and still nobody is involved in combat reconnaissance." He added that ORBs were not being trained as intelligence units. "What is an ORB?" Stalin asked. Proskurov replied, "Separate Reconnaissance Battalion. Each division is allotted one." The ORBs weren't being used properly, he went on, nor were the reconnaissance companies assigned to each regiment. During the Finnish campaign, he noted, "The 7th Army took over the intelligence department of the Leningrad Military District, the other armies had none." Stalin asked what Proskurov would propose. Proskurov suggested following the pattern of foreign armies, placing all intelligence under one staff element: "We should establish a unit in our directorate to handle combat reconnaissance or be left solely with agent intelligence."[26]

Proskurov dealt next with the problem of dissemination. The commanders of the Eighth and Ninth armies, Shtern and Chuikov, complained that they were not receiving reports. It was discovered that Comrade Smorodinov's general staff people considered what was happening in the Eighth Army's sector no business of the Seventh Army and so never passed on the reports. "This is idiotic," thundered Proskurov. "An army commander must know what's happening in an adjacent sector. We must make senior and junior commanders aware of intelligence. . . . We do not have exact figures on how many thousands of lives we lost because of the absence of intelligence."

Stalin did not respond. Probably he did not want to get involved in the question of who was to blame for the horrendous death toll of the Winter War. Instead he changed the subject and asked about an agent in London who had sent reports on a planned British air raid on Baku, but he got no further details. The same man had also reported that 12,000 colored troops were being brought into Romania. Proskurov said the source wasn't an agent but the air attaché, Major General Ivan I. Cherny. Stalin responded by saying, "You argue that he's an honest man. I say that he's a honest man, but a fool!" He went on, "I am afraid that if your agents continue to work like that, nothing will come of their work."[27]

Meretskov interrupted to note that commanders were afraid to get into intelligence because later it would be said of them that they served abroad. Proskurov agreed, observing that "if it's written in your personnel file that you were abroad, it remains there throughout your life." Stalin countered, saying that "we have thousands of people abroad. This is a service." One can imagine the thoughts of those present, all of whom knew that Meretskov and Proskurov were right about the suspicions that attached to persons serving abroad.

Proskurov brought up the difficulties encountered by agents parachuted seventy kilometers behind the lines, including the fact that many agents, like many commanders, were "infected with the idea that they would be greeted with flowers, but it didn't turn out that way." This was a scarcely veiled reference to the Finnish Democratic Republic, which was supposed to enlist the support of the Finnish working class, Stalin's idea. The obvious reference in the presence of others to the failure of his plan must have infuriated Stalin, who then accused Proskurov of sending into Finland Russians with no knowledge of Finnish: "Give the Main Military Council a list of who you've sent and where." Proskurov responded, "I'm glad that you are interested in these questions, because after this things will be better." He added that "it was one thing for a tourist to look at an emplacement but to describe its construction, and its exact location, that's another matter. We had an amusing incident recently. Skorniakov [Nikolai D. Skorniakov, assistant air attaché in Berlin] sent a telegram. But Kulik ordered Skorniakov to send sketches and construction details. But he couldn't provide those details as he wasn't qualified. This problem can't be solved by sending in a tourist." Stalin missed the point and argued that it would be best to have Skorniakov recalled and fully debriefed. Kulik called a recess.[28]

Thus ended Proskurov's part in the conference. Proskurov made no concessions to Stalin, who evinced little understanding of combat intelligence or the manner in which intelligence was collected, analyzed, and disseminated. Stalin obviously disliked the way Proskurov behaved toward him, and time after time he sought to turn the discussion away from serious subjects to frivolous matters. From the manner in which Stalin and others reacted to Proskurov and intelligence issues, it was clear that

Proskurov and his Intelligence Directorate were to be made scapegoats for the failures that led to the disastrous Finnish war. As for Proskurov, in his negative references to various senior officers by name, he seemed ready to take on anyone who in his view maligned the intelligence service. It was, of course, one thing for Stalin and others to use the April conference to blame intelligence for Finnish war errors; it was another to have official recognition of the accusation that the intelligence service was inadequate. The vehicle chosen for this was the act of transfer of the Defense Commissariat from Voroshilov to Timoshenko in May 1940; contained in the act were the reports of the chiefs of central directorates, delivered in the presence of Zhdanov, Georgy M. Malenkov, secretary of the Central Committee, VKP(b), and Nikolai A. Voznesensky, chairman of the State Planning Committee. The paragraph on "The Condition of Intelligence Work" read as follows:

> The organization of intelligence is one of the weakest sectors in the work of the Defense Commissariat. We do not have organized intelligence and the systematic collection of information on foreign armies. The work of the Intelligence Directorate is not connected to the work of the general staff. In the Intelligence Directorate the Defense Commissariat does not have an organ providing the Red Army with information on the organization, condition, armaments, and preparations for deployment of foreign armies. At the moment of assumption, the Commissariat of Defense does not dispose of such information. Theaters of military operations and their preparation have not been studied.[29]

Proskurov's days as Red Army intelligence chief were clearly numbered. But even as these attacks on Soviet military intelligence were taking place, the war in the West suddenly erupted. In early April 1940 the Germans occupied Denmark and Norway, and on May 10 they invaded Holland, Belgium, Luxembourg, and France. On May 15 the Dutch would capitulate and the Belgians would follow suit on May 27. By June 4 British forces had evacuated France; Paris fell on the fourteenth, and on the seventeenth Marshal Pétain ordered French forces to lay down their arms. Stalin's hopes for a long, drawn-out war between Germany and the Allies would be dashed—now he needed to know what Hitler would do next. It seemed unlikely, under these circumstances, that Stalin would move against his intelligence chief, Proskurov.[30]

CHAPTER 6

Soviet Military Intelligence Residencies in Western Europe

In June 1940 the Soviet Military Intelligence Service, still headed by Proskurov, produced two intelligence reports on the events transpiring in Europe. One reflected the German view of the Wehrmacht's successes in France. The other provided the first indication of what Hitler would do after the defeat of France.

On June 4, 1940, Proskurov sent the first report to Stalin. It was based on a visit to the German embassy by Colonel Gerhard Matske, German military attaché in Tokyo. He had stopped off in Moscow on his way back to Tokyo after a two-week stay in May with a German army unit during its campaign in Belgium and northern France. He shared his experiences there with Lieutenant Colonel Hegendorf, German assistant military attaché in Moscow, and other attachés. The source was probably Gerhard Kegel (code name KhVS), an experienced RU agent formerly in Warsaw and now a member of the Trade Section of the German embassy. Kegel would have heard of Matske's account from Hegendorf. The report was sent to Stalin, but we do not know how he or his senior military advisers reacted to it.

Matske said that he was overwhelmed by the speed and force with which the German units had advanced in the Low Countries and France, throwing the defenders off balance. He cited the use of parachute and airborne troops in the capture of the Rotterdam airport and the rapid crossing of the Albert Canal, which prevented the demolition of the bridges.

Matske and Hegendorf commented that the speedy capture of the Liège fortresses was made possible by the German units' opportunity to practice their techniques and test their weaponry in advance. They had used their flamethrower tanks, for example, on similar fortresses in the Czech fortifications in the Sudeten area, which had been given up by the Czechs after the Munich agreement in September 1938. Other equipment included dive bombers that carried 1,700-kilogram bombs, each fitted out with a screeching siren that everywhere demoralized the defenders. Matske attributed the Germans' success to the intensive training their units had received in preparation for the western campaign; the French, by contrast, appeared to have slept through the winter.[1]

Two days after Proskurov sent the first report, he received the second, a telegram from the Soviet military attaché in Sofia, Colonel Ivan F. Dergachev. It forwarded a report from a reliable source on future German plans (by this time it was already clear that the Wehrmacht was near victory in France). According to the report, "the Germans aspired to conclude an armistice with France. Italy would then threaten France militarily and peace would result. After a peace agreement, Germany would, within a month's time, put its army in order and together with Italy and Japan make a sudden attack on the USSR. The purpose would be to destroy communism in the Soviet Union and to create a fascist regime there." The source vouched for the accuracy of this information and asked that it be sent to the Soviet government; the report was forwarded to Stalin, Molotov, and Timoshenko.[2] Within four days after its receipt by Proskurov, Italy attacked the French; on June 22 the French concluded an armistice with Germany and on June 24 with Italy. From German archives we now know that less than a month later Hitler gave orders to his staff to prepare for an invasion of the USSR.

There is no archival record of Stalin's reaction to this second report, but it and the earlier one are but two examples of the fine military intelligence he received. How did the residencies of Soviet military intelligence function over the next year in reporting on German plans and actions? Equally important, how did the RU handle reports when they arrived in Moscow, how were they disseminated, and what were the reactions of their recipients? Although normally reports were regularly distributed to Stalin and other members of the civilian and military leadership, some were withheld or altered, apparently to conform to Stalin's conceptions. There were also occasions when Stalin would react to a report by calling it "disinformation" or even by threatening the source. In this chapter and the two that follow I will examine which of the RU's legal and illegal residencies abroad did the best job of alerting Stalin and the leadership to the German menace.

First, though, a word about the RU source Gerhard Kegel, or KhVS, the German commercial specialist in the German embassy in Moscow. In addition to probably providing the first of Proskurov's reports, he also provided highly prized reports on the trade negotiations between Germany and the USSR, which were always rushed to Stalin, Molotov, and Mikoyan by the RU. On June 21, 1941, Kegel reported that Germany would attack the USSR on June 22 between 3:00 and 4:00 a.m. There is no indication that this report had any impact on Stalin, even though he must have been aware that its source was the same agent who had provided such detailed accounts of the German position in USSR-German trade negotiations. During the spring of 1941, however, when concern over an impending invasion was growing, nothing had been heard from KhVS. It was not until June 11 that he reported that German embassy personnel would be ready to evacuate Moscow in seven days and that the burning of documents had already begun. Given his position and access, it does seem strange that between October 10, 1940 (his last report on trade negotiations), and June 11, 1941, there was no word from him on German preparations for war.[3]

Berlin

Of all the RU residencies whose reports are currently available for study, Berlin had the largest number and was one of the most effective. The residency was headed by the military attaché, Major General Vasily I. Tupikov (code name Arnold), assisted by the air attaché, Colonel Nikolai D. Skorniakov (code name Meteor); their assistants were Vasily Ye. Khlopov, Ivan G. Bazhanov, and Nikolai M. Zaitsev. Zaitsev was responsible for maintaining contact with the illegal Alta (Ilse Stöbe), who handled source Ariets.[4]

A great producer when in Warsaw, Ariets continued in Berlin when he was assigned to the Information Section of the German Ministry of Foreign Affairs. On September 29, 1940, he reported that relations between the USSR and Germany were worsening and that Hitler intended to "resolve problems in the east in the spring of next year [1941]." He named as his source Karl Schnurre, head of the Russian sector of the Foreign Ministry's Economics Department.[5]

It was Ariets who on December 29, 1940, reported that from "highly placed circles" he had learned that Hitler had given orders to prepare for war with the USSR. Specifically, the report said, "War will be declared in March 1941." In the margin of this report, the new head of RU, Filipp I. Golikov, wrote, "Give a copy to the Narkom (Defense Commissar Timoshenko) and the chief of the general staff." He added a note to his staff: "Who are these highly placed military circles? One must elaborate. Concretely, to whom was the order given?" He added, "Demand more intelligible light on this subject; then order them to check it. Get a telegraphic response from Meteor in five days and give it to me." The report was disseminated to Stalin in two copies, to Molotov, Timoshenko, and Kiril A. Meretskov, chief of the general staff. It seemed clear that Golikov was unaware of Ariets's record or his access.[6]

On January 4, 1941, Ariets confirmed that "he had this information from a friend in the military; moreover, it was based not on rumors but on a special order of Hitler that was especially secret and known to only a few people." On February 28, 1941, Ariets followed up with a more detailed report on preparations for war against the USSR: "People involved in the project confirm that war with Russia has definitely been decided on for this year [1941]." Three army groups had been formed under Marshals von Bock, von Rundstedt, and von Leeb, prepared to advance on Leningrad, Moscow, and Kiev. "The beginning of the attack is provisionally set for May 20. To all appearances, an enveloping attack is planned in the Pinsk area with a force of 120 German divisions. Preparatory measures have resulted in the assignment of Russian-speaking officers and noncommissioned officers to various headquarters. In addition, armored trains are being constructed with wide gauges as in Russia." From a person close to Göring, Ariets heard that "Hitler intends to bring in around three million slaves from Russia in order to improve his industrial capacity."[7]

Ariets's information was reasonably accurate. Given his record, it should have established a solid base within the RU Information Department for evaluating reports from other sources on German preparations for an invasion. Unfortunately for the Soviets, Golikov was new and the department had a series of other new chiefs during the period of Ariets's reporting. The result was that it apparently never received adequate consideration.

Vasily I. Tupikov arrived in Berlin in December 1940 to serve as military attaché and legal resident. At the end of April 1941, after observing conditions in Berlin and reviewing reports from residency sources, including Ariets, he addressed an unusual letter to Golikov. "If it turns out that in this presentation of my conclusions I am forcing my way through an open door, that will not discourage me," he wrote. "If I am mistaken in them and you correct me, I will be very grateful." His initial conclusions were: "1. In current German plans for waging war, the USSR figures as the next enemy. 2. The conflict will definitely take place this year." Golikov disseminated the letter to all addressees, including Chief of the General Staff Georgy K. Zhukov, but omitted Tupikov's conclusion.

In an attachment giving the deployment of the German army as of April 25, 1941, Tupikov asserted that the strength of German forces in the west was being reduced while that in the east along the border with the USSR was increasing. These conclusions of the RU's senior man in Berlin reinforced the reporting of Ariets. Golikov did not respond to the letter personally but directed Colonel A. M. Kuznetsov, chief of the First [Western] Department: "In your next dispatch to Tupikov, it will be necessary to answer this letter."[8]

Tupikov did not stop. On May 9 he sent a report to Zhukov and Defense Commissar Timoshenko describing a plan for possible operations of the German army against the USSR. "Defeat of the Red Army," he said, "will be completed in one or one and a half months with arrival of the German army on the meridian of Moscow."[9]

Because GRU would not permit access to its archives, we cannot know what other reports were produced by RU Berlin nor do we know the contents of the correspondence between the RU in Moscow and its Berlin group. Nevertheless, from Ariets's reporting and the position taken by Tupikov in April 1941, it seems clear that this residency had few doubts concerning German intentions. As for Tupikov himself, he was made chief of staff of the Southwest Front upon his return from Berlin and died in the defense of Kiev in the summer of 1941.

Helsinki

The RU legal resident in Helsinki was Colonel Ivan V. Smirnov (code name Ostvald); his assistant was Major M. D. Yermolov. We have only two reports from this residency, dated June 15 and June 17, 1941. They were both based on personal observation and made clear that German troops were arriving in significant numbers. One, from RU source Brand, stated that Finland had begun to mobilize and was evacuating women and children from large cities.[10] The reports were confirmed by a June 18 telegram, found in Federal Security Service (FSB) archives, from the Japanese ambassador in Helsinki to the Japanese ambassador in Moscow informing him of general mobilization that included the calling up of women for work in medical units and food preparation. Defensive installations were going up on the eastern borders, the telegram added, and antiaircraft artillery was being deployed in Helsinki.[11]

London

For some reason, no intelligence reports from the RU residency in London were ever included in the RU material given to academician Aleksandr N. Yakovlev for inclusion in *1941 god*. Nor is there any reference to London in the two-volume work on the GRU by A. Kolpakidi and D. Prokhorov, *Imperia GRU*. This despite the fact that the London RU residency was one of the largest and most productive of RU stations abroad before and during World War II.[12]

The resident and military attaché up until August 1940 was Major General Ivan I. Cherny, who was replaced by Colonel Ivan A. Skliarov (code name Brion).[13] An important moment for the residency came in March 1939, when the Germans occupied Prague and the Czechoslovak government ceased to exist. The British intelligence service, MI-6, organized the escape from Prague of Colonel Frantisek Moravec, head of Czech military intelligence, along with some of his best people and his files. Shortly after their arrival in London they met with the Soviet military attaché, Major General Cherny, and arrangements were made for official liaison. This was later taken up by Cherny's successor, Skliarov. At some point, Moravec was allegedly recruited by Semen D. Kremer and given the code name Baron. This clandestine contact was maintained by Major Shevtsov separately from the official liaison. According to Vladimir Lota, Moravec's recruitment meant that the RU had recruited not just a single agent but the entire intelligence networks of the Czech service.[14]

The most carefully guarded secret in the residency was its penetration of one or more of the British organizations with access to ULTRA, code word for the code breaking of German ENIGMA traffic. Apart from information on German order of battle and troop deployments, these sources could have provided hard reporting from ULTRA on actions by the German Luftwaffe in the fall of 1940 to dismantle communications stations and other arrangements originally created to support a German invasion of the British Isles. These facilities were not to be manned after January 10, 1941, indicating that the Germans had in reality given up their plans to invade England, regardless of what was said in their deception operations. Did Stalin, who fervently believed Hitler would never attack the USSR until he had conquered England, see such reporting? Did he believe it? We do not know.[15]

The best picture of the activities of the RU's London residency in the 1940–41 period comes from the VENONA intercepts of traffic between London and Moscow.[16] The officers of the residency were kept busy covering the effects of German air raids on British armaments production, rail transport, seaports, as well as public morale. They submitted reports on British antiaircraft measures, German bombing techniques, and British army order of battle and organization of defenses against a possible German invasion. Considerable attention was paid to the collection of information on German tactics during the Battle of France from British servicemen who had been involved. In all of this, the residency relied not only on recruited agents but also on help from members of the British Communist Party, or the "friends."[17]

Paris and Vichy

The RU resident in Paris (later in Vichy, after the defeat of France and the establishment of the Pétain government) was military attaché General Ivan A. Susloparov; his assistant was Makar M. Volosiuk, assistant air attaché (code name Rato). Reporting to them were two illegal residents, Henri Robinson (code name Harry) and Leopold Trepper (code name Otto). Robinson, who had been a Soviet agent in France since the 1930s, is believed to have been the source of an April 3, 1941, report from Rato describing the German occupation regime, the three zones existing under it—forbidden, occupied, and unoccupied—their purpose, and the kinds of activities under way in each. The report bears a close resemblance to one prepared by Robinson on January 30. During 1940–41 Robinson submitted a great deal of information on the movement of German troops to the east and their defensive construction along the Atlantic coast. He also reported on French factories working on production orders for the German military, as well as on police controls and documentation in occupied and unoccupied France. In a September 20, 1940, report, Harry doubted that the Germans were serious about invading England because their preparations were much too obvious. On April 4, 1941, Harry stated flatly that the Germans were no longer considering an invasion of England although they would continue their bombing.[18]

As for Trepper, alias Jean Gilbert, he arrived in France in the summer of 1940 and began to develop new cover and acquire sources. He informed resident Susloparov on June 21 that the "Wehrmacht command has completed the transfer of its troops to the Soviet frontier and tomorrow, June 22, will suddenly attack the Soviet Union." When Stalin read this report, he wrote in the margin: "This information is an English provocation. Find out who the author of this provocation is and punish him."[19]

Switzerland

The only other information we have on RU agent sources in Western Europe comes from Switzerland, where the illegal network under Alexander Rado (code name Dora) was active. Although the best reporting from this network came after the German invasion in 1941, some reports were filed in the winter and spring of 1941. On February 21, 1941, for example, Dora sent a report to RU Moscow based on information from the chief of intelligence of the Swiss general staff. According to the source, "Germany has 150 divisions in the east. . . . the German offensive will begin at the end of May." In the margin of the report Golikov wrote, "This is likely . . . disinformation. We must point this out to Dora." Golikov was writing at a time when other sources were reporting on German intentions and the buildup on the Soviet Union's western frontier was continuing apace. One can only conclude that Golikov was aware of Stalin's conviction that Germany would not attack the Soviet Union in 1941 and did not dare publish a report that contradicted him.[20]

On April 6, 1941, Dora noted that all German motorized divisions were in the east. The report of June 2nd is interesting: "All German motorized divisions on the Soviet border are in constant readiness. . . . In contradistinction to the April–May period, preparations along the Russian frontier are being carried out less obviously but with greater intensity." On April 22 subsource Poisson (unidentified) reported to Dora that, according to the chief editor of the newspaper *Basler Nachrichten,* highly placed government officials in Berlin expected the Ukrainian campaign to begin on June 15. Little resistance was anticipated.[21]

Another Dora report, dated May 19, this time from Diane (unidentified), is attributed to the Swiss military attaché in Berlin. It sounds like the sort of gossip one might pick up on the diplomatic circuits and seems filled with standard German deception themes. After commenting that "the information on the proposed German campaign in Ukraine comes from the most reliable German sources and is valid," Diane says that "these sources add that the offensive will only occur when the English fleet cannot enter the Black Sea and when the German army establishes itself in Asia Minor. The next German goal will be the capture of Gibraltar and the Suez Canal in order to drive the English fleet from the Mediterranean Sea." If not deception, the vision of the Germans capturing Gibraltar and driving the British fleet from the Mediterranean was a pipe dream. Franco had refused to allow them to attack Gibraltar through Spain, and the British fleet had administered a severe drubbing to the Italian navy at Taranto.[22]

The last report available from Dora before the invasion was dated June 22 and contained order of battle detail on the German army but nothing on the invasion.[23] This recital of the contributions of the Dora networks confirms that their best work came later.

CHAPTER 7

Soviet Military Intelligence Residencies in Eastern Europe

In Eastern Europe one found the same mix of agent sources as in Western Europe. There were those with good access to knowledgeable sources who reported solid intelligence and provided first-rate reports and, contrarily, those with purely social contacts who repeated gossip or unsubstantiated information based on rumors. Information obtained from the latter sources was, of course, likely to contain German deception. Stalin, however, disregarded the accurate reporting as disinformation. His people paid an extraordinarily precious price for his actions.

Bucharest

The best producer of information in Eastern Europe was the RU residency in Bucharest, headed by Colonel Grigory M. Yeremin (code name Ye-shchenko), whose cover was that of third secretary in the Soviet embassy. Yeremin had previously headed the Romanian/Balkan Section of the First Department at RU Moscow Center. His deputy was Mikhail S. Sharov (code name Korf). The aces among this residency's sources were German embassy press officer Kurt Völkisch and his wife, Margarita (code names AVS and LTsL); other sources generally confirmed and supplemented AVS's reporting. Had Stalin and others in the Soviet political and military leadership taken these Bucharest reports seriously, it is difficult to see how they could not have been aware of German preparations for an invasion of the USSR.

Here is how RU Moscow described the importance of AVS: "AVS has the possibility of close contact with the work of the German embassy in Bucharest. He is aware of all the activities being carried out by the Germans in Romania. He has been directed by German intelligence to maintain contact with Ukrainian anti-Soviet organizations in Romania and knows of their plans and measures directed against the USSR. He has many acquaintances among responsible officials in the German Foreign Ministry and enjoys their confidence. AVS is well acquainted with Gerstenberg, the German air attaché in Romania, who is carrying out special tasks for his government." In recognition of AVS's importance, RU Moscow Center assigned Mikhail Sharov to the residency primarily to maintain contact with him. Sharov's cover as a TASS correspondent gave him broad mobility in the community and a reason to be in occasional contact with AVS or his wife, LTsL.[1]

In view of his access, Moscow Center gave AVS these tasks: "Report on the activities of Germany in Romania, and also on the Anglo-French bloc in Italy. Follow the activities of Ukrainian nationalists in Romania and report on the efforts of Germany to use them . . . against the USSR." His reporting was sent to Stalin, Molotov, Timoshenko, Zhukov, and others in the top leadership. On March 1, 1941, AVS described a visit to Berlin where "many spoke of an impending German attack on the USSR. The Russian department of the German high command is working intensively on this." The report in the Central Archive of the Ministry of Defense (see note 2) gives the full text and repeats word for word the portion regarding an "impending German attack" but, before that, states that "a large scale military operation against the British Isles . . . is considered unlikely because this operation is too risky and would be associated with extensive losses." The final section of the report ends, however, with the statement that rumors of German plans for war against the USSR are being deliberately planted to create uncertainty in Moscow and serve German military goals in the future. The last sentence reads: "The possibility of an attack against the USSR by German troops concentrated in Romania is decisively excluded in Berlin." This report was sent to Stalin, Molotov, Timoshenko, Voroshilov, Dimitrov, Beria, and Zhukov. Each recipient could interpret it as he chose. Stalin probably rejected the idea that Germany had abandoned plans to invade England, an idea that ran contrary to an important element of his conviction, nourished by German deception, that Hitler would not attack the USSR until England had capitulated. He probably discounted the section describing German preparations for attacking the USSR and preferred the last sentence.[2]

On March 13, Kopets, another Bucharest RU residency source, reported that he had asked an SS officer, "When do we go against England?" The officer replied that there were no longer plans for invading England. "The Führer does not now even think of this. We will continue to fight England with our air force and submarines." A second source, Korf, reported that a German major occupying rooms in the residence of a sub-source stated that "we have completely changed our plan. We will move to the east, against the USSR. We will obtain grain, coal, and oil from the USSR and that will enable us to continue the war against England and America." Both these reports confirm AVS on the German decision to abandon plans for an invasion of England.[3]

On March 24, 1941, RU Bucharest forwarded an AVS report that the German ambassador, Baron Manfred von Killinger, who was expected back from Berlin on March 23, had come out the winner in a bureaucratic battle with SS chief Heinrich Himmler over whether Germany should support Romanian dictator Ion Antonescu or the ultranationalistic, anti-Semitic Iron Guard. Himmler and others probably supported the Iron Guard because of its ideology, but Killinger, a very influential senior Nazi Party official who had been named ambassador in 1940, was able to persuade Hitler and Göring that Germany should back Antonescu. AVS also reported that during meetings in Vienna, Göring and Antonescu had discussed Romania's role in the forthcoming war with the USSR. He described the growing chorus of voices calling for war with the USSR. "The German military," according to AVS, "are drunk with their successes and claim that war with the USSR will begin in May."

AVS, having just returned to Bucharest from Berlin, asked embassy counselor Hamilcar Hoffmann on March 26 what he thought of the rumors of an impending war with the USSR. Hoffmann replied by recounting his discussions with Michael Antonescu, nephew of the dictator and minister of justice in his government. According to the nephew, Antonescu was made privy to Germany's plans for war against the USSR by Hitler in January 1941. Detailed discussions in Vienna with Hermann Göring on Romanian mobilization and preparations for war had followed. In Michael Antonescu's view, "Antonescu has promised Germany that Romania will actively participate in the campaign against the USSR. May will be the critical month."[4]

Also on March 26, Colonel Yeremin sent in a report from another source, Nemesh, a retired Romanian staff officer. This report adds weight to those from AVS on German plans for war with the USSR. Nemesh stated that "the Romanian general staff has precise information that in two or three months Germany will attack the Ukraine. The Germans will attack the Baltic States at the same time, hoping for an uprising there against the USSR. . . . The Romanians will take part in this war together with the Germans and will receive Bessarabia." Nemesh also described military preparations under way in Romanian Moldavia. After reading the report, Golikov gave instructions that the contents be checked with Colonel Pavel V. Gaev, chief of the Intelligence Department of the Odessa Military District, who was responsible for covering Romanian matters as well.[5]

On March 30, AVS added to his previous reporting on the meetings between Antonescu and Göring in Vienna. Agreement was supposedly reached stipulating that Germany would provide arms for twenty Romanian divisions and no more. Antonescu wanted to mobilize far more men, but in the German view, further mobilization would threaten spring planting. "In every sector, including that of the German presence in Romania," AVS continued, "the growing threat of the German front against the USSR is becoming more noticeable."[6]

On April 14, AVS reported on the several talks Ambassador Killinger had held with Antonescu after his return from Berlin. On the one hand, he gave Antonescu assurances that Hitler "considered him to be the sole person in the Romanian leadership capable of ensuring the stable development of Romania." On the other hand, he reminded him that Germany alone would determine when "Russia's turn would come." Meanwhile, Romania need not fear a Soviet attack and must not "provoke the USSR." As for Bessarabia, Antonescu would get it back, but Berlin would determine the timing. On April 20 AVS added that preparations for war with the USSR were still moving forward. He noted that Berlin had not wanted Romania to participate in the war against Yugoslavia because it needed the Romanian general staff to concentrate on "the task of military preparations in Moldavia, deploying its troops there with German help." This work was now going forward "in coordination with the German military mission." Also, "German troops now in Yugoslavia will be returned to Romania and concentrated on the Russian front. . . . The date for the beginning of the attack on the USSR will be from May 15 to the beginning of June." This AVS report ended with information on the growing antiaircraft defenses around Ploesti and the arrival from Germany of Ukrainian "emissaries" who would be sent to areas bordering on Bukovina and Bessarabia to "organize espionage and sabotage groups." They would be sent into Soviet areas to "foment peasant uprisings and carry out acts of sabotage."

These AVS reports were substantiated on April 23 by Vrach, another Bucharest RU residency source. A colonel in the German air mission had told him that "one or two powerful air raids will demonstrate Russian impotence . . . beginning the war in May; we will end it in July." Another high-ranking officer explained Germany's victory in these terms: "Our main advantage is that we always maintain the initiative. We will do so in our confrontation with the USSR. From the first blow we will demoralize the Russian army. The most important thing—always keep the initiative." This report ends with details on the deployment of German troops in Romania.[7]

On May 5 the Bucharest RU residency issued another AVS report, quoting an air officer from a Luftwaffe unit stationed in Romania who had just returned from a trip to Berlin: "Whereas before the date for German military operations against the USSR was to have been May 15, in connection with the events in Yugoslavia it has now been moved back to the middle of June." AVS stated that the officer firmly believed in the likelihood of an impending conflict. Gerstenberg, one of AVS's best sources (according to Moscow RU Center), spoke of the impending German-Russian war as "something that goes without saying" and said that "all of his service actions are devoted to this event." He also said as a fact that "the month of June would see the beginning of the war. . . . The Red Army would be defeated in four weeks. German aviation would destroy rail junctions, highways, airfields in the western USSR, in the shortest possible time; the immobile Russian army would be surrounded and split up by advancing German armored units and suffer the fate of the Polish army." Furthermore, Gerstenberg doubted the likelihood of Russian air attacks on Romanian territory because "the location of Russian air units was known to the Germans and they would be put out of action on the first day of the war."[8]

On the basis of his debriefing of a German visitor from Berlin, AVS reported on May 28 that "preparation for the military action of Germany against the USSR is proceeding systematically. . . . Military preparations are going forward like clockwork and make the beginning of the war in June realistic." A key aspect of the report was the care Hitler was exercising not to disclose the exact nature of his plans regarding the USSR in discussion with his allies. Nevertheless, "German measures for a campaign against the USSR are being carried out with great precision. . . . [Alfred]

Rosenberg, who has been chosen over Ribbentrop to deal with the political aspects of the 'Russian complex,' is now working directly with General [Alfred] Jodl [chief of the operations staff of the Wehrmacht high command]. He is taking an active part in preparing for the campaign against the USSR. . . . All preparations are to be completed by mid-June. . . . War against the USSR presents no problem from a military standpoint. . . . In two or three months German troops will be in the Urals." In conclusion, AVS repeated his view that "the Germans are continuing to prepare for war with us."[9]

It was information from the Bucharest RU residency and AVS that provided the basis for the RU special report of June 7, 1941, on "Preparations of Romania for War," which ended with the words: "Officers of the Romanian general staff persistently assert that, in accordance with unofficial declarations of Antonescu, war between Romania and the USSR should begin soon." The report was disseminated to Stalin, Molotov, Voroshilov, Timoshenko, Beria, Kuznetsov, Zhdanov, Zhukov, and Malenkov. Because Romania would never attack the Soviet Union independently, the report should have had an impact. It obviously did not.[10]

Clearly, AVS made an extremely valuable contribution to RU knowledge of German plans and intentions. What happened to him? When the war began, members of the Soviet embassy were interned and then sent back to the USSR. AVS stayed on with the German embassy but lost contact with Sharov, his communications link with RU Moscow. The RU attempted to infiltrate agents into Romania to try to make contact, but its operations failed. AVS and his wife made trips to Berlin, where they contacted Alta, hoping that she might find a way of getting AVS's information to RU. Nothing worked out and Alta herself was arrested by the Gestapo and later executed. As it turned out, she never betrayed AVS and his wife. They remained with the German embassy in Bucharest until the arrival in Romania of the Red Army in 1944, then returned to the USSR.

AVS agreed to continue working for the RU and did so until war's end. When the division of Germany into four zones of occupation was announced, AVS objected to it, claiming that the decision was made in response to a Soviet demand. He refused to continue working with the RU, and he and his family were sent to the GULAG, as confirmed by a January 16, 1952, decree of the USSR Ministry of State Security. They were released only after Stalin's death and were not rehabilitated. In October 2003, when the first of Vladimir Lota's articles on AVS came to the attention of officials in the Belorussian prosecutor's office, their case was reviewed. The 1952 sentence was invalidated and they were rehabilitated posthumously. One son died in the GULAG; a second son survived and today lives in Germany.[11]

Belgrade

Until Belgrade was destroyed by the Luftwaffe and Yugoslavia was overrun by the Wehrmacht in April 1941, the RU residency in Belgrade had excellent contacts with the Yugoslav general staff. This and other sources enabled it to produce valuable reporting both on the situation in the Balkans and on German intentions to invade the USSR.

The legal RU resident in Belgrade was the military attaché, Major General Aleksandr G. Samokhin (code name Sofokl). The assistant military attaché was Colonel Mikhail S. Maslov; secretary to the military attaché was Captain Andrei A. Vasilev. Viktor Z. Lebedev (code name Blok) whose cover was counselor of the political representation, as Soviet embassies were known at the time, was very active in the Belgrade diplomatic community. As the year 1941 began, the residency was responding to requirements from RU Moscow concerning the movement of German troops into Romania and the Balkans generally. A January 27, 1941, report concluded that there were now fourteen German divisions in Romania, thus confirming German interests in protecting Romanian oil and expanding its Balkan position. On the same date, statements by the German ambassador in Belgrade at a closed meeting in his embassy disclosed the link, from the German point of view, between developments in the Balkans and future relations between Germany and the USSR. According to the ambassador, the Balkans must "be included in the New Order in Europe, but the USSR will never agree to this and therefore war between the two is inevitable."[12]

On February 14, the RU residency obtained the Yugoslav general staff's holdings on the location and strength of German army divisions. The report listed 127 divisions in Eastern Europe, 5 in Scandinavia, and 50 along the English Channel. The remainder were in the reserves in Germany, in occupied France (11) and in Italy (5). As for those in Romania, they consisted of 3 tank divisions, 4 motorized divisions, and 13 infantry. In a marginal note, Golikov ordered the Information Department to "disseminate this with a map."[13]

On March 9, 1941, residency agent Rybnikar was told by the minister of the royal court that the German general staff had turned down a plan for an assault on the British Isles; the next task would be the conquest of the Ukraine and Baku, which would take place in April or May of that year.[14]

On April 4, General Samokhin wrote to RU Moscow: "The concentration of German troops all along the border of the USSR from the Black Sea to the Baltic, the ill-disguised revanchist declarations of Romania in regard to northern Bukovina, the movement of [German] 'instructors' to Finland, the benevolent reaction to Swedish mobilization, the new movement of German troops into the Government General [occupied Poland], and finally the fact of the transformation of Balkan countries into [German] allies do not permit us to exclude the thought of German military intentions toward our country, the more so if Germany succeeds in establishing itself on the shores of the Adriatic and Aegean seas." German diplomacy seemed to be telling the Balkan countries, "Keep in mind . . . we are going to begin a war with the USSR, we'll be in Moscow in seven days, join us before it is too late."[15]

That day Samokhin also sent a warning message obtained by RU residency officer Lebedev stating that "the Germans are sending troops into Finland; they are sending a considerable force consisting of ten infantry and three tank divisions into Hungary via Austria and are planning to attack the USSR in May. The point of departure for this will be a demand that the USSR join the Axis and provide economic assistance. . . . Against the USSR the Germans have three groupings: Königsberg under Rundstedt, Crakow under Blaskowitz or List, and a third, Warsaw, under Bock."[16]

Understandably, the Belgrade residency predicted that the German attack on the USSR would begin in April. Given the rapid collapse of Yugoslav resistance (by April 17 the Wehrmacht had crushed all opposition), the residency could not have known of Hitler's decision on April 30 to postpone the invasion of the USSR by four weeks. Nevertheless, the information Samokhin did obtain from Yugoslav sources, while it was still possible to do so, surely confirmed the outlines of German intentions toward the Soviet Union.

Budapest

The RU residency in Budapest clearly illustrates the problems faced by a residency that had no resources other than a few agent sources and social contacts within the diplomatic community and the host government. The legal resident in Budapest was the military attaché, Nikolai G. Liakhterov (code name Mars), who arrived in June 1940. He had an assistant, a secretary, and a chauffeur. The residency had only two agent sources, code names Vagner and Slovak, but virtually nothing is known of their backgrounds and access. The first report available from this residency is dated March 1, 1941, and states unequivocally: "Everyone considers that at the present time a German offensive against the USSR is unthinkable before the defeat of England." This came from the military attaché community, with the Italian attaché stating, "The Germans are preparing four parachute divisions and up to thirty infantry divisions for movement on fast ships as the advance guard of their invasion of England." Inasmuch as Germany had only one parachute division, the Seventh, this drivel appears to have been pure German deception, a cardinal element of which was the notion that Germany could not and would not fight on two fronts—hence, there would be no war with the USSR until England capitulated.[17]

On March 13, 1941, the resident reported this gem obtained from Hungarian military intelligence, to whose offices he had been invited: "Among the diplomatic corps false rumors are circulating about the preparations of Germany, Hungary, and Romania for an offensive against the USSR, about mobilization in Hungary, and about the sending of large quantities of troops to the Soviet-Hungarian border. This is English propaganda." Liakhterov was told to visit the Carpathian Ukraine and see for himself that these rumors were false. When this report was received in Moscow, Golikov ordered the Information Department to tell the residency that its report had been disseminated to the leadership. Advising a residency that one of its reports had been sent "to the leadership" was unusual. Most disseminations were carried out according to standard distribution lists to specific addressees. One can speculate that Golikov acted as he did because he knew the report's labeling of preparations for a German offensive against the USSR as "English propaganda" was how Stalin would view it.[18]

A March 15 report was devoted primarily to German troop movements in the Balkans. On April 24, Liakhterov submitted a breakdown of the German army by divisions; the information was obtained from "colleagues" in the attaché community. There were several errors, as is often the case when rumors reach the attaché community. For example, the report referred to "five parachute divisions . . . of which four are stationed in Norway," when the Germans had only one.[19]

On April 30, the residency reported on the return to Hungary of German divisions that had fought in Yugoslavia. The soldiers stated that after

a short leave they were to be sent to Poland. Rumors continued in Budapest and Bucharest concerning an impending war between Germany and
the USSR. The report also provided information on Hungarian army units
now stationed in eastern Hungary. Although this information was un-
sourced, Golikov ordered that it be included in a May 5 special report,
observing that it was important to discover the destination of German
troops leaving Yugoslavia. A May 1 report noted the movement of German
troops from Belgrade to Poland, while those in Romania were advanced to
the Soviet border. A second section of this report contained this sentence:
"Among German troops rumors are being blown up that in twenty days
England will no longer be considered a military factor and war with the
USSR will be inevitable in the near future." An Information Department
note stated that the first part of the report about the movement of troops
to the Soviet border would be used in special summaries, but not the second part about the inevitability of war with the Soviet Union. This shows
how Golikov and those subordinate to him not only slanted reporting to
please Stalin but omitted reporting any views in opposition to Stalin's
convictions.[20]

The last report available from the Budapest residency was dated
June 15, 1941; it cited agent Slovak as the source. The first paragraph stated
that German troops from Belgrade were leaving for Poland, while those in
central Romania were moving to the Soviet frontier. In the second paragraph Slovak stated flatly: "The Germans will complete their strategic deployment by June 15. It is possible that they will not attack the USSR
immediately, but they are preparing for it. Officers speak openly about it."
Golikov's written reaction: "Let's discuss it." From marginal comments by
the Information Department, it seems that only the first paragraph was
disseminated to Stalin, Molotov, Voroshilov, Timoshenko, and Zhukov.[21]

Prague

After the Germans occupied Prague in March 1939 and made Czech lands
a German protectorate (Slovakia was given its "independence" as a German satellite), the Soviet embassy in Prague became a consulate general.
The legal RU resident in Prague from 1939 to 1941 was Leonid A. Mikhailov (code name Rudolf), who worked in the office of the consulate general
under the alias Leonid E. Mokhov. The residency was extremely active in
running various RU agent nets and maintaining contacts with the Czech
resistance.[22] Two reports, however, bore directly on the impending Ger-

man invasion. On April 15, 1941, the Prague residency reported that "according to an individual in the circle of persons close to German Foreign Minister Ribbentrop, it is known that in the leadership of Germany there has been a discussion of an invasion of the USSR. The date has been provisionally set for May 15th. Preparation for the aggression will be masked as large-scale preparations for a decisive blow against England."[23]

On April 17, 1941 the RU legal resident in Prague forwarded this report from a source in the Skoda firm who was said to have cooperated with the RU out of patriotism following the occupation of his country: "The German high command has ordered an immediate halt to the manufacture of Soviet heavy armaments at the Skoda plants. Senior German officers stationed in Czechoslovakia have told friends that German divisions are concentrating on the western borders of the USSR. It is believed that Hitler will attack the USSR in the second half of June." The source for the report was probably RU residency agent Vladimir Vrana, who was employed in the export division of Skoda soon after the occupation by the Germans. Three days after the report was sent to Stalin, Golikov received it back with Stalin's comments written on it in red ink: "English provocation! Investigate!"[24]

Sofia

In the extent and level of its agent networks, the RU residency in Bulgaria owed much to the traditional ties of language and religion between Russia and Bulgaria. The description of these networks in recently published literature on the RU lists an impressive number of agents and their sources in Bulgarian officialdom and in the country's military forces. At one time Sofia served as the main RU center in the Balkans. One of the best sources was Vladimir Zaimov (code name Azorsky), who had retired as a major general and inspector of artillery in 1936. Zaimov had extensive contacts throughout the Bulgarian armed forces who cooperated with him because of their pro-Russian, anti-German views. In early April 1941, Zaimov reported to Yakov S. Savchenko, the legal residency officer who was his regular contact, that Germany planned to attack the USSR in June. Given the existence of this source and others (some described below), it comes as a surprise that only a small number of reports from the Sofia residency appear in Aleksandr N. Yakovlev's *1941 god.*[25]

The resident and military attaché in Sofia from October 1939 to March 1941 was Colonel Ivan F. Dergachev. His deputy was Leonid A. Sereda (code name Zevs), who arrived in December 1940 and served as acting resident from March to June 1941.[26] The earliest report available from Sofia is a statement on April 27, 1941, by a German general to a Bulgarian prelate that "the Germans are preparing a strike against the USSR. . . . All officers with a knowledge of Russian are ordered to Berlin for special training, after which they will be assigned to the Soviet frontier area. They will be assisted by White émigrés who know the Ukraine."[27]

One of the most startling aspects of later residency reporting is the insistence on a German army presence in Turkey. On May 9 agent Margarit reported that "German troops from western Macedonia are moving through Turkey in officially sanctioned columns to Iraq!" The report then reverted to information on Soviet-German relations: "Germany is preparing to open hostilities against the USSR in the summer of 1941 before the harvest. In two months, incidents will begin along the Soviet-German border. The blow will come from Polish territory, by sea against Odessa and from Turkey against Baku." The resident added that the information on the presence of German troops in Turkey came from agent Boevoy, one of whose sources was Zhurin, head of the Military Justice Department of the Bulgarian Defense Ministry and a member of the High Military Council. Golikov appended this comment in the margin: "Sofia has twice reported that German troops are moving officially through Turkey to Iraq. Is this true?"[28]

On March 14, 1941, source Belvedere provided very good information on a meeting between Tsar Boris and Field Marshall Walther von Brauchitsch and on the Germans' use of flamethrowing tanks in their campaign in Yugoslavia. "There are at least three or four divisions in Turkey en route to Syria," he added. The resident, responding to a Moscow message, stated that he did not "insist on the veracity of these reports" but considered it "necessary to relate that I have received reports of the movement of German troops through Turkey from a third source. The neighbors [here the resident speaks of the NKGB residency] working on the same problem have analogous information." The issue must have somehow been resolved because this is the last time it is mentioned in the available reporting. How it arose is difficult to say. Turkey was not part of the February 15, 1941, German deception program, but Moscow was very concerned about German influence in Turkey. Thus, requests from Moscow for information on German activity affecting Turkey, once transmitted down the line to Sofia residency sources, could have stimulated them to provide the required answers, true or not. In any case, sources Boevoy and Zhurin both reported later that "the German high command has no intention of attacking Turkey."[29]

The May 15 report from another residency network, Kosta, deals with the return of German army units from the fighting in Greece. "Infantry, motorized units of the Twelfth Army, are returning from Greece through Sofia to Romania. . . . From May 20, Bulgarian military units will be sent to Greece as occupation troops."[30] On May 27, 1941, Boevoy reported that "German troops, artillery, and munitions are continuously moving from Bulgaria to Romania . . . en route to the German-Soviet border." In his comment on the report, Golikov ordered the RU resident in Bucharest to "put people along the line of march of the German columns to observe and report on them. Yeshchenko [the RU resident in Bucharest] is behind the events." Here again, Golikov displayed his lack of knowledge of the residency's sources. Boevoy's best source was Zhurin, who was a major general, chief of the Military Justice Department of the Bulgarian Defense Ministry, and a member of the Bulgarian Higher Military Council. It would seem that Golikov or his Information Department could have devised better tasks for Boevoy and the residency's officers than standing by the side of the road and watching German troops drive by.[31]

On June 13 Boevoy reported that "according to information from Zhurin, the Führer has decided to attack the USSR before the end of this month. The Germans have deployed more than 170 divisions on the Soviet border." RU Moscow replied by asking: "Who is the source of this information?" The answer: "This was stated by [Bulgarian] Defense Minister Teodosy Daskalov at a meeting of the Bulgarian Higher Military Council." Clearly, Zhurin was the source of this important report. It is not known how the Soviet leadership reacted to the information.[32]

The last available report from the Sofia residency before the June 22 invasion was provided by the Kosta network. On June 20, 1941, a German emissary said that "a military clash is expected on June 21 or 22. There are 100 German divisions in Poland, 40 in Romania, 6 in Finland, 10 in Hungary, and 7 in Slovakia. There are 60 motorized divisions in all." A courier from Bucharest reported that "mobilization in Romania has been completed, and military operations are expected at any minute."[33]

Bit by bit, a picture developed from reporting by RU residencies in Eastern Europe of German preparations for an invasion of the Soviet Union. Events in Greece and Yugoslavia had thrown off the original timetable, but the reports made clear that there was no letup in these preparations, only a postponement of Day X.

CHAPTER 8

Who Were You, Dr. Sorge?
Stalin Never Heard of You.

The picture provided by the RU residencies in Western and Eastern Europe would be reinforced by reports from Japan, which became the principal playing field for the RU in the Far East in the period immediately preceding the German invasion of June 22, 1941. There was a legal residency in Tokyo under Ivan V. Gushchenko, who was military attaché from February 1940 to June 1942. Two of his subordinates—Sergei L. Budkevich (who served in Tokyo from 1936 to 1941) and Viktor S. Zaitsev (who was employed there from July 1940 to February 1942)—served as links to the residency's "crown jewels," the network created and run by the illegal Richard Sorge (code name Ramsay). Sorge was Stalin's bête noire, forever sending RU Moscow dire predictions of a German invasion of the USSR, even warning Stalin of its exact date. Ironically, Stalin, at war's end, reportedly observed that Moscow had an agent in Tokyo who was worth a "corps or even a whole army." That is not what he said about Dr. Sorge earlier.[1]

Sorge has been the subject of so many books, articles, films, and historical conferences that it would be impossible to cover every aspect of his life in the same detail, but the broad outlines of his biography and a few events are important here. Sorge was born in Baku, Russia, of a German father and Russian mother on October 4, 1895. The family moved to Germany in 1897. Sorge served in the imperial German army in World War I, finished university, and joined the German Communist Party in 1919. In 1924 he went to work for the Comintern in Moscow. He was recruited for Soviet military intelligence by Jan Karlovich Berzin and in 1930 was sent to Shanghai, China, and then in 1933 to Japan. He made a visit to the Soviet Union in 1935, returned to Tokyo, and remained there until his arrest in October 1941 and his execution in November 1944. While working in Tokyo as a journalist for the *Frankfurter Zeitung*, he became a member of the Nazi Party and was completely trusted and accepted by the German military attaché (and later ambassador), Eugen Ott, and other officials of the German embassy. He would often help Ott draft dispatches and was shown sensitive, classified communications from Berlin.

Sorge scored a major triumph in 1938 when he cultivated the German counterintelligence officer sent from Berlin by Admiral Wilhelm Canaris to participate in the Japanese interrogation of NKVD General G. S. Lyushkov, who had defected to the Japanese army in Manchuria. In a telegram to Sorge on the Lyushkov defection, the RU urged Sorge to "do everything and use every available means to get copies of the documents to be received by Canaris's special envoy from the Japanese army. Get copies of the documents received by the envoy from Lyushkov."[2] Sorge promptly copied much of the long report and sent it to Moscow.[3] The Lyushkov debriefing revealed how the NKVD evaluated the defenses of the Red Army in the border area between Manchuria and Mongolia, the state of its equipment, and the low morale of the Soviet forces. Improvements made over the summer and the arrival of General Georgy K. Zhukov, however, enabled the Red Army to defeat the Japanese decisively in September 1939 at the battle of Khalkin Gol on the border between the Mongolian People's Republic and Japanese-occupied Manchuria.

On November 18, 1940, Sorge was one of the first to report on German preparations for war against the USSR; on December 28, he reported that a new reserve army of forty divisions had been created in the Leipzig area.[4] That same day, in messages 138 and 139, he commented that each new arrival at the German embassy from Berlin spoke of the eighty German divisions deployed on the Soviet border with Romania. He stated that the purpose was to influence Soviet policy. If the USSR "begins to develop activities against German interests, as happened in the Baltic, the Germans could occupy territory on a line Kharkov, Moscow, Leningrad. . . . The Germans know that the USSR would not risk this, as the Soviet leadership is aware, particularly after the Finnish campaign, that it will take twenty years for the Red Army to become a modern army like that of Germany."[5] On March 1, 1941, Sorge reported that twenty German divisions had been moved from France to the Soviet border—these were in addition to the eighty divisions already there.[6]

Another series of telegrams described the complications arising from differing Japanese and German interests insofar as relations with the USSR were concerned. A March 10, 1941, message revealed that "the Japanese are interested in a surprise attack on Singapore as a way of giving Japan a more active role in the Anti-Comintern Pact. The Germans, however, would only be interested in a Japanese attack on Singapore if America remained out of the war and if Japan could no longer serve to put pressure on the USSR." On March 15 Sorge reported the contents of a message to Ambassador Ott from Ribbentrop: "I ask you to do everything within your power to persuade the Japanese to commence an immediate offensive against Singapore." Ott added that "the German general staff considers the onset of military operations against Singapore the only guarantee against a Red Army attack on Manchuria."[7] An RU memorandum summarizing several Sorge messages reported on discussions between Ambassador Ott and Prime Minister Fumimaro Konoye of Japan. When Konoye did not raise the issue of an attack on Singapore, the ambassador asked about it. The prime minister remarked that the Singapore question seemed to interest everyone. Later, in a discussion with Sorge, the ambassador asked if Sorge could push the Japanese into attacking Singapore. Sorge, in turn, put the question to the RU in Moscow. In two telegrams dated May 10, one based on a report from the German naval attaché and the other from Ambassador Ott, Sorge made it clear that "as long as Japan continued to receive raw materials from the United States, it would not attack Singapore." Despite German urging for action against Singapore, the Japanese continued to stall.[8]

The principal question, that of German-Russian relations, would not remain in the background for long. On May 2, 1941, Sorge discussed the question with Ambassador Ott and the naval attaché. They agreed that after the completion of the operations against Yugoslavia there would be two critical dates in German-Soviet relations: "The first date—the time for completion of the harvest. After the harvest is in, a war against the USSR can start at any moment, as all that will remain for Germany to do will be to gather the harvest. The second critical moment will be the negotiations between Germany and Turkey. If the USSR creates any difficulties with regard to the acceptance by Turkey of German demands, war will be inevitable." The two Germans then added: "The possibility of war at any moment is very great because Hitler and his generals are convinced that war with the USSR will in no way interfere with the conduct of the war with England. German generals judge the combat capabilities of the Red Army to be so low that they calculate the Red Army will be defeated in several weeks."[9]

On May 5, 1941, Sorge passed on a microfilm of a telegram from Ribbentrop to Ambassador Ott with the news that "Germany will begin a war against the USSR in the middle of June 1941." On May 15 he reported that the war would begin on June 20–22![10] On May 19–20 new German representatives arriving from Berlin were reported by Sorge to have declared that "war will begin at the end of May because that is the time they have been ordered to return to Berlin." They also stated that "for this year the danger might pass" but added that "Germany has nine 'army corps' against the USSR, containing 150 divisions. One army corps is under the command of the well-known [Walther von] Reichenau." Golikov asked whether Sorge meant army corps or armies. "If he meant army corps, then it is not in keeping with our understanding of a corps."[11] This comment does not say much for Golikov's order of battle competence. Reichenau commanded the Sixth Army under Gerd von Rundstedt's Army Group South. It would have been obvious that the Sorge message was intended to mean armies, not corps. Perhaps Golikov was merely needling him.[12] Probably in answer to Golikov's query, Sorge reported on June 13: "I repeat: nine armies with a strength of 150 divisions will begin an offensive at dawn on June 22, 1941."[13] On June 11 a German courier told the military attaché that he was "convinced war against the USSR is probably being delayed until the end of June." Sorge saw the beginning of a communication to Berlin to the effect that, "if a German-Soviet war breaks out, it will take the Japanese about six weeks to begin offensive operations against the Soviet Far East . . . but the Germans consider that it will take more time because this conflict will be both on land and on sea."[14] Ambassador Ott told Sorge on June 20 that "war between Germany and the USSR was inevitable. . . . Invest [Ozaki Hotsumi, the leading Japanese member of the Sorge network] reported that the Japanese general staff was already considering the position it would take in case of war."[15]

Stalin could not abide this ominous reporting from Sorge. When he received the May 19 report predicting an attack by 150 divisions under nine armies by the end of that month, he accused Sorge of being "a little shit who has set himself up with some small factories and brothels in Japan."[16] Stalin's nasty remark shows well enough that he already knew of Sorge. A report from the RU based on Sorge information received by Stalin in late 1936 was returned with the instruction: "I ask you not to send me any more of this German disinformation."[17]

As late as August 11, 1941, when the war Sorge had predicted was overwhelming the Red Army and Sorge's network was straining to respond to Moscow's orders to determine whether Japan would attack the Soviet Far East, a memorandum was prepared at the RU headquarters casting doubt on Sorge's loyalty. It used testimony incriminating Sorge from officers who during the purges had admitted that they were German and Japanese spies; supposedly, they had named Sorge to their German and Japanese interrogators as a Soviet intelligence officer. The memorandum argued that Sorge must be under hostile control as the enemy already knew the truth about him. Each of the three officers named was later rehabilitated.[18] This negative attitude toward Sorge had other consequences. In February 1941, when Soviet military intelligence in Moscow should have been concerned with what Sorge could produce, Golikov informed him that "I consider it necessary to reduce expenses in your office to 2,000 yen per month." On March 26, 1941, Sorge replied: "When we received your orders to cut our expenses in half, we took it as a kind of punishment. You have probably received our detailed telegram in which we tried to show you that cutting [funds] in half . . . is tantamount to destroying our apparatus."[19] Contrast this behavior with that of Golikov's immediate predecessor, Proskurov, when he had to refuse Sorge's request to return to Moscow in June 1939. Proskurov sent this note to the Japanese section of the RU handling the Sorge case: "Think carefully about how we could compensate for Ramsay's [Sorge's] recall. Prepare a telegram and letter to Ramsay with excuses for the delay in replacing him and listing the reasons it is necessary for him to remain in Tokyo. Give Ramsay and the other members of his organization a onetime monetary bonus."[20]

For his part, as late as the early 1960s Golikov apparently still believed Sorge had been under hostile control. In the middle of a screening of the Franco-German film *Wer Sind Sie, Dr. Sorge?* to senior officers, Marshal Zhukov, angry at not having been shown the Sorge reports predicting the war and its exact date, stood up in the theater and called out to Golikov: "Why, Filipp Ivanovich, did you hide these reports from me? Not report such information to the chief of the general staff?" Golikov replied, "And what should I have reported to you if this Sorge was a double, ours and theirs?"[21]

On June 23, the day after the invasion began, RU Moscow sent this peremptory message to Sorge: "Report your information on the position of the Japanese government with regard to the German war against the Soviet Union." His responses to this vital question would be Sorge's last gift to the land of his birth before his arrest on October 18, 1941. Sorge reported fully on Ambassador Ott's frustration during July and August as the Japanese resisted German efforts to obtain a firm answer to the question of whether they would attack the Soviet Far East. On July 10 Sorge reported that "thirty-seven troop transports were on their way to Formosa." He also said that "the Japanese would go ahead with their plans for French Indochina but would at the same time remain ready for action against the USSR if the Red Army were to be defeated." However, Ott told Sorge that "the Japanese would begin to fight only when the Germans reached Sverdlovsk!" In a meeting with Ott, Foreign Minister Yosuke Matsuoka expressed concern that "the Japanese people would experience air raids on the population centers of Japan." Ott said "this would not be possible because the Red Army had only two types of bombers that could raid Japan and return, and neither was yet in the Far East." Comments added to this report by the acting chief of the RU, Major General of Tank Troops Aleksei P. Panfilov, suggested a sea change in attitude toward Sorge. Panfilov wrote: "Considering his great possibilities as a source and the reliability of a significant amount of his previous reporting, this report inspires confidence."[22]

Japanese vacillation concerning an attack on Soviet positions in the Far East was a direct result of the government's decision to delay entry into the Soviet-German war unless it became apparent that the Red Army had been decisively defeated. Actions were taken during the summer of 1941 to strengthen the Kwantung army in the event the Germans succeeded. A much higher priority, however, was the acquisition of sources of key raw materials in the Netherlands East Indies and elsewhere in the South Pacific.

By mid-September it had become clear to Ambassador Ott and his military and naval attachés that there was no hope of Japan's entering the war against the USSR. As one Japanese Foreign Ministry official put it, "If Japan goes to war, it will only be in the south, where it can obtain raw materials—oil and metals."[23] By early fall 1941, Japan saw America as its major foe. As this news sank in at the Stavka (General Headquarters of the Supreme Command) in Moscow, preparations began for the movement of Soviet troops from the Soviet Far East to the Moscow region.

During October and November Stalin transferred eight to ten rifle divisions, along with 1,000 tanks and 1,000 aircraft, from the Far East to the Moscow area. In the early morning hours of December 5, the Soviet

CHAPTER 9

NKVD Foreign Intelligence

In addition to the RU, the principal organization involved in providing intelligence to Stalin from agent sources was the Fifth (Foreign Intelligence) Department of the NKVD's Chief Directorate for State Security (Glavnoe Upravlenie Gosudarstvennoi Bezopastnosti, or GUGB). It began as the Foreign Department of the All-Russian Extraordinary Commission (Cheka) on December 20, 1920. For most of the 1920s it focused on foreign threats to the young socialist state ranging from Russian émigrés to the followers of Leon Trotsky. Gradually it broadened its coverage to include the acquisition of foreign technical secrets. With Hitler's rise to power in Germany, it began to expand its legal and illegal residencies abroad to met the new danger.[1]

The reason the NKVD/GUGB's Fifth Department did not contribute more to what Stalin knew is that it was decimated by Stalin's own purges. Post-Soviet publications by the Russian Foreign Intelligence Service (SVR) emphasize losses suffered earlier by the Soviet Foreign Intelligence Service owing to "repression." This anodyne expression is apparently preferred to the more precise characterizations of the manner in which the purges actually operated. Hundreds of members of the NKVD's Foreign Intelligence Service were arrested, tortured during interrogation to extract confessions based on trumped-up charges, and then either shot or sent to the GULAG. During 1938, for example, almost all illegal residencies were liquidated. Contact was lost with valuable agent sources, and for long periods

no intelligence was received in Moscow. Many legal residencies were reduced to an officer or two, mainly young and inexperienced. Nor did the
Central Headquarters of Foreign Intelligence escape the loss of senior officials, including chiefs of the service. To help the intelligence service recover, party organizations selected individuals from civilian life and the
armed forces, sent them to special schools for training, and assigned them
to positions in the service. The best known of those who became foreign
intelligence officers in this manner was Pavel M. Fitin.[2]

Fitin was born on December 28, 1907, of Russian peasant parents in
the village of Ozhogino, now in Tyumenskaia Oblast, Russian Federation. After finishing primary school, he worked in a rural cooperative in
Ozhogino. Commencing in May 1927, Fitin was chairman of a Young Pi-
oneers Buro and deputy secretary of the District Committee of the Kom-
somol. That year he became a member of the Party.

In June 1928, after completing middle school, Fitin began a prepara-
tory course for higher education run by the Tyumen Regional Education
Department. In August he entered the Institute of Mechanization and
Electrification of Agriculture. After completing the institute's courses in
July 1932, he stayed on as an engineer in the Laboratory of Agricultural
Machines. In October 1932 he became the chief editor for industrial litera-
ture of the Selkhozgiz publishing house. Drafted into the Red Army in
October 1934, he served as a private in the Moscow Military District. He
was demobilized in October 1935 and returned to Selkhozgiz, where he
rose to become deputy chief editor.

In March 1938 the party sent him to the Central NKVD School. He
finished the school five months later and was sent to the Fifth Department,
NKVD/GUGB, as a probationer. A lack of experienced cadres meant Fitin
rose rapidly, becoming case officer, then chief of the Ninth Section (working against Trotskyites and right wingers abroad). On November 1, 1938,
he was named deputy chief of the Fifth Department when Vladimir G.
Dekanozov was promoted to chief. On May 13, 1939, Stalin had Dekanozov transferred to the People's Commissariat for Foreign Affairs (NKID) to
oversee the purge of pro-Litvinov diplomats; Fitin succeeded him in the
Fifth Department, NKVD/GUGB. Pavel A. Sudoplatov, who had been acting chief of the department prior to Dekanozov's appointment, was passed
over for the chief's post but remained as deputy of the department. When
NKVD/GUGB became the People's Commissariat for State Security on
February 3, 1941, Fitin became chief of the First, or Foreign Intelligence,

Directorate, NKGB, which on July 31, 1941, was again placed under the NKVD/GUGB.[3]

The Sudoplatov-Fitin relationship is interesting. The two men were quite different. Sudoplatov was a tough customer who had spent his entire career in the special operations element of state security, responsible for sabotage, kidnaping, and assassination of Stalin's enemies. He had made a name for himself in May 1938 with the murder of Yevhen Konovalets, the Ukrainian nationalist, who was living in Rotterdam. Later, he directed the assassination of Leon Trotsky in Mexico. Sudoplatov clearly resented the fact that Fitin, as a newcomer to intelligence work, was made chief of the service while he remained deputy. Also, Sudoplatov was closely tied to Beria and followed his lead in condemning intelligence reports that ran counter to Stalin's view that Hitler would not invade the Soviet Union. On June 19, 1941, for example, when the Rome NKGB residency reported that the Italian ambassador in Berlin had been told by high-level German military officers that Germany would commence military operations against the USSR between June 20 and 25, Sudoplatov made this marginal comment on the telegram: "It appears that this is strictly disinformation."[4]

Fitin, by contrast, was well liked by his subordinates and considered a thoughtful, kindly chief who had his own approach to any question but was always ready to listen to the views of others. While it is true he was new to the Foreign Intelligence Service, he seemed to have an instinct for it. In his careful, meticulous way, he became a superb manager.[5]

The Fifth Department headed by Fitin in 1939 was unlike the KGB's much larger First Chief Directorate for Foreign Intelligence and Counterintelligence, which emerged during the Cold War. Indeed, even at the time it was outgunned by most of the other departments, all of which were concerned with internal security. These included the First Department, which was responsible for protection of the leadership. The Second, or Secret Political, Department maintained a network of secret agents at all levels of Soviet society. The Third, or Counterintelligence, Department ran agent nets that reported on foreigners, foreign installations, and Soviet citizens suspected of espionage activity on behalf of foreign intelligence services. The Fourth Department operated the system of special departments (*osobye otdely*) responsible for counterintelligence and political reliability in the military forces. Out of a total of 1,484 employees in the GUGB, only 225 were in the Fifth Department, all of them housed in Building No. 2, better known as the Liubianka. The place reeked of "repression."[6]

By February 1941 the GUGB was removed from the NKVD and made an independent People's Commissariat, the NKGB. The Fifth (Foreign Intelligence) Department became the First Directorate, testimony to the growing importance of external intelligence. The other departments of the GUGB were combined into the Second Directorate for Counterintelligence and a Third Secret-Political Directorate. Under Fitin's leadership the Moscow staff of the new Foreign Intelligence Directorate continued to grow. The number of personnel in its foreign residencies numbered 242. The structure of the operational departments was then streamlined, with Germany remaining the First Section. Subordinate to the Fifth Department in 1939 were fourteen geographic sections (*otdeleniia*). The First covered Germany, Hungary, and Denmark, the Second Poland, the Third France, Belgium, Holland, and Switzerland, the Fourth Great Britain, and so on. The Fifteenth Section dealt with technical intelligence; the Sixteenth handled operational technical matters such as documentation and concealment devices.[7]

Unlike Proskurov, the chief of military intelligence, Fitin never had access to Stalin directly. Because his department was subordinate to the NKVD's Chief Directorate for State Security (GUGB), his reporting had to be signed by either Lavrenty P. Beria himself or Vsevolod N. Merkulov, GUGB's chief. Merkulov had served in internal security from 1921 to 1931. In December 1938 he came up to Moscow from party work in the Georgian SSR along with other Beria cronies; in November Beria had become People's Commissar for Internal Affairs. Then, in February 1941, when the People's Commissariat for State Security was created out of the NKVD/GUGB, Merkulov became commissar, with Bogdan Z. Kobulov as his deputy. When Merkulov was absent—as he was, for example, from about June 9 to June 13, 1941—reports to Stalin and other listed recipients were signed by Kobulov. On the few occasions when Fitin met personally with Stalin, Merkulov was always present; it is doubtful that either Beria or Merkulov would have given Fitin permission to see Stalin alone. Even had he been permitted, it seems unlikely that Fitin could have persuaded Stalin to accept the validity of reporting with which he did not agree.[8]

As concern over German military activities on the western frontier grew acute, Fitin was forced to spend more and more time with Pavel M. Zhuravliev, head of the German component in the center. Fitin was personally responsible for relations with Soviet military intelligence. Beginning in the summer of 1940 and continuing through June 1941, there was constant communication between the two organizations. The RU frequently passed specific requirements to the NKGB, after which Zhuravliev's people would adapt them to the capabilities of individual residencies and their sources and send them to the appropriate residency. All exchanges between the RU and the First Directorate had to be approved by Fitin. There is one instance noted in July 1940 in which Fitin passed on to the RU a report from sources in Bratislava, Slovakia, on the Germanization of the Slovakian army. This report Fitin had actually copied by hand.[9]

Another task for which the German Department was responsible was the receipt of reports from the NKVD border troops and their agents and dissemination to the RU and the senior leadership. Evaluating NKGB reporting in May 1941, the RU asserted that it accepted without doubt the increasing German army presence along the Soviet frontier. It pointed out, however, that by moving their troops from one area to another, the Germans may have been attempting to confuse RU estimates. It therefore requested greater precision in identifying units and the nature of their movements.[10] That this guidance was having some effect can be seen in a detailed report to the NKGB SSR from the Belorussian SSR NKGB that provided precise unit identification and organizational structure. Merkulov made a marginal note to Fitin: "Put this together with information you have and prepare the contents of it for the Central Committee VKP(b)."[11]

Unlike Military Intelligence, NKVD/NKGB Foreign Intelligence had never created an analytical component, or "information" unit. It had always relied on the dissemination of reports directly to specific customers, leaving them to decide on interpretation. Stalin insisted on this procedure and made clear that he alone would judge individual reports and their implications. His problem was his limited ability to understand things foreign. Apart from brief trips abroad before World War I to attend party conferences, his first substantive foreign visit was to Iran for the Teheran Conference in 1943. His last was to Potsdam, in the Soviet Zone of Germany in 1945.[12] Already blinkered by Marxist-Leninist ideology and a conspiratorial cast of mind, Stalin was a poor judge of the reporting. The most telling evidence was his fixation on the idea that Hitler could not, would not attack the USSR until he had conquered England.[13] By the spring of 1941, Fitin received increased reporting from his own sources and from other elements of the NKGB and NKVD. In recognition that some capability for analysis needed to be created, the Information Section of the German Department, the NKGB's first analytical component, was formed. It was organized by Mikhail A. Allakhverdov, a veteran Chekist and Central Asian specialist who had just returned from Belgrade, reportedly after an attempt to stage a coup against the pro-German government. Some said he was actually sent there to watch the British run their own coup. It was successful, but the patient died—Hitler immediately overran Yugoslavia.[14]

Allakhverdov's deputy was Zoia Ivanovna Rybkina, who had entered internal security in 1928 and by 1935 occupied the post of deputy resident in Helsinki, where she served until 1939. In 1940 she was assigned to the German Section, where she specialized in the study of German intentions toward the USSR and processed reporting from Berlin residency sources. She was therefore well qualified to become deputy in this first NKGB Information Section.[15]

One of the section's activities was the preparation of a "calendar" of reporting by the two most prolific Berlin sources, Korsikanets and Starshina, on German plans and preparations to attack the USSR. This was to be the final effort of the newly created section before the war began.[16]

CHAPTER 10

Fitin's Recruited Spies

Fitin's foreign intelligence directorate was part of the state security apparatus on which Stalin had always relied. Because this apparatus was headed by men like Beria and Merkulov on whom he believed he could depend, he may have tended to pay special attention to Fitin's reports. Which of Fitin's spies produced the best intelligence reports for Stalin, and did their reports please him? City by city, here is the answer to that question.

Berlin

The Berlin residency began to rebuild after Hitler's ascent to power. A new resident, Boris M. Gordon, arrived in 1934 and began recruiting sources. His most successful recruit was Arvid Harnack, an official in the German Economics Ministry. Harnack had a wide circle of acquaintances, all of them opposed to Hitler, capable of providing access to a variety of intelligence. His development of Harnack (code name Korsikanets) was interrupted in May 1937 when he was recalled to Moscow, where he was arrested and executed on the usual spurious charges. His replacement, Aleksandr I. Agaiants, arrived soon after his departure and began to re-establish contact with various sources, including Wilhelm (Willy) Lehmann (code name Breitenbach), a police official who had volunteered his services in the pre-Hitler period. He was later assigned to Gestapo counter-intelligence operations against the Soviet mission.

Unfortunately for the residency, Agaiants died while undergoing an operation for a perforated stomach ulcer in December 1937. His death left the residency without a chief and with many of its best sources out of contact. In August 1939 the new resident arrived as first secretary and then counselor of the Soviet mission. He was Amaiak Z. Kobulov, whose older brother, Bogdan Kobulov, was a Beria favorite and then a department chief in the NKVD's sinister Chief Directorate for State Security (GUGB). The appointment of an individual who had no foreign intelligence experience, had never been abroad, and spoke no German was typical of the nepotism then prevalent in Beria's NKVD. It was deeply resented by the professional officers in the German component. Although Fitin himself endeavored to contain his displeasure at the appointment, it became evident that if operational discipline and contact with key sources were to be restored, an experienced deputy would have to be assigned to Berlin.

This turned out to be Aleksandr M. Korotkov, an experienced officer who had been active since 1933 as an illegal in Western Europe. It was Korotkov who recontacted Korsikanets on September 17, 1940, using the pseudonym Alexander Erdberg. He would continue to handle this case and then work directly with Korsikanets's friend Harro Schulze-Boysen (code name Starshina), who occupied a major's slot in the intelligence element of the German Air Ministry. The several subsources exploited by these agents included: a member of the Technical Department of the Wehrmacht (code name Grek), the principal bookkeeper of the industrial chemical giant I. G. Farben (code name Turok); a Russian émigré industrialist and former tsarist officer with good contacts in the German military (code name Albanets); a German naval intelligence officer (code name Italianets); an employee of the heavy-machine building firm AEG (code name Luchisty); and a German air force major, liaison officer between the Air Ministry and the Foreign Ministry (code named Shved).

The third person with whom Korotkov was in direct contact was Starik, an old friend of Korsikanets who was able to report on the opposition to Hitler and assist in communications among the group. A review of available declassified reports from Berlin during the 1940–41 period demonstrates that it was this formidable intelligence team that provided the bulk of the information.[1]

The Berlin NKGB residency did an excellent job of source exploitation. In October 1940 Korsikanets reported that "Germany would go to war with the USSR after the first of the year 1941." The initial phase of the operation would be the occupation of Romania. Another source in the German high command told Korsikanets that "the war would begin in six months." In early January 1941, Starshina, the Luftwaffe officer in the intelligence element of the Air Ministry, reported that "an order had been given to begin large-scale photographic reconnaissance flights over the Soviet border area. At the same time Hermann Göring ordered the 'Russian Section' of the Air Ministry subordinated to the active air staff responsible for operations planning." On January 9 Korsikanets reported, "The Military-Economic Department of the Reich Statistical Administration was ordered by the German high command to prepare a map of Soviet industrial areas." Per Starshina, by March 1941 "the photographic reconnaissance flights were under way at full speed. German aircraft were operating from air fields at Bucharest, Königsberg, and Kirkenes in northern Norway. Photos were taken at a height of 6,000 meters. Göring is the 'driving force' in planning for a war against the USSR."[2]

On March 20 Korsikanets learned that "in addition to the occupation forces there was only one active division in Belgium, thus confirming the postponement of military action against the British Isles. Preparation for an attack against the USSR has become obvious. This is evident from the disposition of German forces concentrated along the Soviet border. The rail line from Lvov to Odessa is of special interest because it has European-gauge tracks." On April 2 Starshina described the operations plan prepared by the aviation staff for the attack on the Soviet Union: "The air force will concentrate its attack on railroad junctions in the central and western parts of the USSR, the power stations in the Donetsk basin, and aviation industry plants in the Moscow area. Air bases near Cracow in Poland are to be the main departure points for aircraft attacking the USSR. The Germans consider ground support for its air forces to be a weak point in Soviet defense and hope by intensive bombardment of airfields quickly to disorganize their operations."[3]

On April 14 Starshina heard from a liaison officer on Göring's staff that "German military preparations are being carried out in a deliberately open fashion in order to demonstrate Germany's military might. . . . The beginning of military operations must be preceded by an ultimatum to the USSR to accept a proposal to join the Tripartite Pact. The date for the implementation of this plan is linked to the end of the war in Yugoslavia and Greece." The idea that Germany would first issue an ultimatum was an article of faith for Stalin and his generals (for hadn't wars always started that way?), but it was clearly part of the German deception program. That Starshina passed on this tidbit should not have cast doubt on his purely military reporting. For example, on April 17 he noted that German victories in North Africa caused some to hope that England could still be beaten; "however," he went on, "the general staff is continuing its preparations for operations against the USSR with its previous intensity, as can be seen in its detailed designation of bombing targets." On April 30 Starshina declared that "the question of the German campaign against the Soviet Union has been definitely decided, and it can be expected at any time. Ribbentrop, who up to now has not been a supporter of the idea of war with the USSR, has joined those who are for an invasion of the USSR because he is aware of Hitler's firm resolve in this matter." The NKGB sent this report to the Central Committee, the Council of People's Commissars, and the NKVD.[4]

Starshina prefaced his May 9 report with this statement, evidently intended for Aleksandr M. Korotkov, his case officer: "It is necessary to warn Moscow seriously of all the information pointing to the fact that the question of an attack on the Soviet Union is decided, the jump-off is planned for the near future, and with it the Germans hope to resolve the question 'fascism or socialism.' Naturally, they are preparing the maximum possible forces and resources." After noting that some in the air staff believed May 20 would be the start of the war, while others thought it would be in June, Starshina reverted to his earlier statement about an "ultimatum," saying that it "will include demands for larger exports to Germany and an end to Communist propaganda. As a guarantee that these demands will be met, German commissioners will be sent to industrial and economic centers and enterprises in the Ukraine, and some Ukrainian oblasts will be occupied by German troops. The delivery of the ultimatum will be preceded by a 'war of nerves' with a view to demoralizing the Soviet Union." The report ended with a reference to the diplomatic protest sent by the USSR to Berlin concerning German overflights: "Despite the note of the Soviet government, German aircraft continue their flights over Soviet territory for the purpose of photography. Now the pictures are taken from a height of 11,000 meters and the flights are undertaken with great care."[5]

As a further indication of the seriousness of German preparations for an invasion, on May 11 Starshina reported that "The First Air Fleet will be the main component for operations against the USSR. It is still a paper organization except for units of night fighters, antiaircraft artillery, and the training of components specializing in 'hedge hopping.' Its status on paper does not mean, however, that it is not ready to move, since according to the plan everything is on hand—the organization is prepared, aircraft can be moved in the shortest possible time. Up to now the headquarters for the First Air Fleet was Berlin but it has been moved to the Königsberg area. Its exact location, however, has been carefully concealed." All airfields in the Government General (occupied Poland) and East Prussia had been ordered to be ready to receive aircraft.

On June 11 Starshina reported, "On June 18 Göring will move to his new headquarters in Romania. According to senior officials in the Aviation Ministry and on the air staff, the question of an attack on the USSR has definitely been decided. One should consider the possibility of a surprise attack." In his June 17 report Starshina affirmed that "all preparations by Germany for an armed attack on the Soviet Union have been completed, and the blow can be expected at any time." Presented to Stalin by NKGB chief Merkulov and First Directorate NKGB chief Fitin, this was the report that drew his angry rejoinder that Starshina should be sent back to "his fucking mother."[6]

In the same report, Korsikanets described plans for the German civilian administration for occupied areas of the USSR, to be led by Alfred Rosenberg. His enumeration of the other principal administrators ended with an account of a speech by Rosenberg to his subordinates. In it Rosenberg promised that "the very concept of the Soviet Union will be effaced from geography maps."[7]

The Berlin residency's final contribution to this morbid litany was Willy Lehmann's last report. Lehmann, who had been a residency source since 1929, reported on June 19 that "his Gestapo unit had received an order that Germany would invade the USSR at 3:00 a.m. on June 22, 1941."[8]

The reported timing of the invasion varied, and individual reports contained what later proved to be elements of German disinformation. Taken together, however, the information from these sources should have left no question in Stalin's mind that the German Reich and its formidable war machine were preparing for a massive invasion of the USSR.

Aleksandr M. Korotkov, the officer who reestablished contact with Korsikanets in 1940, went out of channels to write a lengthy letter to Beria dated March 20, 1941. Korotkov reviewed the intelligence provided by Korsikanets and others, including the military intelligence residency, and concluded that Germany was indeed preparing to attack the USSR. Recognizing that trust in Korsikanets was a key element in evaluating his information, he suggested that resident Amaiak Kobulov meet

Korsikanets. Korotkov apparently hoped that by recommending this step he would be ensuring that the Korsikanets material had greater impact. Korotkov knew that Kobulov was "a creature of Beria." But while he wrote about Kobulov respectfully, he knew that Beria would never engage Kobulov in a serious discussion of intelligence matters. Alas, Korotkov seems not to have understood that neither Beria nor Kobulov would ever risk crossing Stalin on the question of Germany's intentions. Kobulov did meet Korsikanets but there is no indication the meeting changed Stalin's mind about intelligence from this or other Berlin sources. In late October 1940 when Korsikanets reported that Germany would go to war against the USSR in the beginning of 1941 and that the first phase would be the German occupation of Romania, Stalin summoned Beria. Knowing Stalin's negative opinion on the issue, Beria announced to him: "I will drag this Korsikanets to Moscow and jail him for disinformation."[9]

The Berlin residency also had a source, code name Yun, covering the American embassy there. Little is known of this source except that he was in contact with Donald R. Hiss, embassy first secretary; L. M. Harrison, second secretary; J. Patterson, first secretary; and Colonel B. P. Payton, air attaché. On April 9 and 10 he reported that these officers were convinced that, soon after the end of the war with Yugoslavia, Germany would invade the USSR.[10]

London

The London residency met the immediate prewar period ready to reap the harvest made possible by the Cambridge Five, whose recruitment and development during the 1930s was a masterpiece of intelligence operations. The intelligence and operational potential of the positions occupied by these sources was breathtaking. John Cairncross (code name List) had managed to become personal secretary to Sir Maurice Hankey, through whose office flowed a bonanza of British government policy and intelligence documents. Case in point, as early as September 1940 List provided the document "Estimate of the Possibilities of War," indicating that Hitler would not be able to invade the British Isles. Because Stalin was convinced that the Germans would not invade the USSR until they had dealt with the British, this report must have been rejected by the Boss. Other items provided by List probably reflected the lack of consensus within the British Joint Intelligence Committee (JIC). There was disagreement as to whether the obvious German deployments along the Soviet frontier presaged invasion or were there to pressure Stalin into new concessions. The apparent JIC belief that the Germans were seeking to force the Soviets into negotiations also fitted Stalin's preconception that war would begin only after an ultimatum. It was just ten days before the attack that the JIC decided that Hitler would in fact invade.

Even if the NKGB had an analytical capability, it seems doubtful that it could have succeeded in comprehending the political forces at work within the British government at this critical time.[11] Some of the List reporting included copies of telegrams sent by Ambassador Stafford Cripps and responses from Foreign Minister Anthony Eden, as well as extracts from various British intelligence reports. Because, on the one hand, the List reporting contained very precise British information on German preparations for war but, on the other hand, also reflected continuing British concerns about new German-Soviet negotiations, it probably reinforced Stalin's conviction that war was unlikely.

Reporting from Anthony Blunt (code name Tony), who managed to enter the British counterintelligence organization, MI-5, where he served as liaison officer with a variety of offices, such as the SIS (MI-6), the Foreign Office, and the War Office must have been of exceptional operational interest to the NKGB residency.[12] Little is available, however, on Tony's reporting on the approaching crisis. What is available presented the same problems of analytical interpretation as that from other Cambridge sources. They can be seen in a report based on the "Soviet Russia" section of a War Office intelligence summary for April 16–23, 1941, that said that "German preparations for war with the USSR continue but so far there is absolutely no proof that the Germans intend to attack the USSR in the summer of 1941." Another Tony report, based on an intercepted telegram to the Japanese Foreign Ministry, would have been of interest to NKGB code breakers as they were already decoding some Japanese diplomatic traffic.[13] Two of Tony's reports related to Finland and foretold Finnish involvement in a war against the USSR on the German side. When compared with reports from the NKGB Helsinki residency (see below), they should have been clear that the Germans had persuaded the Finns to join in the invasion.

Guy Burgess (code name Mädchen) was employed primarily as a "talent spotter and recruiter" and produced little of value in the critical months leading up to June 22, 1941. His great value would come in the postwar period when he became personal secretary to Hector McNeil in the Foreign Office.[14] Kim Philby (code name Söhnchen), for all his notoriety in penetrating the British Secret Intelligence Service, contributed little to Soviet knowledge of German preparations for invasion of the USSR. Söhnchen did not actually enter the SIS until September 1941. Before that he was in Special Operations Executive (SOE), the British service established to support resistance movements in German-occupied Europe. Desperate to determine whether Rudolf Hess had brought specific proposals to the British government for an Anglo-German accord, the center turned to Söhnchen. In his first reply, on May 14, all Söhnchen could report was secondhand information explaining why Hess had tried to contact the duke of Hamilton and a comment by Sir Ivone Kirkpatrick to the effect that, whereas Hess had brought peace proposals, their substance was not known. Söhnchen's next contribution, on May 18, 1941, was obtained from Tom Dupree, deputy chief of the Press Department of the Foreign Office. In the opening paragraph of that message, the London resident, Anatoly Gorsky (code name Vadim), stated truthfully that he still did not have exact information on the aims of Hess's trip to England. After presenting the information he had gleaned from Dupree, Söhnchen added his own opinion that "this was not the time for peace negotiations" but that later Hess might "become the center of intrigue for conclusion of a compromise peace and would be useful to the peace party in England and to Hitler." This statement, plus the somewhat clumsy efforts later by the British government, through the SIS, to persuade Stalin that Hess really did bear peace proposals, had the effect of convincing the paranoid dictator that both the British and the Germans were about to turn against him.[15]

Helsinki

Long before the German invasion, the Helsinki residency played a key role in Soviet-Finnish relations. In April 1938 Stalin gave Boris A. Rybkin, the former NKVD resident there, the task of conducting secret negotiations with senior officials of the Finnish government on matters concerning the Soviet-Finnish frontier. Rybkin had returned to Finland as Soviet chargé d'affaires, still using the pseudonym Boris N. Yartsev. The negotiations did not succeed and Rybkin left when the Winter War began in November 1939.

After the war, Yelisei T. Sinitsyn arrived as resident. Like his predecessor, he became Soviet chargé d'affaires. With this cover, his residency was able to develop impressive sources and provide some of the best information received by the center on the impending war and Finland's role in it. On April 26, 1941, the residency reported that highly placed German officers were convinced of the inevitability of a German attack on the USSR after conclusion of the Balkan operations. It also reported that the Finns believed that Finland's support of Germany was inevitable. By early May, concerns of Finnish involvement deepened. A May 7 report quoted Finnish general staff officers as saying that Germany would do everything it could to bring Finland into the war on its side. An attack against Murmansk would begin by using German troops then stationed in northern Norway, while German air and naval forces would support Finnish attacks in the south. During the Easter season of 1941, German and Finnish staff officers took part in discussions on Finnish army maneuvers. Another report, dated May 10, informed the center that the Germans were actively soliciting the support of Finnish refugees from Karelia (occupied by the USSR after the Winter War), promising that Finland would not only recover lost land but acquire new territories in eastern Karelia and the Kola peninsula. A June 5 report from the residency source Poeta confirmed that the number of German troops transiting Finland would be increased and that German pressure on the Finns to participate in the war was growing. Another source, Advokat, reported that, in response to German demands, partial mobilization had been ordered, large numbers of German troops were on their way, and the Germans had demanded the expulsion of all British subjects from some regions of Finland.[16]

The last shoe dropped when Sinitsyn was told by source Monakh that an agreement had been signed between Germany and Finland on the participation of Finland in the German war against the USSR and that the invasion would come on June 22, 1941. There was no response from Moscow and not until Sinitsyn returned to Moscow from Helsinki did he hear from Fitin what had happened. Fitin had accompanied Merkulov to see Stalin about the contents of a report from Berlin (the report from Starshina). Fitin also presented the Monakh report, noting that this was a reliable source who obtained the information from someone who had attended the signing ceremony. All Stalin said was, "Check it all out and report." Merkulov made no effort to support Fitin.[17]

Warsaw

While none of the other NKGB residencies rivaled Berlin's relentless warnings of the impending German invasion, a few of them had special access and produced items that confirmed the Berlin material. The legal residency in Warsaw fits this description.

In November 1940 NKGB Foreign Intelligence established the residency under Petr I. Gudimovich (code name Ivan); his cover was chief of the office dealing with Soviet property. He was assisted by his wife, Yelena D. Modrzhinskaia (code name Maria), herself an experienced intelligence officer, who arrived in Warsaw on December 15.[18] Ivan's cover duties did not require a large effort. For his cable and pouch communications Ivan had to rely on the Berlin NKGB residency. Nevertheless, Moscow had a very important reason for establishing the Warsaw residency. By the late summer of 1940 it was apparent that Warsaw was becoming the center in German-occupied Poland for the logistical side of the Wehrmacht's preparations for its invasion of the Soviet Union. By placing Ivan and Maria there, Moscow could hope for the recruitment of subsources; at a minimum, the center would have in Warsaw two experienced observers who could move freely in the area. Gradually, the two acquired reporting sources among Poles whose hatred of the German occupiers exceeded their traditional dislike of Russians. By the spring of 1941, Ivan and Maria had concluded that Germany was preparing for war with the USSR. Ivan requested permission to report his findings in person to People's Commissar for State Security Vsevolod N. Merkulov. After listening to him, Merkulov replied: "You are greatly exaggerating. All of this must be verified again. Only after that, perhaps, can your information be reported to the leadership of the USSR."[19]

On April 20, 1941, Ivan went to Berlin and prepared his regular report. On May 5 Stalin, Molotov, Voroshilov, and Beria received the results:

> Military preparations in Warsaw and throughout the Government General are being carried out openly and German officers and soldiers speak completely frankly of an imminent war between Germany and the Soviet Union as though it were already an agreed-upon affair. The war will apparently begin after conclusion of the spring planting season. German soldiers, quoting their officers, claim that the conquest of the Ukraine by the German army will be guaranteed from within through the work of a well-functioning fifth column on USSR territory.
>
> From April 10 to 20, German troops moved eastward through Warsaw without stopping, both during the day and by night. Because of the uninterrupted flow of troops, all movement on the streets of Warsaw was halted. By rail, trains were moving in an easterly direction loaded mainly with heavy artillery, trucks, and aircraft parts. From the middle of April, military trucks and Red Cross vehicles appeared on the streets of Warsaw. German authorities in

Warsaw had been given orders to put air raid shelters in order, black out windows, create first aid teams in each building, and mobilize Red Cross detachments that had been disbanded earlier. All motor vehicles belonging to private individuals and commercial firms, including German ones, had been mobilized for use by the army. Schools had been closed as of April 1 as their buildings were to be used as military hospitals. . . . German troops here were occupied with improving and building new highways leading east. All wooden bridges on all roads to the East were being strengthened with iron beams. River-crossing materials were being prepared along the river Bug.

As long as the Warsaw residency stuck to facts pertaining to its own area, it was right on target. The one false note in its long report was the statement that "the Germans apparently are counting on taking the Ukraine by a direct blow from the west and at the end of May will begin an offensive against the Caucasus through Turkey." This one sentence would have been enough for Stalin to reject the entire message.[20]

CHAPTER **11**

Listening to the Enemy

NKVD/NKGB foreign intelligence was not the only component under State Security Commissar Merkulov that produced valuable information for Stalin on Germany's intentions. We know from the 1977 official classified Soviet history of the organs of state security that in the period leading up to the German invasion the counterintelligence components ran extensive operations against foreign missions in Moscow. These operations involved agent penetrations, telephone taps, the installation of listening devices, and efforts to suborn and recruit members of these missions. Although their principal goal was to identify foreign intelligence officers, monitor their activities, and investigate contacts with Soviet citizens, these operations produced important intelligence as a byproduct. While the "take" from the German embassy and those of Germany's allies was among the very best, operations against the American, the British, and other embassies, as well as against the offices and residences of foreign correspondents, provided supplemental, confirmatory data.[1]

In February 1941, the Chief Directorate for State Security (NKVD/ GUGB) became the NKGB, still under Vsevolod N. Merkulov. Its Third Department became the Second Counterintelligence Directorate, as counterintelligence operations continued and expanded.[2] The head of counterintelligence remained Petr V. Fedotov, a seasoned Chekist who had participated in operations against Chechen tribesmen from 1923 to 1937. By

1939, after the arrival of Beria as head of the NKVD, Fedotov became head of the Secret-Political Department. In September 1940 he was transferred to the Counterintelligence Department.[3]

Under Merkulov, the Third, or Secret-Political, Directorate also used secret informants to uncover and act against anti-Soviet elements in the general population. Those secret-political operations of greatest interest to us in determining the extent of reporting on German intentions were the ones described in chapter 4. These operations were conducted in the newly acquired regions of the Moldavian, Ukrainian, and Belorussian union republics, and the Baltic republics of Lithuania, Latvia, and Estonia, recently incorporated into the USSR.

The Moscow operations of the Second Directorate produced the best information on the intentions of Germany and its allies. At the end of April 1941, the directorate's First, or German, Department sent Stalin a transcript of an April 25 conversation between Colonel Hans Krebs, assistant German military attaché, and his assistant, Schubut. "Well, we've finished the Greeks. Soon a new life will begin—the USSR. Do we plan to call up the entire army?" one voice asks. "Yes." "But they haven't even noticed that we are preparing for war." These remarks and earlier ones in the conversation, about the weaknesses of the Soviet rail and highway systems, should have left no doubt in Stalin's mind of German intentions. Still, this was a rather frank discussion by German officers who must have been aware that they were likely to have had their offices and quarters bugged. Previously their conversations had been guarded. How did this change happen?

The speakers were having their talk in the home of German military attaché General Ernst Köstring. It was a detached house, wholly occupied by the German attachés, hence not as susceptible to normal microphone operations as an apartment would have been. The Soviet counterintelligence officers had earlier recognized the importance of the Köstring residence, and in late April 1941 they had decided to attempt a penetration. They planned to use a neighboring house as a base, explaining to residents of the area that workers were fixing burst pipes that required major repairs. From this base they tunneled unnoticed into the basement of Köstring's home and entered his office, opening his safe, photographing his documents, implanting microphones throughout the house, and removing all traces of their visit. Fedotov himself personally devised the operation. The results meant that from that moment until June 22, Soviet counterintelligence received reports of confidential discussions among the Germans themselves. They also received reports of discussions between the Germans and with their Italian, Hungarian, and Finnish allies.[4]

These conversations, all of which pointed to the likelihood of a German attack on the Soviet Union, were reported to the leadership. On April 26, for example, there is a record of a meeting between a German officer and a person who, from his speech and demeanor, appeared to be an intelligence agent being debriefed by the German. The latter notes: "We must have information on divisions. We have some, but it is far from sufficient. . . . As far as Russia is concerned, here we won't encounter any great difficulties." The agent then claims that the evening before he entertained Russian naval officers at his home who told him that "the Germans will now declare war." The German officer concludes by saying, "I want to give you a small task—penetrate directly into Russian units and collect information."[5] Then, on May 31, 1941, a conversation took place between Köstring and the Slovakian minister. Köstring: "Some kind of provocation must be carried out here. It must be done in such a way that some German will be killed, and that way bring on a war." This comment may have contributed to Stalin's fear of provocation by the Germans. It is more likely, however, that Köstring was extrapolating from the manner in which Hitler orchestrated the onset of the Polish war. In that case, SS troops donned Polish uniforms and attacked a radio station inside Germany.[6]

On May 18, however, the German Department published extracts from coverage of conversations on May 13 and 15 in which German officers make it unmistakably clear that they expect war with the Soviet Union soon. One says: "In the opinion of the Russians, the morale of our troops had been damaged . . . but they [the Russians] are not thinking about what we know, what we're doing. . . . General, we have to begin this war." Another comments: "True, many say that Russian offensive plans are very poorly worked out. That's their weak point. Therefore, our troops must be thrown into a swift attack. Then the Russian troops will be crushed. . . . I think that the Russians will bite their fingernails when we appear suddenly." The excerpts end with these remarks: "The business we are speaking of must remain absolutely secret. . . . The Russians, of course, will be taken unaware. . . . My visit to the Red Army general staff showed me that they suspect nothing."[7]

On June 7 the German Department produced transcripts dated June 5 and 6. Both contained comments reflective of German plans to invade the USSR. The last line of the June 5 transcript read: "We must cut Moscow completely off from Leningrad." On June 6 these remarks were heard: "If we use a large quantity of fighter aircraft here, it will take us only eight weeks." The response: "The Russians have had a breathing space of almost two years."[8]

There were, of course, microphones planted in the installations of other countries. The Finnish transcript of May 12, when taken together with information reports from the First Directorate residency in Helsinki (see chapter 9, above), should have left no doubt in the minds of the Soviet leadership that the Finns would collaborate with the Germans in their war against the USSR. A Finnish official speaking on May 12 stated: "We must stand on the side of Germany because it is the only great power that is close to us."[9]

Microphones continued to provide timely information, supplemented by agent reports on the evacuation of embassy staffs as war drew near. On June 11 an agent of the Third, or English, Department of the Second Directorate reported that the British embassy had received a telegram from the Foreign Office in London ordering the embassy to prepare for evacuation within seven days. On the evening of the eleventh, the burning of documents was said to be under way in the basement of the embassy. On June 18 additional information was received concerning the evacuation of members of the British embassy and their families, as well as thirty-four members of the German embassy. Reports of another wave of departures from the German, Italian, Romanian, and Hungarian embassies noted that the diplomats violated rules by going directly to Inturist, thereby bypassing approved channels. The overheard requests stipulated that all departures take place no later than June 19.[10]

On June 19 the Fourth, or Italian, Department provided information on the situation in the Italian embassy. Ambassador Augusto Rosso visited Ambassador Friedrich Werner von der Schulenburg of Germany, who said that, although he had no concrete information, he thought that war was inevitable. After returning to his own embassy, Rosso first sent a telegram to his wife in Tokyo, telling her to delay her return to Moscow. He then dictated a telegram to Rome asking what Italy would do in the event of a conflict between Germany and the USSR. He also asked for instructions on what to do with Italian property and documents. While American officials were not sure there would be a war, they confirmed to Italian diplomats the American embassy's plans for evacuation. A journalist and correspondent for *Collier's*, Alice Leone-Moats, reported that the wife of the American ambassador, Laurence Steinhardt, was preparing a dacha that, in her words, would serve as a shelter for those foreign diplomats who would remain in Moscow during a war in the USSR.[11]

Three transcripts prepared by the German Department covered discussions held on June 20 that all reflected Germany's intention to attack the Soviet Union. The first noted the puzzling lack of preparedness evident in the city of Moscow: "They are doing nothing, even though they have heard rumors and know of the evacuation of the diplomatic corps." Another contained remarks such as: "It would be very good to begin to fight now. . . . The Russians are afraid of us." A discussion follows about the condition of the road system in various parts of the European USSR. The last transcript involved the call a visiting lieutenant general paid on Defense Commissar Timoshenko and Chief of the General Staff Zhukov. He was received most graciously, but no military topics were touched on. Later in the transcript one person says, "The Russians neither want to fight nor are capable of fighting." "Yes," someone replies.[12]

One of the last and perhaps most poignant transcripts from the microphones in General Köstring's home, was a conversation on June 20 between Ambassador von Schulenburg and Köstring. Von Schulenburg began by saying: "I am in a very pessimistic mood, and while I know nothing concrete, I think Hitler will start a war with Russia. I saw him privately in April and said completely openly that his plans for war with the USSR were sheer folly, that now was not the time to think about war with the USSR. Believe me, because of this frankness, I have fallen into disgrace. I am risking my career and perhaps I'll soon be in a concentration camp." Köstring did not share the ambassador's pessimism with regard to victory over the USSR. Bogdan Kobulov, acting for Merkulov, sent this pathetic report to Stalin, Molotov, and Beria.[13] It is not known if it evoked a response.

The Second Directorate continued to receive reporting from its agents in various foreign embassies. Among the very interesting reports are those provided by the late Russian writer Ovidy Gorchakov. He described an agent (code name Yastreb) who was cultivating a senior officer of the German embassy identified only as "Von B.," treating him to sumptuous dinners and providing him with female companionship, courtesy of the Second Directorate. The purpose of the relationship was his eventual recruitment. But until then, the goal was to elicit as much as possible about the current activity and personnel at the German embassy. Von B. claimed to have been involved in the negotiations for the 1939 nonaggression pact.

He described the scene at the Moscow airport on August 23 when Ambassador von Schulenburg and leading members of the German embassy greeted Foreign Minister Ribbentrop and the German delegation. Among the other informative tidbits provided by Von B. was his contention that German intelligence was aware that after the June 14, 1941, TASS communiqué claiming there would be no war, Beria ordered Lev Z. Mekhlis, head of the Red Army Political Directorate, to spread the word.[14]

Another informant in the German embassy (code name Ernst) might have been a lower-level member of the embassy's administration or a Soviet employee. The information provided by Ernst, while prosaic, made clear that the embassy was preparing for a serious eventuality. On May 19 he reported on a meeting between the Soviet ambassador in Berlin, Vladimir G. Dekanozov (accompanied by his interpreter, V. P. Pavlov), and Ambassador von Schulenburg, who was accompanied by his close friend Gustav Hilger; embassy secretary Gebhardt von Walther was also in attendance. Von Schulenburg tried to warn Dekanozov of Hitler's intention of starting a war with the USSR, but Dekanozov said he was not authorized to listen to such statements and that only Molotov should be involved. According to Ernst, Dekanozov then reported the conversation to Beria, who said that Germany was trying to blackmail the USSR. On June 2 and 3 Ernst passed on conversations with German assistant military attaché Hans Krebs in which Krebs praised Stalin's adherence to the nonaggression pact and the decision by the Soviet Military Council not to call for a higher state of alert. This, of course, seems to have been a furtherance of German disinformation. On June 11, Ernst reported that the German embassy had received orders from Berlin to be ready to evacuate in seven days. The burning of documents had already begun in the basement. As for the June 14 TASS announcement, Ernst said that Molotov had given von Schulenburg a copy before publication. Von Schulenburg expressed the view to many that the communiqué was a wise step.[15]

Another agent (code name Gladiator) covered the Italian embassy. On June 12 he reported that everyone there spoke openly about the forthcoming German invasion. Ambassador Rosso was concerned about his wife, who planned to return to Moscow from a Far East trip (he later decided it made no sense for her to return). On June 20 Gladiator reported that the ambassador intended to leave that day and had made a farewell speech to the Soviet employees.[16]

The American embassy seemed to have had a large quota of Soviet servants reporting to counterintelligence. One (code name Karmen) spoke

English and was apparently a personal interpreter and assistant to the wife of the ambassador. On May 4 Karmen reported on the decision by the ambassador "to lease a large dacha near Moscow." He did this "because he is convinced that the Germans will attack Russia soon, this summer." The renting of the dacha was also reported in a Fourth (Italian) Department transcript on June 19. On May 5 the ambassador's wife told Karmen to see to the packing of the silver, expensive tablecloths, and bed linens for shipment to America.[17]

On June 6 Karmen reported that it was common knowledge in the embassy that U.S. Secretary of State Cordell Hull had sent copies of telegrams from the U.S. ministers in Bucharest and Stockholm to Ambassador Steinhardt. On June 8 Karmen overheard the American journalist Alice Leone-Moats describe a drive to the German embassy's dacha in which Gebhardt von Walther, the embassy secretary, told her the Germans would attack Russia on June 17. According to Karmen, on June 19 Alice Leone-Moats told everyone in the American embassy that von Walther had corrected his earlier statement; he now asserted that the attack would come on June 21, and Leone-Moats felt he expected her to alert the Americans. Looking directly at Karmen, she said, "We are all tired of warning the Russians."[18]

On June 20, a Friday, the American embassy wives and employees were busy packing. Mrs. Steinhardt took Karmen with her on a last round of shopping in the commission stores. She told Karmen that all the women would be flying out of Moscow the next day, she to Stockholm, the others to Teheran. The men of the embassy would go to the new dacha at Tarasovka while journalists would move from hotels in town to places on the city's outskirts. All the foreigners with whom Karmen came in contact predicted that Germany would defeat the USSR in from six weeks to three months. Karmen asked why earlier reports had produced no response and demanded that they be sent to a higher level.[19]

Among the other agents reporting on the American embassy were Verny, a chauffeur with a good command of English who also reported on the plans to lease a new dacha. On June 20 Verny took the ambassador around the outskirts of Moscow to reconnoiter roads that could be used if the city was evacuated. Jack, the ambassador's valet, reported that on June 1 he had helped the ambassador pack three valises. Necessary items were put in the first valise, next to the door; the second accommodated items of lesser importance. The first would be taken if there were only fifteen minutes to leave, the second if they had half an hour, and so forth.[20]

Such minutia was probably typical of the reports Second Directorate agents working in various diplomatic installations in Moscow sent to their case officers, but taken together the details represent the thoughts and actions of foreigners who appear to have been convinced that war with Germany was at hand. Combined with the transcripts from listening devices and telephone taps, the information should have persuaded the recipients—Stalin, Molotov, and Beria—that something vitally threatening was afoot.

There were other indicators as well. On June 14 German authorities issued an order to all German merchant ships not to enter Soviet ports. Those already in Soviet ports were to leave immediately. On June 20 the Leningrad Directorate of the Soviet Baltic Commercial Fleet reported a radiogram, sent in the clear, uncoded, from the freighter *Magnitogorsk* that it was being held in the German port of Danzig for unknown reasons. The Baltic Commercial Fleet message noted that "the *Magnitogorsk* is not responding to our queries. Although we have had no instructions from Moscow, tomorrow, June 22, we will order the *Lunacharsky* to return to Leningrad and the *Vtoraia Piatiletka* to go to Riga." The last German ship to leave Leningrad on June 15 carried the German specialists helping to complete the German cruiser *Luetzow*, purchased earlier by the Soviets. It seems incredible that no one in the Soviet navy's Baltic Fleet became aware of these messages, historically a prime indicator of approaching hostilities.[21]

In addition to controlling the activities of the Moscow operational departments, the Second Directorate oversaw and in some cases directed counterespionage operations in the union republics. For this reason it was kept informed of operations by German military intelligence (Abwehr) in key border areas. One wonders how Merkulov's men interpreted the following report and what they did with it. Coming at the end of a description of German military activities along the frontier were these ominous sentences: "German intelligence is sending its agents into the USSR for short periods—three to four days. Agents being dispatched for longer periods, ten to fifteen days, are instructed that in the event German troops cross the frontier before they are scheduled to return to Germany, they must report to any German troop unit located on Soviet territory."[22] Such reporting shows the need to draw strategic conclusions from simple counterintelligence reports. If the interrogation of captured Abwehr agents reflected briefing along these lines by their handlers, it should have been evident that the Wehrmacht was on the point of invading the Soviet Union.

Taken as a whole, the information obtained from NKGB counterintelligence confirmed that provided by foreign intelligence sources, yet

Stalin and Boris M. Shaposhnikov

I. I. Proskurov, Hero of the Soviet Union

Ribbentrop and Stalin

Semen K. Timoshenko

Georgy K. Zhukov

Ilse Stöbe (Alta)

Arvid Harnack (Korsikanets)

Harro Schulze-Boysen (Starshina)

Willy Lehmann (Breitenbach)

Pavel M. Fitin

Richard Sorge

Ivan I. Maslennikov

Petr V. Fedotov

Grigory M. Shtern

Ernst G. Shakht

Filipp I. Golikov

Yakov V. Smushkevich

Proskurov and his family before his arrest

Lev Ye. Vlodzimirsky

Proskurov's monument

CHAPTER **12**

Working on the Railroad

Before and during the war the Soviet economy functioned much as it had since its creation by Stalin in the first Five Year Plan. Problems in speeding the transformation of the Soviet Union into a modern industrial state were addressed with punitive measures carried out by the economic components of the NKVD's State Security Chief Directorate. Industrial accidents, for example, were reported as sabotage by informants and punished by death or imprisonment. Thus, it is not surprising that the First (Railroad) Department of the NKVD's Chief Transport Directorate (GTU) was charged with improving the performance of the national rail system. Less well known is the important contribution it made to the collection of intelligence on the buildup of German forces in occupied Poland.

As early as July 1939, the GTU began complaining of acts of sabotage on rail lines within the USSR. The perpetrators were never detected. The GTU called for improvements in agent operations at key points such as locomotive repair shops, railroad bridges, marshaling yards, water towers, and so forth.[1] The agent informants operated in classic NKVD fashion, reporting on individuals on train crews or at stations whom they suspected of anti-Soviet attitudes or actual sabotage. When the USSR occupied the western oblasts of Ukraine and Belorussia in the fall of 1939, the rail lines in the area were organized regionally in the Soviet manner. Agent informants were imported from other parts of the USSR or recruited from members of local railroad employee groups. As in other counterintelligence and security situations, their actions also led to the collection of first-rate intelligence on the areas in which these groups operated—in other words, straight from the iron horse's mouth.

In a special report dated July 12, 1940, the GTU gave an early demonstration of what its agents could discover. The report contained information from agents in Hamburg, Lübeck, Stettin, Memel, Tilsit, Königsberg, and Danzig, who asserted that the number of locomotives assigned to haul construction materials, cement, and iron to build fortifications in areas along the Soviet frontier had recently been increased. The report described new seaplane bases at Swinemünde and activity at shipyards in Stettin, providing details on new classes of motor torpedo boats. It was signed by Solomon R. Milshtein, head of the GTU, and sent to Beria, people's commissar for internal affairs, and to Bogdan Z. Kobulov, who as head of the Chief Economic Directorate was responsible for security in industry. Clearly, the report should have been sent to military intelligence (RU) as well.[2]

A July 28, 1940, GTU report reflects the modus operandi of the GTU agent networks. An agent (code name Zagorsky) run by the Belostokaia railroad, went by train to a German border station. Here, he conversed with employees of the German railroad who claimed there were some 30,000 German troops concentrated fifteen kilometers from the station. This information was confirmed by another agent (code name Shibanov). According to a report in early August, agents from the Belostokaia railroad traveled by train as far as the German stations of Malkino and Sedlets, where German troops were being hurriedly moved to the Soviet frontier area. On July 20, for example, two trains unloaded German motorized troops. Each train included flatcars transporting equipment for them. To speed up the unloading of the trains, the Malkino station had a turntable for quickly rerouting the locomotives. Trains from Soviet railroads were not allowed to use this device but had their locomotives turned about by manual switching. "In the past several days German tank units have been unloading at the Sedlets station, after which they move in the direction of the Soviet frontier." The reports were signed by Captain of State Security M. L. Benenson, deputy chief of the First (Railroad) Department, GTU, and stamped with the Milshtein seal. The recipients were the same, Beria and Bogdan Kobulov. Again, there is no indication that this information was passed to military intelligence.[3]

The GTU's agent networks provided significant details on August 16,

1940. A German commission composed of officers and headed by a general arrived in Terespol, Poland, by armored train and inspected the area. An agent (code name Bykov) operating there saw German officers at the railroad station with the number 58 on their shoulder boards. The troops (infantry, artillery, tank units, and cavalry) arrived in large numbers and were quartered in tents near the town of Ostrolenka. It was reported that there were to be eighteen German divisions concentrated in the area around Terespol. Antiaircraft artillery units were located in the Lublin and Demblin areas, and tank units were said to have occupied the towns of Lukov and Sedlets. To economize on fuel, agents reported, one tank towed two others in moving from rail heads. According to German soldiers who spoke to a GTU agent, numerous German troops had arrived from the Western Front and were being quartered in renovated Polish barracks. Agents also reported that on August 2 German demolition teams had blown up old Austrian and Polish fortifications and that construction units were building new works. The report ended with considerable detail on German recruitment of Ukrainian nationalists in the Peremyshl area and the distribution of German propaganda for an independent Ukraine.

A second report, also on August 16, from agents of the Belostokaia railroad emphasized that the movement of German troops to the east continued. On June 29 and 30 two trains containing artillery units were unloaded at the Malkino station. The trains included seventy-four flatcars. On July 31 twelve more flatcars arrived with three-inch and six-inch guns along with cases of shells. About forty trains were unloaded at the Sedlets station, and the troops moved out to positions on the Soviet frontier along the river Bug. A German locomotive engineer told a GTU agent that Germany's locomotives and cars were all tied up with the movement of troops to the Soviet border. The troops were being brought from the French front under the pretext of home leave, but they were not being given leave. Both reports were signed by Captain Benenson and countersigned by Milshtein.[4]

At this point one sees the first indication that military intelligence was receiving copies of these agent reports from the GTU networks. On September 17, 1940, Captain Benenson sent a memorandum to Colonel Grigory P. Pugachev, acting chief of the Information Department, RU general staff. The memorandum transmitted an August 16 GTU report and asked for an evaluation of its information. It is true that a whole month had elapsed, but at least there is an indication of interagency coordination.[5]

As of August 23, agents from the Lvov railroad reported that German troops in the vicinity of Peremyshl were working intensively to construct fortifications along the entire Soviet frontier. Among these were trenches and large ditches into which concrete was poured to reinforce the walls. At the bottom were steel plates for the emplacement of large-caliber field guns. The agents also reported on continuing efforts by the Germans to enlist Ukrainians under the banner of an independent Ukraine. The report, signed by Captain Benenson, was sent to Beria and Kobulov, but this time Vsevolod N. Merkulov, chief, NKVD/GUGB, was included in the dissemination.

Agents of the Lvov railroad reported in late September 1940 that fifteen kilometers west of the Zhuravitsy station the Germans were building a series of strong points along the Soviet frontier consisting of trenches with machine-gun nests. This line was camouflaged. The work was carried out only at night and local residents could enter the area only with special passes. Concurrently, the Germans were working intensively on concrete emplacements near Yaroslava and Rzhesheva. Cement, stones, and iron for these structures were unloaded at the Yaroslava railroad station along with troops, tanks, mortars, and ammunition. Male residents of the region fourteen and older were mobilized for this work. The report, like many others, concluded with information on Ukrainian nationalistic activity supported by the Germans. There is no indication of this report's distribution list.[6]

Indications of the scope of the eastward movement of German forces came from agents of the Lvov railroad, who reported the involvement of numerous troops between August 14 and August 22. At least thirty troop trains a day passed through Warsaw in an easterly direction. Passenger traffic was suspended during this period and residents were subjected to a curfew from 11:00 p.m. to 6:00 a.m. The remainder of the report dealt with the actual deployment of troops at various points along the border and the efforts of the Germans to enlist and control Ukrainians in German units.[7] There is no information on the dissemination of this document, either.

Reports from agent nets of the Lvov railroad revealed increased movement of German troops toward the Soviet frontier during September. At the end of the month, equipment for pontoon bridges began to arrive at Peremyshl. Among German soldiers and their Ukrainian nationalist allies there was much talk of war with the USSR "beginning soon." Mention of bridging equipment certainly should have alerted Soviet intelligence to the fact that this buildup was not solely an exercise in improving German defenses along the Soviet border. Perhaps indicative of the growing importance of the reporting capabilities of the GTU agent networks was the replacement of Captain Benenson as chief of the First (Railroad) Department of GTU by Major of State Security N. I. Sinegubov. In November the same agent nets from the Lvov railroad reported the departure of infantry troops and the arrival of artillery and mechanized units. Distribution was still made to Beria, Merkulov, and Kobulov but was expanded to include Pavel Sudoplatov, Fitin's deputy in the Foreign Intelligence Department of the NKVD/GUGB.[8]

In a special report dated December 27, the GTU provided details on the situation in German-occupied Poland from agents on the Lvov, Belostokaia, and Litovsk railroads. Five airfields had been constructed in wooded areas in the vicinity of Warsaw in accordance with a standard pattern. There were no hangars. A central runway with concrete roads provided for movement of fuel and access to aircraft parking areas hidden beneath the trees. Fuel tanks with 50,000-liter capacity were buried under thirty centimeters of earth. As for troop movements, the report reflected the continuing buildup. In Warsaw itself, about 410,000 Jews had been herded into a ghetto where there was a high mortality rate caused by a ration of only 125 grams of bread per person per day. Polish nationals who lived in the new Soviet border area were being resettled in central Poland and their places taken by *Volksdeutsche*, who by then had been given German citizenship. Crop requisitions by the Germans had caused hunger among the Polish population. Ukrainians, Belorussians, and Russians occupied favored positions and mixed freely with Germans. The report, signed by Sinegubov and released by Milshtein, bore a marginal note from Beria to Fitin and one from Fitin to Zhuravliev, head of the German Section: "Use in a report to the Central Committee." The distribution remained Beria, Merkulov, and Kobulov, but the order to Fitin to use it to prepare a report to the Central Committee suggests that military intelligence would also see a copy. By this time, Fitin's group was charged with reviewing the GTU reports and giving them standard dissemination, including to military intelligence.[9]

In January 1941 the GTU NKVD reported to the leadership on the mobilization readiness of the Soviet railroad system. The various details in the report are undoubtedly based on ones provided by the many agent informants maintained throughout the regional railroads. It began with the statement that the system had a number of "serious abnormalities." The People's Commissariat of Transport Routes (NKPS), it went on, had no mobilization plans. There was still no agreement between the Defense Commissariat (NKO) and the NKPS on plans for military transport in wartime. The NKPS asked the NKO for information on the scope of military transport needs, while the NKO wanted to know the capacity of the railroad systems in the various theaters of operations. In 1940 the NKO gave the NKPS a rough outline of transport needs for sectors of each railroad, on the basis of which the NKPS prepared a provisional mobilization plan that proved totally unrealistic. There was still no centralized plan for the transport requirements of the economy for the first month of war. The commissariats had not yet given the NKPS their freight needs, and the Military Mobilization Directorate of the NKPS had not insisted. There followed a detailed listing of problems in each of the railroads in the western oblasts, as well as special problems. For example, heavy tanks require flatcars with a sixty-ton capacity, but none were built in 1940. The number of locomotives actually present in the western oblasts was less than 75 percent of the number called for by the plan, and there were shortages of many other items that would be needed for restoration of service and rebuilding of depots and other installations in wartime. Finally, mobilization preparations had not even been started in the Baltic region. The report included the names of various officials within the NKPS whose performance in the mobilization area was found to be deficient. It was signed by Beria and the head of the GTU, Milshtein.[10]

A special GTU report of February 10, 1941, noted that the regrouping of German troops along the Soviet frontier continued. Troop trains leaving occupied Poland via Bohemia-Moravia and Austria were said to be on their way to Bulgaria, where they would be employed in operations against Greece. Other troops, leaving the Lithuanian border, were rumored to be going to the "Anglo-German front." It is difficult to know whether rumors of these destinations were correct or simply reflected regroupings intended to confuse and mislead Soviet intelligence. The report went on, however, to describe movement of German troops into areas near the Soviet frontier.

Perhaps more significant were the sightings of a Ukrainian volunteer corps near Lublin, two regiments of which had already conducted maneuvers. Another Ukrainian volunteer corps was being formed in Warsaw. As for construction of military installations, the report noted continued triangulation surveys preliminary to establishing artillery firing points. The work on new airfields described in earlier reports was proceeding, as was work on concrete emplacements, which in some areas was under way at night under floodlights. This activity was supported by special construction trains consisting of twenty-seven flatcars, eighteen freight cars and ten passenger coaches. The flatcars carried construction material, and the coaches engineer troops. In some sectors railroads had been completely militarized. All civilian employees had been replaced by German military personnel, the report concluded.

The capacity of some lines was being expanded as new lines were built. Reports on February 14 and 27 seem to be the last ones issued by the GTU. They claimed that the Germans were still raising troop levels along the border and enumerated these increases by area. Several trains had arrived with French and Belgian tank cars containing gasoline that was emptied into reservoirs hidden in nearby forests. Lines of artillery firing points along the Lithuanian SSR border were camouflaged and surrounded by barbed wire entanglements. Also reported was the use of track rails covered by concrete to protect bomb shelters. More sectors of railroads in occupied Poland near the Soviet frontier were being militarized, with civilians discharged and German troops taking over. Blackout curtains were being installed and practice blackouts undertaken. As for conditions in the Government General of Poland, certain foods were growing scarcer. Sugar, tea, and coffee were no longer to be had. As in previous reports, much attention was paid to the activities of Ukrainian nationalists. All Ukrainian schools were teaching the geography of the new "independent Ukraine," and rumor had it that six hundred leading Ukrainian nationalists had been sent to Berlin for training as future leaders.[11]

Because we know that at one point Fitin was told to prepare a report for the Central Committee VKP(b) using material from GTU sources, it is likely that GTU agent informants continued to collect intelligence under local NKGB control and had their reports published by Fitin's First Directorate. An unsigned report dated March 31, 1941, from the NKGB to the Defense Commissariat on movement of German troops toward the Soviet border resembles earlier reports of the GTU. The report states only that the information is from "agent information available to us." There are more than twenty-one numbered paragraphs, some of which give specific numerical designations for German troop units, and most contain some reference to the movement of troop trains at various railroad stations.[12]

Proof that these GTU agents were taken over by local NKGB components can be found in a report of June 12, 1941, by the Lvov Oblast Directorate of the NKGB, all elements of which were provided by agents employed by or involved in the operation of the railroads. Portentously, the last sentence reads: "As of June 10, 1941, in Peremyshl and Shuravitsakh all local railroad men will be fired; transport will be fully operated by [German] military units."[13]

CHAPTER 13

The Border Troops Knew

One security component in the Soviet establish-ment was ideally situated to observe and report on the progress of the German buildup across the frontier. This was the Chief Directorate of Border Troops (GUPV), whose forces covered every kilometer of the west-ern borders of the USSR from the Barents Sea to the Black Sea. Although the border troops regard May 28, 1918, as their official founding, it was not until 1939 that a separate directorate was established. Throughout the 1920s and 1930s, the border troops were included administratively with troops responsible solely for internal security. Their official history main-tains that throughout these years their main concern was protection of the Soviet regime against "spies, saboteurs, and terrorists," whether dis-patched by anti-Soviet émigré organizations or foreign intelligence ser-vices. This responsibility extended to interception of smugglers or any persons attempting to enter the USSR illegally. This is the version featured in the exhibits and lectures at the Border Troops Museum in Moscow, but it is hardly an accurate reflection of border troop activities. Nor does it account for the extensive network of border zones and physical obstacles patrolled by the border troops inside the Soviet state frontier. The reality is that the GUPV was just as concerned with keeping Soviet citizens from leaving the country as it was in apprehending enemy agents infiltrating border areas.[1]

The border troops did not escape the 1937–38 purges. With the movement of the Soviet frontier westward in 1939, however, they reorganized and expanded. Their strength rose by 50 percent during 1939–40; armaments improved and increased. Still, the shift to new western borders resulted in considerable disruption of routine. It required, among other things, the creation of new agent nets for coverage of the areas opposite each of the newly established border troop districts along the Finnish frontier, on the seacoast borders of the newly acquired Baltic States, in the new oblasts of western Belorussia and the Ukrainian SSR, and along the Romanian frontiers of the Moldavian SSR. Arrests of German intelligence (Abwehr) agents increased from 28 in the first quarter of 1940 to 153 in the same period in 1941. Similar increases were noted in cross-border movement of groups such as the Organization of Ukrainian Nationalists. In the period leading up to June 1941, as new Red Army units moved into the western border areas, new liaison and communications arrangements had to be established between military units and the border troops. These arrangements were described in a Politburo directive of June 22, 1939.[2]

By the end of 1940 there were eight border troop districts (*okruga*) in the area between the Barents Sea and the Black Sea. These districts were located within the territories of the five western military districts: Leningrad, Special Baltic, Special Western, Special Kiev, and Odessa. The overall strength of border troops in these districts was approximately 100,000. Almost half the troops were stationed in the Ukrainian and Belorussian districts. Under the eight Border Troop districts there were forty-nine detachments. Each detachment (*otriad*) had from 1,400 to 2,000 men. Their organization and armaments followed a standard pattern: a deputy commander for intelligence, an intelligence department, and from four to five border commands (*komendatury*), each with four or five outposts (*zastavy*). The district also had a reserve, or maneuver, group of up to 250 men who could be rushed to critical areas if needed. In this connection, it was the large-scale infiltration of sizable numbers of hostile sabotage and intelligence teams in the 1940–41 period that caused the border troops their greatest difficulty and had the most severe impact on the security of the Red Army's infrastructure. In the Belorussian and the Ukrainian border troop districts, the distance between outposts was from eight to ten kilometers, a bit more in other areas. The border troops had no tanks or artillery. In 1941 their light weaponry would be upgraded to include more heavy machine guns, mortars, and antitank rifles.[3]

Border Troop Locations

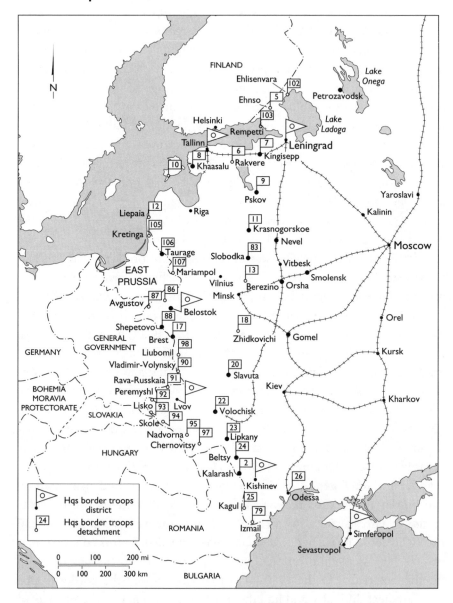

Shows the cities in which the headquarters of the Leningrad, Baltic, Belorussian, Ukrainian, Moldavian, and Black Sea border troops districts are located. Their numbered subordinate detachments are shown along the frontier.

As early as March 1939, border troop units received orders to create additional intelligence posts so as to improve the level of cross-border intelligence activity. On October 25, 1940, an order was given to establish new intelligence posts within the ten-kilometer border zone along the frontier between the USSR and German-occupied Poland. They were to consist of three officers and were to be located in large population centers; their basic activity was to be daily operational work directed at uncovering illegal border crossers and their accomplices.[4]

Between the summer of 1940 and June 1941, intelligence on the armed forces of Germany and its allies concentrated on the Soviet border presented a major concern for the border troops. It was imperative to collect information on German "force structure" and preparations for offensive operations. It was also imperative to collect information on the Abwehr's plans for infiltrating Soviet frontier areas with agents or teams of agents and then to intercept and apprehend them.

The border troops relied on observation by moving patrols and from fixed towers or camouflaged observation and listening posts (the listening posts were particularly effective at night). Regular patrols meant the troop outposts became totally familiar with the physical features and human activity in the areas across the border from them. Further information came from the debriefing of deserters and refugees from the German occupation and from interrogation of spies and saboteurs, many of whom were recruited by the Abwehr from the local population. Border troops obtained specifics on the missions of these people and these often reflected German operational plans; the debriefings and interrogations also supplied general data on conditions in occupied Poland and East Prussia and on German military activities.

Although it is known that it was not until July 31, 1940, that Hitler advised his generals of his decision to attack Russia, on July 15 of that year Stalin, Molotov, Voroshilov, and Timoshenko received a startling report signed by Beria.[5] It was based on a special report from Ivan I. Maslennikov, deputy people's commissar of internal affairs for troops. According to the Belorussian border troop district, between July 1 and July 7 seven German divisions arrived in Warsaw and its vicinity and were installed in towns and villages within a sixty-kilometer radius of the city. In most cases, the report provided regimental numbers. These troop movements caused an interruption of passenger service between Warsaw and Lublin. Infantry, artillery, and tanks moved in march formation from Lublin toward the Soviet frontier. Responsibility for guarding the German side of the border had been taken over from German border police by field units of the German army. In addition, the border troops of the Ukrainian SSR had registered the arrival of German infantry and tank units in the border areas in the direction of Peremyshl. Border troop detachments reported that in areas opposite them, "German troops are engaged in constructing defensive positions, placing mines, and improving highways."[6]

There was no special reaction from the top leadership to this report, probably because on July 9, acting on orders from Defense Commissar Timoshenko, Deputy Chief of the General Staff I. V. Smorodinov held a meeting with Ernst Köstring, the German military attaché. Köstring explained that the large numbers of German troops were simply replacements, now that significant contingents of troops were no longer needed in the west.[7] An untrue explanation, of course, but accepted by Stalin and his lieutenants. Another factor that may have had a calming effect was the signing on June 10, 1940, of a Soviet-German convention creating an "Institute of Representatives for Border Affairs" to resolve conflicts. The Soviet representatives were normally border troop officers from the detachment nearest to a specific incident. Between January 1, 1940, and June 10, 1940, there were 22 incidents; between June 10, 1940, and January 1, 1941, there were 187, most of which were resolved in the Soviets' favor. It seemed that as the Germans massed their forces along the border, they were ready to accommodate their Soviet counterparts' wishes. On February 13, 1941, the deputy chief of the border troops of the Ukrainian NKVD, Ivan A. Petrov, reported that "the Germans made a show of ostentatious politeness but in reality they maintained a rather stubborn, well-thought-out line in dealing with these incidents. They preferred to elevate them to the diplomatic level rather than react negatively."[8]

A turning point seems to have been reached in late July 1940, when the commanding officer of the Ninetieth Border Troop Detachment, at Vladimir-Volynsk, received a letter from the German side announcing the arrival of the governor of occupied Poland, Hans Frank, to inspect the frontier in the vicinity of the town of Grubeshev. "Frank and his retinue of about thirty individuals arrived in a convoy of fourteen automobiles, moved up and down along the frontier, and observed the Soviet side of the border through field glasses," reported the chief of staff of the Ninetieth Detachment, who was also a "border representative." After Frank's visit, the buildup of German forces and military construction projects in eastern Poland seemed to increase. German authorities explained that troops "from the French front had arrived in this 'quiet zone' for rest and reorganization." During July and August, "an army headquarters was established in Warsaw, an army corps in the suburbs, as well as eight infantry division headquarters."[9] Undoubtedly as a result of this activity, on December 21, 1940, Beria called for retention in service of 7,000 individuals in the border troops whose terms of service would normally have expired on January 1, 1941.[10]

A report from the Ukrainian border troop district dated January 16, 1941, described a visit on December 9, 1940, by "German army commander Field Marshal Walther von Brauchitsch to troops stationed in the area of Sanok. Sanok is a town in southeast Poland on the river San, approximately twenty-five kilometers from the border. The troops were drawn up in formation to meet him." The remainder of the report described arrivals of new troop trains and the construction of antiaircraft installations, narrow-gauge railroads, and station facilities with platforms.[11] A January 24, 1941, report from Lieutenant General Ivan A. Bogdanov, commander of the border troops of the Belorussian NKVD, summed up the German troop presence in the Warsaw area as follows: "An army headquarters in districts along the frontier, headquarters of eight infantry divisions, a cavalry division (in the Ternopol area), twenty-eight infantry regiments, seven artillery regiments, three cavalry regiments, a tank regiment, and two pilot training schools." Bogdanov devoted much attention to the creation of the new convention for resolving border incidents.[12]

While learning more about the German forces opposite them, the border troops continued to apprehend agents dispatched from Abwehr operations bases in Königsberg, Warsaw, and Cracow. Through careful interrogation of these agents, it was relatively simple to learn their missions. More important, it was possible to distinguish between those that were routine peacetime intelligence collection on Soviet defenses and those that were obviously intended to pave the way for German offensive operations within the Soviet Union. An excellent example of the latter can be found in a January 18, 1941, memorandum from Lieutenant General Maslennikov to State Security Commissar Merkulov. "Recently a number of incidents have been noted in which German intelligence organs located in the Government General have given orders to agents sent by them into the USSR to bring to Germany samples of oil, motor vehicle and aviation gasoline, and lubricants," the memorandum opened, going on to describe four cases during December 1940 and January 1941. Two were in the area of the Ninety-first Border Detachment in Rava-Russkay, Ukrainian SSR, and two in the area of the Seventeenth Detachment in Brest-Litovsk, Belorussian

SSR. The agents captured by the Ninety-first Detachment stated that they were told "to acquire samples of the fuels and lubricants in use in Soviet industry and transport facilities." The agents who figured in an arrest on December 22 were told that "their samples must be large enough to permit analysis." Maslennikov commented that "three of the agents were already in Moscow, where they had been transferred on orders of Bogdan Z. Kobulov, deputy state security commissar, because of the large amounts of Soviet currency in their possession." The memorandum ended: "Claiming lack of knowledge, the arrested persons were unable to give the reason for German intelligence interest in our petroleum products and why they were needed." Merkulov responded with this instruction in the margin: "We must clarify the reason for these tasks."[13] Clarify? It must have been obvious to both Maslennikov and Merkulov that the collection of samples permitted the Germans to determine whether the fuels available in the USSR would be suitable for use in their vehicles and, if not, what modifications or additives would be necessary. The use of multiple agent missions to obtain this information strongly suggested that the Germans planned to be operating on Soviet territory in the near future. In the atmosphere of Moscow, however, neither man wished to suggest this in writing, even as a possibility. They were well aware that Stalin was convinced that the Germans would not attack the Soviet Union in 1941. Nevertheless, we know from German accounts of their operations in the first few days of the invasion that German motorized units prized the Soviet fuel dumps they captured. The First Panzer Division, low on fuel as a result of its rapid advance into the Baltic States, must have been overjoyed when it came on a large, intact fuel depot.[14]

Maslennikov continued to forward border troops reports on German troop movements. Perhaps to subtly underscore the threat, he now added parenthetically the distance from the border of each locality cited in his reports. On February 23, 1941, he reported "the departure of two motorized divisions from Cracow (145 kilometers from the border) to the Carpathians. On February 4 60 tractor-drawn heavy guns and six field radio stations arrived in Kholm (28 kilometers from the border). Three trains arrived in Lublin (45 kilometers from the border), each with 30 platform cars loaded with armored vehicles and heavy trucks. In the area opposite the Seventeenth Border Troop Detachment at Brest-Litovsk, German authorities have taken over school buildings to house troops." The report was disseminated to Beria, Merkulov, and Golikov, the new head of military intelligence.[15] By March, reporting from both border troop units and

NKGB agent sources began to be issued by the NKGBs of the respective union republics. A March 27, 1941, report from the NKGB Belorussian SSR covered troop movements, use of schools for troop housing, mobilization of reservists in East Prussia, assignment of new recruits to specific infantry regiments, details on areas of concentration of German units (many with unit designations and street numbers), and military construction, including road improvements, new roads, airfields, and fuel storage dumps. The last section dealt with rumors prevalent in the border areas of the Belorussian SSR, most of which predicted a German assault on the USSR. The report was signed by the people's commissar for state security, L. F. Tsanava. Merkulov, the recipient, wrote these instructions in the margin: "To Comrade Fitin: 1. Prepare a summary report of the military information for the Defense Commissariat. 2. Inform the Central Committee and the Council of People's Commissars that the number of troops on the border has increased and that this has been reported to Defense. Dated 28.03." Sudoplatov noted: "Sent to Timoshenko under No. 809/m of 31.03.41." The delay in forwarding the report demonstrates that no real sense of urgency existed at the top levels of the organizations involved.[16]

April saw a great increase in reporting. The chief of border troops in the Ukrainian SSR signed six individual reports. Lieutenant General Maslennikov sent Beria five. Also, as evidence of increasing concern and tension, reports from subordinate border troops and NKGB offices were incorporated into special reporting by union republic and national NKGB commissariats. On April 9 Pavel Ia. Meshik, head of the Ukrainian SSR NKGB, signed a special report on German troop movements that began: "According to our information from various sources, from the beginning of 1941 and particularly recently, the German command has been carrying out a large-scale movement of troops from Germany to the territory of the Government General and then to the borders of the USSR."[17] On April 10 the Foreign Intelligence Directorate of the USSR NKGB sent a summary report to the RU "on the concentration of German troops." According to the directorate, "information from agent sources and statements by border crossers have established that the concentration of units of the German army on the border of the Soviet Union is continuing. At the same time, there is accelerated construction of defensive positions, airfields, strategic branch rail lines, highways, and dirt roads." This low-key statement could be open to many interpretations.[18]

A somewhat more dramatic and revealing report came to Fitin on April 12 from the NKGB Ukrainian SSR. It was based in large part on the debriefing of a former junior officer in the Polish army who had also served abroad as a vice consul. According to him, "the transfer of large German units, the movement of munitions, and the completion of airfield construction on the Soviet frontier began in January 1941 and expanded intensively in April. In the beginning of February 1941 the so-called French Southern Army, which had been located in the southern part of Poland, was moved by rail to the river San in the direction of Peremyshl and deployed about forty kilometers from the USSR border. The tanks and mobile river-crossing pontoon bridges of this army moved independently. In the first half of March, the so-called Northeast Ninth Army, which had been brought from France to the Cracow area, spent two days there and was then sent by rail to Lublin. In the second half of March, fresh troops from Germany, mostly Bavarians, arrived in Sanok and Krosno." This broader picture of German troop movements was followed by local detail confirming much of the other reporting received in April.[19]

The tone sharpened a bit later in April. Meshik addressed a report to the personal attention of Nikita S. Khrushchev, the first secretary of the Ukrainian Communist Party, that said: "Agent reporting and debriefing of border crossers establishes that the Germans are intensively preparing for war with the USSR, for which purpose they are concentrating troops on our borders, building roads and fortifications, and bringing in munitions." Much of the rest of the report was a plea to Khrushchev to allow him to take measures against Ukrainian nationalists to prevent them from becoming "a fifth column" in wartime. Using VCh, an encrypted speech system, Meshik sent virtually this same message to Merkulov by telephone on April 20.[20]

Despite the growing concern evident in the reports of the first months of 1941, there was still no urgency in disseminating them at the top level of the regime. A special report sent from the Ukrainian SSR NKGB to Merkulov at NKGB USSR on April 16 bears the marginal notation: "Sent to Golikov . . . on April 20, 1941." The dilatory distribution of reports may well have been the result of shoddy bureaucratic practices, but it may also have reflected a reluctance on the part of all involved to be accused of provoking a war.[21] Still, even Lavrenty P. Beria could not continue to ignore the reports flowing into his office. On April 23 he signed and sent a report to the Central Committee VKP(b), the Council of People's Commissars (SNK), and the Defense Commissariat (NKO) summarizing German troop movements between April 1 and April 19 in East Prussia and the Government General. "In these areas," the report said, "the arriving troops consisted of a large headquarters, three motorized divisions, six infantry divisions, up to twenty-one infantry regiments, two motorized regiments, nine to ten artillery regiments, seven tank and four engineer battalions, a motorcycle battalion, two companies of bicyclists, and more than 500 motor vehicles."[22]

Reporting by border troop units and summaries by their higher headquarters during May reflected the same patterns observed in April, albeit in greater scope and intensity. Of the twenty reports examined for this period, the majority were from the NKVD of the Ukrainian SSR. Most dealt with activities opposite border troop detachments stationed in the areas from Brest-Litovsk in the Belorussian SSR to Chernovitsy in the Ukrainian SSR. Report after report described the constant arrival of new German troops, munitions, and other supplies. Most of these movements were conducted at night. There were also signs of greater boldness. German officers now observed Soviet concentrations openly through field glasses and photographed them from positions just hundreds of meters away. The German authorities placed greater restrictions on civilians, prohibiting them from using the railroads, for example. All schools were now closed and occupied by German troops. In several areas, troops were reportedly confiscating cattle, grain, and other agricultural products and shipping them to Germany. Maslennikov reported that for the first time German authorities were stopping or delaying Soviet trains bound for Germany. They even stopped some with exports, which were provided for under Soviet-German trade agreements. Most of these incidents probably occurred because there were military activities under way that the Germans did not want the Soviet train crews to see.[23]

On May 15 Major General Vasily A. Khomenko, chief of border troops, Ukrainian SSR district, reported an increase in agents dispatched by hostile services.[24] Maslennikov reported that between May 10 and May 16 border troop detachments captured seven agents trained and dispatched by an intelligence organ of the German high command in Berlin. On May 16 the Germans sent over a group of four armed agents charged with reporting on targets in Drogobych Oblast. According to Khomenko, "One of the agents arrested had the mission of delivering to German intelligence samples of gasoline and kerosene produced in the Western oblasts of the Ukrainian SSR." It would appear, then, that the Germans were continuing to collect petroleum samples.

On May 30 Maslennikov sent Merkulov the results of the debriefing of four Wehrmacht deserters. Their testimony provided additional background on Wehrmacht deployment and force structure. While the report noted some weaknesses in German morale, it concluded with the comment: "In the event of a war between the USSR and Germany, the majority of soldiers are convinced that the Germany will be victorious." A copy went personally to Marshal Zhukov.[25]

Soviet border troops had been working diligently to provide information on the growing German menace since the summer of 1940. Some academic analysts in the Russian Federation, critical of the performance of Soviet intelligence in this pre–June 1941 period, have pointed out that it was not until May 24, 1941, that the Chief Directorate of Border Troops of the NKVD declared: "Concentrations of troops and work on the construction of military installations in the border zones of neighboring states demand of us knowledge of every detail. At the present time, intelligence must be organized by us in such a way that every incident, no matter how insignificant it may seem, is noted and kept under continuing observation." Considering the flood of information obtained from border troop operations well before and immediately after the issuance of this directive, the delay may have resulted as much from Soviet bureaucracy as from the reluctance within Beria's NKVD to issue an order that obviously took the German threat seriously.[26]

In the first week of June 1941, it appeared that Beria was beginning to accept the warnings of a German attack as reality. On June 2 Sergei A. Goglidze, a longtime colleague of Beria's and the special representative of the Central Committee and Soviet government in the Moldavian SSR, reported the latest from the Soviet-Romanian border area: the commander of a Romanian border unit had "received orders from General Antonescu to clear the mines from all roads, bridges, and sectors close to the border. These were mines that had been laid in 1940–41. At present all bridges have been cleared of mines and they are now starting to clear them in the sector along the Prut River." Goglidze added that "among Romanian officers there is talk of military operations by German and Romanian forces beginning on June 8. For this purpose, large troop units have been moved up to the border. This movement has been confirmed by two sources." Furthermore, "the Romanian Ministry of the Interior has ordered local authorities to prepare their offices for evacuation to the Romanian interior." The message conveyed by the removal of the mines from roads and bridges leading to Soviet territory seemed clear. The Germans intended to use these facilities in their invasion of the USSR.

The same day, Beria reported to the Central Committee and the Council of People's Commissars (in other words, to Stalin) on order of battle information from border troop detachments. Noteworthy was the identification of two army groups and two armies, one the sixteenth and the other an army commanded by General Reichenau, in eastern Poland. Also included was the movement of the Thirty-fifth Infantry Division from Bulgaria to East Prussia, the presence of Hitler—accompanied by Göring and Admiral Erich Raeder—at maneuvers by German naval forces in the Baltic Sea, and the inspection of the Soviet border by German general officers on May 11 and 18. The most alarming part of the report was the presence "at many points close to the frontier of pontoons, canvas, and pneumatic boats. The largest quantities were found along the axes of the approach to Brest and Lvov." No one could seriously argue that this equipment would be left, exposed to the weather, until sometime in 1942 when Stalin believed that Hitler might finally attack the USSR.

Beria followed up on June 5 with a similar report: "On May 20 the headquarters of two infantry divisions, the 313th and the 314th, Marshal Göring's personal regiment, and the headquarters of a tank unit were identified in Bialo-Podliaska, 40 kilometers west of Brest." In an area "33 kilometers northwest of Brest, pontoons and parts for 20 wooden bridges were stored." This section on the Soviet-German border contained additional order of battle information and word that, as of May 20, Luftwaffe units were active at some of the airfields constructed near the border. The section on the Soviet-Romanian border reported that "parts of two German divisions coming from Greece and Germany have been deployed along the border. . . . 250 aircraft were seen at the airfield at Buzey, 100 kilometers northeast of Bucharest." Also, "as of June 1–5, the Romanian general staff ordered all military personnel on leave and all reservists up to 40 years of age to report to their units." The report was sent to Stalin with a notation that the general staff had been informed.

While still reporting on Wehrmacht movements and activities (including the first cases of German infantry opening fire on border troops patrols), Major General Khomenko and the Ukrainian border troop district became embroiled in a controversy with the Soviet general staff that reflected the atmosphere of caution at the top military command levels in Moscow. On June 9 Khomenko reported that the chiefs of Red Army fortified districts had received orders to occupy forward defense positions. Maslennikov passed this information on to the general staff. On June 10 Zhukov sent this message to the Military Council of the Kiev Special Military District (KOVO): "The chief of border troops of the NKVD, Ukrainian

SSR, reported that the chiefs of fortified districts have received orders to occupy forward positions. For a report to the defense commissar, inform us of the basis for the order to the fortified districts of Kiev Special Military District to occupy forward positions. Such action could provoke the Germans into an armed confrontation fraught with all sorts of consequences. Revoke this order immediately and report who, specifically, gave such an unauthorized order." This was followed on June 11 by a telegram from Zhukov to the commanding general, KOVO: "The defense commissar [Timoshenko] has ordered: 1. The zone of forward defenses will not be occupied by field or fortified district forces without a special order. Guarding of the installations will be accomplished by a system of sentries and patrols. 2. The orders given by you on occupying forward positions are to be immediately canceled. Check the execution of this order and report by June 16, 1941." It would appear that the order had been issued by Colonel General Mikhail P. Kirponos, commanding the KOVO. Given the quantities of intelligence available to him from the border troop detachments in his area on the German forces opposing the KOVO, the order made sense. The action by Timoshenko and Zhukov must have been initiated at the request of Stalin, whose strategy was to avoid any actions that might "provoke" the Germans. Kirponos was to die in battle attempting to lead his forces out of a German encirclement in September 1941.

On June 12, an outpost of the Ninety-second Border Troop Detachment at Peremyshl reported "a field telephone cable on the Soviet side of the river San that appeared to have emerged from the river. The troops then detected a cable with four leads running into the water at the shoreline on the German side." On the Soviet side the four leads went in four directions: "One went 400 meters and was connected with our telephone line; the second ran for 200 meters and was fastened to the rail of a railroad track; the third paralleled the second and was also fastened to a rail; the fourth, 80 meters in length, went to our barbed wire fence. There were also footprints leading to the water line."[27] The incident was reported by Lieutenant General Maslennikov and, according to him, was resolved by the border institute, with the Soviet side represented by Colonel Yakov O. Ageichik, chief of staff of the Ninety-second Detachment. The representatives agreed that the cable ran from the German side to the Soviet side. There is no information on any further action. This case, like those of the petroleum samples, the machinery for adapting Western railcars to the Soviet gauge, and the camouflaged river-crossing equipment, should have made it absolutely clear that the Germans intended to invade in the very near future.

CHAPTER **14**

Proskurov Is Fired

In July 1940, a little less than a year before the German invasion, Stalin dismissed Ivan I. Proskurov as his military intelligence chief, replacing him with a man who had no intelligence experience. Stalin's reasons have never been officially revealed and he probably never committed them to paper in any detail. Nevertheless, several motives seem plausible.

Among the grounds Stalin certainly had was his resentment and anger at Proskurov for his behavior at the April 1940 conference on the lessons of the Finnish war. It didn't take long for the story of the clash between Stalin and Proskurov to get back to RU headquarters. One officer related:

> At one of the meetings of the Politburo and the Military Council, the problems of the Soviet-Finnish war were discussed. The unpreparedness of our army, the enormous losses, the disgraceful tramping around for two months in front of the Mannerheim Line, and much else had become known to the people as a whole. Abroad they spoke of [these problems] in a loud voice. Stalin and his coterie had to save face. The Politburo and Military Council meeting was dedicated to ensuring that this was somehow done. After a stormy debate they decided that the reason for all our misfortunes in the Soviet-Finnish war was the poor work of Intelligence. . . . To dump everything on Intelligence was not a very original device. No government, not a single minister of defense or commander in chief, would ever admit his guilt in the event of a defeat.

In this Stalin was also not very original. He decided to use Intelligence and Lieutenant General Proskurov personally to get himself out of the situation. Proskurov, however, would not accept the accusations directed against him. He knew that the troops had all the necessary information on the Mannerheim Line, that the reason for the failure lay elsewhere, and he boldly argued with Stalin, naming the real reasons for the failure.[1]

Proskurov's performance at the April conference was in keeping with his behavior throughout his military career. One of his subordinates, Lieutenant Colonel Maria I. Poliakova, who had served in the RU since 1932, recalled that, after the signing of the Nazi-Soviet Nonaggression Pact, Stalin and the Defense Commissariat became even more critical of RU reporting than usual. On one occasion Proskurov returned from a visit to the general staff in a bad mood, exclaiming, "What do they take us for—fools? How could this be disinformation?" He continued to express himself openly and forcefully whenever the occasion required.[2] Once, in May 1940, at a meeting with the deputy defense commissar, Proskurov declared, "No matter how painful it is, I must say that no other army has such disorderliness and a low level of discipline as ours."[3]

Later that month he addressed a commission of the Defense Commissariat and the Central Committee on the effects of repression. His remarks were as forthright as ever: "The past two years have been a period of repression of alien and hostile elements in agent directorates and intelligence organs. During these years organs of the NKVD have arrested more than two hundred persons, replacing the entire leadership, including chiefs of departments. During the period when I was in command in the central apparatus alone and its subordinate units, 365 persons were dismissed for political and various other reasons. Three hundred twenty-six new persons were hired, the majority of whom were without intelligence training."[4]

Stalin would have found it difficult in any case to work with a subordinate as regularly outspoken as Proskurov, but he must have been furious at the manner in which Proskurov behaved toward him in public. Another reason might have been the tension between Proskurov and Stalin's newly appointed defense commissar, Semen Timoshenko, who had developed considerable dislike for Proskurov from the Finnish war experience. Timoshenko could never forget Proskurov's inspections of his front opposite the Mannerheim Line, nor could he forgive Proskurov's report to Stalin on the scandalous losses his people suffered. According to Proskurov's sarcastic description of Timoshenko's approach, "instead of artillery preparations for the attacks, it was a 'calvary charge.' Instead of bombing strikes by aviation, it was 'fix bayonets!'" Proskurov made his conclusions and recommendations carefully. He consulted Dimitry M. Karbyshev, a well-known military engineer, about the Mannerheim Line fortifications. He also proposed setting up airfields on frozen ice, closer to the front.[5]

In memoirs of retired RU officers who knew Proskurov, the shadow of Timoshenko is cast in strange ways. One officer recalled Proskurov as "an impetuous young man whose rank as deputy defense commissar went to his head." He noted "Proskurov's criticism of Timoshenko for the unsatisfactory training of intelligence units and groups" and observed that "Proskurov did not know how to get along in the system, and when Timoshenko became defense commissar he zeroed in on Proskurov and had him dismissed from the RU."[6] Another former intelligence officer recalled that "Proskurov was assigned to the RU to improve morale and discipline after the purges, and he was quite successful in this." In the officer's view, "the bad blood between Proskurov and Timoshenko began when Proskurov arrived in Leningrad during the Winter War and was not met by either front commander Timoshenko or his deputy. When Proskurov later met with Timoshenko he apparently made a negative comment on this discourtesy. Timoshenko was not pleased by this and he nursed a grievance against Proskurov. One of the things he did after becoming defense commissar was to relieve Proskurov of his position as chief of the RU."[7]

One reason behind Stalin's action might have been the June 6, 1940, report from the RU Sofia residency that Proskurov sent to Stalin, which suggested that Germany would conclude a separate peace with France and then, together with Italy and Japan, attack the USSR. The effect of this report on Stalin can be imagined. No longer able to rely on a prolonged European war, he was planning new actions in the Baltic to secure that area for the USSR. Would Hitler actually trash the nonaggression pact and turn on the Soviet Union? Here again Proskurov was presenting Stalin with very unpalatable news.[8]

Was this the reason Proskurov was summoned to see Stalin in the Kremlin on June 7? Proskurov met alone with Stalin between 5:15 and 6:10 p.m. that day. After he left, a large group assembled in Stalin's office at 7:20 p.m. It included Timoshenko, Shaposhnikov, Meretskov, Smorodinov, and Voroshilov, none of whom could have been well disposed toward Proskurov after the unplesantness of the April conference.[9]

Proskurov was not formally relieved of his duties as head of military intelligence until July 27, 1940, when he was placed at the disposal of the defense commissar.[10] The last intelligence reports he signed were dated June 19 and June 20 and described increases in German troops on the borders of Lithuania. By July 15 RU special summaries were being signed by Filipp I. Golikov, Proskurov's successor. Apparently this change was not publicized, because on July 22 Fitin, chief of foreign intelligence for the NKVD, addressed a memorandum to Proskurov reporting movement of German troops into the Government General. Fitin had not yet received the word.[11]

Given the timing, Proskurov's dismissal could have been related to Hitler's July 16 "Führer Directive No. 16," calling for an attack on England, code name Sea Lion. When Stalin learned of the directive, he is said to have asked Proskurov if the Germans could really invade the British Isles. "An invasion of this kind," Proskurov explained to his leader, "depends on four important conditions: German aviation must first establish air superiority; ensuring control of the sea, at least in the area of the landing, and securely pinning down the British Fleet in the Atlantic Ocean and the North Sea; the availability of sufficient shipping tonnage for the landing; the possibility of overcoming coastal defenses and the degree of opposition of the English troops in the interior." Proskurov went on to say that "only if they meet all four conditions can the Germans count on success. If they miss only one, they will not have a chance." He then examined each point, noting the problems faced by the Germans and predicting that it would take at least three more months to complete preparations, by which time weather conditions would make the operation impossible. This negative assessment greatly angered Stalin, and that day Proskurov was relieved of his post.[12]

Proskurov's reported answers reflected reality. Admiral Erich Raeder, commander in chief of the German Navy, said that the plans were unrealistic, that "the operation entailed the greatest dangers, that there was a serious possibility that all of the troops engaged in the operation might be lost." The German naval staff made these points to the supreme command of the armed forces in a July 19, 1940, memorandum:

> a. The French ports . . . were badly damaged in the recent fighting or are in other ways unsuitable.
> b. The part of the Channel selected for the actual crossing presents great problems because of weather conditions, tides, and rough water.
> c. The first wave of the invasion would have to be landed on the open English coast, and there are no suitable landing craft for such a landing.

d. The waters for this crossing can not be made or kept absolutely free of enemy mines.

e. The vessels in which the troops and their supplies are to be embarked can not even be assembled in the embarkation ports until absolute mastery of the air has been achieved.

f. . . . Up until now the British have never thrown the full power of their fleet into combat. But a German invasion of England would be a matter of life or death for the British, and they would unhesitatingly commit their naval forces in an all-out fight for survival."[13]

In September 1940 the Luftwaffe carried out its first raids on London. The attacks by German bombers were preceded by waves of fighters. On September 15 the raids were turned back with heavy losses, demonstrating that the RAF could still achieve air superiority. On September 17 Hitler announced "the postponement of Sea Lion until further notice."

In the final analysis, why was Proskurov fired? The one overriding reason seems to have been Stalin's awareness that he could not control the man. Proskurov would pursue his own views on a subject even if they ran counter to Stalin's position. This was evident in the confrontation between Stalin and Proskurov at the Finnish war conference and in Proskurov's insistence on sending him intelligence reports that did not conform to his views.

To others of his associates in the RU days, Proskurov possessed qualities that would never have endeared him to Stalin. According to one, "he was modest, sociable, honest, principled, brave, and very straightforward in his judgments. He quickly caught on to the work and was a talented leader. Many of the intelligence operations he started were to last throughout the war." Another said, "Proskurov had a sharp mind and a tenacious memory." He recalled a trip he took to Western Europe at Proskurov's request in March–September 1939: "I reported on the residents I met, that is, those who were still there [not purged]. I noticed that as I spoke Ivan Iosifovich squeezed his cheekbones, muscles in his face twitching." Under Proskurov, moreover, agents were kept on whereas under Golikov a second wave of repression began; that was why Proskurov would not let Richard Sorge return to the USSR. And not only Sorge. When officers who were recalled despite his efforts had their stays in Moscow extended, Proskurov himself would meet with them, without advertising the fact, calm them down, and give them the latest news.[14]

Who was the man who replaced him? Filipp Ivanovich Golikov was born on July 16, 1900, in the village of Borisovo, near Shadrinsk, in

Kurganskaia Oblast. His father was a medical practitioner in the village who passed his socialist beliefs on to his son. Young Golikov won a scholarship to the gymnasium in Kurgan and after the October Revolution joined the First Krestiansky Rifle Regiment, known as the Red Eagles. He attended military agitator courses in Petrograd, then was assigned to the Tenth Moscow Rifle Regiment of a special brigade of the Third Army on the Eastern Front. In August 1919 he became an instructor-organizer in the Political Department of the Fifty-first Division. His official biography in the *Soviet Military Encyclopedia,* from which these facts are taken, says that "after the civil war, until 1931, he was engaged in party-political work." Since the civil war in the European part of the country had pretty much ended after the conclusion of the Polish campaign and the subsequent defeat of Peter Wrangel in November 1920, ten full years of Golikov's life were devoted to political assignments, the exact nature of which are still not clear.[15] In 1931 he attended an unidentified military school, becoming commander of the Ninety-fifth Rifle Regiment of the Thirty-second Rifle Division. From 1933 to 1936 he commanded the Sixty-first Rifle Division of the Volga Military District. During this time he also pursued correspondence courses with the Frunze Military Academy. He then commanded the Eighth Separate Mechanized Brigade until 1937, when he was put in command of the Forty-fifth Mechanized Corps in the Kiev Military District.[16]

Then, suddenly, he was made a member of the Military Council of the Belorussian Military District. There was something very strange about this assignment. Military councils normally consisted of the commanding officer, his first deputy, and a political "member." Depending on the circumstances, this member might be a high-ranking political commissar or even the senior party secretary in the district. Why, after seven years of command assignments with a rifle regiment, a rifle division, a mechanized brigade, and finally a mechanized corps, was Golikov sent to this key military district as the member of its military council? In any case, it was in this capacity that he encountered Georgy K. Zhukov, then commanding the Third Cavalry Corps. Under the direction of Lev Z. Mekhlis, chief of the Political Directorate of the Red Army and the main scourge of the Red Army during the purges, Golikov was laying the groundwork for a purge of the command elements of the Belorussian Military District. Relying on allegations made by repressed officers under hostile interrogation, Golikov accused Zhukov of friendships with former enemies of the people and hostility toward political workers. Zhukov found support in others in the

Belorussian Military District's command structure and his command of the Third Cavalry Corps was confirmed, but he would never forget Golikov and the way he tried to send him to "Beria's basements."[17]

In November 1938 Golikov was given command of the Vinnitsa Army Group in the Kiev Special Military District, and in 1939 that of the Sixth Army. This latter assignment was not by chance. The mission of the Sixth Army was to occupy the city of Lvov and the surrounding area. As noted earlier (chapter 4), the Lvov area was known to have been of interest to the Germans, even though the demarcation line agreed on in the secret protocol to the Nazi-Soviet Nonaggression Pact gave it to the Soviets. Stalin was determined to get there first. Even more important, Lvov was the center of the Ukrainian independence movement, with thousands of adherents in the area, many of whom had received training from the Abwehr. To ensure an orderly transition to Soviet rule within the Ukrainian SSR, the Sixth Army and its Political Department would have to cooperate closely with the NKVD. Thus, this assignment did not require extensive combat experience. It required political sensitivity and knowledge of how the Soviet system worked. Golikov was a perfect choice. While he himself likely saw Stalin as a guardian angel, Stalin surely saw in him an individual on whom he could rely completely.

When Golikov became the new head of military intelligence, the subordination and designation of the service were changed. Under Proskorov it had been the Fifth, or Intelligence, Directorate of the Defense Commissariat, and Proskorov bore the title of deputy defense commissar. On July 26, 1940, an order of the Defense Commissariat on the structure of the general staff placed the Intelligence Directorate in the general staff, where it was called RU GS KA, or Intelligence Directorate, General Staff, Red Army. Golikov was designated deputy chief of the general staff, subordinate to the chief of the general staff, then Meretskov. (Zhukov would replace him as chief of the general staff in January 1941.)[18]

The most important department in the RU was the Information Department, responsible for producing intelligence summaries and special reports. Its chief also served as deputy to the directorate chief. When Golikov arrived in July 1940, the acting chief of the Information Department was Grigory P. Pugachev. He was succeeded by Nikolai I. Dubinin, who left because of illness in February 1941, to be replaced by Vasily A. Novobranets, who had joined the RU in April 1940 under Proskurov and, since April 1940, had been deputy chief of the Information Department for Eastern Countries. Golikov did not get on well with Novobranets, quarreling over Novobranets's view that German troop deployments on the western borders presaged a German offensive against the USSR. In April 1941, a new chief arrived, Major General N. S. Dronov. His last assignment had been as chief of staff of an army group in the Odessa Military District, and his only previous experience had been as a commander or staff officer with the troops. So Golikov's deputy, the chief of the most important department in the directorate, would be, like Golikov himself, an officer with no intelligence experience. (In October 1941 Dronov would leave the RU to become chief of staff of the Tenth Army, the very army to which Golikov would also be assigned that fall. These two babes in the intelligence woods must have gotten on well together.)[19]

Golikov's office was on the third floor of the building at Znamenski 19, one of a complex that housed the NKO, the general staff, and the Political Directorate of the Red Army. His officers described him as a short person, round faced, with close-cropped blond hair and piercing blue eyes. According to one, he always wore a strange smile whether he approved or disapproved of work done by a subordinate. "He never gave straightforward orders or directions but always left it up to the subordinate. If he was not satisfied, he would say, 'I never gave you orders like that' or 'You did not understand me.'" Golikov let it be known to his officers that he would report directly to Stalin. Above all, he seemed always concerned that RU information be consistent with Stalin's views.[20]

CHAPTER 15

Golikov and
Operation Sea Lion

As head of military intelligence from July 1940 to June 1941, Golikov was responsible for the dissemination of reports from RU field residencies; he also supervised the preparation of periodic intelligence summaries or analyses based not only on RU agent reports but on all information available from all elements of the government, including the Foreign Affairs Commissariat. Significant in Golikov's treatment of this information was his emphasis on German operations against England. Aware that Stalin was convinced that Hitler would not attack the Soviet Union until he had defeated England, Golikov used every opportunity to reinforce this view and to label any warnings of an imminent German invasion of the Soviet Union as disinformation originating in England, America, or Germany.

In 1965 historian Aleksandr M. Nekrich asked Golikov about the analyses prepared under his supervision: "Abroad much is written about the warnings the Soviet Union received through various channels of the impending attack. The impression has been created that the first warning came in March 1941 [a report given by Undersecretary of State Sumner Welles to Konstantin A. Umansky, the Soviet ambassador to the United States]. Is this true?" Golikov replied:

No, it wasn't like that. The first warnings came from Soviet military intelligence well before March 1941. The Intelligence Directorate

carried out an enormous amount of work in the collection and analysis of information from various channels on the intentions of Hit-
lerite Germany, particularly and most of all its intentions toward the
Soviet government. Along with the collection and analysis of extensive agent information, the RU carefully studied international information, the foreign press, public opinion, military-political and
military-technical literature from Germany and other countries, and
so forth. Soviet military intelligence had reliable and proven sources
of secret information on a whole series of countries, including Germany itself. Therefore, the American report was not and could not
have been news to the political and military leadership of our country, beginning with I. V. Stalin.[1]

In describing the RU's performance and Stalin's reaction, Golikov was
less than candid. The March 1941 warning did occur, however. The information was obtained by Sam E. Woods, a gregarious commercial attaché
at the American embassy in Berlin, who had established good contacts in
the German resistance and was able to follow German preparations for the
invasion of the USSR from late July 1940 to the signing of Plan Barbarossa. Although Woods's reporting brought the usual bureaucratic criticism in Washington, by early 1941, it had been confirmed by American
code breakers who had read messages between Tokyo and the Japanese
ambassador in Berlin. President Roosevelt ordered that the Soviets be
informed. Sumner Welles notified Ambassador Umansky on March 20. A
telegram to Ambassador Laurence Steinhardt stated that "the Government
of the United States, while endeavoring to estimate the developing world
situation, has come into the possession of information which it regards as
authentic, clearly indicating that it is the intention of Germany to attack
the Soviet Union." When Stalin saw the translation of the message, he
wrote on it, "Provocation!"[2]

Later, on April 15, 1941, Steinhardt met with his regular contact,
Solomon A. Lozovsky, a deputy in the Foreign Affairs Commissariat, and
told him, "I consider it my duty to inform you and ask that you inform
Molotov: 'Beware of Germany. . . . There is more to it than simple rumors;
it would be madness for Germany to take this step, but they can do it.'"
Lozovsky replied, "I do not believe that Germany will attack the Soviet
Union. . . . In any case, the USSR is always ready and will not be taken
unaware."[3]

On June 5, Steinhardt and Lozovsky had a long meeting on many
issues affecting Soviet-American relations, principally those involving the
Baltic States. For the Soviets, an important problem was the arrest in April

1941 and detention of Gaik B. Ovakimian, ostensibly an employee of the Soviet trading company AMTORG but actually the head of the NKGB residency in New York. At meeting's end Steinhardt again brought up the danger of a German attack on the USSR. Lozovsky stated that "the Soviet Union remains calm in the face of all kinds of rumors about an attack on its borders. The Soviet Union will meet it fully armed. If there are people who might try, then the day of an invasion of the USSR will be the unhappiest in the history of the country attacking the USSR."[4] This apparently was their last meeting. Ironically, Lozovsky, a staunch Soviet patriot, was executed in August 1952 for crimes against the state in connection with the investigation of the Jewish Anti-Fascist Committee. Laurence Steinhardt, the highest-ranking Jewish diplomat in the U.S. State Department, died in a plane crash in March 1950 while serving as ambassador to Canada.[5]

Warnings from Great Britain remained tentative through 1940, becoming explicit only at the beginning of 1941. Back on June 24, 1940, Churchill had expressed to Stalin his hope for friendly relations between Great Britain and the Soviet Union, making clear that his government would not give up the fight against Nazi Germany and that its longer-term goal was to liberate those countries of Europe under German domination.[6] On July 3 the Soviet ambassador, Ivan M. Maisky, met with Churchill, who reiterated his determination to resist Hitler but said he had no idea when the German attack on Great Britain would come. Earlier, in a June 22 telegram to Molotov, Maisky had declared that the decision of the Churchill government to continue the fight despite the fall of France was supported by the British people. Although the group around Chamberlain still existed, it would not risk open opposition to the Churchill government. To judge from VENONA information, the RU residency would spend much of its time during 1940 reporting on the effects of German bombing and its impact on popular morale.[7]

As a concluding comment and perhaps as a warning, Churchill repeated to Maisky at their July 3 meeting a statement by the French politician Pierre Laval to an American journalist: "Hitler has nothing against France. Hitler hates the Bolsheviks and is waiting only for the appropriate circumstances to deliver the fatal blow." Maisky responded: "You can be sure that the USSR can take care of itself at any time and in any circumstances."[8]

It seems doubtful that Churchill intended Laval's words as a serious warning. In any case, it would have been lost in the tedious exchanges during the remainder of 1940 over various problems caused by the Soviet incorporation of the Baltic States. Even a long discussion on December 27 between Maisky and Anthony Eden, newly ensconced in the Foreign Office, intended by Eden as a gesture of friendship, degenerated into arguments over Baltic gold and freighters. By this time, of course, Operation Barbarossa was on track.[9]

In the new year, things changed. On February 12, 1941, Eden told Maisky that in the last two weeks the number of German troops in Romania had grown rapidly and that all the airfields in Bulgaria were in the hands of the Germans. In March the British government tried to persuade the Soviets that the German advance into the Balkans and the Near East represented a threat to both countries. It was time to create an atmosphere of trust, to look less to the past and more to the future. On March 6, 1941, the British ambassador, Sir Stafford Cripps, told Andrei Vyshinsky, deputy commissar for foreign affairs, of rumors that Germany was preparing to attack the USSR and that its actions in the Balkans were designed to protect its Balkan flank. Cripps believed the rumors were based on Hitler's rejection of the plan for the invasion of the British Isles, and he proposed the mounting of strong opposition to Germany."[10]

On April 19 Cripps handed Vyshinsky a copy of an April 3 letter from Churchill to Stalin that read in part: "I have at my disposal sufficient information from a reliable agent that when the Germans considered Yugoslavia caught in their net, that is, after March 20, they began to transfer three of their five tank divisions from Romania to southern Poland. As soon as they learned of the Serbian revolution, that transfer was revoked. Your Excellency will easily understand the meaning of these facts." We know now that this information was based on ULTRA, the British program for breaking the ENIGMA code used by the Germans.[11]

On June 3, 1941, Maisky reported to Moscow in a telegram a conversation in which Eden had told him that the British government had precise information about a recent concentration of German forces on Soviet borders, mainly in the Ukrainian region. Churchill considered the buildup a prelude to an attack against the USSR. Eden added, under instructions from the British government, that if German air forces in the Near East turned against the USSR, British air forces could go on the offensive and provide assistance. On June 13 Eden, again acting under instructions from Churchill, repeated his warning to Maisky of an increased concentration of German troops on Soviet borders and reaffirmed the British government's position in the event of a German invasion of the USSR. The government was prepared, Maisky said in his telegram to the Foreign Affairs Commissariat, to "provide us with the full assistance of its air forces in the Near East, which can be reinforced from Great Britain, send a military mission to the USSR composed of people with experience of war with Germany for the purpose of imparting that experience to us, and develop to the maximum economic cooperation, using for that purpose a route through the Persian Gulf or through Vladivostok if the position of Japan will permit a route through that city." Eden, Maisky reported, had asked that his declaration be immediately transmitted to Moscow.

On June 21, Maisky sent the Foreign Affairs Commissariat a statement by Ambassador Cripps, now in London, to the effect that "an armed conflict between Germany and the USSR is inevitable in the near future" and that "he considers it his duty to take all steps necessary so that in case of such a conflict close contact between England and the USSR will be established from the first moment, allowing the British government to render without delay the assistance of which Eden spoke on June 13." On June 16 Sir Alexander Cadogan, acting on instructions from Eden, had given Maisky a detailed briefing on the German troop units concentrated on the Soviet border. The total came to 115 divisions, not counting those from the Romanian army. Also included in the briefing were detailed descriptions of German troop arrivals during April and May in Poland, Moldavia, and northern Bukovina, as well as in Norway and Finland.[12]

The details on German troop deployments contained in the Eden-Cadogan briefings were undoubtedly based on disguised versions of UL-TRA matrial. The RU residency, however, had its own source or sources in the British intelligence establishment, who obtained ULTRA items in their original form. Theoretically, then, it might have been possible for Golikov's people to compare the original reports with the sanitized versions provided by Eden. If the RU Moscow had indeed been able to compare them, it would certainly have tried, but in no case could Eden's warnings have been dismissed as "British disinformation."

In the category of diplomatic warnings there are also the messages Ambassador Dekanozov sent to Moscow from Berlin. They would explain the note Beria sent to Stalin on June 21, 1941, demanding the "recall and punishment of our ambassador in Berlin, Dekanozov, who keeps on bombarding me with 'disinformation' about the alleged preparation of an attack on the USSR. He has reported that the 'attack' will begin tomorrow."[13]

On December 5, 1940, even before he presented his credentials to Hitler, Dekanozov had received an anonymous letter that began: "Next spring Hitler intends to attack the USSR. The Red Army will be destroyed by numerous, powerful encirclements." Voluminous details followed, many of which considered the assistant air attaché, Nikolai D. Skorniakov, credible. A report of the letter was sent to Molotov, who forwarded it to Stalin on December 24 with the comment "Comrade Stalin—for your information."[14]

On March 16, 1941, Dekanozov wrote to inform Molotov of increases in German fortifications and troops on the Soviet border: "In mid-January units of the Fourth Army arrived from Finland and were quartered on the outskirts of Warsaw and closer to our border. . . . Every day trains pass going east with armaments (weapons, shells, motor vehicles, and construction materials)." In an attachment to the letter, Dekanozov sent a "German-Russian phrase book intended for German soldiers," explaining that "there is information that these phrase books have been distributed to all German soldiers on the German-Russian border."[15] On March 28, Dekanozov's secretary received a call on the city telephone line. The caller said in German, "Around May a war will begin against Russia," and hung up.[16]

On April 4 an encoded telegram transmitted to Moscow the contents of a letter prepared by Dekanozov the day before: "Prompted by recent reporting from Korsikanets and Starshina, Dekanozov wishes to give Molotov the latest information bearing on German anti-Soviet activities." He described the increase in obvious surveillance of Soviet diplomats in Berlin and complained that the Germans were engaged in a "war of nerves," instilling in the population at all levels rumors of an inevitable war with the USSR. He listed several examples, five of which emphasized the Ukraine as the main target and one that quoted a German officer as saying, "Let's beat England and then go against Russia." These all reflected German deception themes. The other examples reflected reality. One quoted a German officer who said the "friendship" between Germany and the USSR would last less than three months. Dekanozov also reported on increasing German military activity as seen during a trip to Königsberg by an assistant attaché. Referring to the German-Russian phrase book he earlier sent to Moscow, he noted the presence of phrases like *hands up*, suggesting the book was not intended as a guide for friendly tourists. Also, visitors to the Consular Section all told stories of the growing danger to the USSR of Germany and of troop movements east. In addition to the rumors, Dekanozov reported the increasing difficulties the Soviet trade delegation in Berlin was having with the German firms fulfilling orders; some had even stopped accepting orders under the trade agreements. Dekanozov repeated his earlier theme that the rumors reflected German efforts to put pressure on the Soviet government, but he asked, "Is this all that the Germans are after? Judging by a number of factors, they are seriously considering an imminent confrontation with us, an invasion of the USSR, even during the war with England." Judging by this comment, Dekanozov appears to have broken ranks with the Stalinist position that Germany would never attack the Soviet Union until England was defeated.

Dekanozov then demonstrated that he followed intelligence matters closely by discussing the cases of "K" and "S" (Korsikanets and Starshina). He reported a conversation with their case officer (this would have been Aleksandr M. Korotkov), who had persuaded him that they were devoted to the Soviet cause. If their reports on the imminence of a military conflict were believable, Dekanozov commented, "should we not, based on this, envisage special tasks for them in the event contact is lost?" He suggested that the NKGB residency provide better guidance to Moscow as to the importance or value of individual reports. It is hard to imagine how Molotov received these comments, knowing that Stalin held these sources in contempt precisely because they were predicting a German invasion.[17]

On June 4, 1941, Dekanozov told Molotov that beginning in early May several new elements had been observed in the German press and in public opinion. Parallel to the rumors of the imminence of war between Germany and the USSR, other rumors were being quoted of a rapprochement, on the basis of either extensive concessions to Germany by the USSR or a division of "spheres of influence." Dekanozov quoted a number of newspapers in Germany and countries under German control. Singling out the rumors about German "leasing of the Ukraine," he asked, "What's this about? Why are the Germans spreading such rumors about the position of the Soviet Union?" Dekanozov's answer was that the Germans wished to picture Soviet policy in a distorted form. In this way, Dekanozov claimed, the Germans "are continuing to prepare the ideological (and actual) preparation for war against the USSR."[18]

On June 13 Dekanozov sent Molotov a telegram laying out the latest views of the officers of the Soviet mission in Berlin on the growth of German military strength in the Soviet border area. He began by suggesting that responsibility for carrying on Germany's war against England in Africa would be given to Germany's "vassals," France and Italy, thereby preserving its forces in Europe. He described the efforts of the mission to observe German troop movements to the east by rail since the end of April. There were at least 140–150 divisions on the Soviet Union's western frontiers, he contended, with another 30–40 divisions between the border of the Government General and Berlin. He concluded by presenting the observations noted between 7:00 p.m. on June 12 and 7:00 a.m. on June 13 along major rail routes. Trains moving east were loaded with troops and equipment, and no troop trains were seen returning from east to west. Dekanozov's telegram reflected the combined efforts of the mission, the RU, the NKGB, and the embassy and trade delegation officers, but there is no indication if Molotov gave it further distribution.[19]

On June 15 Dekanozov followed up on his earlier messages "on the concentration of German troops on the Soviet frontier" by citing statements from foreign military attachés that confirmed these reports. The Danish and Swedish attachés stated that there were more than one hundred divisions along the Soviet frontier and that the movement of troops was continuing without interruption. Some still believed these troop deployments were to put pressure on the Soviet Union, but the Swedish attaché had no doubt that they were serious preparations for war with the USSR. Foreign observers also pointed to the movement of German troops and material into Finland.[20] Certainly this report and the others from Dekanozov indicating the imminence of war with Germany would have been enough to prompt Beria to write the letter he did to Stalin calling for Dekanozov's recall and punishment.

The last message from Dekanozov came on June 21, the day before the invasion. A portion reads as follows: "Before dinner, I declared to Comrade I. F. Filippov, TASS correspondent and embassy worker, that there was no reason for alarm and panic; we cannot give our enemies cause for action and we must distinguish between truth and propaganda. Neither Ribbentrop nor his closest associates are in Berlin, where we have marvelous summer weather. The NKVD representative, Akhmedov, received a report from a source that states that allegedly tomorrow, Sunday the twenty-second, Germany will invade the USSR. I told him and his chief, B. Kobulov, not to pay any attention to this sort of false report and advised them to go off on a picnic tomorrow."

If this message is genuine, there are several things wrong with it. First, the tone is completely unlike that of the messages Dekanozov had been sending to Molotov over the past two months. Next, Dekanozov would have known that Filippov was an NKGB officer and contact for the source Litseist, a double agent under Gestapo control. He would not have said that he was a TASS employee. He also would have known that Akhmedov was a member of the RU residency and not the NKVD or the NKGB. Finally, Dekanozov would also have known very well that Akhmedov's boss (had Akhmedov actually been NKGB rather than RU) would have been not B. Kobulov but A. Kobulov. Thus, the errors must have been deliberate. Perhaps Dekanozov could not encipher this message and had to send it in the clear, knowing that the recipients in Moscow would focus on the June 22 date and not worry about the errors, which were probably put there to confuse the Germans.[21]

In addition to Dekanozov's messages from Berlin, the Information Department of the RU issued intelligence summaries once per month between July 1940 and June 1941. These were compiled and signed by the chief of the department and then approved by the chief of the RU, Filipp I. Golikov. The summaries were disseminated to all members of the Politburo, the Defense Commissar, the general staff, the central military establishment, the staffs of military districts, and troop units, down to the staffs of corps. The department also issued various reference books, manuals, and reports on the military-economic potential of individual countries and the possible scale of deployment of their armies, or "mobilization memoranda. Finally, there were special reports classified top secret (*sovershenno sekretno*), which were signed by the chief of the RU and disseminated to a list of recipients established by Stalin that apparently included, apart from Stalin himself, Molotov, Malenkov, Beria, Voroshilov, Timoshenko, and the chief of the general staff (Meretskov until February 1, 1941, then Zhukov). In addition to publishing disseminations, the Information Department maintained close contact with the general staff. For example, an officer of the Operational Directorate of the general staff, Lieutenant Colonel S. I. Guneev, was specially designated to maintain contact with the RU, visiting at least once each week, receiving the latest information, and entering it on his maps. He would then brief the chief of the general staff and, afterward, officers of the Operational Directorate. Officers from other directorates of the general staff could also visit the RU for information updates.[22]

As of June 15, 1940, the RU counted seven infantry divisions and two cavalry regiments in East Prussia and twenty infantry divisions and four cavalry regiments in former Poland. On July 4, the RU agents and those of the Intelligence Departments of the Western and Kiev Special Military Districts detected 860 troop trains moving from the west to East Prussia, former Poland, and Austria. Given these movements, German troop strength in these areas was believed to be thirteen infantry divisions (two motorized), two tank brigades, and up to 3,000 naval infantry in East Prussia; twenty-eight infantry divisions, one tank regiment, an unidentified tank unit, and five cavalry divisions in former Poland; and twelve to thirteen infantry divisions in Austria.

One summary listed fifty-three to fifty-four divisions as of July 16. NKVD Foreign Intelligence also reported "seven infantry divisions in the Warsaw area. The movements from west to east are continuing." The summary cited the foreign press and the German military attaché in Moscow as saying that these movements were occasioned by German units returning to their former barracks areas.[23]

On July 20, 1940, the RU sent a summary of "Events in the West," signed by Golikov, to Defense Commissar Timoshenko. Its stated purpose was to note increases in German troop strength in East Prussia and former Poland after the movement of troops from the west. Despite varying estimates of troop strength, the increases were impressive and clearly a warning that the German buildup constituted a threat to the Soviet Union.

On December 10 the RU issued a special report on the appearance in Romania of a group of sixteen to seventeen German divisions under General Johannes Blaskowitz and on German intentions to create a new group in the protectorate (former Czechoslovakia). The report predicted that the Germans would resolve the Balkans problem in the early spring. Another special report, dated December 14, described German plans for mobilization of reservists between the ages of twenty and forty who had been deferred for reasons such as work in the defense industry, illness, and wounds not fully healed. The number of mobilized divisions would come to 300,000 men. In the second half of November, the report asserted, the Germans began the creation of three to five tank divisions, three to five air divisions, and a significant number of antiaircraft units. The new units were equipped with captured weapons.[24]

The German section of a special report, also dated December 14, on "Mobilization Measures of Contiguous Capitalist Countries" stated that the German high command was doing everything it could to increase the strength of its present eight-million-man army. Beginning in October 1940, a supplemental mobilization had netted 1.5 million men, of whom 750,000 went to the army and the rest to defense industries. In January 1941 men between the ages of forty and forty-five were to be called, along with those recovering from wounds. There was also information on the creation of twenty-five infantry, five tank, and five motorized divisions, to be completed by March 1, 1941.[25]

A lengthy March 11, 1941, special report on the "Direction of Development of the German Armed Forces and Changes in Their Condition" was signed by Golikov but must have been prepared by the RU Military-Technical and Economic Department. Its section on increases in strength assessed the number of divisions as of September 1940 at about 228, of which fifteen to seventeen were tank divisions and eight to ten motorized. During the winter of 1940–41, twenty-five new infantry divisions, five new tank divisions, and five new motorized divisions were created. In addition, five of the existing infantry divisions were reorganized as motorized divisions. Thus, as of March 1 the number of divisions in the German army reached 263, of which 221 were infantry, 22 tank, and 20 motorized.

A chart in the report also indicated that as of September 1, 1940, a total of 102 divisions were deployed in the "West" (not further defined), seventy-two in the "East," twenty-two in the "Southeast," and thirty in the reserve. As of March 1, 1941, the number of divisions in the "West" were reduced to ninety-two, those in the "East" to sixty-one, while those in the "Southeast" had risen to sixty-two. The number carried in the reserves fell to thirteen. Thirty-five newly created divisions were noted in the second section of the chart but not located. These numbers and locations reinforced Stalin's view that England remained Hitler's primary concern; that is why in 1940 45 percent of all German divisions were located in the "West" and why in 1941 40 percent were still located there. As for the "Southeast," the number of divisions deployed there rose by forty-two. This increase probably confirmed Stalin's conviction that the main German axis of attack would be south of the Pripet Marshes and into Ukraine. He was, of course, wrong. The main German thrust came north of the Pripet.[26]

The March 11 report also stated that the number of German military aircraft had nearly doubled since October 1, 1940, to 10,980. Here again Stalin's fixation with England is reflected. Whereas in October 1940, the Luftwaffe carried 4,000 aircraft in the "West," by March 1, 1941, the number had reached 8,030. According to the March 11 report, there were only 700 German aircraft on the Soviet border on March 1, the same number as in September 1940. The remainder of the March 11 study discussed improvements and modernization of aircraft, tanks, and antitank and long-range artillery. It also concluded that the Germans had the capability to employ chemical weapons, having acquired new chemical shells from captured Czech stocks and possessing ample protective gear for their own troops. Perhaps the most interesting aspect of this primarily technical report is its comment on a German program for the construction of fortifications paralleling the Soviet frontier with the Government General. This work began soon after the Polish defeat and the fixing of the new border in 1939. The report found that "despite the intensive character of the work on fortifications . . . all are still under construction and will take at least a year to complete."[27]

On March 20, 1941, Golikov signed a document entitled "Opinions on the Organizational Measures and Variations of Combat Actions of the German Army against the USSR," which he distributed to the defense commissar, the Council of People's Commissars (SNK), and the Central Committee of the VKP(b). Unlike the special reports from the RU that he signed, this study was a *doklad*, a formal publication that was supposed to represent all the information available on a specific subject. Unfortunately, the document is highly slanted. It began: *"The majority of agent reports concerning the possibility of war with the USSR in the spring of 1941 come from Anglo-American sources, the goal of which at present is without a doubt to worsen relations between the USSR and Germany."* Golikov underscored this and other sentences (shown in italics), apparently to appeal to Stalin's suspicious, conspiratorial nature and his conviction that the Anglo-Americans wished either to provoke a conflict between Germany and the USSR or to make common cause with Hitler to destroy the "first socialist state." The report went on: *"Recently, English, American, and other sources speak of the preparations for an alleged German invasion of the Soviet Union.* Of all the statements received by us recently, the following deserve attention." The report then set forth sixteen numbered paragraphs containing a variety of hearsay remarks and rumors from foreign military attachés, journalists, and the foreign press. There are one or two that vaguely resemble statements from NKGB sources Korsikanets and Starshina, such as, "Göring allegedly has agreed to make peace with England and attack the USSR." Eleven items sound the theme "Germany will attack the USSR after a quick victory over England." Only two reflect an American source, the American minister in Bucharest, who is quoted as saying, "If the Germans don't have success in England, they will be compelled to carry out their old plans for the seizure of Ukraine and the Caucasus." He also cites the Romanian foreign minister as trying to persuade him "to have President Roosevelt introduce a plan for peace between the USSR and Germany." There is no way to tell where these and other quotations in the report came from.[28]

The report presented three possible versions of a German invasion of the USSR. The first was the one contained in the anonymous letter the report says Dekanozov received on December 15, 1940. (Dekanozov actually received the letter on December 5, 1940.) One blow would come from

Lublin, along the Pripet, to Kiev; the second from Romania, between Jassy and Bukovina, along the Teterev River; and the third from East Prussia to Memel, Villing, the Berezina River, and then along the Dniepr River to Kiev. The letter writer's version of a German attack bore no resemblance to the actual Barbarossa plan.

The second version was taken from a December 1940 document produced by the Kiev Special Military District giving the deployment plans for the Southwest Front in 1940. It described Germany's hoped-for invasion of the Ukraine, an action that would take place only after Germany has won its struggle with England: "There would be attacks along three axes: (a) from East Prussia into the Baltic States, . . . with Finland joining Germany to recover lost territory; (b) through Galicia and Volyn, with Germans supported by Ukrainians and Romanian troops also seeking to recover lost territory." This version concluded with the statement "In the other sector, secondary attacks will be carried out for the purpose of clearing the remaining territory."

The third version was that provided by Ariets via Alta on February 28, 1941. It called for the creation of three army groups under Marshals von Bock, von Rundstedt, and von Leeb and directed at Leningrad, Moscow, and Kiev. "The beginning of the attack," he reported, "is provisionally set for May 20." When the invasion actually came, von Leeb commanded Army Group North (Leningrad), von Bock Army Group Center (Moscow), and von Rundstedt Army Group South (Kiev).

Golikov's report went on:

Apart from these documents, according to information from other sources, it is known that the plan for attacking the USSR will consist of the following:
a. After the victory over England, Germany, attacking the USSR, proposes to deliver blows from two flanks: an envelopment from the North (they have in mind Finland) and from the Balkan peninsula. [Leaving aside the proviso "after the victory over England," this statement bears no resemblance to Barbarossa as Ariets described it and the Wehrmacht executed it.]
b. The director of a German commercial firm declares that the invasion of the USSR will occur from Romania. For this the Germans will build a *highway from the protectorate* [former Czechoslovakia] *through Slovakia and Hungary in order to move troops to the Soviet frontier.* Hungary and Romania have permitted Germany to use all their railroads for the movement of troops and have also permitted her to build new airfields, bases for motorized units, and warehouses

for ammunition. Hungary has permitted Germany to use part of its airfields. All of Romania's troops and military equipment have been placed at the disposal of the German command.

c. A Yugoslav military attaché declares that, after solving the Balkan question, it is difficult to know where the Germans will direct their attacks, but he is personally convinced that this will precede an invasion of the USSR. The very fact that the Germans are now at the Dardenelles is a direct act against the USSR. In general, Hitler has never changed his program, outlined in the book *Mein Kampf*, and that program is his basic goal for war. Hitler uses friendship as a means of attaining the possibility of solving the task of reconstructing Europe.

d. From the reporting of our military attaché on March 14, there are persistent rumors circulating in Romania that Germany has changed its strategic war plan. A German major said to our source, "We are completely changing our plan. *We are moving east, to the USSR. We will take from the USSR grain, coal, oil.* Then we will be invincible and can continue war with England and America." Colonel Rioshanu, a friend of the Romanian defense minister told our source in a personal conversation that the *main staff of the Romanian army, together with the Germans, is busy working out a plan for war with the USSR, the beginning of which should be expected in three months.* The Germans are afraid of an action by the USSR the moment they go into Turkey. Wishing to prevent danger from the USSR, the Germans want to take the initiative and strike the first blow, seizing the most important economic regions of USSR. The first of these is the Ukraine.

e. *According to a report from our military attaché in Berlin, from information of a fully trustworthy source, the beginning of military operations against the USSR should be expected between May 15 and June 15, 1941.*

These points were followed by two conclusions: "1. On the basis of all of the opinions cited above and possible versions of actions in the spring of this year, I consider that the most likely date for the beginning of actions against the USSR will be the moment of victory over England or the conclusion of an honorable peace for Germany. 2. Rumors and documents speaking of the inevitability of war this spring against the USSR must be rated as disinformation coming from English and even, perhaps, from German intelligence.[29]

Golikov's March 20 doklad was probably the worst intelligence document he produced during his service as chief of the RU. It bore no relationship to reality. It was intended to appease Stalin, to reassure him that his view of Hitler's intentions was correct and that Germany would not go to war until after the defeat of England. This is why Golikov labeled all reporting to the contrary as British or German deception. He cited only a very few of the agent reports or union republic NKGB summaries that specifically predicted a German invasion, instead carefully assembling those reports that confirmed the Stalinist view. Were these among the ones that Stalin pointed to when he told Timoshenko and Zhukov that he had his own documents?

Golikov's reports continued up to the day of the invasion. An April 4, 1941, special report documented the steady movement of German troops to the East during March; it was distributed to the military, including Timoshenko, Zhukov, Meretskov, and Nikolai F. Vatutin.[30] An April 16 special report documenting movement between April 1 and April 15 was the first one to note the arrival of river-crossing equipment in the area southeast of Brest-Litovsk, but the implications were not discussed.[31]

Golikov's May 5, 1941, special report conceded an increase in the number of German divisions in the Soviet border zone (from 70 to 107) and predicted a further increase as troops were brought back from operations in Greece and Yugoslavia. The report still insisted that the Germans had sufficient troops to develop operations against England in the Near East, Spain, and North Africa.[32]

A May 15 special report continued in the same vein: "The regrouping of German troops in the first half of May was characterized by continuing strengthening of those against the USSR along the entire western and southwestern borders, including Romania. It was also characterized by a further strengthening of forces for action against England in the Near East, Africa, and Norway." The report noted that "according to recent information, four to five divisions are preparing for movement through Spain to carry out operations against Gibraltar." It appears that neither Golikov nor his head of the Information Department, Dronov, heard of the meeting between Hitler and Franco on the Franco-Spanish border on October 23, 1940, in which Franco turned down all of Hitler's suggestions for military cooperation.[33]

This special report claimed eight to ten German parachute divisions, with one division or two in Greece, five to six divisions on the coast of France and Belgium, and two divisions within Germany. This was totally inaccurate information. As of May 15, the Luftwaffe's only parachute division, the Seventh, was preparing its three parachute regiments and one air landing (glider) regiment for an attack on Crete. (The assault was originally planned for May 17, but it was postponed to May 19 and finally took place on May 20.) The British, with their access to ULTRA, were fore-warned of the attack plans. As a result, even though the Germans even-tually succeeded in capturing Crete, the Seventh Division suffered heavily, causing Hitler to abandon this approach to land warfare. Why did the RU persist in listing eight to ten airborne divisions (including five to six on the coast of France and Belgium) in its German order of battle? The only logical answer lies in Stalin's conviction that Hitler still intended to invade England. Airborne divisions would be essential for such an operation, the reasoning went. Golikov, therefore, obligingly made five to six divisions available.[34]

The allocation of German divisions in the May 15 RU special report formed the basis for the section on enemy forces contained in the famous mid-May plan entitled "Considerations of a Plan for the Strategic Deploy-ment of the Armed Forces of the Soviet Union in the event of a War with Germany and Its Allies." The first paragraph of this document read: "At present, Germany (according to information from the Intelligence Direc-torate of the Red Army) has deployed around 230 infantry, 22 tank, 20 motorized, 8 airborne, and 4 cavalry divisions—about 284 divisions. Of these, as of May 15, there were up to 86 infantry divisions, 13 tank, 12 motorized, and 1 cavalry—a total of 112 divisions—concentrated on the borders of the Soviet Union. It is assumed that under certain political conditions, Germany could, in the event of an attack on the USSR, array against us up to 137 infantry, 19 tank, 15 motorized, and 5 airborne divi-sions, for a total of 180 [sic] divisions." The remaining 104 German divi-sions were allocated as in the May 15 special report, including 40 infantry, 2 cavalry, 1 tank and 2 airborne divisions in Denmark, Belgium, Holland, and France.

The author of these "considerations" gives these reasons for proposing a new strategic deployment: "Inasmuch as Germany at the present time holds its army mobilized, with rear services deployed, it has the capacity to precede us in deployment and to deliver a surprise attack. In order to prevent that (and destroy the German army), I consider it necessary that in no case should we give the initiative for action to the German command. We should preempt the enemy in deployment and attack the German army at that moment when it will be in a stage of deployment and will not yet have succeeded in organizing the front and the coordination of arms and services." This plan, although prepared for the signatures of Timoshenko and Zhukov, was apparently never signed and was rejected by Stalin. In any case, it was totally unrealistic. The three German army groups were moving into position, and communications plans within these formations were well advanced. Those troops designated to form the lead elements would begin their movement to their jump-off areas on June 10.[35]

A May 31, 1941, special report continued to emphasize German operations against England. Among actions undertaken by the German command in the second half of May with forces released from the Balkans, the first cited was "renewal of the western groupings for the struggle against England." An "increase in the strength of the forces against the USSR" came second. The number of divisions earmarked for action on all fronts against England totaled 122 to 126, while those against the USSR totaled 120 to 122. The penultimate paragraph reported: "As far as the front against England is concerned, the German command . . . [is] continuing concurrently its movement of troops to Norway, . . . having in view the execution of the main operation against the British Isles." This assertion was pure poppycock. By May 31 evidence existed that the increase in German forces in Norway was most likely related to German-Finnish cooperation in planning for war against the USSR. This Golikov report, with its deliberate distortions concerning England, was also disseminated by name to Timoshenko and Zhukov, plus others on the normal dissemination list.[36]

On June 5, 1941, Golikov issued a special report on Romanian preparations for war, ending with this sentence: "Officers of the Romanian general staff are insistent in declaring that, in accordance with an unofficial declaration of Antonescu, war between Romania and the USSR should begin soon." A June 7 special report on the same subject stated that new mobilization measures could bring the Romanian army to a strength of one million men and thirty divisions. Both reports went to Timoshenko and Zhukov.[37]

The latter report covered increases in Poland on the Soviet border and concluded: "Considering Romanian mobilization as a means of strengthening Germany's right flank in Europe, SPECIAL ATTENTION must be paid to the continued strengthening of German troops on Polish territory." Do these capital letters signify growing concern within the RU?

CHAPTER 16

"We Do Not Fire on German Aircraft in Peacetime"

Notwithstanding intelligence reports describing the buildup of German troops along the Soviet borders, there was an even more serious threat. That one, too, affected the border areas but now it was in the skies above them. Very probably the single greatest error committed by Stalin between the summer of 1940 and June 22, 1941, was his decision to allow the Luftwaffe freedom to conduct unlimited reconnaissance flights over the Soviet Union. Fearing that preventive action by Soviet air defenses would "provoke" Hitler, he issued strict orders against it. He would not change his views even after Soviet intelligence provided him with precise evidence that the flights were part of a German program to procure aerial photographs of Soviet fortifications, troop installations, airfields, and communications and supply facilities throughout the entire theater of impending operations. Because of Stalin's misjudgment, Soviet losses in the early hours of the war were magnified as German bombers systematically destroyed each of the targets reconnaissance had identified, including the aircraft of the border military districts.

The leadership of the Red Army understood the importance of defending Soviet airspace against hostile reconnaissance. It understood, too, the need to protect its aircraft from destruction so as to provide its ground forces the support they would require in the event of war. At a conference of senior Red Army commanders held in Moscow on December 23–31, 1940, Defense Commissar Timoshenko declared that the "decisive effect of aviation [in offensive operations] lies not in raids on the enemy's rear but in coordinated action with troops on the field of battle."[1] The commander of the Kiev Special Military District and future chief of the general staff, General Georgy K. Zhukov, also emphasized the role of aviation: "Army commanders and their chiefs of air forces should take special care not to permit their aviation to be destroyed at their airfields. The best means of doing this is a surprise attack by our aviation on the airfields of the enemy and the dispersed disposition of our aviation on airfields with camouflaged equipment and antiaircraft defenses."[2]

The role of aviation was further amplified by Pavel V. Rychagov, chief of Red Army air forces, who outlined these tasks for air units in a war: gain air superiority, cooperate with the troops on the battlefield, protect the troops, act against the operational/strategic reserves and rear services of the enemy, provide intelligence based on aerial reconnaissance, and ensure the success of parachute drops and airborne landings if they are employed. Rychagov cautioned that "basing of the large numbers of aircraft required to accomplish these tasks demands a well-developed network of airfields, and at each airfield on average there should be no more than twenty-five aircraft."[3] While a consensus certainly existed on these issues within the Red Army leadership, actions to support that consensus were almost totally lacking. It would not be until June 19, 1941, for example, that a decree of the Council of People's Commissars and the Central Committee VKP(b), would call for "camouflage of aircraft, runways, tents, and airfield equipment."[4]

Basing was especially problematic in the western border districts, where forty-eight of the Red Army's seventy air divisions were located in 1941. These units were expected to bear the brunt of the Luftwaffe's anticipated effort to achieve air superiority. The poor condition and unsuitable locations of the air units in the border districts made it much easier for the Germans to succeed. Many Soviet airfields were only ten to thirty kilometers from the frontier. Fighter aircraft and bombers were often based at the same airfield. Takeoff while under attack was made difficult by the large number of aircraft jammed together. Many air regiments had just received new aircraft, but this meant that both new and old planes were crowded onto the same fields; moreover, there were not enough pilots to man all these aircraft. In the Baltic Military District, 118 aircraft were without aircrews; in the Western Special Military Districts, the number was 430, and in Kiev 342. Antiaircraft systems were weak, and camouflage measures had not yet been carried out. In the Baltic Military District, air units received orders to conduct training flights over the night of June 21–22; as a result, the majority of bomber regiments were in the midst of postflight inspection and refueling—their pilots having been released to sleep—when the Luftwaffe attacked them. In the Western Special Military District, fighter planes were dispersed along the entire length of the border. The Ninth Mixed Aviation Division, which had just received 262 MIG 1s and MIG 3s, was particularly close to the border; 420 new PE-2 bombers were assigned to the bomber regiments of the Ninth and Eleventh Mixed Aviation Divisions. The aircrews were just beginning to master these new aircraft.

At 11:00 p.m. on June 21, enemy saboteurs cut the telephone wires between the Western Special Military District's air force headquarters and its air divisions and their regiments. The situation was made worse by the lack of contact with the service of air observation, warning, and communications (VNOS), which had yet to begin to function effectively. The air forces of the Kiev Special Military District were also unprepared. Because VNOS was not working properly, aviation units based on fields close to the border did not receive warnings in time.[5] At the December 1940 conference, the problems of VNOS had briefly been addressed by Filipp I. Golikov, chief of military intelligence, who pointed out its importance, noting that an advancing mechanized corps, for example, could be wiped out by enemy dive bombers unless it received warning of their approach. There were not enough VNOS posts to guarantee early warning, and those that existed were badly trained and equipped. Their sole means of communications was telephone lines; they did not possess radios. German early warning systems, Golikov observed, were far superior to those of the Red Army.[6]

Despite general agreement at the December 1940 conference on what was needed to upgrade the aviation components of the border military districts, little was done, and what was done was done badly. In fact, it was the Germans who appear to have implemented on their side of the border the very programs the conference speakers prescribed. For example, they repaired and modernized existing Polish airfields and constructed new fields and landing strips, many with underground facilities for fuel and munitions storage. To compound the problem, aerial photoreconnaissance, conducted over many months, enabled the Germans to observe Soviet efforts to improve their frontal aviation posture. The Luftwaffe's surprise attack delivered massive blows to Soviet forward airfields with great precision, depriving Soviet ground forces of air support when they needed it most.

Incidents of German overflights of Soviet territory were detected as early as September 1939 but were probably not considered a serious problem. The border between the USSR and German-occupied Poland was initially a military demarcation line, and German pilots could easily justify losing their way. By early 1940, however, Soviet border troops had settled down along the new frontier and begun to act against these overflights, which had taken on the character of organized aerial reconnaissance. On February 10, 1940, a German aircraft entered Soviet airspace to a depth of two kilometers. Border troops opened fire with machine guns and the aircraft returned to German territory. On February 11 there were three more incidents, the last one involving the return flight of one of the aircraft. Here again the border troops opened fire and the aircraft disappeared into German airspace.[7] The situation worsened on March 17, when a flight of thirty-two German aircraft, both fighters and bombers, entered Soviet airspace in the area of the Eighty-sixth Border Troop Detachment in the Western Special Military District. A border guard unit opened fire on the aircraft as they were returning. An aircraft was hit and came down fifty meters from the border; one crewman was killed and a second fatally wounded. In reporting the incident, the Belorussian border troop district noted that there had already been twelve violations of Soviet airspace in that region alone since December 1939. In one case, a Soviet fighter crashed trying to force a German aircraft to land. The Soviet pilot was killed. The report concluded with a request that instructions be given to border troops in the event of continuing violations of Soviet airspace. The NKVD USSR brought the matter to Stalin's attention. As if to underline the urgency of the problem, another incident occurred in the area of the Kiev Special Military District on March 19. Five German aircraft described as reconnaissance types crossed the border and headed east. Soviet fighters scrambled but reported they could not find the Germans. The headquarters of the Sixth Army reported the aircraft as having landed on Soviet territory. It turned out that one aircraft had run out of fuel, tried to land, and was damaged; the other four landed safely and their pilots explained that they were on a training flight, had lost their bearings, and were low on fuel. The incident was reported to Beria by the NKVD deputy responsible for troops, Ivan I. Maslennikov.[8]

It did not take long for Stalin to react. On March 29, 1940, Beria issued NKVD Directive No. 102 to all border troop districts on the western frontier: "(1) In case of violations of the Soviet-German border by German aircraft or balloons, do not open fire. Limit yourselves to preparing a report on the violation of the state frontier. (2) Immediately lodge an oral and written protest on each border violation with the appropriate representative of the German command concerned with border service. (3) Chiefs of border troops must take measures to present to the Chief Directorate of Border Troops not only urgent reports but also documents and all correspondence relating to violations of the state frontier."[9]

Apparently unconvinced that the directive would stop the trigger-happy border troops from provoking the Germans, Beria followed up on April 5 with a new order regarding the use of firearms anywhere on the Soviet-German frontier. This order annulled a 1938 order calling on border troops to fire on border violators without concern for whether their bullets fell on "the territory of a neighboring nation." Now border troops would "strictly see to it that bullets do not fall on German territory." In the event, thousands of heavily armed saboteurs and diversionists entered the western oblasts and republics in the period leading up to the invasion, and numerous firefights erupted as border troops tried to intercept them. Where the order was not ignored, many of the intruders succeeded. It is clear, therefore, why, on the night of June 21–22, 1941, they managed to cut hundreds of the telephone lines in the western military districts.[10]

Violations of Soviet airspace continued throughout 1940. On May 26 Vasily A. Khomenko, chief of the Border Troops Directorate of the NKVD Ukrainian SSR, reported on Germans photographing Soviet border zones, particularly their road nets.[11] Border troop commanders complained that "the recent orders to the border troops and Red Army covering forces have reduced their role to that of passive observers whose protests are ignored. German representatives admit to the violations and promise to report them but nothing happens. The overflights continue more persistently than ever."[12]

Obsessed with the idea that if he did not provoke Hitler there would be no war, Stalin disregarded these complaints. In fact, on June 10, 1940, a Soviet-German convention was signed on "Procedures for Regulating Border Conflicts and Incidents" that virtually invited the Germans to continue their aerial reconnaissance without fear of possible consequences. According to point 5, article 5, of the convention, "in the event of a border violation, officials of one side or the other will initiate an investigation. If it is determined that the border crossing (overflight) was unintentional (loss of orientation, malfunction of the aircraft, lack of fuel, etc.), the person crossing or flying over the border is subject to immediate return." For the next year, these procedures imposed serious restraints on Soviet border troops,

Red Army units, and interceptor aircraft. At the same time, they embold-
ened the Luftwaffe not only to increase the number of overflights but
actually to land at Soviet airdromes for a closer look at their facilities and
aircraft.[13]

NKVD deputy Ivan I. Maslennikov signed over fifteen reports on airspace violations between March and December 19, 1940. These reports
were normally sent to Stalin, Molotov, and Timoshenko. On only one occasion that we are aware of did a military district try to adhere to an order,
issued back in January 1940 and sanctioned by Aleksandr M. Vasilevsky of
the General Staff Operational Directorate, to open fire immediately on any
aircraft violating Soviet airspace. On April 20 a brigade commander on
Maslennikov's staff telephoned the Belorussian Special Military District
(BOVO) to inquire whether the district had received the NKVD order of
March 29. He didn't get an answer; instead, the BOVO colonel to whom he
was speaking announced that, after the NKVD order was issued, BOVO
had checked with the general staff to see if the January order was still in
force. A written confirmation was received, signed by Deputy Chief of the
General Staff I. V. Smorodinov. There is nothing further available on this
question, but it seems unlikely that resistance to the March 29, 1940, order
continued.[14] It is known that, in his reports on German violations of Soviet
airspace, Maslennikov began inserting this ritual phrase: "The aircraft
were not fired on." Diplomatic protest was unsuccessful. On October 26,
1940, for example, Andrei Vyshinsky, deputy commissar for foreign affairs,
presented an aide memoire to Ambassador von Schulenburg describing
incidents on October 22 and 23 and asking the German government to take
appropriate steps to ensure no further violations of Soviet space by German aircraft. There is no indication that the Germans paid the least bit of
attention.[15]

An NKVD report sent to the leadership on March 20, 1941, noted that
"for the period October 16, 1940 to March 1, 1941, thirty-seven German
aircraft violated Soviet airspace. In that same period six Soviet aircraft
inadvertently violated German airspace." No explanation was given for the
Soviet actions. "The flights of German aircraft are in most cases carried
out over the construction of fortified areas, obviously for intelligence purposes. These aircraft fly over USSR territory up to distances of three to six
kilometers on the average, but in some cases as far as eighty kilometers. . . .
Whenever these violations occur, the border troops protest them. German
authorities do not deny that violations have taken place but claim they
arise from the fact that there are many military flying schools near the

border and student pilots easily become disoriented." The report closed with this sentence: "Despite these explanations by German representatives, violations of Soviet airspace continue."[16]

Whoever drafted that NKVD report was right on the money. Confirmation that these were intelligence flights came from Harro Schulze-Boysen (code name Starshina), who passed the information to Arvid Harnack (code name Korsikanets) in January 1941. This arrangement continued until the end of March, when Korsikanets's case officer, deputy resident Aleksandr M. Korotkov, began to handle Starshina directly. In judging Starshina's reporting, one must remember that Korsikanets, Korotkov, and the officers in the NKGB Foreign Intelligence Directorate in Moscow were unfamiliar with German air force terminology or operations. Often the right questions were not put to Starshina or the information he provided was incorrectly interpreted when it was disseminated to the leadership in Moscow. Nevertheless, his reporting on the Luftwaffe's photo reconnaissance program, when considered in the light of Germany's continuing violations of Soviet airspace, should have convinced the leadership that more was involved than navigational errors by student pilots.[17]

Starshina's first report described a large-scale effort to photograph the entire border area of the western USSR, including Leningrad and Kronstadt, using improved cameras. The results would be used to produce accurate maps of the USSR and to further operational planning. The squadron performing the photo reconnaissance was known as Revelstaffel, after its commander, Revel. Its main base was at Oranienburg, where it was carried on the books as a squadron engaged in experiments in high-altitude flight. It flew its reconnaissance missions from bases at Bucharest, Königsberg, and Kirkenes in northern Norway. The photography was carried out at an altitude of 6,000 meters and the films were of excellent quality. Starshina also reported that, according to the German military attaché in Stockholm, in mid-April the Soviet government had protested to the Finns that the Germans were overflying Finland to reach Soviet airspace. The Finns advised the Germans of the Soviet protest and asked if German aircraft could bypass Finnish territory. At the same time, the Finns promised the Germans that if their aircraft passed over Finnish territory flying from Kirkenes in Norway, the Finns would not fire on them. The Finns' positive attitude was the result, Starshina believed, of the close cooperation between the German and Finnish general staffs in drawing up plans for operations against the USSR.[18]

According to postwar German sources, high-altitude reconnaissance over the USSR was ordered by Hitler in October 1940 and carried out by Lieutenant Colonel Theodor Rowehl's unit beginning in February 1941. (Starshina's "Revel" was a Russian transliteration of the German "Rowehl"). One group operated from East Prussia and covered Belorussia, using HE-111 aircraft. The second covered the Baltic States with DO-215-B2 aircraft made by Dornier. The third, operating from Bucharest with HE-111 and DO-215-B2 aircraft, covered areas north of the Black Sea. From Cracow and Bucharest, a "'special squadron of the Research Center for High-Altitude Flying' covered the area between Minsk and Kiev. They employed special Junkers models, the JU-88B and JU-86P—magnificent machines capable of reaching 11,000 and 15,000 meters respectively. . . . These aircraft were equipped with pressurized cabins, with engines specially tuned for high-altitude flying, with special photographic equipment, and a wide angle of vision. . . . The plan worked smoothly. The Russians noticed nothing." These German descriptions of the program confirm Starshina's reporting and provide greater technical detail. They are wrong, however, with regard to the start of the overflights and in the belief that the "Russians noticed nothing." They certainly did notice, but given Stalin's refusal to respond to these provocations, nothing was done about them.[19]

As of early January 1941, Starshina reported, Göring ordered the "Russian Department transferred from the Air Ministry to the so-called active element of the air staff, which works on plans for military operations." By early April, plans were developing for a bombing campaign as part of the invasion: "Air attacks will focus on important military and economic objectives; however, because the Soviet Union is such a vast territory, in its operational plans the Luftwaffe will concentrate on key rail junctions in the central USSR where north-south and east-west lines intersect. Other early targets of German bombing will be electric power stations, particularly in the Don Basin. Targets in Moscow will include engine building and ball bearing plants, along with enterprises of the aviation industry."

On March 28 and April 21, 1941, the Foreign Affairs Commissariat protested German overflights in notes to the German Foreign Office. The April 21 protest noted eighty violations and described an April 15 incident at Rovno in which a German plane was forced to land by Soviet fighters. On it "were found a camera, some rolls of exposed film, and a torn topographical map . . . of the USSR, all of which gives evidence of the crew's purpose."

The April 21 note also reminded the German Foreign Office of "the statement that was made on March 28, 1940, by the assistant military attaché of the embassy of the USSR in Berlin to Reich Marshal Göring. According to this statement, the People's Commissar for Defense of the USSR made an exception to the usual very strict measures for the protection of the Soviet border and gave the border troops the order not to fire on German planes flying over Soviet territory *so long as such flights did not occur frequently.*" I emphasize this last phrase to highlight the pathetic nature of the Soviet response to these constant German provocations. As for Starshina, he reported on May 9 that "despite the Soviet diplomatic note [probably the April 21 note], photo reconnaissance flights are continuing. The only concession made by the Luftwaffe has been to raise the altitude for photography to 11,000 meters and order the aircrews to take greater care." The photo reconnaissance flights continued, however, and increased in intensity up to June 22. No one in the Soviet leadership, the military, or the security services could ignore these flights, yet no references to them or to their implications appeared in any of the periodic special reports by Golikov. When Stalin later cursed Starshina for his June 17 report, part of his anger may well have arisen from the agent's continual reminders of the real purpose of the German overflights.[20]

Between April 19 and June 19, 1941, there were 180 violations of Soviet airspace compared with 80 between March 27 and April 18. Violations occurred nearly every day in June, each one marked by a memorandum report to the leadership from the NKVD deputy for troops, Ivan I. Maslennikov. In addition, he forwarded summaries of border troop reports on the movements of German troops ever closer to the border. Even Beria joined in with a June 12 memorandum to Stalin and Molotov. After enumerating the increasing number of violations, he commented: "Violations of the border by German aircraft are not accidental, as can be shown by the direction and depth of these flights over our territory. In many cases German aircraft fly over our territory for distances of up to 100 kilometers or more, particularly in the direction of areas where defense construction is under way or over the locations of large Red Army garrisons." Beria concluded this section of his memorandum with an account of the incident at Rovno. The report was sent to the attention of Stalin and Molotov.

As the tempo of airspace violations increased, there were indications that Soviet fighter pilots were growing tougher. On June 19 three German aircraft were forced to land by Red Army fighters although no shots were fired. On June 20 a German bomber was intercepted near Brest-Litovsk by a Soviet fighter and signaled to follow it. When the bomber ignored the signals, the interceptor fired a warning burst from his machine gun. The

German returned the fire and managed to make it back across the border. The Soviet pilot was not hit and returned to his base.[21] Senior Red Army commanders of covering forces along the border voiced concern about these intrusions over Soviet defensive positions. The commander of the Twelfth Army in the Kiev Special Military District sent a written request for instructions "on when it was permitted to open fire with antiaircraft weapons on German aircraft." Maksim A. Purkayev, chief of staff of the district responded: "You may open fire if (1) special directives to that effect have been given by the Military Council; (2) mobilization has been declared; (3) the plan for a covering force has been put into effect, so long as there are no special prohibitions; (4) it is known to the Military Council of the Twelfth Army that we do not direct fire from antiaircraft artillery on German aircraft in peacetime."[22]

Although it has become clear with the declassification of documents from the prewar period that it was Stalin who insisted on the orders not to fire on German aircraft, some retired officers cited other reasons for the failure to halt German aerial reconnaissance. For example, Marshal Matvei V. Zakharov, in 1941 chief of staff of the Odessa Military District, claimed that the aircraft could not be intercepted because Soviet interceptors could not follow them across the frontier and the Red Army did not have sufficient antiaircraft artillery to shoot them down. Moreover, the VNOS posts were ineffective in warning air defense of the approach of hostile aircraft. Nowhere in his treatment of German violations of Soviet airspace does Zakharov admit that it was orders from the top that made it possible for the Luftwaffe to operate with impunity over the USSR.[23]

As the invasion grew nearer, the intensity of German air activity increased. There were eleven cases on June 19 and thirty-six on June 20. On the twentieth, the violations included five from Finland; although the nationality of the aircraft was not given in the NKVD reporting, all the planes entered Soviet airspace from Finland and returned to Finland after completing their missions. One violation took place from Romania. Among those incidents attributed to German aircraft, one involved thirteen German bombers that entered Soviet airspace at a height of only 300 meters, went a distance of 4.5 kilometers, then returned to German territory after spending only four minutes over the USSR. Pilots and bombardiers cannot do better than to have a very safe but quick look at the targets they are getting ready to bomb. Three airspace violations were reported on June 21, the day before the invasion, each of them involving two engine bombers that entered the USSR at low altitudes. After traveling distances of from six to ten kilometers, they returned to German territory, very probably having reconnoitered their specific targets. That these flights were not accidental can be seen in the June 21, 1941, message to Moscow of the chief of staff of the Western Special Military District: "German aircraft with loaded bomb racks violated the frontier June 20."[24] Never in the history of modern warfare had an aggressor been given a unique opportunity like this to photograph its victim's defenses.

On June 29, seven days after the invasion, *Pravda* announced that the total number of German violations of Soviet airspace in the period leading up to the war was 324. The existence of these overflights was never made public before the German attack.[25] The brave statements made by senior Soviet commanders at the December 1940 conference were so much bluster, however well meant at the time. All these men, from the defense commissar to the general staff to the commanders of the western military districts and the armies under them, realized that to have permitted German aerial reconnaissance up to the evening of the invasion was sheer insanity.

CHAPTER **17**

German Deception
Why Did Stalin Believe It?

Without examining the full dimensions of Germany's artful program of deception, one cannot entirely understand the tragedy of June 1941. As Barton Whaley's seminal work first noted, it was not random noise that prevented Moscow from divining Hitler's true intentions.[1] Rather, it was the dissemination, through myriad channels, of bits and pieces of information based on very specific deception themes, some of which were designed by Hitler himself. The entire program was executed under Abwehr control, and it involved virtually all components of the German government, although in each component only a few officials were briefed on their roles in spreading deception. The program was pursued with precision and bureaucratic thoroughness. Whaley's study, important as it is, was written in 1973, before the release of much of the archival and other material on the pre-1941 period that has become available since the breakup of the Soviet Union in 1991. This information, combined with German archival data, provides a much more detailed picture of German deception themes and how they confirmed Stalin in his belief that Hitler would not attack the USSR in 1941.

A February 1941 directive of the high command of the German armed forces (OKW) made clear that the invasion of England, or Operation Sea Lion, was a major element of the deception program. This directive spoke of strengthening "the already existing impression of an impending invasion of England."[2] The theme, present in diplomatic and intelligence reports as early as July 1940, continued through the rest of that year.[3] Stalin was greatly dismayed by the swift German victory over France and the British expeditionary forces on the Continent, seeing his hopes dashed for a drawn-out war with the consequent exhaustion of both of the belligerents. Nevertheless, he still believed there would be no danger of a German attack on the Soviet Union, as long as Germany was at war with England. He remained wedded to the concept that Germany would never risk having to fight on two fronts. He didn't realize that this was not a serious problem for Hitler because, after the evacuation of the British forces from Dunkirk, there were no British troops left on the Continent and the French army no longer constituted a threat of any kind. A German invasion of England was the only hope Stalin had that Germany would become so entangled in a major struggle with England that it would delay for a year or more active military operations against the USSR.

Despite Hitler's decision on September 17, 1940, to postpone the invasion of England, throughout the spring of 1941 German deception programs continued to stress the "English invasion first" theme. On May 12, when the OKW issued orders for the implementation of the second phase of the deception program to coincide on May 22 with the concentrated movement of Wehrmacht military rail traffic to the east, that theme still predominated.[4]

One of the specific recommendations of the May 12 directive was to spread the idea that the forthcoming airborne attack on Crete was to be a "general rehearsal" for the invasion of England. In his diary, Propaganda Minister Joseph Goebbels gleefully described running in the official newspaper, the *Völkischer Beobachter,* an article entitled "Crete as an Example" that suggested that the attack on Crete was a prelude to the invasion of England. Deliberately withdrawing the issue of the newspaper as soon as it had been delivered to foreign embassies reinforced rumors of an impending assault on England.[5]

The airborne component of the battle for Crete was not an auspicious success. The British learned of plans for this operation well in advance through ULTRA. The volume of ULTRA messages must have been considerable, and it is difficult to see how the RU London residency sources privy to ULTRA could have been unaware that the German Seventh Airborne Division had been badly beaten by the defenders. While the Germans finally gained control of Crete, the paratroop victory was not one that could serve as an example of what would happen were an airborne assault on England undertaken. The Seventh *Flieger* Division, the only one Hitler possessed, had been virtually destroyed, and according to General Kurt Student, the leader of Operation Mercury, Hitler was very unhappy, believing that "the days of paratroops were over."[6]

On May 24 and 25 Goebbels noted in his diary that "our distribution of rumors concerning an invasion of England is working." Back in Moscow, meanwhile, Stalin's new military intelligence chief, Filipp I. Golikov, kept the English invasion myth very much alive. He included it in his periodic intelligence summaries, while at the same time describing reports pointing to an imminent German attack on the USSR as "German or English deception."[7]

How was it possible for Golikov to make such statements without being questioned on their substance? As has already been noted, the London RU residency was probably the most prolific of any RU component in the 1940–41 period and during the war itself. Thanks to the VENONA releases of ULTRA decrypts, we have obtained examples of their messages to Moscow. Their reporting on British victories in the aerial warfare of 1940 and on the decision of the Luftwaffe in the late fall of 1940 and January 1941 to close down facilities in France and the Low Countries intended to support Sea Lion demonstrated that the invasion of Britain had been abandoned. Other information on Germany's real military plans, as reflected in ENIGMA traffic, was very likely passed to RU headquarters. In the face of this and other reporting from reliable sources, Golikov's actions are difficult to understand except in the context of his toadyish behavior toward Stalin and his deep fear of him. As for his subordinates, they were all aware of the fate that awaited them were they to confront Golikov.[8]

Another important deception theme, "defense against a Red Army offensive," was plausible during the early stages of the German buildup along the Soviet frontier, when Wehrmacht units, newly arrived from the west, began construction of what were, in fact, purely defensive works such as trenches, machine gun nests, barbed wire, and even artillery emplacements. Linked to the defensive theme were statements by German officials to the effect that the troops were returning to former garrison areas, or were sent east to be beyond the range of British bombers. These essentially benign explanations for the movement of German troops to the Soviet border area began as early as July 9, 1940, when General I. V. Smorodinov, Soviet deputy chief of the general Staff was told by German military attaché General Ernst Köstring, that there would be large-scale troop movements in Poland and East Prussia, ostensibly because the German army would be demobilizing older units. Köstring said that units with younger groups would be brought in while other units returned to permanent garrisons. None of these explanations seemed valid. As the German concentrations grew, large amounts of river-crossing equipment appeared, and modified locomotives arrived equipped with devices enabling them to change track carriages to the Soviet gauge. German intentions then became clear.[9]

From January to June 1941, a number of reports from RU and NKVD/NKGB foreign intelligence reflected deception on the operational level. These reports all pointed to the "Ukraine as the main axis and principal goal of the German attack." The purpose of the deception, obviously, was to mask the decision under Barbarossa to launch the main blow north of the Pripet Marshes, along the Brest-Minsk axis. This is where the major German thrust actually came. The Red Army, though, had concentrated its largest forces in the Ukrainian Special Military District after Stalin decided in fall 1940 to change the strategic deployment plan worked out by the general staff. This plan had correctly anticipated the main German attack north of the marshes.[10] Stalin objected because he felt the Germans' main objective would be the grain and manufacturing centers of the Ukraine, which they would need in the event of a protracted war. Apparently, he did not realize that Hitler had no intention of becoming bogged down in a protracted war. He counted, unrealistically, on a "lightning war." Nevertheless, the change was made as Stalin wished on October 5, 1940. Consequently, the Germans wanted to ensure that the Soviet general staff did not change its mind about where the main blow would fall.[11] Hence their inclusion in their deception program of the Ukraine as their primary objective.[12] As in the Finnish war, Stalin refused to accept professional military advice.

In a memoir published in 1989, Marshal Matvei V. Zakharov described the fateful decision to deploy the Red Army's largest formations south of the mouth of the river San. He, too, noted Stalin's reasoning (that Hitler would need Ukrainian resources for a protracted war) but failed to observe that Hitler really hoped for a blitzkrieg and had no plans for a drawn-out conflict. According to Zakharov, it was probably the frequent changes in general staff leadership that permitted this error in deployment to occur without challenge. He concluded his defense of Stalin's position by citing an April 2, 1941, Starshina report that claimed that the Germans would open the war with a "lightning blow against the Ukraine." Whatever Stalin's reasons for the change, it was an incredible mistake.[13]

As the date for the invasion drew nearer, German deception took on

new forms: "ultimatums, negotiations, and the concept that the Wehrmacht presence on the Soviet borders was solely there to pressure the
USSR in accepting German demands." An analysis of the agent reports
received by SS Oberfüher Rudolf Likus in Ribbentrop's Special Bureau
demonstrates that as of May 15, 1941, foreign diplomatic and press officials in Berlin were convinced that negotiations were under way between
Germany and the USSR. They thought that Germany had placed specific
demands on the Soviet Union, such as transit rights for German armed
forces through the USSR, a German lease of the Ukraine, and transfer of
control of portions of the Baku oil fields to Germany. Belief in the existence
of serious negotiations, even a visit to Berlin by Stalin, was strengthened
by rumors that a Berlin flag company was busy sewing red flags for a
forthcoming visit by the Soviet leader.[14] As for the ultimatum aspect, references to it were found in portions of reports from Starshina, the NKGB
source in the Luftwaffe Intelligence Department. On May 9 Starshina described conversations with officers about likely dates for the invasion;
some officers, he reported, believed Germany would first issue an ultimatum demanding increased agricultural and industrial deliveries and a stop
to communist propaganda (at the same time, Starshina noted that preparations for the invasion were going forward at an accelerated tempo).[15]
A month later, on June 9, Starshina and Korsikanets noted increasing
rumors of a German lease of the Ukraine and a visit by Stalin to Berlin.
They suggested that these rumors were being circulated by the Ministry of
Propaganda and the military command to mask preparations for the invasion of the USSR and to ensure maximum surprise. On June 11 they reported that "competent circles say the question of an invasion of the USSR
has been decided. It is necessary to reckon with a surprise attack. It is not
known whether Germany will make some demands on the USSR before-
hand." On June 16 Starshina reported that "all preparations by Germany
for an armed attack on the Soviet Union have been completed, and the
blow can be expected at any time." There was no mention of an ultimatum
in his report.[16]

Still, Stalin appeared desperate to enter into negotiations—anything to
delay an attack. If negotiations had to be preceded by an ultimatum, so be
it. While the German deception machine was feverishly spreading word of
negotiations, however, it continued to rebuff all efforts by the Soviet government to open a dialogue on an official basis. This silence in the face of
rumors that negotiations were under way frustrated the Soviet leadership
and contributed to their paralysis of will.

The Soviets were not without their own deception operation, of course. Although, according to Barton Whaley, the Germans were the first to institutionalize deception when they created a disinformation service in the German army shortly before the end of World War I, the new Soviet government was not far behind. On January 11, 1923, a Special Bureau for Disinformation was created within the State Political Directorate (GPU), its task to "break up the counterrevolutionary plans and schemes of the enemy."[17] Aimed at domestic opponents as well as those abroad, it created notional opposition organizations that identified and neutralized anti-Soviet elements within Soviet Russia and their links with Western intelligence services and émigré organizations. These operations, or "active measures," as they were known to the Soviet services, continued through the 1920s and 1930s. One such operation was apparently directed at Germany in the period before the German invasion of June 1941.

In early 1941, August Ponschab, the German consul in Harbin, began forwarding messages to the Foreign Ministry in Berlin containing what appeared to be German translations of circular telegrams sent from the Foreign Affairs Commissariat in Moscow to its diplomatic missions in the Far East. These telegrams included portions of messages from Soviet embassies in Berlin, London, Paris, Washington, Ankara, and so forth. The ostensible purpose of the telegrams seems to have been to keep Far Eastern missions abreast of events affecting Soviet interests elsewhere in the world.[18] When these messages arrived in Berlin, they were placed in the Russian section of the personal file of Ernst von Weizsäcker, state secretary in the German Foreign Ministry. There were no marginal notes on the messages, nor was there any indication that their content had any effect on Hitler's plans to invade the USSR or on the Germans' own deception program.[19]

Overall, the intent of the messages seems to have been to warn Germany of the growing problems confronting it, while at the same time making clear that the USSR would "resist" any "intimidation" by Germany or Japan. We do not know how this operation was carried out, what NKGB elements controlled it in Moscow, who actually prepared their detailed and lengthy telegrams, and how these were cleared by Molotov or Stalin. In any event, there is no indication the effort had the slightest impact on Hitler's determination to invade the Soviet Union.[20]

Parallel to these messages, the final acts of German deception were being played out in Berlin with the initiation of unofficial secret talks between Vladimir G. Dekanozov, the Soviet ambassador in Berlin, and

Otto Meissner, a longtime Russian specialist in the German Foreign Ministry. On the Soviet side, these negotiations, which covered many of the
questions raised in the Ponschab telegrams, reflected the hope that serious, official talks would ensue. For Hitler, they served only to keep Moscow's hopes for delay alive until German forces had completed their move
into attack positions. Nothing concerning these secret talks between Dekanozov and Meissner has ever appeared in official Foreign Affairs Commissariat communications or in foreign policy archives (AVP). The major
source of information on them is the memoirs of Valentin Berezhkov, a
Soviet diplomat who served in Berlin under Dekanozov. As the Dekanozov-
Meissner talks broke off, a Ponschab message referred, in one of the last
attempts at deception, to the temporary closing of the Siberian railroad.
Perhaps the threat was intended to persuade Berlin to renew the talks.
There was never any hope of that. Hitler had made up his mind.[21]

Soviet intelligence dissemination practices may have inadvertently
contributed to the success of the German deception program. Both Defense Commissar Timoshenko and Chief of the General Staff Zhukov complained that they were not shown all the available intelligence.[22] An examination of intelligence reports and summaries between February 1, 1941—
and June 22, 1941, reveals that both men received more than has been
generally known but that indeed they were not given all the information
they should have been. The problem was the chaotic dissemination system. Timoshenko and Zhukov received sixteen reports as joint addressees.
As defense commissar, Timoshenko received ten reports while Zhukov was
the sole addressee on only two reports.[23]

Another collection of reports derived from border troop units. Of thirteen such reports, Zhukov was included as an addressee on only one, Timoshenko on seven. Beria sent one of these reports, on the apprehension of
German agents by border troops, only to Stalin. Given the counterintelligence nature of the report, a limited distribution might have made sense.
Another report, however, also signed by Beria and sent only to Stalin,
contained details on the concentration of German and Hungarian troops
and air units on the Soviet frontier during May 1941. Certainly this information would have interested Timoshenko and Zhukov. Stalin insisted on
reading individual agent reports sent to his office, dismissing them as
disinformation if they were at variance with his views.[24]

There was only one place in the Soviet intelligence world where analysis was supposed to be undertaken, and that was the Information Department of Soviet military intelligence. That department was controlled by

Golikov, who had demonstrated that he would accept Stalin's direction without question. Every report arriving at RU headquarters in Moscow from a field residency source had to be passed on by him before it could be disseminated—and only then as he directed. Two instances illustrate the problem. First, a report from a source in the German embassy in Bucharest ended with the comment that "a German move to the east in the near future is excluded"; rumors that Germany would attack the USSR "are being spread deliberately with a view to causing uncertainty in Moscow." Golikov ordered the report distributed to Stalin, Molotov, Timoshenko, Voroshilov, Dimitrov, Beria, and Zhukov.[25] By contrast, a May 6 report from Richard Sorge contained this paragraph: "German generals evaluate the combat readiness of the Red Army so low that they estimate the Red Army will be destroyed in the course of a few weeks. They believe the defense system on the Soviet-German border is extraordinarily weak." Golikov ordered this paragraph excised before distribution of the report.[26]

Whereas neither Timoshenko nor Zhukov was on the distribution list of every report produced by Military Intelligence, State Security, or the border troops, Golikov made sure they received each of his special summaries. Here Golikov persisted in repeating the German deception theme that an invasion of England was Hitler's primary objective. The penultimate paragraph of the May 31, 1941, summary read: "The German command has rather quickly restored its main dispositions in the west, continuing concurrently its movement of troops to Norway, . . . having in view the execution of the main operation against the English Isles."[27]

Some historians believe that Stalin readily accepted German deception and refused to heed his own intelligence warnings because of his own secret plans for a preventive war against Germany. Naturally, these plans and preparations had to be concealed from the Germans lest they disrupt them. This is why he found so attractive the German insistence in its deception program on defeating England before turning east and why he rejected the advice of those who wished to respond forcefully to the threatening German army buildup, the constant reconnaissance flights, and so forth.

The idea that Stalin intended to attack Germany in July 1941 is put forward by Viktor Suvorov in his book *Ledokol: Kto nachal vtoruiu voinu?* (*Icebreaker: Who Started the Second World War?*).[28] Suvorov claims that Stalin failed because Hitler got wind of the plan and launched Operation Barbarossa, a preemptive strike. This thesis started a controversy that continues, but most historians in Russia and abroad reject it as unsupported by evidence, while there is overwhelming archival and other data demonstrating that the Red Army was incapable of mounting an offensive of the magnitude required. Nevertheless, some historians have defended the idea. Those who do so in Germany, for example, see in it grounds for supporting the view that Hitler's Barbarossa was simply his reaction to Stalin's own plans.

Understandably, it has been in Russia that *Icebreaker* has had the greatest impact. For many Russians the theory permits them to retain their faith in Stalin, answering as it does, or at least appears to, the question of how Stalin could have trusted Hitler. *Icebreaker* argues that he didn't trust him but, on the contrary, was preparing to do him in on a schedule of his own choosing. For others, victims of Stalin's terror, *Icebreaker* confirms their view that Stalin was intent on spreading communism throughout Europe.[29]

Mikhail I. Meltiukhov proposes that Stalin planned to attack German forces in Poland and East Prussia in mid-June 1941. Another historian, Boris Shaptalov, repeats the Suvorov theme that Stalin was completely taken in by German deception that Hitler would never fight a two-front war.[30] Stalin was undoubtedly deceived by the Germans, whether or not he ever intended to strike them first. Thus, those who advance the thesis of *Icebreaker* as a way of absolving Stalin from responsibility for the debacle of June 1941 must also concede that he was totally fooled by German disinformation.

Double agents and a dupe like Amaiak Z. Kobulov abetted Germany's designs. Appointed NKVD/GUGB resident in Berlin on August 26, 1939, Kobulov had never served abroad, spoke no German, and lacked any experience in intelligence operations. But note the date of his appointment—it was only three days after the signing of the Nazi-Soviet nonaggression pact and four days before the German invasion of Poland; in this critical period, Stalin and Beria wanted to have a man in Berlin whom they could trust completely. His fitness for the job was of little concern. Naturally, the professionals in the German Section of Foreign Intelligence in Moscow objected, but since Fitin had been in charge of the department only since May 1939 and was still proving himself, there was little chance of stopping the appointment.

Over the next year, the Gestapo had ample time to study Amaiak Kobulov, to surveil his daily routine as he moved from his residence to his office in the Soviet embassy complex on Unter den Linden, and to note the contacts he made in diplomatic and press circles. He kept a high profile (he was promoted from secretary to counselor) and there is little doubt that the Gestapo knew precisely who he was. As a resident he was fairly ineffectual, but recalled to Moscow in June 1940 for a review of his work, he rejected all criticism, apparently feeling that he had sufficient protection from his brother, Bogdan, and from Beria to do as he pleased. Nevertheless, he was urged to try to develop new agent sources.

It came as something of a surprise, then, when in early August 1940 NKVD Moscow received an urgent message from him describing a meeting he and a TASS correspondent had with a young Latvian journalist, Oreste Berlinks. The TASS correspondent was I. F. Filippov (code name Filosof,), a member of the NKVD Foreign Intelligence residency in Berlin whom Kobulov, knowing no German, used as an interpreter. Berlinks had been a correspondent of the Latvian newspaper *Brive Zeme* but, now that the newspaper was no longer being subsidized by the German Foreign Ministry, he needed financial assistance. According to Kobulov, Berlinks was well disposed toward the incorporation of Latvia into the USSR and was willing to share with Moscow information he obtained from the Foreign Ministry. Ten days later, on August 15, Kobulov surprised Moscow with the news that he had "recruited" Berlinks and given him the code name Litseist. There followed some biographic data on Litseist. NKVD Moscow instantly realized that this operation posed a problem because Kobulov was able to send information from this new source directly to Stalin and Beria, bypassing NKVD specialists. Their concern grew as they began to receive the results of checks on Litseist's background from NKVD Latvia. It appeared that Litseist was anti-Soviet and had spread pro-Nazi propaganda. The Berlin residency was cautioned to keep this in mind in its dealings with him.

Amaiak ignored these warnings and continued to meet with Litseist. The information he began receiving covered topics such as German plans to invade England, Hitler's concern that Germany not become involved in a two-front war, the existence of a split within the Nazi hierarchy over the question of Soviet-German relations (with the military urging war against Russia and Hitler playing a restraining role), the German need for an independent Ukraine whose grain could feed all of Europe and for Soviet oil. His information also supported the contention that the presence of German troops on the Soviet border was a defensive measure occasioned by a Red Army buildup. Litseist's reports, particularly on German reluctance to become involved in a war in the east until England was defeated, were all sent directly to Stalin by Beria and later by Merkulov when he became head of NKGB. They were apparently very well received, reinforcing as they did Stalin's conviction that a conflict with Germany could be delayed until at least 1942. One might wonder whether it was not a folder of Litseist reports that Stalin showed Timoshenko and Zhukov on June 13, 1941, when he refuted their intelligence on German troop concentrations by saying "I have other documents."[31]

Although it must have been apparent to officers in the German Department of the NKGB Foreign Intelligence Directorate that these reports were at odds with other information on German intentions and capabilities, not until 1947 did Soviet Intelligence learn that the Litseist case was a carefully targeted part of a much broader German deception program. In that year a former Gestapo officer who had been assigned to work with the Ribbentrop Special Bureau as part of his regular work with foreigners residing in Berlin was interrogated by Soviet Counterintelligence. He stated that "the Latvian Berlinks, a German agent, was planted on Amaiak Kobulov, a counselor of the German embassy whom the Gestapo knew was conducting intelligence operations." Berlinks was "recruited" by Kobulov, he said, and "for a long time we supplied him with disinformation that he passed to Kobulov." Berlinks reported that he had gained the confidence of Kobulov, who told him "that all his reports went directly to Stalin and Molotov."[32] Obviously, Hitler considered Kobulov a useful channel for the passage of information to Moscow. It worked like this, said the Gestapo officer: "Ribbentrop prepared the material, then passed it to Hitler. The material would then be given to Berlinks for delivery to Kobulov with Hitler's sanction." The archives of the Ribbentrop Special Bureau confirm this information. A December 30, 1940, report sent to Hitler and Ribbentrop by Rudolf Likus of the Special Bureau reads: "Our informant in the Soviet Russian embassy was called in by embassy counselor Kobulov at 7:30 this evening and given four important tasks, one of which was an order from Comrade Stalin to obtain the text of the speech given by the Führer on December 18 before several thousand military school graduates. Kobulov said the speech was not publicized in the German press, but portions available to the Kremlin allegedly displayed an anti-Soviet tendency. Stalin is interested in this and wishes to be convinced that there were no such tendencies. The agent, who works for the GPU, must obtain the text." Ribbentrop commented in the margin: "We can brief the agent any way we wish." Walther Hewell, Ribbentrop's liaison officer with Hitler's office, also commented: "The Führer wants you to collect such information regularly from the Soviet embassy."[33]

We now know that the German deception program confused many well-placed RU and NKGB foreign intelligence sources whose access to very good information was rendered suspect by disinformation spread without their knowledge by individuals within their organizations. Stalin probably never knew or suspected that through Amaiak Kobulov Hitler was playing him for a fool.

Still, were all these deception operations enough? Enough, that is, to persuade Stalin to cling stubbornly to his apparent conviction that Hitler would not attack the Soviet Union until he had dealt with England? It seemed evident, as the spring of 1941 unfolded, that more and more information indicated that the German forces on the Soviet frontier were planning to invade. Senior Soviet military leaders were growing uneasy; even members of Beria's clique, such as Dekanozov, were predicting war. To hold out as Stalin did, right up to the moment bombs began to rain down on Soviet cities, he must have been convinced that there would be no German invasion. To be this confident, he would have had to have special information, a card that in his view trumped everything he was shown predicting such an invasion. If Stalin did not have such assurances, possibly from Hitler himself, then his behavior in May and June 1941 was completely irrational. It is one thing to be deceived (and Hitler was a master of deception) but quite another to adhere stubbornly to one's personal interpretation of events, thereby threatening the existence of the Soviet state and the lives of its citizens.

CHAPTER 18

Secret Letters

In 1965–66 Konstantin M. Simonov, the renowned Soviet war correspondent, writer, editor, and poet, conducted several interviews with retired Marshal Georgy K. Zhukov. At one point, Zhukov recalled a meeting with Stalin at the beginning of January 1941 concerning the large numbers of German forces in the Government General (German-occupied Poland). Stalin told Zhukov he had "turned to Hitler in a personal letter, advising him that this was known to us, that it surprised us, and that it created the impression among us that Hitler intended to go to war with us." In reply, Hitler sent Stalin a letter, also personal and, as he underlined in the text, confidential. He wrote, said Zhukov, that "our information was correct, that there actually were large troop formations deployed in the Government General," These, Hitler explained, "are not directed against the Soviet Union. I intend to observe the [nonaggression] pact strictly and swear on my honor as a chief of state that my troops are deployed in the Government General for other purposes. The territories of western and central Germany are subject to heavy English bombing and are easily observed from the air by the English. Therefore, I found it necessary to move large contingents of troops to the east, where they can secretly reorganize and rearm." Insofar as Zhukov was aware, Stalin believed this letter.[1]

This reference to correspondence between Hitler and Stalin was not published until 1987. Apparently, the only archival reference to an exchange of letters between Hitler and Stalin is a May 9, 1941, report of a

meeting between Ambassador von Schulenburg of Germany and the Soviet ambassador to Berlin, Dekanozov, then on leave in Moscow. Dekanozov had proposed that "a joint German-Soviet communiqué be prepared
refuting rumors of tension in German-Soviet relations and also refuting
the possibility of war between the two countries. Von Schulenburg feared
there was not enough time to negotiate a joint communiqué and urged
that Stalin write a letter to various chiefs of state in which he referred to
his new position as chairman of the Council of People's Commissars and
stated that the USSR would pursue a policy of peace with all countries. In a
separate letter to Hitler, he would discuss the proposed communiqué, advising him of the contents. Von Schulenburg added that if Stalin sent such
a letter Hitler would send a special aircraft for the courier and the whole
affair would move forward very quickly."[2]

On May 12, 1941, Dekanozov received very specific written instructions from Stalin and Molotov for his response to von Schulenburg: "I
spoke with Stalin and Molotov concerning von Schulenburg's proposal for
an exchange of letters in connection with the necessity of quashing the
rumors of worsening relations between the USSR and Germany. Stalin
and Molotov have no objection in principle to such an exchange of letters
but consider that such an exchange should be carried out only between
Germany and the USSR." Not, it would seem, with countries other than
Germany. (If the two leaders were actually in correspondence, Stalin had
no intention of revealing it.)[3]

Lev Bezymensky, a Russian historian and war veteran, describes a
meeting he himself had with Zhukov in 1966 in which the subject of Hitler-
Stalin letters arose. According to Bezymensky, Zhukov commented:

> Sometime in early June I decided to try again to convince Stalin of
> the accuracy of the intelligence reports on the approaching danger.
> Until then Stalin had turned aside similar reports by the chief of
> the general staff. . . . Defense Commissar Timoshenko and I brought
> along staff maps with the locations of enemy troops entered on
> them. I made the report. Stalin listened attentively but remained
> silent. After the report he sent us away without giving us his opin-
> ion. . . . A few days passed and Stalin called for me. . . . He opened a
> case on his desk and took out several sheets of paper. "Read," said
> Stalin. . . . It was a letter from Stalin to Hitler in which he briefly
> outlined his concern over the German deployments, about which I
> had reported a few days earlier. . . . Stalin then said, "Here is the
> answer. Read it." I am afraid that after so many years I cannot exactly
> reproduce Hitler's words. But this I do remember precisely: . . . I read

the TASS communiqué in the June 14 issue of *Pravda* and in it, to my amazement, I discovered the same words I had read in Hitler's letter to Stalin in Stalin's office. That is, in this Soviet document, I found printed Hitler's very arguments.

Stalin's evident purpose in releasing the June 14 TASS communiqué was to prompt a response from Hitler. The communiqué opened by blaming England for spreading rumors that Germany and the USSR were "close to war." According to these rumors, "Germany has made territorial and economic demands on the USSR and negotiations are now under way leading to closer relations between the two countries. Ostensibly the USSR has rejected these demands, as a result of which Germany has deployed troops along the Soviet borders with a view to attacking the USSR." The communiqué declared that "Germany has made no such demands on the USSR and both sides are steadfastly observing the terms of the nonaggression pact. Rumors that Germany intends to break off relations with the USSR have no basis in fact. The recent movement of German troops, freed from operations in the Balkans, to eastern and northeastern Germany has other motives having nothing to do with Soviet-German relations. Rumors that the USSR is preparing for war with Germany are untrue and provocative. Attempts to portray the summer maneuvers of the Red Army as hostile to Germany are absurd." That many of these themes, such as England's blame for rumors of war, were reflected in Hitler's letters should come as no surprise. What was unexpected about the TASS communiqué was the unreal manner in which it portrayed the state of Soviet-German relations just eight days before the Nazi onslaught.

This account differs substantially from that of Simonov in his reporting of the interviews in which Zhukov spoke of meeting Stalin in January 1941. Simonov also does not say that Stalin actually showed Zhukov both his letter to Hitler and Hitler's reply. Bezymensky claims that there are no archival records of the Stalin-Hitler correspondence but notes that they may have been destroyed. He quotes German archives to show that at the end Hitler ordered his private correspondence with heads of state destroyed.[4]

A 1997 novel on the immediate prewar period entitled *Groza* refers to this correspondence in considerable detail. Its author, Igor Bunich, claims that "from October 1940 to May 1941 Hitler sent Stalin six personal letters. Only two have been found, one dated December 3, 1940, and the second May 14, 1941." None of Stalin's replies have been found. In his December 1940 letter, Hitler advises Stalin that he intends "no later than the summer of the coming year" to resolve the English question by "seizing and occupying the heart of the British Empire—the British Isles." Referring to his statements in an earlier letter that German troops were assembled in an area of the Government General inaccessible to English aviation and intelligence for reorganization and training, he acknowledges that this has aroused in Stalin "understandable anxiety." He goes on to say that "rumors of a German invasion of the USSR are being deliberately circulated by the appropriate German offices" as a way of "keeping Churchill and his circles in ignorance of our precise plans." Hitler closes by proposing a personal meeting with Stalin "at the end of June–beginning of July 1941."[5]

Although the December letter contains references to the usual deception themes, nothing can match Hitler's personal letter to Stalin of May 14, 1941. According to the author of a November 2003 article in *Krasnaia Zvezda*, it was intended by the Nazis to "misinform the leadership of the USSR concerning its true intentions. The German Führer himself was involved in this action. It endeavored to exploit the Soviet leader's long-standing distrust of the ruling circles of Great Britain, his efforts to put off the beginning of the war at any price, and his belief that the English leadership planned to push Germany into attacking the USSR."[6]

In the excerpts in the article, Hitler again explained the presence of German troops on the Soviet border as protection from British aircraft even though they had given rise to rumors of a conflict "between us." Hitler assured Stalin "on my honor as a chief of state" that these rumors could be completely ignored. They "are being spread by English sources," he asserted, admitting, though, that with so many troops concentrated in the area a conflict could break out "without our wishing it." He feared, he said, that "some of my generals might deliberately embark on such a conflict in order to save England from its fate and spoil my plans."

Hitler then advised Stalin that "by approximately June 15–20 I plan to begin a massive transfer of troops to the west from your borders." He asked Stalin "not to give in to any provocations that might emanate from those of my generals who might have forgotten their duty. And, it goes without saying, try not to give them any cause. If it becomes impossible to avoid provocation by some of my generals, I ask you to show restraint, to not respond but to advise me immediately of what has happened through the channel known to you."

The phrase noted by Zhukov, "on my honor as a chief of state," would seem to authenticate the excerpts in the *Krasnaia Zvezda* article. The issue, however, is more complicated. The excerpts also appear, word for word, in

Bunich's novel, which purports to reproduce the entire text of the letter. (English translations of both the December 1940 and the May 1941 letters can be found in appendix 2.)[7]

Zhukov told Simonov that Hitler responded to a letter Stalin wrote at the beginning of 1941 expressing concern over the presence of large numbers of German troops in Soviet border areas. Hitler's December 31, 1940, letter may have been that response. The phrase "on my honor as a chief of state" appears not in that letter, however, but in the May 14, 1941, letter, the last one from Hitler. This confusion is not surprising since Zhukov's memory may have dimmed, but he may also have been repeating what Stalin told him. Zhukov's statements to Simonov do indeed reflect Hitler's explanations for the German troop presence in Soviet border areas, but no mention is made of Hitler's intentions toward Great Britain, which figure prominently in both letters. Stalin may not have wished to reveal an aspect of German military planning that Hitler expected him to keep confidential; on the other hand, if Lev Bezymensky's recollection of his 1966 meeting with Zhukov is correct and Zhukov did read portions of the Hitler-Stalin correspondence in June 1941, it is surprising that Zhukov said nothing to either Simonov or Bezymensky of Hitler's statements about attacking England. Zhukov would have immediately understood their significance.

The May 14 letter, then, might be seen as the final masterpiece in a gallery of disinformation. By confiding in Stalin that some of his generals might launch an unauthorized provocative attack and asking Stalin not to respond in kind, Hitler virtually dictated the scenario Stalin followed in the first hours after the invasion. By the same token, it was tragic for the Soviets that Timoshenko, Zhukov, and those around them—knowing what they knew of the extent of German preparations and aware, as military professionals, that an offensive across thousands of kilometers could never have been undertaken as a "provocation" by a few dissident German generals—could not change the views of their stubborn leader. At a minimum, these Hitler letters, if genuine, demonstrate that Aleksandr Solzhenitsyn was right when he wrote that Stalin, who trusted no one, did in fact "trust Adolf Hitler."[8]

There is another aspect of the May 14 letter that demands attention. The penultimate paragraph reads: "I thank you for having agreed with me on the question known to you and I ask you to forgive me for the method I have chosen for delivering this letter to you as quickly as possible."[9] Very likely the "method . . . for delivering" the letter refers to the unscheduled flight on May 15, 1941, of a Junkers transport to Moscow. In the Bunich novel, it is depicted as a courier plane carrying the letter to Stalin.[10] In any case, a German JU-52 aircraft made its way through Soviet airspace, undetected and apparently unauthorized, and, against all regulations, landed at the central airfield. Here it was not only allowed to land but also refueled for its return trip and permitted to leave Soviet airspace. These actions were obviously at Stalin's behest. Kept in the closest secrecy, the official permission extended to the plane was unknown to all but a very few. This intrusion of Soviet airspace immediately became a sensation within the defense establishment.[11]

According to a statement by the Defense Commissariat, because of poor organization the early-warning posts of the Fourth Separate PVO (National Air Defense) Brigade of the Western Special Military District detected the JU-52 only after it had penetrated twenty-nine kilometers into Soviet airspace. Mistaking the JU-52 for a commercial aircraft, a DC-3, on a routine flight, they failed to notify anyone of the intrusion. Although the Belostok airport had been informed of the JU-52 flight (we do not know by whom), it did not pass the information on to PVO or to the Ninth Mixed Air Division (responsible for interception) because its communications were down. Similarly, senior officers of PVO Moscow did not learn of the flight until May 17 even though a PVO Moscow duty officer had been advised by a Civil Air Fleet dispatcher that the aircraft had passed over Belostok. In addition, the Defense Commissariat report went on, the Red Army air forces took no measures to halt it. Moreover, the chief of staff of the air forces, Major General Pavel S. Volodin, and the chief of the First Department of the staff, Major General Vladimir D. Grendal, knew that the aircraft had crossed the frontier without authorization. They not only failed to take measures to detain it but assisted its flight to Moscow by giving orders to PVO to ensure its safe arrival and by permitting it to land at a Moscow airfield. How could this have happened? Whatever the truth of the matter, the incident was treated as a major failure of the air defense system and the Red Army's air forces.[12]

On June 7 Colonel General Grigory M. Shtern, the air defense chief, was arrested. (Chief since March 19, he had assumed his new position only to discover that air defenses were in abysmal shape.) On June 10, the Defense Commissariat, in NKO Order No. 0035, reprimanded Volodin and Grendal for having given the "JU-52 unauthorized permission for the flight and for landing in Moscow without having checked its right for such a flight."[13] On June 27 Volodin was arrested, and on October 28 he was shot without trial along with Shtern and others.[14]

It seems evident that for a transport aircraft the size of the JU-52 (note that it had been mistaken for a Douglas DC-3) to have flown through Soviet airspace unchallenged from the western border to Moscow would have been a near miracle. For it to have landed safely in Moscow, been refueled, and been allowed to leave soon after its arrival without a major PVO investigation seems incredible. It can be postulated, therefore, that Stalin, who was awaiting a response from Hitler to one of his letters, gave the order to allow the JU-52 to proceed to Moscow, land, and be refueled for its return flight. He would not, of course, have said a word about a communication from Hitler. When the story of the "unauthorized" JU-52 flight began to leak out, causing an outcry in PVO and the air forces, Stalin acted immediately to take advantage of the situation, moving first against Shtern, whom he had long disliked, and then against Volodin. As air forces chief of staff, Volodin may have known that Stalin was behind the safe arrival and departure of the flight. By the time of Volodin's arrest on June 27, five days after the invasion, Stalin would have realized he had been cruelly deceived by Hitler. The flight was testimony to that fact. It was imperative he get rid of Volodin, who knew too much and could not be allowed to survive. Farfetched? Not if one considers Stalin's passion for conspiracy and his ability to wait patiently for the right moment and then act quickly to achieve his ends. He would never have allowed it to become known that he had been naïve enough to have fallen for Hitler's disinformation.[15]

CHAPTER **19**

The Purges Revived

When Proskurov was relieved of his position as chief of military intelligence back in July 1940 and an order came down placing him at the disposition of the Defense Commissariat, he became a man without a job.[1] An order of this type was issued when Stalin or the top military brass had not yet decided on an officer's next assignment. For a man with the energy and determination of Proskurov, this distance from the action was hard to take. The fact that the air forces were undergoing a reorganization favored by many senior officers made it that much harder. He wanted to be part of the planning. A decree of the Council of People's Commissars dated July 25, 1940, ordained that the air division would be the basic organizational structure of the Red Army's air forces.

This changeover was to be fully completed by January 1, 1941, and would involve an increase of over 60,000 personnel in the Red Army air forces. Proskurov would surely have learned of the reorganization from his friends in the air forces, particularly those with whom he had served in Spain. Although he could not participate in the implementation of the new decree, he must surely have followed the action closely, even from afar.

Still, he very much wanted a new assignment and he must have pushed hard to get one. Therefore, it was no surprise when word came of a September 9, 1940, order appointing him deputy chief of aviation for the Far Eastern Front. Nothing happened, however; written on the original of the document were these words: "Hold until further notice."[2] Instead, on Octo-

ber 23 Proskurov was appointed deputy to the chief of the Main Directorate of Red Army Air Forces for Long-Range Bombardment Aviation.[3] On
October 29 Proskurov attended what appears to have been a meeting of the
Main Military Council at the Kremlin, apparently to discuss the forthcoming changes in long-range bombardment aviation.[4] Then, on November
5th, a decree of the Council of People's Commissars created independent
long-range bombardment aviation divisions under the control of a new
assistant to the chief of the Main Directorate of Red Army Air Forces.
Proskurov would occupy this post. In addition to specifying the designations and locations of the new long-range bombardment (DD) divisions,
the decree called for creation by March 1, 1941, of sixteen new airfield-
engineering battalions and fifty-three aviation-technical companies.[5] This
last proviso was a direct reflection of lessons learned in the Finnish war:
both Pavel Rychagov and Yevgeny Ptukhin had complained of the short-
age of good airfields and the lack of airfield construction and mainte-
nance units.[6]

How did Proskurov receive this prestigious assignment when we know
he was no favorite of Stalin and not at all liked by Timoshenko? The answer must have been his very close friendships with the two top officers in
the Red Army's air forces. One, Yakov V. Smushkevich, was the assistant
chief of the general staff for aviation.[7] Proskurov's other patron was the
chief of Red Army aviation, Rychagov.[8] With such backing, it was no wonder that Proskurov was given his new responsibilities. But it was true, too,
that Stalin had a propensity for allowing his victims to remain at liberty or
even to advance while he waited patiently for the right opportunity to
destroy them. Proskurov, of course, was unaware of Stalin's ultimate intentions and that Rychagov and Smushkevich were also on Stalin's list.
Bombers were his specialty and he was delighted to be back in his favorite field.

Rychagov and Proskurov both knew that the principal task of the new
bomber organization would be training aircrews in flights at night and in
poor weather conditions. Rychagov recalled from his experience in the
Finnish war that such training was a major problem. If a pilot crashed an
aircraft while practicing instrument flying or landings and takeoffs from a
small airfield, the accident investigators would try to make the unit commander appear to be undisciplined or suspicious.[9] Because the accident
investigations were run by more than one organization, the voice of the
unit commander was seldom heard. In Rychagov's view, a great many mis-
takes were made in air force training because "we were afraid of crashes,

accidents, and incidents."[10] Proskurov understood this and was determined to create training programs for the bomber regiments that would
come as close as possible to approximating combat conditions. Still, he
had to deal with issues created by the bureaucratic machinery of the Defense Commissariat. At the end of December 1940, Proskurov attended the
conference on the way the German army functioned in the Polish and
French campaigns of 1939 and 1940. In early January, at one of the war
games, he played the role of a front air force commander on the Western
side. On January 29, 1941, he attended a meeting in Stalin's office presumably to discuss the games. Also present were Timoshenko, Semyon
Budenny, Kulik, Meretskov, Zhukov, Voroshilov, and others. The air forces
were represented by Rychagov, Pavel F. Zhigarev, and Proskurov.

Training remained Proskurov's major concern. The story is told that
when Proskurov inspected a bomber regiment at Zaporozhe, the commander reported that "his unit was ready to undertake any mission, day or
night, under any weather conditions." When midnight came Proskurov put
the brigade on alert, and he heard the same story from the commander.
When he then ordered the regiment to undertake a mission at the bombing
range at Rostov-on-Don, some 300 kilometers to the east, it turned out that
there were only ten aircrews in the entire regiment capable of the mission.
On their return flight three aircraft misjudged their altitude and crashed.[11]
The loss of aircraft during training affected not only the long-range bomber
regiments but the entire air force. At a meeting with Stalin in early April
1941, possibly the session at which Molotov and Zhdanov were also present, Rychagov attributed the accident rate to the fact that Stalin made the
aircrews fly in "coffins." Stalin replied, "You should not have said that."[12]
Rychagov had sealed his fate.

This was not the first time the problem of accidents plaguing the air
forces would arise at the highest levels of the party and government. For
example, in May 1939 the Main Military Council held a two-day session
that resulted in a lengthy order by the defense commissar on "Accidents in
Units of the Red Army's air forces." A draft of the order was circulated at
the council meeting, and comments were requested. Proskurov, then a
member of the council, formally objected to a paragraph on flight schools
that "eliminated training in aerial gunnery and high-altitude flights." He
insisted that such training be retained because it permitted instructors to
better evaluate trainees' ability.[13]

By April 9, 1941, the Politburo discussed the aerial accident rate. It asserted that not only was the rate not being reduced but it was increasing. Its report pointed out that two to three aircraft per day were being lost to crashes and that the leadership of the air forces did not seem ready or able to deal with the situation, nor could it enforce the flight rules. The cause of these accidents, according to an excerpt of the Politburo meeting, was "simply a lack of discipline." The report cited cases in which aircraft and lives were lost because unit commanders insisted on having their aircrews fly in bad weather. It singled out Rychagov for having attempted to conceal the lack of discipline and the laxity causing these accidents. The Politburo then issued a joint decree of the Central Committee of the VKP(b) and the Council of People's Commissars:

1. Remove Rychagov from his post as chief of the Red Army's air forces and as deputy people's commissar for defense, as he is undisciplined and unable to fulfill his responsibilities as chief of the air forces.
2. Send Colonel Mironov [chief of the operational flight section of the air forces staff] to trial for having given a criminal order, obviously disregarding the elemental rules of flight.
3. Place the discharge of the responsibilities of chief of the air forces of the Red Army on First Deputy Chief Comrade Zhigarev.
4. Propose that Timoshenko present to the Central Committee VKP(b) a draft order of the Main Military Council in the spirit of this decree.

Nowhere in the excerpt is the state of training of aircrews raised as a possible cause of the rise in the accident rate. This same excerpt from the Politburo protocol reprimanded Timoshenko for having attempted, in an April 8 report, to assist Rychagov in concealing shortcoming in the air forces.[14]

The next step in this deadly bureaucratic farce was a memorandum from Timoshenko to Stalin presenting the draft of an order to be issued by the Defense Commissariat in the name of the Main Military Council, as directed by the Politburo decree. The memorandum was signed by Timoshenko and Zhukov, as chief of the general staff. The date "12/IV/41" is written in by hand to the left of Timoshenko's signature line. The memorandum shows two attachments. The first is a draft order in five copies; the second is a draft order "with corrections" for Zhdanov and Malenkov, also in five copies. Over this copy of the memorandum, in a very bold hand, is a note to Timoshenko from Stalin: "I agree, with the proviso that in the order there be included a paragraph on Comrade Proskurov, that Comrade Proskurov also be tried along with Comrade Mironov. That would be the honest and just thing to do."[15]

Rychagov was dismissed on April 12, 1941, and enrolled in the General Staff Academy; he was replaced by his deputy, Zhigarev, who would later become a chief marshal of aviation.[16] As for Proskurov, that same day the Defense Commissariat issued Order No. 0022–41 relieving him of his position as deputy to the chief of the Red Army air forces. The order also sent Mironov and him to trial for giving a criminal order "violating the elementary rule of the flying service" and resulting in deaths and injuries. No trial was held, but the actions ascribed to Proskurov and Mironov were recorded in their personnel records as "obviously criminal behavior."[17]

Proskurov, however, was not one to remain silent for long. On April 21 he sent a memorandum to Stalin and Zhdanov "on the subject of aviation training for war." He recalled Stalin's conclusion following the Finnish war "that the troops had not been trained under conditions approaching those of combat" and pointed out that "the main shortcoming in aircrews' training . . . was their inability . . . to operate safely in poor weather conditions and at night." He noted their lack of adequate weapons training and intelligence preparation; most aircrews could not locate their targets even in large populated areas. Citing comments by reserve officers of the Civil Air Fleet who were specialists in night flights and instrument navigation, he said that "under existing flight rules in the air forces, they would not be able to fulfill the tasks given to them. The limitations are too great. They have visited aviation units and are convinced that the commanders have too great a fear of flying in poor weather or at night. At the same time, all understand that without realistic training we cannot do battle with a serious adversary. The task is clear: whatever happens, we must break down this fear and force the units of the air forces to train under conditions approaching actual combat."

Proskurov described how

> the Germans by tens and hundreds fly for considerable distances in poor weather conditions. Also, the English fly by the hundreds against heavily defended positions in poor weather and at night . . . and they fulfill their assigned tasks. When will our aviation be capable of safely carrying out similar mass flights? Are our pilots or aircraft worse than those abroad? This question, Comrade Stalin, has tormented me and other air force commanders. When I took over the leadership of long-range bomber aviation, I received a concrete task—during 1941 to make the units of long-range aviation capable

of carrying out combat missions at the maximum range of the aircraft in poor weather conditions and at night. As of December 1940, there were 2,000 aircrews in high-speed bombers. Only 231 flew at night; 138 could fly in poor weather conditions and 485 were trained in instrument flying. During the last four to five months of winter flight training, we worked intensively on raising the quality of flight training in high-speed bombers. We did so in poor flying weather, with limitations on fuel and lubricants and with poor motors (many aircraft have been or are still undergoing repairs). By the middle of April the figures cited above had CHANGED. Now 612 crew fly at night, 420 fly in poor weather conditions, and 963 crews have been trained for instrument flying. I understand, however, that this training is manifestly inadequate. The latest figures characterize the capabilities of the majority of crews to fly in poor weather and at night, but only from their own airfields. Training in real long-range flights is still in the future.

This turning point in the quality of training has been accompanied by a large increase in the number of flight accidents—serious accidents, and there are many, it is true, but the interests of the work demand that we continue to increase the intensity of flight work. . . . Serious warnings and orders . . . will force the command of the air forces to pull itself together but at the same time reinforce the fear of accidents and therefore reduce the tempo of quality training.

Dear Comrade Stalin, we have never in the history of aviation had a case where a commander was tried for poor training of a unit subordinate to him. Therefore, people involuntarily choose between the lesser of two evils and reason thus: 'For shortcomings in training I'll be reprimanded or, in the worst case, demoted, but for accidents or catastrophes I'll be tried.' Unfortunately, more than a few commanders reason this way. Such attitudes exist and will continue to exist until subordinate units are faced with the same responsibilities for combat training as for accidents. I am convinced of this as recently I have spent more time at the unit level.[18]

Proskurov's memorandum, which made it clear that the accidents were primarily the result of poor training, may well have had some effect on Stalin. On May 4, 1941, he signed a Politburo proposal that Comrade Bochkov, USSR procurator, review the cases of Proskurov and Mironov inasmuch as their past meritorious service in the Red Army argued for their sentences being limited to "a public reprimand."[19] Stalin's approval of this proposal probably occurred not because he regretted his actions but because the memorandum made him realize that Proskurov could be a dangerous opponent if provoked. He knew he could not control the man.

Poor Proskurov. His logic was impeccable but it contradicted Stalinist thinking. Accidents had to be blamed on someone, regardless of reasons; he and Rychagov were the scapegoats at hand. In Stalin's view, though, the net needed to be cast wider. Should not all those with Spanish connections be looked on with suspicion as members of a conspiracy to sabotage the air forces?

Once again Proskurov was without a job. Visiting him on June 18, 1941, his close friend and former navigator, Gavril M. Prokofev, found him in very poor spirits and assumed that his depression was connected to his failure to obtain a new assignment. Perhaps, but there were also sinister events in train during April, May, and June about which he would probably not have spoken to Prokofiev. A series of arrests were taking place that he knew would eventually center on the circle of air force officers who had fought with him in Spain. At first it had appeared that technical and engineering officers were the target, but then, on April 1, Ivan F. Sakrier, Doctor of Technical Sciences and chief of the Armaments Directorate of the Red Army's air forces was arrested.[20]

After Sakrier, it was the turn of Petr K. Nikonov, military engineer, first rank, who had been the chief of the Eighth Directorate of Red Army Aviation. Based on Sakrier's testimony, he was accused of participating in an anti-Soviet conspiracy but refused to admit to the charge.[21] A few days later another military engineer, Grigory F. Mikhno, was arrested. Under hostile interrogation, he admitted to having been recruited by Sakrier and having engaged in sabotage to disrupt armaments production for the air forces.[22]

On May 18 another technical officer, Colonel Georgy M. Shevchenko, chief of the Scientific-Testing Proving Ground for Aviation Armaments of the air forces, was arrested. He was accused of membership in an anti-Soviet conspiracy on the basis not only of Sakrier's testimony but of later testimony by Aleksandr D. Loktionov and Rychagov, who would be arrested on June 19 and 24, respectively. Both were former chiefs of the Red Army's air forces.[23]

On May 23 Major General Aleksandr I. Filin, chief of the Scientific Research Institute of the Red Army Air Forces was arrested. This time the testimony of Yakov V. Smushkevich, Spanish veteran and twice a Hero of the Soviet Union, and of Grigory M. Shtern, former chief of PVO (National Air Defense) and one-time chief Soviet adviser in Spain, was used in accusing Filin of sabotage. Filin made no admissions.[24]

Now Stalin's assault on Spanish civil war veterans began in earnest. On

May 30, Major General of Aviation Ernst G. Shakht was arrested, perhaps partly as a result of Proskurov's April 21 memorandum criticizing earlier training procedures. In early May the Politburo decreed that the air force commanders of the Orlov and Moscow Military Districts, Major General P. A. Kotov and Lieutenant General Petr I. Pumpur, be relieved because the state of combat training in their districts was unsatisfactory; the decree read: "The pilots flew very little; they had not mastered night and high-altitude flights, weapons firing, aerial combat, and bombing." Kotov ended up as an instructor in a military academy and survived. Pumpur did not. On May 27 he was accused of having tried to make Shakht, "who was considered untrustworthy and a suspicious character," his deputy. The Politburo asked Anatoly N. Mikheev, head of military counterintelligence, to investigate Shakht.[25] Born in Switzerland of German parents who supported the Russian Revolution, Shakht came to the Soviet Union in 1922 and two years later completed the Borisoglebsky Aviation School. During the 1930s he commanded an aviation unit that supported the Red Army Air Forces Directorate and often piloted for its commander, Yakov I. Alksnis, who was later executed as an enemy of the people. In 1936 Shakht volunteered for service in Spain and commanded the First Bombardment Squadron (his replacement in that command was Proskurov). His friendship with Alksnis and his service in Spain, "where he certainly made contact with Germans," combined with his foreign birth and his German parentage, were sufficient evidence for the NKGB Military Counterintelligence Service to confirm his guilt.

Pumpur, a Hero of the Soviet Union who had commanded fighter aviation in Spain, was arrested on June 1, two days after Shakht. On June 4, 1941, the Politburo issued a decree that "satisfied an NKGB request that before the Pumpur case was tried in court it be turned over to the NKGB for investigation." Extreme physical torture produced the desired admission from Pumpur that he had been recruited into an anti-Soviet conspiracy plot by Yakov V. Smushkevich. Pumpur later repudiated his "confession."[26]

The arrest of Nikolai N. Vasilchenko, the assistant inspector general of the Red Army air forces, took place on June 1. The testimony used against him came from former military intelligence chiefs Uritsky, Berzin, and Orlov, all victims of the 1937–38 purges. On June 4 Major General of Aviation Pavel P. Yusupov, assistant chief of staff of the Red Army air forces, was arrested. He admitted to having been recruited by Smushkevich into an anti-Soviet military conspiracy in 1939. Other members of the conspiracy included Fedor K. Arzhenukhin (a lieutenant general of aviation), Rychagov, and Volodin. On June 6 the NKGB returned to the technical staff and arrested Volko Ya. Tsilov, a military engineer, first rank, and section chief of the Scientific-Testing Proving Ground for Aviation Armaments. He admitted to having been recruited by Shevchenko into a conspiracy to sabotage the production of new arms for the air forces. Also arrested on June 6 was Sergei G. Onisko, a military engineer, first rank, who was a department chief of the Scientific-Testing Proving Ground for Aviation Armaments. He, too, was found guilty, on the basis of Shevchenko's testimony, of sabotaging the aviation armaments program.[27]

Major General Aleksandr A. Levin, deputy commander of the air forces of the Leningrad Military District, was arrested on June 7. Arrested by the Cheka back in 1918 on suspicion of anti-Soviet activity, he had left the party in 1921 because he disagreed with Lenin's New Economic Policy. Reinstated in 1932, he commanded the Stalingrad School for Military Pilots, where he taught Alksnis. Levin remained a close friend until the end. Proskurov, too, trained at the Stalingrad school while he was director. Levin was accused of having been a spy by testimony from Shakht and of participating in an anti-Soviet conspiracy by the testimony of others, including Rychagov. In throwing Levin in with this group of aviation officers and technical personnel, the NKGB investigators may have been counting on his early record to strengthen their case.[28]

The same day, June 7, Colonel General Grigory M. Shtern, Hero of the Soviet Union, who succeeded Jan Berzin as chief Soviet military adviser to the Spanish republican government, was arrested. Shtern had served in the Far East, where he participated in battles with the Japanese at Lake Khasan and then at Khalkin Gol. He also commanded the Eighth Army in the Finnish war, after which he returned to the Far East. On March 19, 1941, he was appointed head of National Air Defense (PVO), which had earlier been virtually ignored by the Soviet leadership. Shtern's arrest left the PVO leaderless at a critical time. (It would not get a new chief until June 19, when Nikolai N. Voronov was moved in from the Artillery Directorate, to which he returned in July.) Some believe that the arrest was prompted by the failure of PVO to challenge an unauthorized flight of a German transport plane into Moscow's airspace on May 15. This seems unlikely. Rather, Shtern's arrest had been planned in advance, part of a broader program to eliminate the most outspoken of Soviet military leaders and to blame them for problems in military aviation. In Shtern's case, the crime was speaking of Stalin's scandalous neglect of air defense.[29]

Evidence that scapegoating of armaments industry officials had reached its zenith came when the people's commissar for armaments, Boris L. Vannikov, was himself arrested on June 7 and relieved of his position two days later. In his memoirs Vannikov recalls Stalin's comment to him that "there are many scoundrels among military engineers. . . . They will soon be arrested." Criticizing his own behavior and that of many of his colleagues, Vannikov writes, "We did not display firmness or adhere to principles, we fulfilled requests that we knew would be harmful to the state. Here we displayed not only discipline but a desire to avoid repression."[30]

The arrest on June 8 of Yakov V. Smushkevich demonstrated that this was a planned operation and not a spur-of-the-moment action. Smushkevich was in the hospital recovering from an operation on his leg necessitated, ironically, by injuries suffered in a 1938 air crash when Stalin honored him for his service in Spain by naming him commander of the May Day air parade. Smushkevich's arrest was a major event. He was well known, respected, and admired not only by his air forces colleagues but by others in the armed forces and the civilian government. Zhukov, under whom Smushkevich ran the air forces in the battle of Khalkin Gol, thought highly of his ability as a commander and pilot. Admiral Nikolai G. Kuznetsov, who had been naval adviser in Spain, knew him well and placed great trust in him, as well as in Shtern, Rychagov, and Proskurov. Aleksey I. Shakhurin, commissar of the aviation industry during the war, speaks warmly of Smushkevich in his memoirs.[31]

The arrests continued. On June 17 Konstantin M. Gusev, commander of the air forces of the Far Eastern Front, was apprehended. He was accused of having been involved in an anti-Soviet military conspiracy by Smushkevich but refused to confess. His arrest was followed by that of Aleksandr D. Loktionov, former commander of the Baltic Military District and head of the Red Army's air forces. It seems likely that Loktionov's arrest was related to Stalin's displeasure at Loktionov's responses to questions Stalin put to him at a March 1938 meeting of senior air force officers and members of the party and government leadership. The meeting, which took place during the purges, dealt with air accidents. Loktionov's replies emphasized the problems caused by the loss of experienced commanders, their replacement by younger, untrained officers, and the unsatisfactory condition of aircraft delivered to air units. Stalin bullied Loktionov but Loktionov did not change his story. As we saw in Proskurov's case, Stalin never forgot a person whom he could not dominate.[32] Arrested the same day as Loktionov was Pavel A. Alekseev, deputy commander of the air forces of the Baltic Military District. Under interrogation he admitted that he had been recruited into an anti-Soviet military conspiracy by Loktionov; others involved in the alleged conspiracy were Smushkevich, Sakrier, Filin, Pumpur, and Gusev. Alekseev confessed to having sabotaged the arming of the air forces by accepting incomplete and inadequate aircraft from builders and delaying the provision of air units with new equipment.[33]

On June 19, just three days before the Nazi onslaught, the orgy of arrests came to a temporary halt. By this time it must have become evident to Beria and NKGB chief Merkulov, whose investigative unit was responsible for these cases, that the Germans were up to something. Reports from the border troops on the movement of Wehrmacht units ever closer to the state frontier and the dramatic increase in Luftwaffe reconnaissance overflights could not be ignored. Nevertheless, the interrogations of those arrested during April, May, and June went on. One group consisted of technical specialists, some of whom were already confessing to having sabotaged the armaments program of the air forces. The second group was made up of general officers of the Red Army Air Forces, as well as Colonel General Shtern, who had headed PVO. Of this latter group, several had served in the Spanish civil war. Had they remained at liberty, they would have continued in service and risen higher in rank but would also have been unwelcome witnesses in any subsequent inquiry into the performance of the air forces.

As for Proskurov, as of June 18 he still had no assignment. His friend Prokofev, who was visiting, claims he overheard one side of a telephone conversation in which Proskurov pleaded with Stalin for a job, any job, even in Odessa. After he hung up, Proskurov complained that it was "the bald one" (Timoshenko) who had told Stalin that he was being "capricious, disdainfully rejecting numerous offers of appointments."[34] Unbeknownst to him, on May 30, 1941, Major General B. P. Belov, chief of the Personnel Directorate of the Red Army air forces, had sent a top-secret memorandum to Pavel F. Zhigarev, Rychagov's replacement as chief of Red Army air forces. The subject was "The Confirmation of Hero of the Soviet Union Lieutenant General of Aviation Ivan Iosifovich Proskurov as Chief of the Air Forces and Chief of the Aviation Department of the Seventh Army." The memorandum read in part: "Proskurov was relieved of his position of assistant chief of the Chief Directorate of Red Army air forces by Order No. 0022–41 of the Defense Commissar because of accidents in the units of bomber aviation. . . . I consider the employment of Comrade Proskurov as chief of the air forces of an army, and specifically as chief of the air forces of the Seventh Army, necessary. . . . I hereby apply for confirmation of

Comrade Proskurov as chief of the air forces and chief of the Aviation Department of the Seventh Army."[35] This was apparently the assignment for which Proskurov had been waiting. It was a demotion, but he had said he would accept any position, "even in Odessa." Why then, on June 4, was Belov deprived of his rank as major general of aviation for "violating procedures in the selection of cadres and placing in leadership positions unproven and politically doubtful people"?[36] There seems to have been some confusion about Proskurov's appointment as head of aviation of the Seventh Army, which at the time was subordinate to the Leningrad Military District. Was he one of the "unproven and politically doubtful people" whom Belov recommended?

While all these arrests were taking place, Stalin continued to deceive himself about German intentions and to deprive his country of the very officers it needed on the eve of the invasion. Meanwhile, Proskurov, apparently unaware of Belov's fate, heard on June 19 that he was to head the Seventh Army, then stationed in Petrozavodsk, northeast of Leningrad. He planned to leave for his new assignment on Sunday evening, June 22.

On the Eve

On Friday, June 20, with rumors of an imminent German attack growing more persistent, Proskurov decided to visit military intelligence headquarters and get the facts. There is no indication he spent any time there with his successor, Filipp I. Golikov. This is not surprising, as Golikov's reputation for manipulating intelligence information to conform to Stalin's theories was by this time well known to most of the RU officers. Instead, Proskurov went to the office of Colonel Ivan A. Bolshakov, who headed the German desk.[1] Proskurov's purpose was obviously to discuss the situation with officers who had been handling information reports from the field—from the RU components and other intelligence and security services, including the NKGB Foreign Intelligence Service. He probably would have been particularly interested in the report from source Brand of the RU Helsinki residency on Finnish mobilization measures.[2] Perhaps of even greater interest would have been the report by Admiral Arseny G. Golovko, commander of the Northern Fleet, concerning the overflight on June 17 of the fleet base at Polyarnyi by German aircraft flying at very low altitude. Antiaircraft batteries were ordered to open fire but did not. When the admiral asked a battery commander why he disobeyed the order, he was told that the troops had been warned for so long to avoid provocations that they were afraid to act.[3] Proskurov could have been reminded of an incident on June 18 in which fear of being accused of spreading panic affected the way in which a German defector's information was handled. The defector, who had struck a superior officer and feared a court martial, had appeared in the area of the Fifteenth Rifle Corps, at Kovel, in the northwest corner of the Ukrainian SSR. He stated that the Wehrmacht would attack at 4:00 a.m. on June 22. When the corps commander reported this information to his superior, he was told, "You're sounding the alarm in vain."[4]

Proskurov might well have seen the startling report from Starshina, the NKGB's source in the German Air Ministry, that "all the preparations by Germany for an armed attack on the Soviet Union have been completed, and the blow can be expected at any time." This report was received at 6:00 a.m. on Monday, June 16 and by midday had been disseminated to the Central Committee. It was sent to Stalin and Molotov on June 17 under a letter of transmittal from People's Commissar for State Security Merkulov. We know that Pavel M. Fitin, who prepared the formal report sent to Stalin by Merkulov, took care to see that his reports were sent to the RU.

Proskurov was probably also shown two reports by Richard Sorge from June 15, one declaring that "the war will start in late June," the other that "the attack will occur along a broad front at dawn on June 22."[5] He may also have been shown reports from border troop units. One such report, dated June 18, described the movement of German troops into jump-off positions. (Postwar examination of German documents confirmed that divisions of the First Echelon of the German forces began to move at night into their attack positions at this time.)[6]

One report that Proskurov probably never saw but that as an aviator he would have greatly appreciated was prepared by Colonel G. N. Zakharov, commander of the Forty-third Fighter Division, who had made a reconnaissance flight of the entire length of the border during the daylight hours of June 19. He reported to his superiors, Dimitry G. Pavlov and Ivan I. Kopets, that the evidence was indisputable: the Germans were getting ready to attack in the very near future. Pavlov and Kopets rejected that conclusion and the report was never sent.[7] The failure to forward it is inexplicable. A reconnaissance flight at this time would have told Red Army defenders a great deal about the nature and location of the forces poised to attack them. Whereas the Germans normally maintained a high degree of camouflage discipline, some actions that were hard to conceal, such as moving river-crossing equipment into place, were necessary if the attack was to take place as scheduled.

Although he could not have seen this particular report, Proskurov heard and saw enough during his visit to alert him to the imminent danger facing his aircraft. While still at military intelligence headquarters, he went to a secret communications telephone and called the chief of staff of the Seventh Army's air forces. He told him of the near certainty of a German invasion in the next few days and ordered him to move all aircraft to reserve fields at once. He gave this order even though Stalin had expressly forbidden any actions that the Germans might consider a provocation.[8]

Proskurov spent Saturday, June 21, preparing for his departure. The city seemed deserted as many Muscovites took advantage of the beautiful early summer weather to leave for the weekend. The next day, Proskurov, his wife, Aleksandra Ignatievna, and his two daughters, ages eight and fourteen, planned to have a picnic, but for some reason Proskurov kept delaying their heading out. At noon, Molotov went on the air to describe the fighting that had been under way since dawn. This was the first most people heard of the German attack and the shock was palpable. Proskurov left immediately for the Defense Commissariat. He returned later in the afternoon, picked up his gear, and said good-bye to his daughters. Then he and his wife went to the train station and he departed. His family never saw him again.

At the Liubianka, the week of June 16 began for Pavel M. Fitin with the arrival of the message from Berlin containing the prediction by Starshina that the attack would come at any moment. Korsikanets added to the impact of the report by listing the German officials assigned to occupation duties in various Soviet cities and ended by quoting Alfred Rosenberg, who gave this group their final instructions: "The very idea of the Soviet Union must be wiped from the map!"[9] This report was sent to Stalin on June 17 by People's Commissar for State Security Vsevolod N. Merkulov. After Stalin read it he ordered Merkulov and Fitin to report to him in his Kremlin office. An article in *Krasnaia Zvezda* describing their visit puts the time as 12:00 noon on June 17. This is strange because the journal registering Stalin's visitors that day indicates that no one was received by Stalin until Molotov arrived at 8:15 p.m. Then at 8:20 p.m. Merkulov and his deputy, Bogdan Z. Kobulov, arrived, remaining until 9:00 p.m. There is no mention of Fitin. It would have been most unusual, in any event, for Stalin to have come to his Kremlin office by noon from his dacha at Kuntsevo. The times of Stalin's arrival at his Kremlin office in the week leading up to the German invasion varied, but the earliest hour noted in the journal is 4:00 p.m. Other historians have confirmed that it was Stalin's habit to come to the office in the evening hours, work late into the night, and return to his dacha toward morning to sleep.[10] This incident and others cause us to question the degree to which the journal accurately reflected all of Stalin's visitors. As for the Merkulov-Kobulov visit, that may have been related to the report, also sent to Stalin on June 17 by Merkulov, on the results of the operation to remove some 40,178 "anti-Soviet, criminal, and socially dangerous" persons from Lithuania, Latvia, and Estonia. Merkulov was apparently absent from Moscow from June 11 to June 17. His absence was probably caused by his involvement in the planning and execution of this operation. Kobulov acted for Merkulov during his absence.[11]

In any case, when Merkulov and Fitin arrived at Stalin's office, his secretary said only, "He is waiting for you." Stalin greeted them with a nod; he did not ask them to be seated and remained standing himself. Merkulov said not a word, leaving it to Fitin to explain the background of the report. Stalin termed it "disinformation" and directed them to check its veracity and give him the results.[12] Fitin returned to his office and called in Pavel M. Zhuravliev, chief of the German Department; Mikhail A. Allakhverdov, head of the newly formed Information Section of the department; Zoia Rybkina; and Yelena D. Modrzhinskaia, an NKGB intelligence officer in Warsaw.[13] He briefed them on the session with Stalin and ordered them to review all the reporting from Starshina and Korsikanets. On the basis of their review, they put together a so-called *Kalendar* of reports, beginning in September 1940, that included the date of each report, the source and subsources, and a précis of the contents. By including the names and job descriptions of the subsources, the analysis demonstrated that Starshina and Korsikanets had access to a wide circle of well-placed collaborators. From the *Kalendar,* which Zhuravliev and the others finished on Friday, June 20, it was evident that as of the summer of 1940 the Germans had every intention of invading the USSR in the spring or early summer of 1941. When Fitin read it he must have realized that Merkulov would never send it on to Stalin because it completely contradicted the his conviction that Hitler would not attack. Consequently, Fitin sent it back to the German Department with this note to the chief: "Comrade Zhuravliev: You keep this. P. Fitin."[14]

Meanwhile, on Thursday, June 19, Fitin's German Department was overwhelmed by a lengthy report from the Belorussian NKGB providing details on final preparations for a German assault. It was normal practice for Fitin's directorate to use such information in summary reports disseminated to the Council of People's Commissars and the Central Committee VKP(b).[15] They put the work on the summary aside when they received a cable from the Berlin NKGB residency containing an alarming report from one of Berlin's oldest and most reliable agents, Wilhelm Lehmann (code name Breitenbach). Lehmann, a Berlin police officer, had been a Soviet agent since September 1929. In 1930 he was transferred to the police element working against the Soviet presence in Berlin. When the Nazis came to power, he found himself in the counterintelligence element of the Reich Main Security Office (RSHA). Because of his reporting on Gestapo counterintelligence efforts, which by 1939 amounted to fourteen volumes in NKVD archives, the Berlin residency was able to protect its operations and run them securely. He was also responsible for security and counterintelligence operations in the German armaments industry. His reporting was considered so valuable that from 1934 to 1937 he was handled by Vasily M. Zarubin, one of the NKVD's most celebrated illegals. (He was better known in the United States under the name Zubilin when he served there as resident from 1941 to 1944.) In 1935 and 1936, Zarubin amazed Moscow when he forwarded reports from Lehmann on the experimental work on rockets being done by Wernher von Braun and others.[16]

In 1939 the sudden death of the Berlin resident, Aleksandr I. Agaiants, resulted in the loss of contact with Lehmann. It was reestablished in September 1940 by Aleksandr M. Korotkov, who became deputy resident. Lehmann, who had risen to become a Hauptsturmführer in the Gestapo, was still responsible for the security of defense industries throughout Germany. After recontact, he was turned over a new case officer, Boris N. Zhuravliev (code name Nikolai). So high was the regard in which the service held Lehmann that on September 9, 1940, Beria himself sent a telegram to Berlin outlining the security rules for handling this valuable source. Because of his position, Lehmann was able to furnish the residency with copies of virtually every document of interest produced by his department of the RSHA. On June 10, 1941, for example, he delivered to his case officer a secret report by RSHA chief Reinhard Heydrich on "Soviet Subversive Activities against Germany." The real blockbuster, however, was his report on June 19 of information received by his Gestapo unit that Germany would attack the USSR on June 22 at 3:00 a.m. The information was considered so important by the residency that it was sent by cable that same evening through the ambassador's channel to ensure it would reach Moscow as quickly as possible. Apparently this report, like so many others, was considered "false and a provocation." How could this have happened? Lehmann's years of service and the value of his reporting were well known even to Beria. Obviously, Beria had no intention of confronting Stalin over the report, and so it must have been suppressed.[17]

After the war began, Lehmann's case officer, Zhuravliev, returned to the Soviet Union along with the other members of the Soviet embassy. Contact was lost, and although Moscow Center tried several times to get back in touch by parachuting radio operators into Germany, nothing seemed to work. From U.S. Army records it appears that one of these radio operators was doubled and gave the Gestapo the parole for making contact with Lehmann. The Gestapo sent one of its own men, who held several meetings with Lehmann, posing as an RU agent. He received secret Gestapo information intended for the Soviets from Lehmann, who was arrested and executed in secrecy. His colleagues were told he had been killed in the line of duty in East Prussia. Lehmann's wife was given the same story and she duly received her widow's pension. The Germans were evidently determined to keep secret the fact that Lehmann had been a Soviet agent.[18]

Over the weekend of June 21–22 Fitin went to his dacha near Tarasovka, west of Moscow. Early on Sunday morning, he received a telephone call from the NKGB ordering him to return to Moscow immediately. As his car headed toward Moscow, he encountered groups of high school students celebrating their graduation. At the sight of them, he asked himself, "Was Starshina wrong?" When he entered the building, the duty officer told him that German troops had crossed the border with the USSR. People were still reluctant to say *war*. Strangely, at these words, Fitin felt himself the happiest of men. Although it was certainly unusual for anyone to greet war in a happy state of mind, Fitin knew that if he had been wrong about Starshina, he would no longer be among the living.[19]

It is difficult to know what the chief of the RU general staff, Filipp I. Golikov, was up to in the days before the invasion. The last RU special report for which we have an archival reference was dated May 31, 1941, for the period up to June 1. It maintained the fiction that England was Germany's main target. It was followed by two special reports on Romania. In the period between June 15 and the beginning of the war, we have five reports from RU residencies reflecting archival documents. Marginal comments on two of them indicate Golikov was active. One, dated June 15, was a report from source Ostvald of the RU residency in Helsinki on the arrival at Finnish ports of two motorized German infantry divisions that were then shipped to the north of the country by train. No fewer than 2,000 motor vehicles and 10,000 motorized infantry and special troops were concentrated in the area of Rovaniemi, in central Finland.[20] Finland declared war on the USSR on June 26.

The report on German troops in Finland was followed by two reports from Sorge in Tokyo on June 17. The first said the Japanese had not yet had a response from the Americans to the Japanese offer to negotiate or a clarification of the American proposal to mediate in the Chinese conflict. Foreign Minister Yosuke Matsuoka asked Ambassador Eugen Ott to relay to Ribbentrop his concern over rumors of an impending German-Soviet war. He saw a German occupation of England, rather than war with the USSR, as the only way to keep America out of European affairs. The second Sorge report predicted that a war between Germany and the USSR was being delayed until the end of June. He noted that the German embassy had sent a report to Berlin stating that in the event of a German-Soviet war, it would require six weeks for the Japanese to begin an offensive against the Soviet Far East; the embassy believed, however, that it would take them longer.[21]

On June 20 a report from Kosta, a source of the Sofia RU residency, reported a conversation with the senior German representative, who stated that hostilities were expected on the June 21 or 22. Another report arrived from Sorge in RU Tokyo on June 20 stating that the German ambassador believed war between with the USSR was inevitable. This cable was handled by Mikhail F. Panfilov, deputy chief of the Information Department, not by Golikov.[22]

In a 1969 article entitled "The Lessons of War," Golikov insisted that the most important of all reports was "Report No. 5 of June 15, 1941, which gave precise figures for the German troops facing each of our border regions—Baltic, Western, and Kiev—from 400 kilometers deep into German territory. We also knew the strength of the German troops in Romania and Finland." Golikov continued: "From the RU intelligence reports we knew the date of the invasion, and every time Hitler put it off (mainly because his troops were not ready), we reported this to our leaders. We found out and reported all the strategic blueprints for the attack against the USSR drafted by the German general staff, the main one being the notorious Barbarossa plan." As there is no archival reference to "Report No. 5," it seems probable that it is a creature of Golikov's imagination. Likewise his claim for its handling, given his usual treatment of RU reporting.[23]

While Stalin still placed his trust in Hitler, many Soviet senior officials were seriously concerned over the growing evidence of German intentions to invade the Soviet Union. The border troops, for example, must have been persuaded of the danger by their own excellent reporting because on June 20, the chief of the Belorussian border troops district issued an order aimed at strengthening border defenses. All training exercises were to be canceled until June 30; personnel involved in such exercises were to return to their units, and all leaves were canceled. Border troop posts at the most vulnerable points in the line were to be reinforced and strengthened.[24]

Timoshenko, who in May 1940 had replaced Voroshilov as defense commissar, had instituted a series of reforms, including the creation of nine new mechanized corps in July 1940 and the authorization of twenty more in February 1941, but it became apparent that these new units were "understrength in manpower, equipment, and logistical support," their personnel "largely untrained." These deficiencies existed throughout the Red Army, particularly in the western border military districts, and were exacerbated by Stalin's refusal to accept the intelligence reports of German troop deployment along the Soviet frontier. Neither Timoshenko's reform programs nor preparations to meet the German threat could succeed given the paralysis imposed on the military leadership by Stalin's indecision.[25]

With the situation on the border growing more alarming, in April and May 1941 the general staff had quietly moved individual units from the Far East and other military districts to the west. Although Stalin had rejected as provocative Timoshenko and Zhukov's idea of a preventive attack (there is no record that Stalin actually received a copy of the plan, but Timoshenko and Zhukov discussed the concept with him), by mid-May he allowed them to move twenty-eight divisions, nine corps headquarters, and four army headquarters to the border districts. These armies were to take up their positions in the Kiev and Western Special Military Districts by June 1–10. Three additional armies were to be deployed to the west, but only one had reached the outskirts of Moscow by June 22. Although close to 800,000 conscripts were called up, they were inadequately supplied. The extraordinary delay in moving these covering forces into place and providing them with the weapons, equipment, and transport they needed would be a crucial factor in the days ahead.[26]

Commanders of troops already deployed along the frontier were aware of the growing danger and tried to obtain from Timoshenko and Zhukov permission to take measures locally to increase combat readiness. Their requests were turned down. Whenever an individual commander risked taking actions he felt would improve his defenses, there was a good chance the NKGB special counterintelligence departments assigned to every troop unit or the local border troops would notice and report him to Moscow. One June 11, for example, Mikhail P. Kirponos, commanding the Kiev Special Military District, received a telegram from Zhukov demanding an explanation for a report that the chiefs of the fortified area units had received orders to occupy forward defensive positions. In a report to the defense commissar, Kirponos was to explain "on what basis the units of the fortified areas of his district received an order to occupy these forward positions." Such actions, Zhukov informed him, "can provoke the Germans to armed conflict and are fraught with all kinds of consequences. . . . Immediately cancel this order and report who gave this unauthorized order." Kirponos received a second message from Zhukov the same day directing him to confirm the execution of Zhukov's order and to report back by June 16.[27] In another instance, Zhukov learned that Fedor I. Kuznetsov, the commanding general of the Baltic Special Military District, had raised the level of readiness of his air defense system "without the sanction of the defense commissar." Zhukov ordered the change in the level of readiness rescinded because the actions involved—which included enforcement of blackout in the cities of the district—could "cause damage to industry, give rise to various rumors, and upset the public."[28]

After the war Timoshenko and Zhukov explained that Stalin had "strictly warned them of the necessity when improving defenses of taking maximum precautions in order not to provoke the Germans into armed conflict."[29] They both knew the dangers inherent in opposing Stalin. It is ironic that on June 16 Stalin signed a decree as chairman of the Council of People's Commissars and secretary of the Central Committee of the VKP(b) complaining that "the provision of armaments to fortified areas under construction is proceeding unsatisfactorily" and ordering various military districts and industrial enterprises to meet a deadline of no later than the first quarter of 1942.[30]

There can be little doubt that both Timoshenko and Zhukov were fully aware of the importance of camouflage in protecting aircraft, airfields, and support structures. It would not be until June 19, however, that Stalin would sign a decree calling for camouflage of aircraft, runways, tents, and airfield support structures and directing the chief of the air forces, Pavel F. Zhigarev, to complete these tasks by July 30, 1941. The same day, June 19, Timoshenko and Zhukov signed an order implementing the decree but extending it to cover ground forces weapons (tanks, artillery, etc.), transport, warehouses, and other structures. The order made clear that the purpose of camouflage was to ensure that "airfields and the aircraft stationed there do not attract attention from the air."[31] These directives were too little and too late. Everyone from Stalin on down to the Defense Commissariat, the general staff, the border troops, the military districts, and those officials in the People's Commissariat for Foreign Affairs who had to prepare and present protests knew full well that the Luftwaffe had been carrying out an extensive reconnaissance program over Soviet territory for the past year.

The offices of the Operations Directorate of the general staff offered a stark contrast to the quiet, sunny streets and parks of the capital. Telephones were busy as staff officers from the military districts and major commands called in with reports from their front-line units of German troops now concentrated directly on the border and preparing to attack. Changes were still being made in front organizations, and other assignments were under consideration. A draft decree in preparation on June 21 called for creation of a Southern Front, to be commanded by the commanding general of the Moscow Military District, Ivan V. Tyulenev, and with headquarters in Vinnitsa, in the southeastern Ukraine. The member of the front's Military Council would be Aleksandr I. Zaporozhets, who had been head of the Chief Directorate for Political Propaganda of the Red Army; he would be replaced in that position by Lev Z. Mekhlis, a devoted Stalinist, who would retain his position as People's Commissar of State Control. The last two paragraphs evidently assumed war was imminent because they entrusted Zhukov with overall leadership of the Western and Southwestern Fronts and Kiril A. Meretskov with responsibility for the Northern Front. This draft, signed by Malenkov on June 21, was very strange as regards the Zhukov and Meretskov assignments. Zhukov, still chief of the general staff, was not sent to Kiev to check on the Southwestern Front until the afternoon of June 22. It would not be until June 26 that Stalin recalled him to Moscow and sent him to the Western Front, where he stayed until June 30 interviewing members of the front staff. How could Malenkov had known in advance what Zhukov would be doing on June 22 and 26–30?[32]

The case of Meretskov is even stranger. As a former Soviet adviser in the Spanish civil war, he had already been mentioned in the continuing interrogations of civil war veterans arrested in April, May, and June 1941. Was his assignment as a high command representative to the Northern Front for real (he did, after all, have considerable experience fighting Finns), or was it a trick to get him out of Moscow and arrest him later?[33]

Between 6:00 and 7:00 p.m. on June 21, Stalin, Molotov, and other members of the Politburo gathered at Stalin's Kremlin apartment. According to Anastas Mikoyan, who was there, "the atmosphere was tense. Stalin still held to the view that Hitler would not begin a war."[34] About 9:00 p.m. Zhukov, who was in the general staff offices, received a call from

Maksim A. Purkayev, chief of staff of the Kiev Special Military District, reporting that a German deserter had just come over with disquieting news. The deserter, one Alfred H. Liskow of the Twenty-second Engineer Regiment, testified that on June 21 his platoon commander, a Lieutenant Schulz, explained to the soldiers that that night, after artillery preparation, the river Bug would be crossed with rafts, boats, and pontoons. Liskow, who apparently considered himself a Communist and a supporter of Soviet power, decided to flee and report the news. At this, Stalin ordered Timoshenko and Zhukov to come to the Kremlin. He was suspicious, though, asking whether "the Germans might have sent him over to provoke us." The others believed the report and prevailed on Stalin to bring the troops to combat readiness "just in case." Stalin insisted on caution in formulating the order.[35] While those assembled were debating whether to send a warning message, at 10:00 p.m. the chief of staff of the Baltic Special Military District, P. S. Klenov, reported that the Germans had completed the construction of bridges across the river Neman, they had evacuated all civilians from an area up to twenty kilometers from the border, and their troops had apparently occupied jump-off positions for an invasion. In addition, the chief of staff of the Western Special Military District, V. E. Klimovskikh, reported that the German barbed wire entanglements that had been present earlier in the day had been removed in the evening, while in the nearby woods the sound of motors could be heard.[36]

This is what those assembled at the Kremlin finally agreed on:

I am transmitting an order of the people's commissar of defense for immediate execution:

1. On June 22–23 1941, it is possible there will be a surprise attack by the Germans on the fronts of the LVO [Leningrad Military District], PriBOVO [Baltic Special Military District], ZapOVO [Western Special Military District], KOVO [Kiev Special Military District], and OdVO [Odessa Military District]. The attack may start with provocative actions.

2. The task of our troops is to not respond to any provocative actions that might result in serious complications. At the same time, the troops of the LVO, PriBOVO, ZapOVO, KOVO, and OdVO, must be in full combat readiness to meet a sudden blow by the Germans or their allies. I ORDER:

a. During the night of June 22, 1941, secretly occupy firing positions in the fortified areas along the state frontier.

b. Before dawn on June 22, 1941, disperse to reserve airfields all aviation, including troop aircraft, carefully camouflaging it.

c. All units bring themselves to combat readiness. Troops are to be kept dispersed and camouflaged.

d. Bring air defense to combat readiness without calling on additional staff. Prepare all measures for blackout of cities and installations.

3. Take no other measures without special permission.

Although this document was signed by Zhukov on June 21, it was not received in the signal center until 1:45 a.m. on June 22 and was not sent to the troops until 2:25–2:35 a.m. It remains one of the strangest military orders in history. Instead of delivering a straightforward warning and a code-word order to execute defensive plans, it quibbled about provocative actions. The result was that many units did not receive the order at all and were taken by surprise.[37] Stalin and his visitors continued to discuss the situation but most of them left by 10:20 p.m. Beria, at 11:00 p.m., was the last to leave. Stalin followed later, returning to the Kuntsevo dacha at about 1:00 a.m. He went right to bed but would be awakened within a few hours by Zhukov's telling him that the war had begun.[38]

CHAPTER **21**

A Summer of Torture

At dawn on Sunday, June 22, 1941, the Germans invaded the USSR. It would take Stalin, who had rejected as disinformation the scores of intelligence reports predicting the attack, several hours, even days, before he could bring himself to acknowledge war's reality. He would never admit that Hitler had successfully deceived him. Much of his concern, as the Red Army suffered its tragic losses on the battlefields, would be to ensure that others, then in prison, who knew or suspected the truth of his culpability would never live to testify against him.

Although the exact date and even the hour of the German invasion had been reported by Soviet intelligence sources, it was only the arrival of a German deserter on the evening of June 21 that finally alerted the Kremlin to the reality of a Wehrmacht attack at dawn the next day. The deserter was immediately brought to the headquarters of the Ninetieth Border Troop Detachment in Vladimir-Volynsk, on the border of German-occupied Poland. Even before the interrogation was finished, all could hear the sound of artillery fire. The commander tried to call out, but the telephone lines had already been cut. This was the work of the hundreds of saboteurs dispatched by the Abwehr in the days before the attack or dropped from aircraft that night.[1]

The artillery fire heard by the border troop detachment commander was repeated along the entire western border of the USSR from the Baltic to the Black Sea. Masses of German armor and infantry moved into the

Soviet Union toward their assigned objectives. In accordance with operational plans drawn up on the basis of aerial photos obtained during a year of unopposed photo reconnaissance, the Luftwaffe sent its aircraft against Red Army air bases, command centers, warehouses, troop concentrations, and other targets, destroying the heart of the air capability of the border military districts and giving the Germans complete air superiority. Thereafter they were able not only to continue their precision attacks against well-defined strategic and tactical targets on the ground but also to support their advancing columns by strafing those Soviet units trying desperately to hold off the enemy.

As news of the German assault by land, sea, and air reached the general staff, Zhukov called Stalin. When he finally got through to him, there was a long silence, with only the sound of heavy breathing on the other end. At last Stalin responded. He asked Zhukov to tell his secretary, Aleksandr N. Poskrebyshev, to assemble the Politburo for a meeting at the Kremlin. Meanwhile, the general staff informed all military districts and major commands of what was happening. At 5:45 a.m. Stalin was joined by Molotov, Beria, Timoshenko, Mekhlis, and Zhukov. Stalin was still trying to come to grips with Molotov's account of the meeting he had just had with von Schulenburg. The ambassador had given Molotov a brief note complaining of the "intolerable threat to Germany's eastern borders brought about by the massed concentration of Red Army forces" and declaring that "the German government considers it necessary to take military countermeasures." Although not a formal declaration of war (which was not Hitler's style), the note and the ongoing German attacks should have made it clear, even to Stalin, as taken aback as he was, that the war predicted by so many had finally started.[2]

Stalin agreed with his military leaders that a new directive had to be given to the border military districts. It would be issued in the name of the Defense Commissar Timoshenko and countersigned by Malenkov:

1. Troops in full strength and with all the means at their disposal will attack the enemy and destroy him in those places where he has violated the Soviet frontier. In the absence of special authorization, ground troops will not cross the frontier.
2. Reconnaissance and attack aircraft will locate the concentration areas of enemy aircraft and the deployment of his ground forces. Bomber and ground-attack aircraft will destroy with powerful blows the aircraft on enemy aerodromes and will bomb the main concentrations of ground forces. Aviation strikes will be mounted to a

depth of 100–150 kilometers in German territory. Königsberg and Memel will be bombed. No flights over Finland and Romania are to take place without special authorization.[3]

This directive bore the unmistakable imprint of Stalin's lingering hope that the attacks were either the work of German generals endeavoring to force Hitler into a full-scale war with the USSR or Hitler's way of pressuring him into new concessions. Hence the absence of any language in the new directive that declares a state of war or calls for full mobilization. And how to explain the incomprehensible order to ground troops to attack the invading Germans but not to set foot on enemy soil? The only explanation for why Timoshenko and Zhukov consented to this strange directive must have been their fear of Stalin, combined with their nearly total lack of accurate information on the state of their own forces. Communications with front-line units, never good to begin with (many units lacked radios) and already badly damaged by sabotage and air attacks, were being further degraded by continuing air strikes. That part of the directive instructing Soviet air units to attack German air fields and troop concentrations was particularly unrealistic. On the first day of the war, the Soviets lost 1,200 aircraft, a large number of which were never able to take off from their bases. The raids on Königsberg and Memel were accomplished by long-range bombers of the First Aviation Corps of the reserve of the high command operating from bases in the interior but without fighter cover. On their return flights, the bombers were intercepted by German fighters and three were shot down.[4]

Beginning at 7:30 a.m., other members of the Politburo gathered along with Georgy Dimitrov and Dimitry Z. Manuilksky of the Executive Committee of the Communist International. All those assembled felt that Stalin needed to address the people by radio immediately. According to Mikoyan, who was among those present, "Stalin refused and said, 'Let Molotov do it.' We all opposed this; the people would not understand why, at such a crucial historical moment, they would hear not Stalin, first secretary of the Central Committee of the party and chairman of the government, but rather his deputy. It was important to us that an authoritative voice be heard with a call to the people: 'All rise up for the defense of the country.' Nevertheless, our efforts to persuade him came to nothing. Because Stalin so obstinately refused, we let Molotov speak, which he did at 12:00 noon." Molotov began his speech by saying he had been directed by Comrade Stalin to address the people and ended by asking citizens to "close

Operation Barbarossa, June 22–September 30, 1941

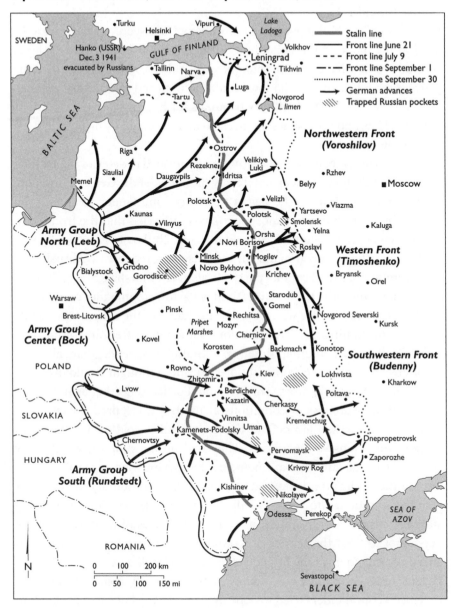

The main axes of the German attacks during the summer of 1941

ranks around our glorious Communist Party, around our great leader Comrade Stalin."[5]

Even before Molotov spoke, a number of top-secret decrees were issued in the name of the Presidium of the Supreme Soviet. One declared martial law in selected union republics and oblasts. A second outlined the procedures whereby martial law would be imposed by military authorities. Another established military tribunals for hearing cases of violations of martial law and imposing sentences, to include death by firing squad, on those found guilty.[6]

At the front, meanwhile, the situation continued to deteriorate. Despite rumors that Stalin was incapacitated by the shock of the German invasion, by 1:00 p.m. on June 22 he began to act as commander in chief, even though by right that was Timoshenko's role. Worried that the front commanders were not up to their jobs, Stalin sent Zhukov to Kiev as a "representative of the high command" in response to a request by Khrushchev, first secretary of the Ukrainian party. He also sent Marshals Shaposhnikov, Voroshilov, and Kulik to check on Dimitry Pavlov, commander of the Western Front. Zhukov asked who would be in charge of the general staff while he was gone; Stalin said, "We'll get along somehow." After Zhukov had left, Timoshenko issued another directive, at Stalin's insistence, that called for an offensive by all three fronts, action that Stalin thought would drive the enemy from Soviet territory. This irrational order, reflecting as it did Stalin's total unawareness of conditions at the front, required Soviet units, struggling desperately to defend themselves and avoid encirclement, to prepare for offensive operations. They had no air support, were under constant German air bombardment, and had serious shortages of fuel and ammunition. The air attacks had not only destroyed military materiel but resulted in damage to scarce medical supplies, destruction of dressing stations, clinics, and hospitals, as well as shortages of qualified medical personnel to treat the hordes of wounded. Moreover, the loss of experienced commanders at the brigade and division levels as a result of Stalin's vicious 1937–38 purges was taking its toll as newly installed but inexperienced commanders tried to cope. Because of the failure of the civilian economy to supply the quotas of trucks, tractors, and horses called for in mobilization plans, many units suffered critical shortages in transport. It is no wonder the offensives failed miserably in the Western and Northwestern Front areas. Indeed, they actually contributed to the rapid disintegration of these commands. It was only in the Southwestern Front that an armored counteroffensive was carried out with some success.[7]

These early directives mandated by Stalin were half measures taken too late to affect the outcome of the frontier battles. On June 22, 1941, the Presidium decreed the mobilization of men subject to military service in a number of military districts; this action, too, should have been taken much earlier. By June 25 the Wehrmacht had advanced as much as 150 miles along the principal axes of advance, and continuing air strikes made mobilization difficult. Because the Luftwaffe continued to destroy warehouses holding uniforms, individual weapons, and equipment, as well as ammunition dumps, newly mobilized men could not be properly outfitted. Nor was it easy to move these reinforcements to their new units. The railroads came under constant air attack. Main and secondary roads were jammed with civilians from the border areas fleeing blindly east from the combat zone, often in columns stretching for as far as twenty-five miles. Military vehicles, artillery, and marching Red Army units trying to reach the fighting were blocked for hours. All these concentrations of humanity were mercilessly strafed by German aircraft.[8]

The main German effort was the responsibility of Army Group Center, under Field Marshal Fedor von Bock. With its fifty divisions and with panzer (tank) groups on each flank, it was the largest and most powerful of the three German army groups committed under Barbarossa. Facing it was the Western Front, commanded by Pavlov, who had served as an armored force adviser in the Spanish civil war. Although an RU officer who served with Pavlov in Spain had on record criticized his personal qualities and questioned his fitness for command, Pavlov had made a good impression on Stalin when he was appointed commanding general of the Western Special Military District. Beginning in mid-June, Pavlov had repeatedly asked for permission to occupy defensive structures in the newly built fortified areas. But permission had been denied.[9]

The night before the German assault, Pavlov was in Minsk attending the theater. He was convinced by the rhetoric from the Kremlin that the Germans had no intention of starting a war. The attack, therefore, came as a total surprise to him. Although the border troop detachments on the frontier offered fierce resistance and the air forces of the front did their best to contest control, they were overwhelmed by the Luftwaffe. On the first day, the Western Front lost 738 aircraft, or 40 percent of its entire force. The Germans were able to outperform Soviet pilots, and their machines were technically superior.

Shocked by the losses incurred by his units, the commander of the front's air forces, Ivan I. Kopets, another Spanish War veteran, committed suicide. Dimitry A. Lestev, chief of the Propaganda Directorate of the front, reported "At 5:00 p.m., June 22, Kopets killed himself in his office. The suspected cause of this suicide was cowardice and the losses suffered by aviation. Command of the front air forces has been taken over by Major General A. I. Taiursky." Ironically, at about 2:00 a.m. on June 22, before the Germans attacked, Kopets and Taiursky, his deputy, had advised Pavlov that the air forces had been brought to complete combat readiness and had been dispersed to reserve airfields in accordance with Timoshenko's orders.[10]

The air forces' defeats in the Western Front produced another tragic incident that reinforced the impression that these forces were simply not ready to deal with Göring's Luftwaffe. The commander of the Ninth Mixed Air Division of the air forces of the Western Front, Sergei A. Chernykh, was so devastated by the division's loss of most of its aircraft on the ground that he fled. He was found later in Bryansk and immediately shot.[11] The problems in the Western Front were indeed catastrophic, yet Moscow had very little idea of the real situation. Thus, on June 26 Stalin ordered Zhukov to leave Kiev, go to the Western Front, and try to determine what needed to be done. After spending three days with front commanders, Zhukov realized that they had lost control and had little idea of the conditions their troops were facing. In constant action for the past several days, under continuous attack by Stukas (German ground-attack aircraft) of the Luftwaffe's Second Air Fleet, the troops of the Western Front no longer constituted an effective force.

Minsk fell on June 28, and on June 30 Stalin relieved Pavlov. He was later arrested and charged with responsibility for the losses suffered by the front. By July 7 he was undergoing interrogation. Order No. 378, dated July 6, 1941, for the arrest of Pavlov had been signed by Boris S. Pavlovsky, deputy chief of the investigative unit of the Third Directorate (Counterintelligence) of the Defense Commissariat, countersigned by Timoshenko, and sanctioned by USSR prosecutor Bochkov. The order stressed Pavlov's membership in an anti-Soviet conspiracy. Still later, in approving and signing Pavlov's death sentence, Stalin directed that "all that nonsense about conspiratorial activity be dropped. . . . Then all fronts should be advised of this sentence so they will know all defeatist behavior will be punished mercilessly." (This one statement by Stalin makes it obvious that he not only knew of the arrests and torture but was aware that the routine charges of conspiracy were fabrications.)[12] Pavlov was replaced briefly by Andrei I. Yeremenko, then by Timoshenko, with Mekhlis as the member of the front's Military Council. One of Timoshenko's first acts was to arrest other members of the front command as responsible for the catastrophe in Belorussia.[13]

One cause of the Western Front's calamitous defeat was the weakness of the Northwestern Front, which was formed from the Baltic Special Military District, encompassing the newly acquired Baltic republics. Facing the Northwestern Front was Ritter von Leeb's German Army Group North. It was strengthened by the attachment of the Third Panzer Group from Army Group Center. The Germans were stronger than the Soviet Northwestern Front in personnel, artillery, and tanks. The numbers of aircraft on both sides were even, but the balance was upset by the losses suffered by the Soviets. In addition, the Soviet commander of the Northwestern Front, Fedor I. Kuznetsov, was a passive individual with relatively little command experience.[14] He had replaced Aleksandr D. Loktionov, who had been arrested on June 19. Earlier, Loktionov had commanded the Red Army's air forces and later had become the first commander of the new Baltic Special Military District.[15] A July 8, 1941, report sent to Stalin by military counterintelligence stated that "in the first several hours after attacks by enemy aircraft, Kuznetsov forbade his aircraft to take off and destroy the adversary. The result was that units of the front air forces were late in entering combat, by which time a significant portion of the aircraft had already been destroyed on the ground." The report concluded that "the air units of the Northwestern Front air forces are incapable of active combat operations." The delays were probably due to Stalin's insistence that Soviet commanders not provoke the Germans. It seems unlikely that they would have occurred had an experienced officer such as Loktionov remained in command.[16]

Pavlov was asked under interrogation: "Who was guilty of allowing the breakthrough on the Western Front?" He replied that "the basic reason for the rapid movement of the German troops into our territory was the obvious superiority of the enemy in aviation and tanks. Besides that, Lithuanian troops were placed on Kuznetsov's [Baltic Special Military District] left flank and they did not want to fight. After the first pressure on the Baltic left flank, the Lithuanian units shot their commanders and ran away. That gave German tank units the possibility of striking me from Vilnius."[17]

It was not just the Lithuanian units that created problems for the Northwestern Front. The populations of the entire Baltic area actively supported the Wehrmacht, showing German troops the locations of Red Army positions, with the result that these units were battered by Luftwaffe ground-attack aircraft. Large numbers of the officers and enlisted men of the Twenty-second Estonian Rifle Corps deserted to the Germans, making it impossible for commanders to provide accurate reports of losses. Mass desertions to the enemy were not confined to the Baltic. The Twenty-sixth Army of the Southwestern Front reported that after two weeks of combat it had lost nearly 4,000 of its personnel to desertions, chiefly those of western Ukrainians. Similar problems existed in the Thirtieth Army of the Western Front, where many of the troops reported as missing were actually deserters of Belorussian nationality. In the same time frame, the 325th Division of the Tenth Army purged its ranks of 446 persons of Ukrainian, Belorussian, and Baltic nationalities.[18] So much for the advantages gained by Stalin from the forcible incorporation of these territories into the Soviet Union. The attitudes of these people were undoubtedly also affected by the forced removal of thousands of "anti-Soviet persons" from the Baltic republics in the days just before the German invasion.

The Northern Front, formed from the Leningrad Military District, was relatively calm because the Finns had not yet declared war on the USSR even though the Germans were using Finnish territory to launch air raids and conduct intelligence forays into the Soviet Union. When General Kiril A. Meretskov, who had been designated the General Headquarters representative to the Northern Front, arrived in Leningrad on the morning of June 22, the officers who met him looked glum. The reason, they said, was "The war's started." The military district commander was not there to greet him, nor did he appear at the meeting that afternoon of the Military Council of the district. Nevertheless, with Meretskov's help the council worked out plans for the defense of Leningrad. On June 23 Meretskov was recalled to Moscow, having been named a consultant to the Stavka, along with Marshal Kulik, Marshal Shaposhnikov, and others. This assignment was evidently a pretext to bring Meretskov back to Moscow because on the evening of June 24 he was arrested in Stalin's outer office and taken to the Liubianka.[19] Three months later, after a summer of bitter fighting to hold back the Germans, fighting in which the experienced Meretskov could not take part, Leningrad came under a siege that would cost the lives of hundreds of thousands of its citizens.

On August 28, 1941, Meretskov wrote to Stalin from his isolation cell in the interrogation section of Lefortovo prison asking that he be allowed to serve in any position at the front. Stalin, knowing that he desperately needed experienced field commanders, pardoned him and released him in September 1941. He was the only general officer arrested in the purge operation of April–June 1941 who survived and held important commands during the war.[20]

The former chief of the air forces, Lieutenant General Pavel V. Rychagov, had been removed from his post by Stalin in April 1941 and sent to the General Staff Academy. When war broke out he was on leave at a Sochi sanitarium; he was recalled to Moscow that day. Upon his arrival on June 24 he was arrested on the basis of an order signed by Bogdan Z. Kobulov, deputy narkom for state security. The arrest order was not sanctioned by a prosecutor. Rychagov's wife, Major Maria Petrovna Nesterenko, herself a well-known aviator, was also arrested.[21] Of Nesterenko it was said that "being Rychagov's beloved wife, she would not have been unaware of his traitorous activities." Rychagov had fought in Spain as a volunteer pilot and later commanded the Soviet volunteer air group operating against the Japanese air force in China. Considering the massive losses in flight personnel on the first day of the war, an officer with Rychagov's experience would have made a significant contribution to the Soviet side had he been free to do so.

When the new commander of the air forces of the Northern Front's Seventh Army, Ivan I. Proskurov, arrived in Petrozavodsk, capital of the Karelian ASSR, on June 23, 1941, the situation was relatively quiet. Finland had not yet joined Germany in attacking the USSR. On June 24, however, Moscow advised the Northern Front that German and Finnish troops were now deployed on Finnish territory preparatory to attacks on Leningrad and the capture of Murmansk and Kandalaksha in the north. To disrupt these plans, on June 25 Moscow ordered air strikes against eighteen enemy airfields in Finland. A total of 487 sorties were flown, resulting in the destruction of thirty enemy aircraft on the ground and eleven in aerial combat. The attacks continued the next day. They evidently provided the pretext Finland needed to announce that a state of war existed between Finland and the USSR. Finland's twenty-one divisions would join the Germans in an attack on Leningrad from the north.[22]

In this perilous situation, why did People's Commissar for State Security Vsevolod N. Merkulov send a telegram to the NKGB of the Karelian ASSR on June 27 ordering the immediate arrest and movement to Moscow of Ivan I. Proskurov, commander of the air forces of the Northern Front's Seventh Army, Proskurov, whose service in the Spanish civil war made him one of the few senior air officers with combat experience against the Germans?[23]

The arrests of Meretskov and Proskurov were not decided at the last minute. They formed part of a much broader operation by Stalin to rid himself of a number of senior officers whose independence of spirit and sense of combat brotherhood he could not tolerate. Stalin knew that he had to remove them as potential future witnesses to his abject policy of kowtowing to Hitler. Stalin could not abide criticism in any form, lest it reveal the truth behind his actions, and these were officers who, unlike the myrmidons with whom he normally surrounded himself, would always tell it like it was. They were, for the most part, officers who had served in Spain as advisers or volunteer pilots. Even after their return from Spain, they would greet one other with "Saludo, Companero" as they passed in the corridors of the Defense Commissariat.

While the carnage continued on the battle fronts and the Red Army fell back in disorderly retreat from the Wehrmacht's attacks, the brutal interrogations of those arrested in the period from April through June 1941 on suspicion of espionage or anti-Soviet activity went forward. These were directed by Lev Yemelyanovich Vlodzimirsky, chief of the Investigative Unit for Especially Important Cases of the NKVD. Responsibility for this regime of torture did not, however, begin or end with Vlodzimirsky. It began at the top with Stalin and continued down through the NKVD/NKGB chain of command.

Vlodzimirsky reported daily to Beria on his progress. Beria in turn kept Stalin advised. During the first weeks of the war as one battle after another was lost, Beria would generally be among the last to leave Stalin's Kremlin office, allowing him plenty of time to review cases of special interest to Stalin.[24] It has become fashionable among some historians to declare that the wave of arrests and vicious interrogations on the very eve of the war were Beria's work and that Stalin was not involved. This is not true. Beria kept Stalin informed on all matters dealing with the fates of arrested persons. For example, on January 16, 1940, Beria sent Stalin a list of 457 persons, 346 of whom were to be sentenced to be shot. The remainder were to receive sentences of not less than fifteen years in the GULAG. On September 6, 1940, Stalin received another list from Beria, this one containing the names of 537 persons, of whom 472 were to be shot and the remainder sentenced to terms of not less than fifteen years.[25] In each case Stalin would merely note, "Received from Comrade Beria." This notation indicated approval.

Did Stalin condone the use of physical torture on these men? The answer to this question can be found in the testimony of scores of individuals who were investigated in the 1937–38 purges. The late O. F. Suvenirov lists over 140 officers who testified to the physical torture and beatings they underwent after their arrest. Their testimony and that of many, many others confirm Khrushchev's statement at the Twentieth Party Congress that "the confessions of many arrested persons accused of hostile activity were obtained by means of harsh, inhuman torture."[26]

On November 17, 1938, a joint decree of the Council of People's Commissars and the Central Committee VKP(b) called attention to the many excesses and shortcomings in the work of the NKVD and the prosecutors. It stipulated that arrests could not be carried out by the NKVD without the sanction of the prosecutors, who were instructed not to permit arrests without justification. They were also made responsible for ensuring the proper conduct of preliminary investigations by the NKVD.[27]

Although the decree nowhere mentioned physical force and torture in investigations, the fact that NKVD interrogators made frequent use of them was well known to the party officials who, along with prosecutors and NKVD officials, constituted the infamous "troikas," extrajudicial arrangements frequently used during the purges to speed up the process. Party secretaries at all levels now insisted that NKVD officials follow the letter of the new decree in conducting investigations, and they sought the dismissal and trial of many senior NKVD officials in their jurisdictions for having participated in abusive and illegal behavior. The scapegoating of the NKVD went on right down to the regional level.[28] Stalin, however, while not unhappy to see NKVD witnesses of the purge years disappear, was unwilling to deprive his investigators of the tools they needed to produce results. On January 10, 1939, he sent a coded telegram to party and NKVD officials in union and autonomous republics and in regions. "The Central Committee VKP(b) explains that physical coercion has been used in the practice of the NKVD since 1937 with the permission of the Central Committee," the telegram said, noting that all "bourgeois" intelligence services used physical coercion. "The Central Committee considers physical coercion a completely correct and useful method, and it must absolutely continue to be used in the future, as an expedient against obvious and armed enemies of the people." This telegram, sent in the name of the Central Committee and signed by Stalin, demonstrates that the beatings and torture that were used at the height of the purges could be employed again, all in his name.[29] The Boss would not tolerate dissent or show pity for those who opposed him in any way. During the Great Purges he would personally approve the execution of thousands as on December 12, 1938. According to Dmitri A. Volkogonov, a monstrous "record" was established on that date as Stalin and Molotov sanctioned the arrest of 3,167 persons.[30] Stalin's behavior in dealing with those he considered his enemies did not change in the early months of the war.

That he was aware of the use of torture on those arrested in the latest wave of arrests cannot be doubted. Two of those he released, Vannikov and Meretskov, were both physically abused. In Vannikov's case, testimony given by investigators A. A. Zozulov and Ivan I. Matevosov described how Boris V. Rodos threw him on the floor, then jumped on him, shouting "Tell, tell all." According to Matevosov, the order was given to obtain testimony from Vannikov implicating others. The protocol signed by the barely conscious Vannikov was actually prepared by Rodos.

On December 22, 1938, about a month after Beria became People's Commissar for Internal Affairs, a new investigative unit was created in the NKVD headed by Bogdan Z. Kobulov. Some idea of how the new unit functioned can be seen in its handling of the investigation of Foreign Affairs Commissariat officials following the dismissal in early May 1939 of Foreign Affairs Commissar Maksim M. Litvinov. (Litvinov was dismissed because he was Jewish and favored cooperation with the West against the Nazi menace.) One such official was Yevgeny A. Gnedin, a relatively young man who had risen to the position of head of the Foreign Affairs Commissariat's press department and was one of its most respected members. He was arrested on the night of May 10–11 and brought to his first interrogation by Kobulov at 3:00 a.m. Gnedin rejected the accusation that he was a spy as laughable and seemed confident of an early release. At 10:00 a.m. he was again summoned for interrogation but this time taken directly to Beria's office. Kobulov was also there, and he and Beria conferred briefly in Georgian. As Gnedin sat next to Beria's desk, Beria told him in a loud voice that according to Kobulov he was a foreign spy. When Gnedin again denied the charge, saying "I'm not a spy," Kobulov struck him a sharp blow and several NKVD toughs burst into the office and joined in pummeling him. At this point, Beria shouted, "Lie down." Gnedin lay down on his back. Beria ordered him to turn over, and when Gnedin hesitated, the NKVD officers roughly turned him over and began to beat him with rubber truncheons. Above the din could be heard the voice of Beria shouting "Don't leave any marks!"[31]

By February 1941 the investigative unit established in 1938 had been expanded and become the Investigative Unit for Especially Important Cases. Lev Vlodzimirsky, a Siberian native and former sailor who had been a member of the secret police since 1928, became the head.[32] The interrogators in his unit were nearly all veterans of the purges. Among his senior interrogators and deputies were Rodos and Lev L. Shvartsman, both well known for their brutality. Rodos was tried in 1956 for cruelty toward prisoners under interrogation. Among those who testified against him was Marshal Meretskov who described the beatings he received. Apparently Rodos delivered a blow hard enough to break one of Meretskov's ribs and send him to the floor crying in pain.[33]

Although Shvartsman's reputation as a ferocious interrogator was every bit as horrific as Vlodzimirsky's and Rodos's, according to one prisoner he did not look the part: "He was stout, his face pale from lack of sleep, and if one had passed him on the street he might have seemed an overworked engineer from a large factory."[34] Nevertheless, Shvartsman could be a nasty customer. The story is told that when Grigory M. Shtern was arrested, his initial interrogation, given his previous rank, was handled by Beria's first deputy, Merkulov, in Merkulov's office. Shvartsman was also present. Merkulov asked Shtern to tell about his crimes and Shtern replied that he had committed no crimes against his country. At this Shvartsman rose from his chair and hit Shtern in the face with an electric cable, severing his right eyeball from its socket. Shtern fell to the floor. Merkulov looked reproachfully at Shvartsman and at the blood on the expensive carpet. Shvartsman apologized to Merkulov, explaining that he had intended to hit Shtern in the neck but missed. With that he called the guards, who bandaged Shtern's eyes and drove him off to the Sukhanovka, probably the worst of all the NKVD prisons in the Moscow area.[35]

No longer able to withstand the pain, Shtern declared at a June 27 interrogation session that yes, he was "a member of a military-conspiratorial organization and a German agent." At the end of the protocol of interrogation, however, Shtern wrote this declaration in his own hand: "I made the foregoing statements during the interrogation, but none of it corresponds to reality and it was made up by me, that is, I was actually never an enemy, an agent, or a conspirator."[36]

Routine interrogations were held at irregular intervals so prisoners could not anticipate them. Beatings with fists or rubber truncheons, accompanied by kicks to the body if a prisoner fell down, were standard. Senior NKVD and NKGB officials also participated in these beatings. When the Meretskov interrogations began, for example, Beria, Merkulov, and Vlodzimirsky all took part, after which Shvartsman and investigators Zimenskov and Sorokin joined in.

Prisoners were also made to stand for hours without moving until their bodies were wracked with pain. Rodos once said to a prisoner, "They say of us that we use Asiatic methods of conducting investigations; we'll show you that this true!"[37] Perhaps the most brutal aspect of these interrogations was the infamous "confrontation" (*ochnaya stavka*), in which two prisoners were brought face to face so that one of them could hear the other's accusations against him or her. With appropriate safeguards, such confrontations are not uncommon in other jurisdictions. It is instructive, however, to learn how Vlodzimirsky went about arranging for a confrontation in early July 1941 between Rychagov and Smushkevich, both Spanish War veterans and service colleagues. He sent interrogators to Rychagov's cell to "prepare" him by brutally beating him. One result of this treatment was to puncture Rychagov's eardrum and lead him to exclaim that he could not longer be considered a pilot. When Smushkevich was brought in, it was apparent that he, too, had been severely beaten many times.[38]

Many of the air force officers and Spanish civil war veterans arrested in May–June 1941 appear in the so-called Stalin lists (*Stalinskie Spiski*) compiled by Memorial, a Russian association dedicated to preserving the history of human rights abuses in the USSR and honoring the victims. The entries provide biographic detail, the accused's position and rank at the time of arrest, the date of arrest, testimony of accusers, and admissions, if any, by the accused. It is these records that provide the basis for the descriptions of arrests and interrogations in chapter 19. In nearly all these interrogations, the main target was Colonel General Yakov V. Smushkevich. Some of the accused named him as their recruiter into an anti-Soviet conspiracy. Smushkevich himself testified to some officials' membership in that conspiracy. Considering the pain he suffered and the likelihood of threats against his daughter, Rosa, it is no wonder he confessed.[39]

Other persons with records in Memorial's Stalin lists were shown to have been recruited by Aleksandr D. Loktionov, the former head of Red Army air forces and commanding general of the Baltic Military District. On June 16, 1941, Loktionov wrote to the prosecutor: "I am subjected to enormous physical and moral torture. The prospect of the interrogations I have described makes my blood run cold. To die, knowing that I was not an enemy, drives me to despair. . . . I am writing my last words—a cry from my soul: let me die an honest man working for my motherland, the Soviet Union. I beg my government—save my life. I am not guilty of treason." This letter evidently did not help Loktionov. On July 15 he was brought to a confrontation with Meretskov, who tried to persuade him to confess. When Loktionov refused, he was beaten again in Meretskov's presence.

Although beatings continued, as of August 10 he still refused to admit guilt. It is evident that what he said under duress, including that he had recruited others, was untrue.[40]

Strangely, another name missing from Stalin's lists and from the interrogation summaries printed in them is that of Lieutenant General Proskurov. The reason is not clear; we know, however, that Proskurov endured his summer of torture, because we have his indictment: "On the basis of the material in his file, Proskurov is accused of membership in a military conspiratorial organization, the tasks of which were to conduct work aimed at defeating republican Spain, lowering the combat readiness of the air forces of the Red Army, and increasing accidents in the air forces." The indictment, signed by the senior investigator of the Investigative Unit for Especially Important Cases and by Deputy Chief Shvartsman, was released by the unit chief, Vlodzimirsky. A note in the protocol of Proskurov's interrogation read: "Proskurov refused to admit his guilt." To the very end, Proskurov would not dishonor himself by giving his tormentors what they wanted.[41]

CHAPTER **22**

The Final Reckoning

Hindsight enables us to savor the final irony of the German invasion of the USSR in June 1941. It was a colossal blunder by Adolf Hitler that denied the Wehrmacht the capture of Moscow and preserved Stalin's power. The Austrian corporal, whose ability to outfox Stalin resulted in the deaths of millions of Soviet citizens, demonstrated that he, like Stalin, suffered from delusions that condemned him to make wrong choices in the summer of 1941.

By the end of July 1941, the city of Smolensk had been captured against very strong Soviet resistance. By mid-August, Army Group Center's two panzer groups, under Colonels General Heinz Guderian and Hermann Hoth, stood poised to resume the offensive. Their goal was Moscow, now only a few hundred kilometers away. Then, on August 21, Hitler issued this order: "The most important objective to be achieved before the onset of winter is not the capture of Moscow but the seizure of the Crimea and of the industrial and coal-mining regions on the Donets [in the Ukraine]." Army Group Center officers were aghast. They knew that if their armored forces were diverted to the south, there would be no hope of resuming the Moscow offensive before weather conditions worsened. They chose Guderian to try to change Hitler's mind by explaining that "Moscow was the heart of the Soviet political system, a major industrial complex, its communications center, and above all, the hub of the entire railroad system. The fall of Moscow would decide the war." The response to his plea was vintage Hitler. His generals "understood nothing of wartime economics. . . . We need the grain of the Ukraine. The industrial area of the Donets must work for us instead of for Stalin."[1] Of course, Hitler's vision of millions of docile Ukrainians working for Greater Germany in the farms and factories of their country was delusional. To a great extent it was rendered so by Stalin's "scorched earth" policy and the massive relocation of industrial facilities, equipment, and workers eastward. Most important, however, was the adverse reaction of the population to the atrocities committed by the German occupiers, turning potential allies into enemies. Could not Hitler understand that these atrocities were animated by his racist attitudes toward all Slavs, who were "a mass of born slaves who feel the need of a master?"[2]

Despite his misgivings at Hitler's insistence on abandoning the offensive against Moscow, Field Marshal von Bock, the commander of Army Group Center, had no alternative but to comply. His panzer units were committed to the drive against Kiev, capital of the Ukraine. Kiev fell on September 19. On September 26 the battle ended with the destruction of five Soviet armies and the capture of 665,000 Soviet prisoners. Contributing to this tremendous loss of men and equipment was Stalin's stubborn refusal to allow the Southwestern Front to withdraw until it was too late. The man who "knew" Hitler would not invade was still rejecting advice from the military professionals, who in turn were afraid to cross him.[3]

Suddenly, as though intoxicated by the enormity of the victory in the Ukraine, Hitler ordered a resumption of the offensive against Moscow with the code word designation Typhoon. It began on October 2, well over a month later than planned by Army Group Center. For von Bock and his generals it was a huge gamble forced on them by Hitler. Their armored and motorized vehicles, already weakened by the battles for Smolensk, had deteriorated further in the long marches and battles of the Kiev encirclement. Supply lines were stretched thin, and shortages worsened. Furthermore, while the weather was fine the first week of October, no one knew how long it would take for autumn rains and winter cold to begin. Nevertheless, by October 14 German panzers had succeeded in capturing two heavily defended key cities, Vyazma and Bryansk. In so doing they encircled and took 663,000 more prisoners and much equipment. But their luck with the weather ran out and they found themselves bogged down in mud. Still, they struggled on and by October 19 had taken Borodino, the historic Napoleonic battlefield. They had also captured Mozhaisk, a hundred kilometers from Moscow.

Operation Typhoon

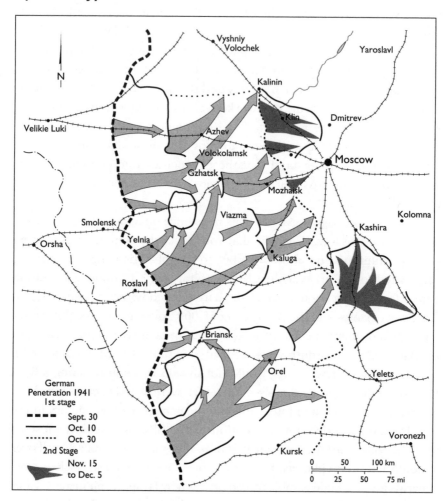

The German assault on Moscow as it developed in October–December 1941

On October 12, two days after Zhukov had replaced Ivan S. Konev as commander of the Western Front, the Stavka had watched nervously as the fresh Siberian Thirty-second Rifle Division was chewed to pieces by the Germans at Borodino. That day the Convoy Service of the Chief Directorate for Internal Troops, USSR NKVD, received a telegram directing the removal of thirty-nine "especially dangerous state prisoners" from the NKVD internal prison. One of them was I. I. Proskurov.[4] It seemed that no one wanted to risk having such criminals fall into German hands, so they were being moved.

Fear that Moscow's defenses might not hold was everywhere. That same day, October 12, Operation Typhoon was closing in on Kalinin, a city just north of Moscow on the suburban railroad and a key sector in the Moscow defense system. The unhindered German advance was made possible by the failure of Kalinin's authorities to organize its defense. The extensive defensive works constructed during the summer of 1941 by thousands of volunteers were left unoccupied. Four home guard units had been created, but they had not been trained and would melt away at the first shots. When the Thirtieth Army established its command post in Kalinin on the morning of October 13, its arrival seemed to be a signal for the civilian population as well as party members, the NKVD, the police force (militia), and the fire brigades to flee in panic toward Moscow. Although by plan only family members were to be evacuated, nearly everyone left, from workers to directors of enterprises, taking with them the motor transport that should have been given to the military. About two-thirds of the residents of Kalinin left town.[5]

By the evening of October 13, the Germans occupied the western outskirts of Kalinin. Fires started by German air raids and by saboteurs were allowed to burn unchecked. In the absence of the militia, looting of food stores and warehouses began in earnest. When the military commander demanded that the chief of the Kalinin Oblast NKVD order his subordinates to return to the city, he threw up his hands and said there was nothing he could do. Finally, checkpoints were organized south of the city by the military. Among those stopped from continuing on to Moscow were 1,500 Red Army junior officers and soldiers. Nevertheless, many, both civilians and military people, got through, and their stories of the German advance and the chaos in Kalinin must have contributed to the sense of panic that began to grip Moscow. NKGB awareness of the Kalinin situation was probably also behind the decision to move Proskurov and other prisoners out of Moscow.[6]

As the Germans drew nearer to Mozhaisk on October 15, the Politburo sat in continuous session, receiving reports on conditions in Moscow and at the front lines. By late afternoon it had decided to defend the city but to evacuate the government, the diplomatic corps, and other key institutions to Kuibyshev (now Samara). Late that evening Molotov notified members of the diplomatic corps of the plans for evacuation. The news spread quickly and by the next day public order and party discipline began to fray. Crowds waited impatiently at railroad stations for trains that never came. Some officials used their official cars and headed east. Looting occurred at bakeries and food stores. Some offices and factories were unable to function as their workers were absent, tending to their own affairs.

On the evening of October 16 the central offices of the NKVD were evacuated to Kuibyshev. As of October 17, it was confirmed that a number of "especially dangerous state criminals were being convoyed from the NKVD internal prison in Moscow to the internal prison of the NKVD in-Kuibyshev."[7] There could now be no doubt that their relocation was related to the chaotic situation in Moscow and at the front. That day Moscow Party First Secretary A. S. Shcherbakov told Moscow citizens in a radio broadcast that the city would be defended "to the last drop of blood." Nevertheless, by October 19 Mozhaisk and Maloyaroslavets had fallen, increasing Muscovites' terror. Most were familiar with these cities and the many beautiful towns and villages in the region, where some had their country dachas. That evening the State Defense Committee (GKO) met to review the situation, deciding that NKVD General Pavel A. Artemev would be responsible for "the approaches to the city and for the city itself." His report on conditions in Moscow shocked the members of the GKO, and they agreed to his recommendation that martial law be established.[8] Amid this feverish activity, Beria found time to send a trusted courier, Demian Semenikhin, to Kuibyshev with Order No. 2756B listing various prisoners and instructing those in authority: "Discontinue investigation, do not send to trial, shoot immediately."[9]

At his trial in 1955, L. F. Bashtakov, the senior officer in charge of this group of special prisoners, insisted that before Beria's order was received in Kuibyshev, "Shvartsman had orders to finish the interrogations, prepare the dossiers, and send the indictments to Moscow." The order to proceed with the executions was unexpected, clearly reflecting the chaos in the capital. It has been said that Beria acted on his own, but it seems highly unlikely that he would have taken this step without touching base with Stalin. Back on September 6 he had asked Stalin to sign an order for the execution of 170 dangerous prisoners being held in the Orel NKVD internal prison. (Orel was in the path of the impending offensive against Moscow and was captured by the Germans on October 3.) As for the specially dangerous group in Kuibyshev, its senior officers were well known to Stalin personally. He knew he could take no chances of their escaping in the confusion that would ensue even as far away as Kuibyshev were the Germans to take Moscow.[10]

It took some time to locate the prisoners on his list. According to journalist Arkady Vaksberg, lower-ranking interrogators had not been informed of the Beria order and were continuing their work. Prisoner Arzhenukhin was still being interrogated on October 27, and Maria Nesterenko's interrogation by Ya. M. Raitses was under way on the morning of October 28 when Senior Major Rodos broke in, shouting: "Let's go!" Shortly thereafter five trucks left the prison.[11] The release of these prisoners to the custody of a member of an NKVD USSR special group was provided for in Order No. 7/2–5017 from the chief of the First Special Department of the NKVD USSR to the chief of the NKVD internal prison in Kuibyshev.[12] It would appear that Bashtakov was that person. The "October massacre" would soon begin.

October 28 also saw the Germans take Volokolamsk, a Sunday's outing away from central Moscow. There was still no assurance that Moscow could be held. If it fell, forcing an ignominious departure by Stalin and his cronies, his position would be threatened. No chances were to be taken, and the secrecy of the prisoners' removal was total.

After leaving the prison, the trucks proceeded to a settlement then called Barysh, on the outskirts of Kuibyshev, where a walled compound contained dachas used by the Kuibyshev Oblast NKVD directorate during the summer months. According to Vaksberg, the prisoners were executed and their bodies buried there. Afterward, a list of those executed was drawn up (see appendix 3). An act dated October 28, 1941, and signed by Bashtakov, Rodos, and Semenikhin stated that those listed had been executed in accordance with Order No. 2756 B from Beria.

The list is bizarre (see appendix 3). Fourteen of those named were air force or air defense senior officers or individuals connected with weapons development. Others were completely unrelated. For example, David A. Rozov was the deputy people's commissar for trade and the former head of AMTORG, the trading company in New York well known as a cover for Soviet intelligence officers. Dmitry A. Bulatov was secretary of the Omsk Oblast Party Committee. The most puzzling name on the list was that of

Filipp I. Goloshchekin, who was complicit in the assassination of Tsar Nicholas II and his family. Also on the list were Maria P. Nesterenko, Aleksandra I. Savchenko, and Zinaida P. Rozova. Five other persons were later added to the first list of twenty. One of them was Mikhail Sergeevich Kedrov, an old Bolshevik born in 1878 who had been arrested in 1939 and now found himself facing death with this group.[13]

There is another version of the story. It hardly seems credible yet it demonstrates the difficulty of establishing the truth about a historical event of this importance in the absence of archivally accurate, officially released information. This second version describes a telephone call received early on October 26, 1941, by the stationmaster in Barysh, a rail junction hundreds of kilometers southwest of Kuibyshev city in what was then Kuibyshevskaya Oblast (now in Ulyanovskaya). The call was from Senior Major of State Security Boris V. Rodos (one of the most sadistic of the team investigating the generals): "Tomorrow at 11:25 a classified train, 00/A, will pass through your line on its way to us in Kuibyshev. I order you to ensure it is given a green light. You'll answer for this with your head!" When the train arrived in Barysh, however, it was stopped and shunted off to a siding because the station had received a warning of an impending German air raid. An offer by townspeople to feed the passengers was rejected by the NKVD guards. The "passengers" were the generals.

When, many years later, it became known that the prisoners had been executed in a place called Barysh, a reporter visited and tried to reconstruct the scene. From the rail siding a path led across the tracks to an abandoned sandpit some three to five kilometers away. Relatives of the reporter told him that it had been the favorite play area of a group of boys who had made their "headquarters" in an abandoned hut. On the night the train was held at the siding, shots were heard from the sandpit. The next day, the boys went out to look. They found nothing—not their headquarters, not the homemade catapult and crossbows they had left there the day before. The place had been flattened. They swore they found many recently fired cartridge cases on the ground, and thereafter the rumor went around that people had been executed.[14]

In 1988 the periodical *Literaturnaia Gazeta* published an article by Vaksberg about the site at Kuibyshev. The first publicly available information on the secret execution, the article caused quite a stir. After it appeared, an editor from Samara Radio and a worker at a local museum apparently found the place of execution and burial. The former NKVD dacha compound had been razed and the spot reportedly turned into a children's park. When workmen dug into the area they found evidence that bodies had been buried there. A marker was erected—a symbol really, because no one knew who was buried where. Then in 1991 a Samara journalist, Viktor D. Sadovsky, apparently working with Memorial, arranged to honor the victims. Many of their relatives attended. Proskurov's only surviving daughter, Lidia Ivanovna, was there, along with Rosa Smushkevich, the daughter of Yakov V. Smushkevich.[15]

Supporting the contention that Beria would not have ordered the October 28 executions on his own is the action he took with regard to other prisoners sentenced to death. These were prisoners whose sentences still required approval of the military collegium of the USSR Supreme Court and the Central Committee of the party before the NKVD could proceed with executions. On November 15 Beria sent Top-Secret Memorandum No. 2865/c to Stalin explaining the situation and asking that the NKVD be permitted to proceed with the executions of those condemned to death. He also requested that in the future NKVD special boards (*osobye soveshchaniia*) have the right to deal with cases of serious crimes and to pronounce appropriate sentences up to death. These decisions of the boards would be considered final. Within two days, Stalin issued a State Defense Committee decree authorizing virtually word for word the actions requested by Beria. On January 29, 1942, Beria sent Stalin a list of forty-six persons, most of whom had been arrested in April–June 1941. Included were Red Army air force generals who had served in Spain and were closely associated with those who had been shot on October 28: Lieutenant General of Aviation Konstantin M. Gusev, commander of air forces, Far Eastern Front; Lieutenant General of Aviation Yevgeny S. Ptukhin, commander of air forces, Kiev Special Military District; Lieutenant General of Aviation Petr I. Pumpur, commander of air forces, Moscow Military District; and Major General of Aviation Ernst G. Shakht, deputy commander of air forces, Orlovsky Military District; and others.

To Beria's request, Stalin replied: "Shoot all those named in this list." An NKVD special board met on February 13, 1941, passing a sentence of death on the men, and on February 23, Red Army Day, they were executed.[16]

What became of the three principals in the events described in these pages?

Pavel M. Fitin worked throughout the war as head of NKVD/NKGB foreign intelligence. His directorate concentrated on the collection of information in allied and neutral states rather than in those countries under

German occupation; its most productive residencies were London, New York, Washington, and Ottawa. London's agents were undoubtedly the best sources on allied planning for the postwar occupation of Germany, already of major interest to Stalin. They also contributed information on Allied development of atomic weapons, a topic that by 1944–45 was of increasing concern to Stalin and that Fitin's people therefore gave top priority. By early 1945, according to historian David Holloway, "Soviet intelligence had a clear, general picture of the Manhattan Project." In February 1945, People's Commissar of State Security Merkulov, still Fitin's boss, reported to Beria that "research by leading British and American scientists had shown that an atomic bomb was feasible." By June 1945, Fitin's sources provided details on the plutonium bomb that would soon be tested. It was the success of this test in New Mexico in July that convinced Stalin of the strategic importance of the atomic bomb.[17] On June 15, 1946, however, the architect of the clandestine collection programs that had made this knowledge available to Soviet scientists, foreign intelligence director Pavel M. Fitin, was summarily dismissed and placed at the disposal of the Personnel Directorate, USSR Ministry of State Security (MGB).

Why? By mid-1946 Fitin had become a highly experienced and effective intelligence chief. His contributions during and at the end of the war had been outstanding. He had never become involved in political power plays that could have irritated Merkulov, Beria, or Stalin. He knew his position and accepted it as a good Stalinist bureaucrat. Nevertheless, in the weeks before the German invasion he had undoubtedly become a burr under the saddles of both Beria and Stalin. Thus, in March 1946 when the USSR abandoned the proletarian designation "people's commissariat" and created new "ministries" in the Western fashion, they probably saw their chance. It seemed logical that the former head of military counterintelligence, Viktor S. Abakumov, who was now the minister of state security, should have the right to choose his own team, including a new chief of foreign intelligence. Out went Fitin. It was claimed that his personal life was not suitable for a chief of intelligence—he had begun living with a much younger woman, a well-known sports figure. (They were married in 1963 and remained so until Fitin's death in 1971.)[18] A friend recalls that after his dismissal (which also involved the loss of his official apartment and dacha) he sorely missed being at the heart of the action and lived in straitened circumstances.[19]

Fitin's next assignment, from September 1946 until January 4, 1947, was as deputy MGB representative in Germany. The reason for the assignment is unknown.[20] In January 1947 he was sent to Sverdlovsk as the deputy chief of the MGB oblast directorate, serving there until September 1951. This was a distinct demotion. Beria reportedly ordered him fired from State Security without a pension "because he lacked sufficient years of service," but Fitin managed to be assigned to the MGB ministry in the Kazakh SSR. When Stalin died in March 1953 and Beria once more headed the security services, he lost the Kazakh ministerial post and was sent back to Sverdlovsk, where he remained until July 1953. By that time Beria had been arrested. For some reason, Fitin was dismissed from the MGB in November 1953 as "unsuitable for the service."[21]

In 1954 Fitin did what many others before and after him did when forced out of the service at an early age: he obtained a position with the Soviet system of state control, where he served until 1959. Then he became director of a photographic *kombinat* (combine) under the Union of Soviet Societies for Friendship and Cultural Relations with Foreign Countries. He probably got the first job through the intercession of friends; the second job suggests intelligence connections. Of the three principal characters, Fitin represents a type most common to Soviet society. He did his job as well as or even better than expected and insisted on sending reports to Stalin that consistently predicted a German invasion. When rebuffed, he kept quiet.

Filipp I. Golikov belonged to another group, one that would do anything to remain in the good graces of the leader. As chief of the RU, Golikov suppressed or altered analyses of the German threat to fit Stalin's mistaken ideas. In addition to the RU assignment, Golikov carried out a number of tasks for the political leadership. Not only did he serve Stalin, but he managed to hang on under Khrushchev.

In July–September 1941 Stalin had Golikov visit London and Washington to assess the extent of Anglo-American assistance and cooperation.[22] The trips were relatively brief, intended not to delve into the details of British and American plans to assist the Soviet Union (America was not yet in the war) but to gauge how serious these capitalist countries were about providing help to a Communist country. Golikov's trip to London on July 8–13 suggested the British were not sanguine about Soviet chances against the Germans. Stalin hoped for greater success in dealing with the Americans so on July 26 Golikov flew to the United States, where he was received by President Roosevelt. He doubtless reported very positively on the meeting.

After his return from his trips, Golikov asked Stalin for a field command, which he received. The descriptions of his actions in various command positions that appear in his official biography in the *Soviet Military Encyclopedia* do not always correspond to reality. He was relieved of virtually every combat assignment he was given or found another by appealing to Stalin. When he was deputy commander of the Stalingrad Front, for example, he was accused of cowardice by Nikita Khrushchev, then political member of the front's Military Council. In October 1942 Golikov was given command of the Voronezh Front but was relieved in March 1943 at Zhukov's urging. In April 1943 Stalin made Golikov head of the Defense Commissariat's Chief Personnel Directorate and started him on the hunt for prisoners of war and displaced persons.[23]

In October 1944 he was appointed plenipotentiary of the Council of People's Commissars for Repatriation Affairs but retained his position as head of Red Army personnel. Many thousands of Soviet citizens were now in Allied hands, and the number was growing daily. These people—former prisoners of war and individuals who had been sent to Germany as laborers during the war—were not all eager to be repatriated. Many of them refused to return to their homeland. This intransigence was anathema to Stalin, which is probably why he directed Golikov to supervise the activities of the Soviet repatriation missions in Germany, the United Kingdom, and elsewhere in Western Europe. The VENONA project recovered the texts of some of Golikov's telegrams to these missions. In one he admonishes his people not to "slip into accepting the American, British, and French" definition of Soviet citizens as "refugees." He urges them to disrupt "the plan to send our people to settle in other countries" and demanded they increase their political work among Soviet citizens. At one point, Golikov admits that "the work is not easy."[24]

At a meeting of senior military leaders in November 1945, Stalin argued that Zhukov was attempting to claim that he was the sole architect of victory; in March 1946 Stalin recalled him from Germany. There followed a series of moves engineered by Stalin but left to the new deputy minister of defense, Nikolay A. Bulganin, to execute. In June 1946 an expanded session of the Main Military Council was called to discuss the Zhukov case. The meeting opened with testimony from Chief Marshal of Aviation Aleksandr A. Novikov that Zhukov had frequently spoken against Stalin's wartime leadership. (Typically, Novikov testified nine years later that he had been arrested in April 1946 and tortured until he agreed to sign the accusations against Zhukov.) Golikov, then head of the Personnel Directorate, was among those present. He had prepared a notebook detailing his view of Zhukov, replete with personal details, and he spoke to this at the meeting. By the end of the meeting, every member of the Politburo also spoke against Zhukov, virtually in chorus, and he was assigned—exiled might be a better term—to the militarily unimportant Odessa Military District. Golikov had extracted his first pound of flesh from Zhukov, whom he blamed for his troubles in command during the war, but his guidance came from Stalin.[25]

In 1949–50 Golikov reportedly participated in the work of a commission called for by Stalin to investigate the so-called Leningrad affair, in which the Leningrad party leadership was suspected of acting independently of central party control. The commission determined that Colonel General Iosif Vasilevich Shikin, head of the Chief Political Directorate of the Soviet Army, was a member of the "Vosnesensky opposition," and Shikin was removed from his position. When Golikov was replaced by Aleksei A. Yepishev as head of the Chief Political Directorate just one year after his elevation to marshal of the Soviet Union in 1961, it was reportedly because of pressure from the Leningrad party organization, which resented his role in the Leningrad affair.[26]

With the death of Stalin and the demise of Beria, Zhukov became defense minister once more and was instrumental in ensuring Khrushchev's victory over Stalinist hard-liners Molotov, Kaganovich, and others in the June 1957 party plenum. But later that year Khrushchev saw in Zhukov a rival for control of party and state institutions, and in October, while Zhukov was making an official visit to Yugoslavia and Albania, he was dismissed as defense minister. At this point, Golikov, then commanding the Military Academy of Armored Troops, wrote Khrushchev to the effect that everyone at the academy supported his actions against Zhukov. In January 1958 Khrushchev appointed Golikov director of the Main Political Directorate of the Soviet armed forces. Although Khrushchev knew, of course, of Golikov's cowardly actions at Stalingrad, he also knew that Golikov hated Zhukov and could be relied on in this political post to eliminate Zhukov's influence. After removing Zhukov from the party Presidium and Central Committee and arranging his retirement in March 1958, Golikov did everything possible to isolate him and prevent old friends from visiting him. In recognition of Golikov's role in the elimination of Zhukov, Khrushchev promoted him to marshal of the Soviet Union in 1961. But Khrushchev was removed as first secretary in October 1964, and in 1971 he died. Golikov was replaced as head of the Main Political Directorate in 1962. He died in 1980, reputedly "shunned by his fellow marshals."[27]

Finally, there is the fate of Ivan I. Proskurov. In the fall of 1941, his wife, Aleksandra, and his two daughters were sent to Kuibyshev with only the clothes on their backs (everything else had been confiscated). They were housed with strangers. Aleksandra and her older daughter, Lidia, were subjected to continuing interrogation, after which Aleksandra was arrested and imprisoned. The girls were left on their own until December 1941, when their mother and they were transferred by prison train to Petropavlovsk in north Kazakhstan. Here, Aleksandra was given documents identifying her as the wife of Ivan Proskurov, enemy of the people, and she and her daughters were exiled to a remote village. She remained there with her younger daughter, Galina, suffering severe hardship and illness, until Ivan Proskurov's posthumous rehabilitation on May 11, 1954. Meanwhile, their older daughter, fifteen-year-old Lidia, decided to risk returning to Moscow; after a harrowing journey in wartime conditions, she made it. She was helped in obtaining official permission to remain in the city through the intercession and assistance of famed polar air explorer Major General of Aviation Mikhail V. Vodopianov, a friend of her father's.[28]

In a cemetery not far from the Yu. A. Gagarin Air Force Academy in the town of Monino, a suburb of Moscow, there is an unusual grave site. A large, impressive monument bears a photograph of Proskurov and the words "Hero of the Soviet Union Lieutenant General of Aviation Ivan Iosifovich Proskurov, Commander of Bomber Aviation" and "Proskurova Aleksandra Ignatievna." At the base of the monument are the words "From the Ministry of Defense USSR." But the general does not lie here. No one really knows where his remains are buried.

Aleksandra died in 1990. At her request, her ashes were placed in an urn and interred at the site.

Conclusion

Will the Future Be a Repeat
of the Past?

The characterization of Stalin that emerges from this book is at variance with that advanced by many American, European, and Russian historians. It seems doubtful that Stalin's foreign policy followed the conventional patterns of nineteenth-century diplomacy. Some have said that his August 1939 treaty with Nazi Germany, which succeeded in delaying German aggression for over a year, enabled Stalin to improve the USSR's defensive posture somewhat. There were improvements, but Stalin hesitated until it was too late to take the steps urged on him by his military professionals. Actually, Stalin's underlying motivation for the 1939 treaty was to render the German conquest of Poland inevitable. This, he hoped, would result in a major conflict between Germany and Poland's allies, France and Great Britain. His reasoning was based on Marxist-Leninist doctrine, which held that such a conflict would exhaust the principal European capitalist powers, creating a revolutionary situation that the USSR could exploit to eliminate the German threat and expand Soviet power throughout the Continent.

Another view justifying the nonaggression pact was advanced by Soviet propaganda and is still held today in official publications in the Russian Federation. Stalin was convinced that throughout the 1930s the foreign policy of France and Great Britain, supported by America, was based on acceptance of Hitler's demands in the hope he would turn against the Soviet Union. This policy culminated in the infamous Munich agreement of September 1938 between Germany and Italy on the one hand and France and Great Britain on the other to render Czechoslovakia helpless in the face of German military force. Neither Czechoslovakia nor the USSR was party to the negotiations, which Stalin saw as constituting another, even more dangerous phase in the West's anti-Soviet program. Stalin continued to distrust the Western powers and their warnings of Hitler's intentions throughout the period between Poland's defeat and June 22, 1941. Stalin's rejection of these warnings and his pathological antipathy toward the West were motivated in great part by his belief that Western leaders were totally anticommunist on ideological grounds, hence determined to pursue anti-Soviet goals. From the late 1920s until the purges of 1937–38, reporting received by Stalin from Soviet intelligence sources and diplomats in Great Britain, France, the United States, Poland, Czechoslovakia, and elsewhere constantly reinforced these views.[1]

Many individuals and groups in Great Britain, France, and America indeed feared the spread of communism, but Stalin seemed unable or unwilling to understand the reasons underlying the West's attitudes toward Soviet communism. His coercive collective farm policy, the famine that followed, and the brutal purges of 1937–38 were observed by many in the West with concern and apprehension. Moreover, the French and British people's fear of war, based on memories of the horrendous losses in 1914–18, disposed their governments to succumb to Hitler's demands even though many, such as Winston Churchill, recognized the danger and spoke out for a more vigorous anti-Nazi position. Later, in September 1939, when Great Britain declared war on Germany and Churchill joined the cabinet, it was virtually inconceivable that this stalwart anti-Nazi would have joined Hitler in an attack on the USSR. As for America, Roosevelt would never have departed from his anti-Hitler, pro-British stance to urge attacks on the USSR. Stalin had little grasp of the political realities in Western countries and his prejudices were increased by reporting from Soviet ambassadors and intelligence residencies in London, Paris, and Washington that pandered to and magnified his fears. How must intelligent men such as Ivan M. Maisky in London and Solomon A. Lozovsky in Moscow have felt when they parroted the party line in their discussions with American and British diplomats in the spring of 1941? To do otherwise would have meant their deaths.[2]

None of Stalin's hopes came to fruition, largely because of unforeseen events. The occupation of Denmark and Norway, followed by the rapid collapse of Dutch and Belgian defenses, the total defeat of the British expeditionary force, and the collapse of the French army—all during April, May, and June 1940—destroyed the possibility of the long conflict he had envisioned. The most important reasons, however, for the failure of the Marxist-Leninist scenario and the tragedy of June 1941 were to be found in Stalin's personality, his gross errors of judgment, and the ideologically warped system he created. For example, his "recovery of the tsarist patrimony" is often cited as a positive result of the 1939 treaty with Hitler. Why then did Stalin immediately alienate the populations of the territories he acquired through it by brutally imposing the Stalinist system on them? Was this not the action of an ideologue indifferent to the fact that these people had never known Soviet communism and that the harsh methods used in implementing it would create recruits for German sabotage and espionage? Or did he believe that his position and that of his system would never be secure unless he could impose it on them?

Stalin's personal responsibility for the monumental losses of the war years, particularly those suffered in the first tragic months of the war, cannot be minimized or denied. It is unfortunate, however, that successive Soviet governments consistently concealed the truth and that the Russian Federation continues to withhold archival evidence that would undoubtedly clarify Stalin's actions.

Nikita S. Khrushchev's "secret speech" of 1956 did not tell the whole story. The Soviet leaders who replaced him soon began to rally round the dead Boss, refusing to allow full access to the records or permit the publication of material critical of Stalin's actions in the prewar period. In the immediate post-Soviet period some criticism appeared, but because it lacked essential archival detail much of it was unconvincing, and it ignored the most serious Stalinist actions and errors. In recent years, defense of Stalin and the punitive organs on which he and his system depended has become more widespread in Russia, while access to key archives or their public release has virtually ceased. Incredible though it may seem, archivally sourced material that was officially released and published in the mid-1990s was later reclassified by some agencies and denied to researchers in its original form even though these researchers possessed specific archival references.

Defenders of Stalin's role have blamed the extensive, comprehensive German deception or disinformation program for his refusal to accept intelligence from his own services that reflected German intentions to invade and for his insistence that no actions be undertaken by his military professionals that might provoke the Germans to attack. There can be no doubt that the German deception effort, led by Hitler himself, was highly effective. Not only did it mislead Soviet intelligence and diplomacy, but Hitler appears to have personally reassured Stalin that Great Britain, not the Soviet Union, was Germany's principal enemy. While Stalin shared some of these assurances with his top military leaders, he apparently never revealed precise details or the extent to which he believed, and indeed acted on, them in matters vital to his country's defense. How to explain his incredible toleration of the yearlong Luftwaffe reconnaissance program that doomed his air forces to destruction on June 22, 1941, and left his unprotected troops open to murderous strafing? Or his naïve belief that the attacks that came at dawn that morning were the work of recalcitrant Wehrmacht generals acting against Hitler's wishes? Had Stalin discussed these questions frankly with his top military leaders, they might have been able to disabuse him of some of his convictions. But this was not Stalin's style. He was convinced that he possessed the only correct information on German intentions, and he kept it to himself, saying only to his top leaders: "I have other reports."

Leaving aside Stalin's poor judgment or naïveté in trusting Hitler, an important reason for the success of German deception lay in the system Stalin had created. The weight of evidence furnished by the Soviet intelligence and security services and confirmed by the observations of agents in the railroads and of the border troops was overwhelming. In fact, the only rational explanation for this information—the massing of bridging equipment, the equipping of locomotives with devices enabling them to adapt to the Russian railroad track gauge, the instructions to Abwehr agents to collect samples of Soviet fuel and lubricants—was the prospect of an imminent German invasion. If Stalin did not accept this information, however, it simply could not be acted on. He alone was the final arbiter of what constituted valid intelligence. Few professional officers would risk confronting Stalin. The memory of the terror of the 1930s was too recent and the military leadership at the very top was too aware of the new wave of arrests taking place during April, May, and June 1941. On the other hand, individuals such as Berlin military attaché Tupikov and Beria's friend Ambassador Dekanozov persisted in reporting bad news, even knowing Stalin's likely reaction.

Another aspect of Stalin's treatment of intelligence was his criteria for selection of personnel. Over the years he preferred men he could dominate and rely on to do his bidding not only in intelligence but in the military, the government, and the economy. Stalin's preference for keeping around him men such as Voroshilov, who feared him and would always defer to him, was well known. Apologists for the foreign intelligence service of state security have complained that the service never had an analytic capability. Its sole function was the collection and dissemination of raw reports to the leadership. But in its Information Department, Soviet military intelligence had an analytic component that for some years produced analyses based on a variety of sources ranging from its own and state security agent reporting to overt information derived from foreign periodicals. In July 1940 Stalin fired Ivan I. Proskurov as head of military intelligence. Proskurov's independent outlook and determination to tell the truth as he saw it never endeared him to Stalin. To replace him, Stalin brought in a political general, Filipp I. Golikov, who was appointed to ensure that Information Department reports and summaries faithfully mirrored Stalin's convictions. Up until the invasion, Golikov manipulated available information in such a way as to make it appear that the Wehrmacht was still deploying its forces to attack the British Isles. Golikov himself said in a conversation with Viktor Anfilov in 1965: "I admit I distorted intelligence to please Stalin because I feared him."[3]

Obviously, then, it was Stalin's insistence on accepting German deception as truth, his rejection of valid intelligence from his own services, and his failure to recognize that the warnings from Western powers, themselves threatened by Hitler's aggressiveness, were both accurate and well intentioned, that led to the debacle of the summer of 1941. Nevertheless, one might wonder how it was that the Red Army, on whom the Soviet people had always counted to repel aggression, collapsed so quickly. There were many reasons: the superiority of the seasoned German forces arrayed against them, their lack of training, adequate transport, and effective logistics. Overshadowing and aggravating these shortcomings was the uncertainty caused among the military by public pronouncements such as the June 14, 1941, TASS communiqué that there was no danger of war. Even more debilitating was the fear and distrust that pervaded Red Army ranks at all levels. The root cause of this feat was the wave of repression that engulfed the army in 1937–38, when thousands of experienced officers perished as enemies of the people.

Beyond Stalin was the system he created. Defenders of his actions in the purges claim that it was necessary to rid the army of a potential fifth column. More likely they were motivated by his determination to eliminate anyone who opposed him or might oppose him. As the numbers of officers lost in this modern inquisition mounted, Stalin drew on the party for replacements, however green, and urged that junior officers be advanced regardless of their degree of experience. What he and many of his closest associates failed to understand was how the purges affected the spirits of those who survived. The atmosphere of terror paralyzed the will of even the best of those still serving and affected their performance on the summer's battlefields. Stalin seemed as indifferent to this aspect of the earlier purges as he was to the effect of those conducted during the months of April, May, and June 1941.[4]

These later arrests reveal much about Stalin's modus operandi. Many of the victims were from the defense industry or from the technical side of the air forces. They were primarily scapegoats for problems in aviation, and their purging fit the pattern Stalin had established years earlier to blame others for problems caused by the furious pace imposed by his industrialization programs. Most of the other victims, several of whom he had known well professionally and had personally promoted, were active air force officers. Many of them had also served in the Spanish civil war. Their service abroad and their independent ways made them anathema to Stalin. Moreover, they knew too much about Stalin's failure to deal with the German menace. He did not, however, move quickly to eliminate them as a group. His approach resembled that of a skillful deep-sea fisherman who, after his strike, plays out sufficient line to persuade his prey that it is free, continuing until he decides it is time to end the game. So Stalin often decided to rid himself of an individual but allowed that person to be appointed to an important position first; then, when circumstances seemed right, he pulled the line in, that is, had the person arrested. All this under circumstances that did not point to him as the instigator. Thus, he waited until Proskurov arrived at his new assignment north of Leningrad to have him arrested and returned to Moscow arrest even though hostilities with Finland had just begun in earnest. It was a matter of complete indifference to Stalin that he had deprived the Northern Front of the one who had met Germans in air combat in Spain and knew the Finnish theater intimately. Stalin's priorities were to get rid of men like Proskurov. What Stalin knew was that they knew too much.

This record of Stalin's actions in the prewar period may seem yet another attack on the man and his record. There is no need for such an attack here: Martin Amis, Miklos Kun, and others have recently undertaken that task in greater depth and detail.[5] The blame for the catastrophe of 1941 falls not only on Stalin but on the system of government by fear that he created over the years. If action had to be taken on a given problem, it was

Stalin who had to intervene, threatening punishment. But when, in 1941, collective farms did not deliver their quotas of serviceable trucks and tractors to newly mobilized Red Army units and tank factories failed to produce their quotas of new T-34 tanks, Stalin's threats were to no avail. Fear had its limits, as Stalin, mesmerized by Hitler's deceptive tactics, seemed unable to act.

The late Oleg Suvenirov in the conclusion to his epochal work, *Tragedia RKKA, 1937–1938*, asks why no one was punished for committing the murders of the purges. He points out that the huge losses of 1941–42 were the direct result of the purges. True, but the struggle to avoid any serious accounting for those losses and for the mindless terror unleashed by Stalin continues. On May 29, 2000, for example, the Military Collegium of the Supreme Court of the Russian Federation decided that a number of Beria's henchmen were not guilty of treason. As a result, the death sentences and confiscation of property pronounced on Pavel Meshik, former interior minister of the Ukrainian SSR; Vladimir Dekanozov, the minister of internal affairs of the Georgian SSR; and Lev Vlodzimirsky, the vicious head of the USSR MVD Investigative Unit for Especially Important Cases were lifted. They were found guilty only of having exceeded their authority. This judicial action and the many articles since then by veterans of the security organs reflect efforts by veterans of the Soviet punitive organs, as well as recent retirees from the Federal Security Service and Foreign Intelligence of the Russian Federation, to demonstrate that they and their predecessors acted only for the good of Soviet security. They consider this Soviet period a normal, albeit blemished, era of Russian history that should be honored.

What of the future? The "victory" of President Putin in the 2004 elections signaled a victory for those who would prefer to forget the crimes of the past. Moreover, Putin's reliance on former KGB colleagues to staff key posts in his government and his actions to bring important media entities such as television under his control suggest a return to the methods of yesteryear. An example of the increasingly authoritarian methods favored by Putin and his associates is the failure of Russian authorities to clarify the history of the immediate prewar period through the release of pertinent archival material. This is a scandal and a disservice to the Russian people. The Russian government should make the truth available openly and directly. Historians call on it to do so.

Organization and Functions of Soviet Military Intelligence

The two operational departments of Soviet military intelligence, East and West, and their subordinate sections responsible for individual countries, oversaw and directed the work of the RU residencies (*rezidentura*) abroad. Among the important residencies in the East were Tokyo and Shanghai. There were, naturally, many more under the West Department—for example, Washington, New York, London, Paris, and Berlin. The officers heading these components had to become familiar with the military, political, and economic situation in the countries concerned. They also had to know the operational environment facing the residencies, that is, the effectiveness of indigenous counterintelligence, as well as the backgrounds and degree of access to information of agent sources. The "legal" residencies were located within Soviet missions and consisted of the military and air attachés, plus other officers under various civilian covers such as TASS, the trade delegation, and components of the embassies.[1] The attachés exploited their official positions to elicit information from other attachés, officials of the host country, and influential citizens. Officers under other legal cover controlled agent sources who were fully aware of their affiliation with Soviet intelligence. They also handled "illegal" residents, who maintained contact with those particularly valuable agent sources who, for security reasons, could not meet with members of the Soviet mission. Illegal residents were generally trained and experienced people documented as non-Soviet foreigners living and working under commercial or other cover they had themselves devised.

Communications between RU Moscow and legal residencies abroad were the responsibility of the operational departments, which used radio, commercial telegraph, and the diplomatic pouch. The messages dealt with administrative matters concerning the residency's activities and its agent assets. Many of the personnel problems had to be resolved by the RU chief himself. For example, in June 1939 Proskurov became involved in deciding whether the famous illegal resident in Tokyo, Richard Sorge, would return to Moscow or remain in Japan; he also had to approve an extraordinary monetary award to Sorge and members of his group.[2] Most of the traffic between Moscow and the field concerned intelligence requirements and information reports from individual sources. When these reports were received, they were examined by the appropriate country desk, which had to be ready to respond to questions about them from the Information Department or from the RU chief himself. The chief might then determine the dissemination. An important aspect of report production and dissemination was the need to protect the identity and security of the agent source. If the source description was too vague or the reliability of the source not properly indicated, the impact of a report could be lessened. Case in point, the first word of Hitler's decision to invade the USSR in the spring of 1941 came to the RU on December 29, 1940, from a source who "heard from well-informed circles" that Hitler had given the order to prepare for war against the USSR. The report was disseminated to the defense commissar and the chief of the general staff but made little impression. This was unfortunate for the Soviets because the agent was highly placed in the German Foreign Office, had good contacts among the German military, and had been a productive RU source since the mid-1930s. He followed up with reports on January 4 and March 20, 1941, that reinforced his initial information. To some degree, the failure to recognize the importance of this report may be related to the changes of personnel at the head of the RU and also in the Information Department brought about by the purges. But the principal culprit was Golikov, who had no background in intelligence and was normally disposed to doubt sources predicting an invasion, in deference to the views of the Boss.[3]

Another RU collection capability rested in the intelligence points (*razvedpunkty*) of the intelligence departments of the military districts located on the Soviet frontier. There were a number of these points within each military district, and their purpose was the creation of agent networks in areas across the state frontier for which the military district was responsible. Information from these agent sources was forwarded to the military district intelligence departments, where it was incorporated into the intelligence summaries prepared by the departments and forwarded to the RU. Some have argued that the level of agents acquired by the intelligence points was too low for them to have obtained the information needed to persuade the Soviet leadership of the German danger.[4] For example, none of the agents were able to obtain documentary evidence from the headquarters of the German units along the frontier. The problem was that many officers in military district intelligence departments, aware that Stalin would reject reports predicting a German invasion, refused to accept information of this kind from intelligence points. After the German attack, some intelligence point officers reported the problem to NKVD Special Department investigators.[5]

Analysis of incoming reports, the production of finished intelligence summaries and special reports, and the preparation of intelligence requirements was the responsibility of the RU Information Department. Within the department various sections dealt with individual countries or groups of countries, the First Section with Germany; the Second with Poland, the Baltic States, and Romania, and so forth. Despite the importance of this department and the obvious need for continuity, there were frequent changes during Proskurov's time as chief. Grigory P. Pugachev apparently headed the Information Department from 1939 to December 1940, when he was replaced by Nikolai I. Dubinin, who was in turn temporarily succeeded by Vasily A. Novobranets, whom Proskurov had brought into the department as deputy chief for the Far East.[6] The RU chief was personally involved in decisions on dissemination of important individual reports. After receiving a report, the chief might request clarification from the operational department on certain aspects before sending it on. He invariably signed the reports himself. When Proskurov was chief, he sometimes sent two or three reports to Stalin under a single letter of transmittal.

Apart from such standard components as personnel, finance, logistics, communications, and cipher security, the RU had an important Third, or Military-Technical, Department encompassing specialities such as artillery, tanks, aviation, communications technology, and chemical and bacteriological techniques. This department maintained elements in the larger residencies in scientifically advanced countries. Its chief, Aleksei A. Konovalov, had served in military-technical elements since 1935, untouched by the purges. The External Relations Department maintained contact on behalf of the Defense Commissariat with foreign military attachés in Moscow both for administrative purposes and for the obtaining of whatever intelligence it could from these relationships. A good example is the June 21, 1940, report on Franco-German armistice arrangements obtained from German military attaché General Ernst Köstring by the chief of the External Relations Department, Colonel Grigory A. Osetrov.[7]

We know that the RU had a radio intercept capability in the immediate prewar period. On October 26, 1939, for instance, RU chief Proskurov sent a report to the defense commissar based on the intercept of radio communications between the chief of staff of the Japanese Kwantung Army in Manchuria and the Personnel Department of the War Ministry in Tokyo. The subject was the Khalkin Gol fighting, the panic caused among Japanese officers by the Red Army's attacks, and the fact that Japanese unit losses were so heavy some units had to be reactivated.[8]

The RU was able to obtain the results of British code breaking from sources within its London residency as early as 1940, and as of 1942 it initiated its own decryption of German code, having obtained the ENIGMA code machine on the battlefield.[9]

Hitler's Letters to Stalin

December 31, 1940

Dear Mr. Stalin,

I am using the occasion of sending New Year's greetings and my wishes for success and prosperity to you and the people of Soviet Russia to discuss a series of questions that were raised in my conversations with Mr. Molotov and Mr. Dekanozov.

The struggle with England has entered a decisive phase, and I intend not later than the summer of the coming year to put an end to this rather drawn-out question by seizing and occupying the heart of the British Empire—the British Isles. I am aware of the difficulty of this operation but believe that it can be carried out, for I see no other way of ending this war.

As I wrote you earlier, the approximately seventy divisions that I must keep in the Government General are undergoing reorganization and training in an area inaccessible to English aviation and intelligence. I understood from my discussions with Messrs. Molotov and Dekanozov that this has aroused in you understandable anxiety. Beginning in approximately March, these troops will be moved to the Channel and the western coast of Norway, and in their place new units will be assembled for accelerated training. I wanted to warn you of this in advance.

In addition, I intend to use these troops to force the English out of Greece, and for this it will be necessary to move them through Romania and Bulgaria. Those troops that will carry out the invasion of England from Norwegian territory will continue to utilize transit rights through Finland. Germany has no interests in Finland or Bulgaria, and as soon as we achieve our goals in this war, I will immediately withdraw my troops. . . .

I especially want to warn you of the following. The agony of England is accompanied by feverish efforts to save it from its inevitable fate. For this purpose they are fabricating all possible foolish rumors, the most important of which can be crudely divided into two categories. These are rumors of planned invasions by the USSR into Germany and by Germany against the USSR. I do not wish to dwell on the absurdity of such nonsense. However, on the basis of information in my possession, I predict that as our invasion of the [British] Isles draws closer, the intensity of such rumors will increase and fabricated documents will perhaps be added to them.

I will be completely open with you. Some of these rumors are being circulated by appropriate German offices. The success of our invasion of the Isles depends very much on the achievement of tactical surprise. Therefore, it is useful to keep Churchill and his circles in ignorance of our precise plans.

A worsening of the relations between our countries to include armed conflict is the only way for the English to save themselves, and I assure you that they will continue efforts in this direction with their characteristic slyness and craftiness. . . .

For a final solution of what to do with this bankrupt English legacy, and also for the consolidation of the union of socialist countries and the establishment of a new world order, I would like very much to meet personally with you. I have spoken about this with Messrs. Molotov and Dekanozov.

Unfortunately, as you will well understand, an exceptional workload prevents me from arranging our meeting until the smashing of England. Therefore, I propose to plan for this meeting at the end of June–beginning of July 1941 and would be happy if this meets with your agreement and understanding.

Sincerely yours,

Adolf Hitler

May 14, 1941

Dear Mr. Stalin,

I am writing this letter at the moment of having finally concluded that it will be impossible to achieve a lasting peace in Europe, not for us, not for future generations, without the final shattering of England and her destruction as a state. As you well know, I long ago made the decision to carry out a series of military measures to achieve this goal.

The closer the hour of a decisive battle, however, the larger the number of problems I face. For the mass of the German people, no war is popular, especially not a war against England, because the German people consider the English a fraternal people and war between them a tragic event. I will not conceal that I have felt the same way and have several times offered England humane peace terms, taking into consideration England's military situation. However, insulting replies to my peace proposals and the continuing expansion by the English of the field of military operations with the obvious intention of drawing the entire world into war persuade me that there is no other way out of this situation except for an invasion of the Isles and the decisive destruction of that country.

English intelligence, however, has very cleverly begun to use the concept of "fraternal peoples" for its own purposes, applying it to its own propaganda, not without success.

Consequently, opposition to my decision to invade the Isles has drawn in many elements of German society, including individual members of the higher levels of state and military leadership. You are certainly aware that one of my deputies, Mr. Hess, in a fit of insanity, I suppose, flew to London, taking this unbelievable action, to the best of my knowledge, to awaken the English to common sense. Judging by information in my possession, similar moods have struck several generals of my army, particularly those who have distinguished relatives in England descending from the same ancient, noble roots.

In this connection, a special warning is raised by the following circumstance. In order to organize troops for the invasion away from the eyes of the English opponent, and in connection with the recent operations in the Balkans, a large number of my troops, about eighty divisions, are located on the borders of the Soviet Union. This possibly gave rise to the rumors now circulating of a likely military conflict between us.

I assure you, on my honor as a chief of state that this is not the case.

From my side, I also react with understanding to the fact that you cannot completely ignore these rumors and have also deployed a sufficient number of your troops on the border.

In this situation I cannot completely exclude the possibility of an accidental outbreak of armed conflict, which given the conditions created by such a concentration of troops might take on very large dimensions, making it difficult if not impossible to determine what caused it in the first place.

I want to be absolutely candid with you.

I fear that some one of my generals might deliberately embark on such a conflict in order to save England from its fate and spoil my plans.

It is a question of no more than a month.

By approximately June 15–20 I plan to begin a massive transfer of troops to the west from your borders.

In connection with this, I ask you, as persuasively as possible, not to give in to any provocations that might emanate from those of my generals who might have forgotten their duty. And, it goes without saying, try not to give them any cause. If it becomes impossible to avoid provocation by some of my generals, I ask you to show restraint, to not respond but to advise me immediately of what has happened through the channel known to you. Only in this way can we attain our mutual goals, on which, it seems to me, we are clearly in agreement.

I thank you for having agreed with me on the question known to you and I ask you to forgive me for the method I have chosen for delivering this letter to you as quickly as possible.

I continue to hope for our meeting in July.

Sincerely yours,

Adolf Hitler

Note: No archival material has been found to authenticate these documents.—DEM

Those Executed without Trial on October 28, 1941

Colonel Generals

Loktionov, Aleksandr D. Former commander, Baltic Special Military District
Shtern, Grigory M. Commander, Antiaircraft Defense Command

Lieutenant Generals of Aviation

Arzhenukhin, Fedor K. Chief, Military Academy for Command and Navigational Personnel
Proskurov, Ivan I. Chief, Air Forces Seventh Army. Former chief, Military Intelligence
Rychagov, Pavel V. Former chief, Chief Directorate, Red Army Air Forces
Smushkevich, Yakov V. Deputy chief, Red Army General Staff for Aviation

Divisional Engineer

Sakrier, Ivan F. Chief, Armaments Directorate, Red Army Air Forces

Major Generals

Kaiukov, Matvei M. Deputy chief, Artillery Directorate, Red Army
Savchenko, Georgy K. Deputy chief, Artillery Directorate for Political Affairs
Volodin, Pavel S. Chief of staff, Red Army Air Forces

Brigade Engineers

Sklizkov, Stepan O. Chief, Small Arms Directorate, Red Army
Sobornov, Mikhail N. Chief, Experimental Design Sector, Technical Council, NKV USSR

Colonel

Zasosov, Ivan I. Chairman, Artillery Committee

Major

Nesterenko, Maria P. Deputy commander, Separate Special-Purpose Air Regiment. Wife of General Pavel V. Rychagov

Civilians

Bulatov, Dimitry A. Secretary, Omsk Oblast Party Committee
Goloshchekin, Filipp I. Involved in assassination of Tsar Nicholas II and his family
Rozov, David A. Deputy People's Commissar for Trade, USSR. Former chairman, AMTORG
Taubin, Yakov G. Chief, Special Design Bureau, NKV USSR

Wives

Savchenko, Aleksandra I. Wife of Major General Savchenko
Rozova, Zinaida P. Wife of David A. Rozov

Chronology of Agent Reporting

August 27, 1940: RU report from Paris: "The Germans have turned down an offensive against England. Preparations, apparently continuing for such an eventuality, are merely intended to hide the movement of German forces to the east, where there are already 106 divisions."

Fall 1940: The Luftwaffe is ordered to dismantle communications stations and other arrangements originally made to support the German invasion of England (ULTRA).

October 1940: Korsikanets reports that he has learned from one source that Germany will go to war after the first of the coming year and from another source that war will come in six months.

December 7, 1940: Soviet Ambassador Dekanozov receives an anonymous letter saying that "next spring Hitler intends to attack the USSR."

December 29, 1940: Ariets reports: "War will be declared in March 1941."

January 4, 1941: Ariets reports that he has learned from a friend in the military that Hitler has approved an "especially secret" order, known to only a few people, to prepare for war with the USSR.

February 7, 1941: Agent Teffi (NKGB counterintelligence in the Greek embassy in Moscow) reports: "There are growing rumors of a German attack on the Soviet Union. There are two versions. The first is that it will occur after the defeat of England. The second, which is more likely, is that Germany will attack the Soviet Union first."

February 21, 1941: Dora reports from Switzerland that "the German offensive will begin at the end of May."

February 28, 1941: Ariets describes three major German army groups readying for attacks against the USSR. "The beginning of the attack is provisionally set for May 20."

March 14, 1941: A German major tells a military attaché: "We are completely changing our plan. We are moving east, to the USSR. We will take from the USSR grain, coal, oil."

March 20, 1941: Sumner Welles notifies Ambassador Umansky that the United States has authentic information that "it is the intention of Germany to attack the Soviet Union."

March 28, 1941: Ambassador Dekanozov's secretary receives a phone call: "Around May a war will begin against Russia."

April 2, 1941: Starshina describes an air force plan for an operation. "Some think it will come in May, some in June."

April 4, 1941: Harry reports from France that the Germans are no longer considering invading England but will continue their bombing of the country.

April 5, 1941: The Prague RU residency reports that the German invasion has provisionally been set for May 15 and that it will be masked as a large-scale preparation for the invasion of England.

April 6, 1941: Dora learns from highly placed government officials in Berlin that they expect the campaign to begin on June 15.

April 9–10, 1941: Yun, an agent covering the U.S. embassy in Moscow, states that after the war with Yugoslavia Germany will invade the USSR.

April 15, 1941: Ambassador Laurence Steinhardt of the United States meets with Solomon Lozovsky, deputy in the Foreign Affairs Commissariat, and asks that Molotov be informed: "Beware of Germany. . . . There is more to it than simple rumors; it would be madness for Germany to take this step, but they can do it."

April 18, 1941: In his memoirs, I. I. Fediuninski, commander of the Fifteenth Rifle Corps, says that a German NCO came through the Soviet lines on April 18 claiming that the German invasion would come at 4:00 a.m. on June 22. When told, M. I. Potapov, commander of the Fifth Army, said, "You're sounding the alarm in vain."

April 19, 1941: Churchill warns Stalin of Germany's plans to invade.

April 23, 1941: Vladimir Vrana, an RU agent working in the export division of the Skoda plant in Prague, reports: "It is believed that Hitler will attack the USSR in the second half of June."

April 23, 1941: Vrach, an RU Bucharest source who got his information from a colonel in the German air mission, reports the war will begin in May and end in July.

April 26, 1941: The Helsinki residency reports that highly placed German officers are convinced that Hitler will attack the USSR.

May 5, 1941: Richard Sorge passes microfilm of telegram from Ribbentrop to Ott, German ambassador to Tokyo, that says: "Germany will begin a war against the USSR in the middle of June 1941." AVS reports: "The date for German military operations against the USSR was to have been May 15 . . . it has now been moved back to the middle of June." AVS learns from his source Gerstenberg that the "month of June would see the beginning of the war."

May 9, 1941: Tupikov, military attaché and RU legal resident in Berlin, reports: "Defeat of the Red Army will be completed in one or one and a half months with arrival of the German army on the meridian of Moscow." Sofia agent

Margarit reports that Germany plans to attack in June: "Germany is preparing to open hostilities against the USSR in the summer of 1941 before the harvest."

May 11, 1941: Starshina reports that "The First Air Fleet will be the main component for operations against the USSR."

May 15, 1941: Sorge reports that war will begin on June 21 or 22.

June 11, 1941: Starshina reports that Göring will move his headquarters to Romania. "The question of an attack on the USSR has definitely been decided. One should consider the possibility of a surprise attack."

June 13, 1941: Sorge: "I repeat: Nine armies with the strength of 150 divisions will begin an offensive at dawn on June 22." Boevoy, an RU agent of the Sofia residency reports: "According to information from Zhurin [a member of the Bulgarian High Military Council], the Führer has decided to attack the USSR before the end of this month."

June 16, 1941: Starshina: "All preparations by Germany for an armed attack on the Soviet Union have been completed and the blow can be expected at any time."

June 19, 1941: American journalist Alice Leone-Moats tells everyone in the American embassy in Moscow that Gebhardt von Walther, the German embassy secretary, has told her that the attack will come on June 21.

June 19, 1941: Willy Lehmann, Gestapo agent of the RU, reports that the attack will come on June 22 at 3:00 a.m. NKGV Helsinki agent Monakh tells his case officer that war will start on June 22.

June 20, 1941: The Kosta network of the Sofia residency reports that war will begin on June 21 or 22.

June 21, 1941: KhVS (Gerhard Kegel of the German embassy, Moscow) reports that Germany will attack on June 22 between 3:00 and 4:00 a.m. Leopold Trepper, illegal RU resident in Paris, advises Susloparov, the legal resident there, that "tomorrow, June 22, [Germany] will suddenly attack the Soviet Union." That evening, German deserter Alfred H. Liskow says that during the night the river Bug will be crossed with rafts, boats, and pontoons.

Glossary of Spies and Their Masters

Names in uppercase are those of intelligence officers and/or prominent government officials; lowercase indicates recruited agents.

avs: Code name of Kurt Völkisch, German press officer, German embassy, Bucharest

Advokat: Source of Helsinki residency

AGAIANTS, Aleksandr I.: Named resident in Berlin NKVD residency in 1937

AGEICHIK, Yakov O.: Colonel, chief of staff of the Ninety-second Border Troop Detachment. Border institute representative

AKHMEDOV, Ismail G.: RU officer in Berlin

Alta: Code name of Ilse Stoebe, RU agent located in Warsaw and then Berlin

Albanets: Émigré industrialist and former tsarist officer. Subsource for NKVD Berlin residency

ALBERT: Code name of Alexandr RADO, RU chief, Switzerland

ALEKSANDR: Code name of Semen D. KREMER, RU officer in London

ALLAKHVERDOV, Mikhail A.: Organized the Information Section of the German Department, the first analytical component of the NKGB

Ariets: Code name of Rudolf von Scheliha, German counselor of the German embassy, Warsaw. Later with German Foreign Office, Berlin. A recruited RU agent in both locales

ARNOLD: Code name of Vasily I. TUPIKOV, RU military attaché, Berlin

AVS: Code name of Kurt Völkisch, agent in Warsaw and Bucharest

Azorsky: Code name of Vladimir Zaimov, agent of the Sofia residency

Baron: Code name of RU agent Frantisek Moravec, former head of Czech military intelligence

BAZHANOV, Ivan G: Officer of the RU Berlin residency

Belvedere: Agent of the Sofia residency

BENENSON, M. L.: Captain, deputy Chief of the First (Railroad) Department, GTU

Berlinks, Oreste: Gestapo double agent, code name Peter. NKGB code name Litseist

BERZIN, Jan Karlovich: RU officer who recruited Richard SORGE

BILTON: Code name of Ivan M. KOZLOV, RU London residency

BLOK: Code name of Viktor Z. LEBEDEV, RU Belgrade residency

Blunt, Anthony: NKGB agent in British counterintelligence organization MI-5. Code name Tony

BOCHKOV, Viktor M.: Chief of NKVD Special Departments

Boevoy: Agent of the Sofia RU residency

BOGDANOV, Ivan A.: Lieutenant general, commander of border troops of Belorussian NKVD

BOLSHAKOV, Ivan A.: Colonel, head of the German desk in military intelligence

Brand: RU Helsinki agent. Real name not identified

Breitenbach: Code name of Willy Lehmann. Berlin policeman, later Gestapo, recruited by NKVD

BRION: Code name of Colonel Ivan A. SKLIAROV, RU London residency

BUDKEVICH, Sergei, L.: Subordinate of RU resident in Tokyo. Link to SORGE and his network

Burgess, Guy: One of the Cambridge Five. Code name Mädchen

Bykov: Agent run by the Terespol railroad (GTU)

Cairncross, John: NKGB agent. Became the personal secretary to Sir Maurice Hankey, through whose office flowed British government policy and intelligence documents. Code name List

CHERNY, Ivan I.: Major general London RU resident and military attaché up to August 1940

DEKANOZOV, Vladimir G.: Soviet ambassador in Berlin. Aware of RU and NKGB agent reporting

DERGACHEV, Ivan F.: Colonel, RU resident and military attaché in Sofia

DORA: Code name of Alexandr RADO, RU Switzerland

Diane: Subsource of DORA in RU Switzerland

DRONOV, N.S.: Major general named chief of the RU Information Department in April 1941

DUBININ, Nikolai I.: Replaced Grigory PUGACHEV as head of the RU Information Department in December 1940

ERDBERG, Alexander: Alias used by Aleksandr M. KOROTKOV, deputy chief, NKVD/NKGB residency, Berlin

Ernst: Informant in the German embassy, Moscow, possibly a Soviet employee

FEDOTOV, Petr V.: Head of NKVD/NKGB counterintelligence in 1940–41

FILIPPOV, I. F.: NKGB officer and case officer for Litseist, under TASS cover. Code name FILOSOF

FILOSOF: Code name of I. F. FILIPPOV, member of NKVD residency in Berlin

FITIN, Pavel Mikhailovich: Chief of the First (Foreign Intelligence) Directorate, NKGB

GAEV, Pavel V.: Chief of the Intelligence Department, Odessa Military District

GENDIN, Semen G.: Acting chief, RU

GILBERT, Jean: Alias used by Leopold TREPPER, illegal RU resident in Paris

Gladiator: Agent covering the Italian embassy in Moscow

GOGLIDZE, Sergei A.: Longtime Beria colleague and special representative of the CC VKP(b) and SNK in the Moldavian SSR

GOLIKOV, Filipp I.: General who replaced PROSKUROV as chief of the RU. Later became marshal of the Soviet Union

GORDON, Boris M.: Berlin NKVD resident executed in 1937

GORSKY, Anatoly: RU resident in London. Code name VADIM

Grek: Member of the Technical Department of the Wehrmacht. Subsource, NKVD/NKGB Berlin residency

GUDIMOVICH, Petr I.: Head of the new legal residency in Warsaw in 1940. Code name IVAN

GUNEEV, S. I.: Lieutenant colonel, Operational Directorate of the general staff, designated contact with the RU in Moscow

GUSHCHENKO, Ivan V.: Military attaché and resident, RU Tokyo

Harnack, Arvid: German official of the Economics Ministry in Berlin. Recruited by Boris Gordon. Code name Korsikanets

HARRY: Code name of Henri ROBINSON, RU illegal resident in Paris

Hegendorf: Assistant German military attaché in Moscow

Herrnstadt, Rudolf: Correspondent of the *Berliner Tageblatt* in Moscow, where he was recruited by the RU. Moved to Warsaw at the RU's request

HEWELL, Walther: Ribbentrop's liaison officer with the Führer's office

Hirschfeld: Birth name of Ivar Lissner, double agent under control of the Gestapo

Hotsumi, Ozaki: Leading Japanese member of the SORGE RU agent network. Code names Invest, Otto

Invest: Code name of Ozaki Hotsumi, leading Japanese member of the Sorge network

Italianets: German naval intelligence officer, Berlin NKVD/NKGB residency agent

IVAN: Code name of Petr GUDIMOVICH, NKGB legal resident in Warsaw

Jack: Valet to the American ambassador in Moscow, NKVD/NKGB agent

Karmen: NKGB agent in the American embassy, Moscow, who was personal interpreter and assistant to the wife of the ambassador

Kegel, Gerhard: RU agent in German embassy, Moscow. Code names: KhVS, Kurt

KHLOPOV, Vasily Ye.: Assistant to assistant air attaché SKORNIAKOV in Berlin

KHOMENKO Vasily A.: Major general, chief of the border troops district, Ukrainian SSR

KhVS: Code name of RU agent Gerhard Kegel, German embassy, Moscow

KOBULOV, Amaiak Z.: As of August 1939, NKVD/GUGB resident in Berlin. Arrived as first secretary and then counselor of the Soviet mission

KOBULOV, Bogdan Z.: Deputy commissar, NKGB

KOLONIST: Code name of Nikolai B. KUZNETSOV, a covert employee of the NKGB Second Directorate

KONOVALOV, Aleksei A.: Head of Military-Technical Department, RU

KOPETS, Ivan I.: Commander of air units of the Eighth Army in the Finnish war and veteran of the Spanish civil war. Commander of air forces, Western Front, who committed suicide June 22, 1941

KORF: Code name of Mikhail S. SHAROV, deputy resident, Bucharest, under TASS cover

KOROTKOV, Aleksandr M.: Deputy chief, Berlin NKGB residency. On September 17, 1940, he recontacted Korsikanets, using the alias Alexander ERDBERG. Was case officer of Starshina

Korsikanets: Code name of Arvid Harnack, German Economics Ministry in Berlin

KORTER, George: Assistant to August Ponschab, German consul in Harbin

Kosta: Network of agents in the Sofia RU residency

KOZLOV, Ivan M.: Member of the RU residency and the Soviet military mission in London in 1940. Code name Bilton

KREMER, Semen D.: Member of the RU residency and the Soviet military mission in Great Britain in 1940. Code names ALEKSANDR, SERGEI

KRUGLOV, Sergei N.: NKVD deputy commissar

KULIK, Grigory I.: Crony of Stalin, who chose him to chair the conference on the Finnish war

KURT: Code name of Gerhard KEGEL

KUZNETSOV, A. M.: Colonel chief of the RU First (Western) Department

KUZNETSOV, Nikolai G.: Covert employee of the NKGB Second Directorate. Code name KOLONIST

LEBEDEV, Viktor Z.: RU residency officer active in Belgrade diplomatic community. Cover was counselor of Belgrade embassy. Code name BLOK

Lehmann, Wilhelm (Willy): German police official who volunteered his services. Later assigned to Gestapo counterintelligence operations against the Soviet mission. Recruited agent of NKVD/NKGB Berlin residency. Code name Breitenbach

LIAKHTEROV, Nikolai G.: RU legal resident, Budapest embassy. Code name MARS

LIKUS, Rudolf: SS Oberführer in Ribbentrop's Special Bureau

Liskow, Alfred H.: German army defector who crossed over on June 21, 1941, and told of impending invasion

Lissner, Ivar: German journalist recruited by the Abwehr, which promised to allow his Jewish parents to leave Germany

List: Code name of John Cairncross

Litseist: NKGB code name of Oreste Berlinks, Latvian double agent in Berlin under Gestapo control. Gestapo code name Peter

LTsL: Code name of Margarita Völkisch, RU agent in German embassy, Bucharest

Luchisty: Employee of the heavy-machine building firm AEG. Berlin NKVD/NKGB residency subsource

LYUSHKOV, G. S.: NKVD general who defected to the Japanese army in Manchuria

Mädchen: Code name of Guy Burgess

Margarit: Agent of the RU Sofia residency

MARIA: Code name of Yelena MODRZHINSKAIA, NKGB legal residency in Warsaw

MARS: Code name of legal resident of Budapest embassy Nikolai G. LIAKHTEROV

MASLENNIKOV, Ivan I.: Lieutenant general, deputy NKVD for troops

MASLOV, Mikhail S.: Colonel, assistant military attaché, Belgrade

MATSKE, Gerhard: Colonel, German military attaché, Tokyo

MEISSNER, Otto: Longtime Russian specialist in the German Foreign Ministry who carried on secret talks with DEKANOZOV

MEKHLIS, Lev Z.: Chief of the Political Directorate of the Red Army. Active in the purges

MERETSKOV, Kiril A.: Deputy chief of the general staff, 1938–40; chief, August 1940–January 1941. Imprisoned June–August 1941

MERKULOV, Vsevolod N.: GUGB chief, commissar for State Security

MESHIK, Pavel Ia.: Head of the Ukrainian SSR NKGB

METEOR: Code name of Colonel Nikolai D. SKORNIAKOV of Berlin RU residency

MIKHAILOV, Leonid A.: Legal RU resident in Prague. Code name RUDOLF

MILSHTEIN, Solomon R.: Head of the GTU. Became chief, Third (Secret-Political) Directorate, NKGB in February 1941

MODRZHINSKAIA, Yelena D.: NKGB intelligence officer in Warsaw. Wife of Petr I. Gudimovich. Code name Maria

MOKHOV, Leonid E.: Alias of Leonid A. MIKHAILOV, RU resident in Prague

Monakh: Source of Helsinki NKGB residency

Moravec, Frantisek: Former head of Czech military intelligence whose escape was arranged by SIS. Recruited by RU. Code name Baron

Negri: NKGB agent in German embassy in Moscow

Nemesh: RU agent. Retired Romanian staff officer

NIKOLAI: Code name of Boris N. ZHURAVLIEV

NOVOBRANETS, Vasily A.: Replaced DUBININ as acting head of the information department, RU

ORLOV, Aleksandr G.: Acting chief of the RU, May 1938–April 1939

OSETROV, Grigory A.: Chief of External Relations Department, RU

OSTVALD: Code name of Ivan V. SMIRNOV, RU legal resident in Helsinki

OTTO: Code name of the RU illegal resident in Paris, Leopold TREPPER

Otto: Code name of Ozaki Hotsumi of the SORGE agent network

OVAKIMIAN, Gaik B.: Head of the NKGB residency in New York, under AMTORG cover

PANFILOV, Aleksei P.: Major general, chief of the First Department, RU, 1940–June 1941

PAVLOVSKY, Boris S.: deputy chief of the Investigative Unit, Third (Counterintelligence) Directorate, NKO

PETROV, Ivan A.: Deputy chief of border troops of the Ukrainian NKVD

PETROV, Pavel I.: Alias of Konstantin B. LEONTEV

Philby, Kim: Recruited agent of NKGB. Did not enter SIS until September 1941. Before that he was in Special Operations Executive. Code name Söhnchen

Poeta: Helsinki NKGB residency source

Poisson: Subsource of DORA, RU illegal resident in Switzerland

POLIAKOVA, Maria I.: Lieutenant colonel in the RU since 1932

PONSCHAB, August: German consul in Harbin who passed on to Berlin what appeared to be German disinformation

PROSKUROV, Ivan Iosifovich: Aviator and chief of the RU. Served in the Spanish civil war. Hero of the Soviet Union. Arrested on July 27, 1941, and shot without trial on October 28, 1941

PUGACHEV, Grigory P.: Colonel, acting chief of the Information Department, RU general staff, Red Army, 1939–December 1940

RADO, Alexandr: Chief of the RU illegal residency in Switzerland. Code names ALBERT and DORA

RAMSAY: Code name of Richard SORGE, RU illegal resident in Tokyo

RATO: Code name of Makar M. VOLOSIUK, assistant air attaché in Paris

ROBINSON, Henri: RU illegal resident in Paris. Code name HARRY

RODOS, Boris V.: Deputy to VLODZIMIRSKY of NKVD Investigative Unit for Especially Important Cases. Known for his brutality

RUDOLF: Code name of Leonid A. MIKHAILOV, RU resident in Prague

RYBKIN, Boris A.: Former NKVD resident in Helsinki. Pseudonym Boris N. YARTSEV

RYBKINA, Zoia Ivanovna: Deputy to ALLAKHVERDOV in Information Section of the German Department, NKGB

Rybnikar: Belgrade RU residency source

RYCHAGOV, Pavel V.: Chief of main administration of the air forces, RKKA. Arrested and shot without trial on October 28, 1941

SAMOKHIN, Aleksandr G.: Major general, RU legal resident in Belgrade. Code name SOFOKL

SAVCHENKO, Yakov S.: Sofia RU residency officer. Case officer for Vladimir Zaimov

Schulze-Boysen, Harro: NKVD/NKGB Berlin residency agent. Code name Starshina

SEREDA, Leonid A.: Deputy RU resident in Sofia. Code name ZEVS

SERGEI: Code name of Semen KREMER, RU resident in London

SEROV, Ivan S.: Head of NKVD in the Ukrainian SSR

SHAPOSHNIKOV, Boris M.: Chief of the Soviet general staff at various times before and during the war

SHAROV, Mikhail S.: Deputy RU resident in Bucharest under TASS cover. Code name KORF

SHEVTSOV, Boris F.: Major, assistant air attaché in the London RU residency in 1940

Shibanov: Agent run by the Railroad Department, GTU

SHTERN, Grigory Mikhailovich: Colonel general, chief military adviser in Spain, 1937–38. Commander of the Far Eastern Front, January–April 1941. From March 17 to day of arrest, June 7, 1941, was chief of PVO. Shot without trial on October 28, 1941

SHVARTSMAN, Lev Leonidovich: Deputy to Lev VLODZIMIRSKY, chief of the NKVD Investigative Unit for Especially Important Cases

Shved: German air major, liaison between Air and Foreign ministries, NKGB Berlin residency subsource

SINEGUBOV, N.I.: Chief of the First (Railroad) Department, GTU. Major of state security

SINITSYN, Yelisei T.: NKVD/NKGB resident in Helsinki after the Winter War

SIZOV, Aleksandr F.: Major general, RU London residency. In liaison with Polish, Czech, and Yugoslav governments in exile

SKLIAROV, Ivan A.: Successor to Major General CHERNY as RU resident and Soviet military attaché in London. Code name BRION

SKORNIAKOV, Nikolai D.: Deputy RU resident and air attaché in Berlin. Code name METEOR

Slovak: Agent of the Budapest RU residency

SMIRNOV, Ivan V.: RU legal resident in Helsinki. Code name OSTVALD

SMORODINOV, I. V.: Deputy chief of the Soviet general staff

Söhnchen: Code name of Kim Philby, agent, London NKVD/NKGB residency

SOFOKL: Code name of Aleksandr G. SAMOKHIN, RU resident in Belgrade

SORGE, Richard: Soviet RU illegal resident, Tokyo. Ran network of agents. Was arrested on October 18, 1941 and executed in November 1944

Starik: Friend of Korsikanets's who assisted in communications among the members of the NKGB spy network in Berlin

Starshina: Code name of Harro Schulze-Boysen, Berlin friend of Korsikanets's NKGB agent. Occupied a major's position in the intelligence element of the German Air Ministry

STEPANOV: Code name of Aleksandr KOROTKOV

Stöbe, Ilse: Well-known journalist and mistress of Rudolf Herrnstadt. Served as a communications link to Herrnstadt's RU agent network. Code name Alta

SUDOPLATOV, Pavel A.: Deputy chief, NKGB Fifth Department. Deputy to FITIN. Assassinated Trotsky

SUSLOPAROV, Ivan A.: General, RU legal resident and military attaché in Paris

Teffi: Agent of the Third (Counterintelligence) Department of GUGB NKVD. Was in the Greek embassy, probably a Soviet servant or worker

TIMOSHENKO, Semen K.: Defense commissar, commander of the Northwest Front in January 1940

Tony: Code name of Anthony Blunt, NKVD/NKGB residency source in London

TREPPER, Leopold: Illegal resident in Paris. Code name OTTO

TSANAVA, Lavrenty F.: Head of NKVD Belorussian SSR, 1938–41. People's commissar for state security

TSEPKOV, V. G.: Senior investigator of NKVD Investigative Unit for Especially Important Cases

TUPIKOV, Vasily I.: Military attaché in Berlin in 1940. RU legal resident. Code name ARNOLD

Turok: Principal bookkeeper for I. G. Farben, NKGB Berlin residency subsource

Ukrainets: Agent of Ukrainian NKVD

URITSKY, Semen P.: RU chief in Moscow, executed in 1939

VADIM: Code name of Anatoly GORSKY, NKVD/NKGB resident in London

VAGNER: Agent of Budapest RU residency

VASILEV, Andrei A.: Captain, secretary to the Soviet military attaché in Belgrade

VASILEVSKY, Aleksandr M.: In the General Staff Operational Directorate

VERNY: Agent at the American embassy, Moscow

VLODZIMIRSKY, Lev Yemelyanovich: Chief, NKVD Investigative Unit for Especially Important Cases

Völkisch, Kurt: German embassy press officer stationed in Warsaw, later in Bucharest. Recruited agent of RU. Code name AVS

Völkisch, Margarita: Code name LTsL. Agent of RU, wife of Kurt Völkisch. Secretary in the German embassy in Bucharest

VOLOSIUK, Makar M.: Deputy RU legal resident and assistant air attaché in Paris. Code name RATO

Von Scheliha, Rudolf: Recruited agent of RU, counselor in the German embassy in Warsaw. Member of the Information Department, German Foreign Office, Berlin, in 1939. Code name Ariets

Von B.: Senior officer of the German embassy in Moscow under cultivation by Yastreb

VON WEIZSÄCKER, Ernst: German state secretary in the German Foreign Ministry. His personal file contained Ponschab telegrams

VOROSHILOV, Kliment Ye.: People's commissar for defense

VOZNESENSKY, Nikolai: Economist accused of conspiracy against the party leadership in the Leningrad affair

Vrach: Source in Bucharest RU residency

Vrana, Vladimir: Agent of Prague RU residency. Employed in the export division of the Skoda Works

Weiss, Ernest: RU agent in London. Had a number of French contacts

YARTSEV, Boris N.: Pseudonym of Boris A. RYBKIN. NKVD legal resident in Helsinki in 1938

Yastreb: Soviet agent cultivating Von B. at the German embassy in Moscow.

YEREMIN, Grigory M.: RU resident in Bucharest. His cover was that of third secretary in the Soviet embassy. Code name YESHCHENKO

YERMOLOV, M. D.: Major, assistant to RU Colonel Ivan V. SMIRNOV, legal resident in Helsinki

YESHCHENKO: Code name of Grigory YEREMIN, RU resident in Bucharest

Yun: NKVD agent covering the U.S. embassy in Berlin

Zagorsky: Agent run by the Belostokaia railroad (GTU)

Zaimov, Vladimir: Agent of the Sofia residency. Code name Azorsky

ZAITSEV, Nikolai M.: RU Berlin residency. Was responsible for maintaining contact with the illegal Alta who handled Ariets

ZAITSEV, Viktor S.: Subordinate of RU resident in Tokyo. Link to SORGE and his network

ZARUBIN, Vasily M.: One of the NKVD's most celebrated illegals. Known in the United States as ZUBILIN when he served there as resident from 1941 to 1944. ZARUBIN handled Willy Lehmann

ZEVS: Code name of deputy RU resident in Sofia Leonid A. SEREDA

ZHUKOV, Georgy K.: Chief of the Soviet general staff January–July 1941

ZHURAVLIEV, Boris N.: Case officer for Willy Lehman. Code name Nikolai

ZHURAVLIEV, Pavel M.: Head of the German Section of the NKGB Foreign Intelligence Directorate

Zhurin: Head of the Military Justice Department of the Bulgarian Defense Ministry and member of the High Military Council. Source of RU agent Boevoy

ZUBILIN: See ZARUBIN, Vasily M.

Notes

The following abbreviations are used:

AP RF   Archive of the President of the Russian Federation
FSB   Federal Security Service
RGVA   Russian State Military Archive
SVR   Foreign Intelligence Service
TsA   Central Archive
TsA MO   Central Archive of the Ministry of Defense

Epigraph

Miklos Kun, *Stalin: An Unknown Portrait* (Budapest: CEU Press, 2003), 421.

Chapter 1: Stalin versus Hitler

1. Ronald Fraser, *Blood of Spain: An Oral History of the Spanish Civil War* (New York, 1979). See also Ronald Radosh, Mary R. Habeck, and Grigory Sevostianov, *Spain Betrayed: The Soviet Union in the Spanish Civil War* (New Haven, 2001).

2. Winston S. Churchill, *The Gathering Storm* (Boston, 1948), 272.

3. Ibid., 325.

Chapter 2: The Outspoken General

1. RVGA, f. 37976, op. 1, d. 523, 3–4. Proskurov seemed very conscious of his Ukrainian background. In filling out personnel questionnaires during military service he listed Ukrainian as his first language, Russian his second.

2. A. Kopeikin, "Salud, Piloto Ruso," *Aviatsia i Kosmonavtika*, no. 12, 1989, 30.

3. RGVA, f. 37976, op. 1, d. 523; A. Ostrovsky, "Sov. Sekretno. Osobo Interesno," *Sovietsky Voin*, September 1990, 68–69.

4. RGVA, f. 37976, op. 1, d. 523, 51.

5. Ronald Radosh, Mary R. Habeck, and Grigory Sevostianov, *Spain Betrayed: The Soviet Union in the Spanish Civil War* (New Haven, 2001), 261. Berzin left the RU in 1936 to become deputy commander of the Special Red Banner Far Eastern Army for Political Affairs. In 1930 he had been sent to Spain.

6. RGVA, f. 35082, op. 1, d. 536, 2a.

7. Kopeikin, "Salud," 31.

8. Ibid; Radosh, Habeck, and Sevostianov, *Spain Betrayed*, 263, 275.

9. RGVA, Proskurov Service Record (Lichnoe Delo), f. 37976, op. 1, d. 523. See also Who's Who (Kto est' kto), http://www.airforce.ru/staff/who_is_who.

10. Order of the Council of People's Commissars, July 16, 1937, February 22, 1938; Ostrovsky, "Sov. Sekretno." 69. The aircraft was probably the TB-7, which Stalin eventually decided against putting into mass production, opting instead for an increase in ground support aircraft.

11. Ostrovsky "Sov. Sekretno," 68.

12. Telephone interview by the author with Lidia Ivanovna Proskurova, daughter of Ivan Iosifovich Proskurov, October 6, 2002.

13. Telephone interview by an intermediary of the author with Lidia Ivanovna Proskurova, November 2003.

14. I. I. Basik et al., eds., *Glavny Voenny Sovet* (Moscow, 2004), 5–6, 15.

15. Ostrovsky, "Sov. Sekretno," 69. See also http://militera.lib.ru/memo/russian/ponomarev. For a description of Soviet military intelligence organization and functions when Proskurov took over, see appendix 1.

16. For background on the origins and early activities of Soviet military intelligence, see Raymond W. Leonard, *Secret Soldiers of the Revolution: Soviet Military Intelligence, 1918–1933*.

Chapter 3: Proskurov Sets Stalin Straight

1. "Soobshchenie I. I. Proskurova I. V. Stalinu," *Izvestia TsK KPSS*, no. 3, 1990, 216–19.

2. M. Yu. Miagkov, ed., *Mirovye Voiny XX Veka* (Moscow, 2002), book 4, 68.

3. Anthony Read and David Fisher, *Deadly Embrace: Hitler, Stalin, and the Nazi-Soviet Pact* (New York, 1988), 118–19, 138.

4. Ibid., 145.

5. Aleksandr N. Ponomarev, *Pokoriteli Neba* (Moscow, 1980), 68–69. This is the source for the account of the August 1939 talks.

6. Ibid., 73–75.

7. Read and Fisher, *Deadly Embrace*, 141.

8. T. Bushueva, "Proklinaia—Poprobuite Poniat," *Novy Mir*, no. 12, 1994, 230–37. This document was found in the Center for the Preservation of Historical-Documentary Collections, formerly the Special Archive of the USSR (Osobiy Arkhiv SSSR), f. 7, op. 1, d. 1223. According to Bushueva, with whom I spoke by telephone in October 2002, the Special Archive contained documents sent back to Moscow by the occupying Soviet Group of Forces in Germany. The Russian original, if it exists, has never been found.

9. "The False Report Issued by the Havas agency," *Pravda*, November 30, 1939. The Havas release is also mentioned in Viktor Suvorov [Vladimir B. Rezun], *Icebreaker: Who*

Started the Second World War? (London, 1990), 43. Suvorov cites it in defense of his largely discredited theory that Stalin intended a preventive war against Germany.

10. Ivo Banac, ed., *The Diary of Georgi Dimitrov* (New Haven, 2003), 115–16.

11. M. Yu. Miagkov, ed., *Mirovye Voiny XX Veka* (Moscow, 2002), book 4, 199–200.

Chapter 4: Soviet Borders Move Westward

1. Anthony Read and David Fisher, *Deadly Embrace: Hitler, Stalin, and the Nazi-Soviet Pact* (New York, 1998), 334–35. See also I. F. Ivanovsky, ed., *Krasnoznamenny Belorussky Voenny Okrug* (Moscow, 1974), 79–80.

2. A. Z. Bednyagin et al., eds., *Krasnoznamenny Kievsky Voenny Okrug* (Moscow, 1974), 130–34.

3. Read and Fisher, *Deadly Embrace*, 341.

4. Dimitri Volkogonov, *Stalin: Triumph and Tragedy* (Rocklin, 1996), 359.

5. A. A. Grechko et al., eds., *Sovietskaia Voennaia Entsiklopedia* (Moscow, 1974), vol. 2, 585.

6. Volkogonov, *Stalin*, 359. See also Bednyagin et al., *Krasnoznamenny*, 134.

7. S. V. Stepashin, *Organy Gosudarstvennoy Bezopasnosti SSR v Velikoy Otechestvennoy Voine* (Moscow, 1995), book 1, 70–73.

8. Ibid., 79–81.

9. Ibid., 88–90.

10. Ibid., 96, n. 2. See also Pavel Sudoplatov, *Special Tasks* (New York, 1994), 3–29.

11. Stepashin, *Organy*, book 1, 283–87.

12. Ibid., 404–13.

13. Ibid., book 2, 99–100.

14. Ibid., 121.

15. Ibid., 154–55.

16. Ibid., 172–87.

17. Ibid., 234–36.

18. Ibid., 297.

19. Ibid., book 1, 74.

20. Ibid., book 2, 166–70, 172–87.

21. Ibid., 263–64.

22. Ibid., 349–50.

23. Ibid., 138–39. See also Aleksandr N. Yakovlev, ed., *1941 god* (Moscow, 1998), book 2, 394–95.

24. Stepashin, *Organy*, book 1, 110–11.

25. Ibid., 112–13.

26. Ibid., 123–26.

27. Yakovlev, *1941 god*, book 1, 31.

28. Ibid., 42–43, 44–45.

29. Ibid., 177–80.

30. Stepashin, *Organy*, book 2, 79–81.

31. Ibid., 133–34.

32. Ibid., 144–46.

33. Ibid., 162–63, 218–19.

34. Robert E. Tarleton, "Bolsheviks of Military Affairs: Stalin's High Command, 1934–1940" (PhD diss., University of Washington, 2000), 293–94.

35. John Erickson, *The Road to Stalingrad: Stalin's War with Germany* (New Haven, 1999), 68.

36. Stepashin, *Organy,* book 1, 22–28, 31–35.

37. Tarleton, "Bolsheviks," 345.

38. Ibid., 305–06.

Chapter 5: The Finns Fight

1. L. A. Bezymensky, "Sovietskaia Razvedka Pered Voinoi," *Voprosy Istory,* no. 9, 1996, 85.

2. E. M. Primakov and V. A. Kirpichenko, *Ocherki Istorii Rossyskoi Vneshnei Razvedki* (Moscow, 1997), vol. 3, 297–98.

3. Vaino Tanner, *The Winter War: Finland against Russia, 1939–1940* (Stanford, 1957), 3–5.

4. Ibid., 8–9. The Aaland Islands are at the mouth of the Gulf of Bothina, between Finland and Sweden. The Russian Empire obtained control over them in 1809, Sweden occupied them briefly after the Russian Revolution, and in 1921 the League of Nations gave them to Finland, on the condition that they be demilitarized. Moscow's position that it would assent to Finnish fortifications only if they participated became moot as Finland and Sweden were making joint plans for the islands.

5. Ibid., 12–13.

6. A. Kolpakidi and D. Prokhorov, *Vneshniaia Razvedka Rossii* (Moscow, 2001), 341–42.

7. Tanner, *Winter War,* 28–32, 76–80.

8. Ibid., 84–88.

9. William J. Spahr, *Stalin's Lieutenants: A Study of Command under Duress* (Novato, 1997), 221–23.

10. Ivo Banac, ed., *The Diary of Georgi Dimitrov* (New Haven, 2003), 121.

11. Tanner, *Winter War,* 104–05.

12. Ibid., 105. See also M. Yu Miagkov, ed., *Mirovye Voiny XX Veka* (Moscow, 2002), book 4, 160.

13. Tanner, *Winter War,* 105–06.

14. Ibid., 104.

15. Spahr, *Stalin's Lieutenants,* 224; A. I. Gribkov, ed., *Istoria Ordena Lenina Leningradskogo Voennogo Okruga* (Moscow, 1974), 150–54; http://www.mannerheim.fi/10_ylip/e_mlinja.htm (accessed October 17, 2004); V. A. Zolotarev and G. N. Sevostianov, eds., *Velikaia Otechestvennaia Voina, 1941–1945* (Moscow, 1998), book 1, 33.

16. Ibid.

17. E. N. Kulkov and O. A. Rzheshevsky, eds., *Zimniaia Voina, 1939–1940: I. V. Stalin I. Finskaia Kampania* (Moscow, 1998), 1–6. The material taken from the Russian edition was checked against the English-language version, *Stalin and the Soviet-Finnish War, 1939–1940,* ed. Alexander O. Chubaryan and Harold Shukman (London, 2002).

18. Chubaryan and Shukman, *Stalin,* 283.

19. Kopets was later commander of the air forces of the Belorussian Special Military District, which became the Western Front when the war started. Horrified at seeing his aircraft destroyed by the Luftwaffe on the first day of the war, Kopets committed suicide.

20. Chubaryan and Shukman, *Stalin,* 111, 139, 149.

21. Ibid., 180.

22. Ibid., 202–04.

23. Ibid., 198.

24. Ibid.

25. Ibid.

26. Ibid., 200.

27. Ibid., 201.

28. Ibid., 201–04.

29. From the party archives, *Izvestia TsK KPSS*, no. 1, 1990, 203.

30. Although France and Great Britain both declared war on Germany on September 3, 1939, after Hitler ignored their ultimatums, for eight months there was no fighting on land except for a brief French advance into the German border area, which the Germans drove back in two days. Their failure to do anything to assist the Poles resulted in what was termed the "phony war" by the English and "la drole de guerre" by the French.

Chapter 6: Soviet Military Intelligence Residencies in Western Europe

1. Aleksandr N. Yakovlev, ed., *1941 god* (Moscow, 1998), book 1, 20–26.

2. *Izvestia TsK KPSS*, no. 3, 1990, 220.

3. Petr I. Ivashutin, "Razvedka Bila Trevogu," *Krasnaia Zvezda*, February 2, 1991. See also Yakovlev, *1941 god*, book 2, 202, 203.

4. A. Kolpakidi and D. Prokhorov, *Imperia GRU* (Moscow, 1999), book 1, 249. There were twenty-three reports in all from Berlin, eight of which are contained in *1941 god*, along with their archival citations. The remainder are referred to in articles authored by retired GRU officers or journalists specializing in military intelligence.

5. Yakovlev, *1941 god*, book 1, 274.

6. Ibid., 466. General Filipp I. Golikov replaced Proskurov as RU head in July 1940.

7. Ibid., 508, 683.

8. Ibid., book 2, book 2, 113–18. The Western Department is the element within the RU responsible for administrative support to the Berlin RU residency. In his *Grand Delusion: Stalin and the German Invasion of Russia* (New Haven, 1999), Gabriel Gorodetsky states that it was Golikov who "sought from the military attaché . . . an overall appraisal of German intentions." There is no indication that Tupikov's letter was in response to a request from Golikov. Rather it was the cri de coeur of a man who felt his residency's reporting was being ignored in Moscow.

9. "Sovietskaia Voennaia Razvedka Nakanune Velikoi Otechestvennoy Voiny," *Novaia i Noveishaia Istoria*, no. 1, 1995, 55.

10. Yakovlev, *1941 god*, book 2, 366, 383.

11. Ibid., 383.

12. Considerable detail on the RU London residency has appeared in V. M. Lure and V. Ya. Kochik, *GRU. Dela i Liudi* (Moscow, 2002), and in Vladimir Lota, "Sekretny Front Generalnogo Staba," *Krasnaia Zvezda*, November 2, 2002.

13. Among the other members of the residency (often serving concurrently as members of the Soviet military mission in Great Britain) were Semen D. Kremer; (code names Aleksandr, Sergei,); assistant air attaché Major Boris F. Shevtsov; assistant army attaché Major Anatoliy Lebedev; Ivan M. Kozlov (code name Bilton); Major General Aleksandr F. Sizov, military attaché to the Polish, Czech, and Yugoslav governments in exile; and various code clerks, chauffeurs, and secretaries.

14. Lure and Kochik, *GRU. Dela i Liudi*, 83. It is hard to distinguish between Moravec's role as an ally engaged in official exchange and the claim that he was secretly recruited and run as an agent. In *Special Tasks* (New York, 1994), 223, Pavel Sudoplatov claims that Moravec (whom Sudoplatov called Muravitz) was recruited by the NKVD resi-

dent in London, Ivan A. Chichaev, who also dealt with representatives of the intelligence services of allied governments in exile. Leaving aside the question of Moravec's relations with the Soviet services, he was without question in continuing and close contact with MI-6 and also the British Special Operations Executive (SOE). See David Stafford, *Churchill and Secret Service* (New York, 1997), 240–41, and John H. Waller, *The Unseen War in Europe* (New York, 1996), 232, 233, 234, 235.

15. Stafford, *Churchill*, ch. 11.

16. The so-called GRU messages between London and Moscow are only a small part of the 2,900 Soviet intelligence messages decrypted by American and British cryptologists and released to the public beginning in July 1995. The project had several different code words over its lifetime, but its declassified version is known by VENONA.

17. VENONA, "GRU Messages between London and Moscow," Historical Monograph 5, 4–5.

18. Yakovlev, *1941 god*, book 2, 17. See also Thierry Wolton, *Le Grand Recrutement* (Paris, 1993), 319–71.

19. A. G. Pavlov, "Sovietskaia Voennaia Razvedka Nakanune Velikoy Otechesvennoy Voiny," *Novaia I Noveishaia Istoria*, no. 1, 1995, 59.

20. Yakovlev, *1941 god*, book 1, 676.

21. Alexander Rado, *Pod psevdonimom Dora* (Moscow, 1976), 90.

22. Yakovlev, *1941 god*, book 2, 224.

23. Rado, *Pod psevdonimom Dora*, 90.

Chapter 7: Soviet Military Intelligence Residencies in Eastern Europe

1. Vladimir Lota, *Krasnaia Zvezda*, March 27, 2004, 5.

2. Ibid. Based on textual comparisons, this report from the Lota article is likely the same as the one dated March 1–2, 1941, from the Central Archive of the Ministry of Defense of the Russian Federation, op. 24119, d. 1, 296–303, and cited in Aleksandr N. Yakovlev's *1941 god* (Moscow, 1998), book 1, 706, 708.

3. Yakovlev, *1941 god*, book 1, 768–69, 775–76.

4. Ibid., 788–89, 797.

5. Ibid., 798.

6. Ibid., 805–06.

7. Ibid., book 2, 77–78, 98–99, 107–08.

8. Ibid., 170–71. See also Lota, *Krasnaia Zvezda*, March 27, 2004, 5.

9. Yakovlev, *1941 god*, book 2, 271–72.

10. Ibid. See also Lota, *Krasnaia Zvezda*, March 27, 2004, 5.

11. Lota, *Krasnaia Zvezda*, March 27, 2004, 5. It is not clear why the Belorussian authorities took an interest in the case of AVS and his family.

12. Yakovlev, *1941 god*, book 1, 572.

13. Ibid., 650.

14. Ibid., 736. Vladislav Rybnikar (a true name) was the editor of the influential Belgrade newspaper *Politika* (V. M. Lure and V. Ya. Kochik, *GRU Dela i Liudi* [Moscow, 2002], 97).

15. Yakovlev, *1941 god*, book 2, 24.

16. Ibid., 24–25. The names of the commanders of the German "groupings" were evidently mixed up. "Königsberg" would have been Army Group North, and it was commanded by von Leeb. "Warsaw" would have been Army Group Center, and its commander was indeed von Bock. "Crakow" was probably Army Group South, and the commander was

von Rundstedt, not Blaskowitz or List. The report confirmed other information, however, to the effect that there were three main axes of attack, as first noted by Ariets from Berlin.

17. Yakovlev, *1941 god*, book 1, 704.

18. Ibid., 710.

19. Ibid., book 2, 112. In a marginal note, Golikov pointed out that there were several errors in the report but he did not mention the number of parachute divisions.

20. Ibid., 128–29, 150.

21. Ibid., 365. It seems likely that Golikov's written reaction to this report, which he knew went counter to Stalin's views and wishes, was registered for the record only. In any case, the chief of the Information Department, Dronov, ordered only the first paragraph included in a special report.

22. Lure and Kochik, *GRU Dela i Liudi*, 91–92.

23. A. G. Pavlov, "Sovietskaia Voennaia Razvedka Nakanune Velikoy Otechestvennoy Voiny," *Novaia I Noveishaia Istoria*, no. 1, 1995. Unfortunately, there are no archival references or indications in the article as to how Golikov reacted to the report's comments about deception. They are, however, the most accurate and straightforward description of the "English invasion" phase of German deception seen in reporting by any residency.

24. Ismail Akhmedov, *In and Out of Stalin's GRU* (Frederick, 1984). See also Lure and Kochik, *GRU Dela i Liudi*, 92.

25. Lure and Kochik, *GRU Dela i Liudi*, 75–82.

26. Ibid., 75, 76.

27. Yakovlev, *1941 god*, book 2, 121.

28. Ibid., 179–80.

29. Ibid., 198–99.

30. Ibid., 211.

31. Ibid., 266.

32. Lure and Kochik, *GRU Dela i Liudi*, 76.

33. Yakovlev, *1941 god*, book 2, 398.

Chapter 8: Who Were You, Dr. Sorge? Stalin Never Heard of You.

1. V. M. Lure and V. Ya. Kochik, *GRU. Dela i Liudi* (Moscow, 2002), 234, 355, 389, 395.

2. Sorge case materials, intercepts by Ministry of Communications and government of Korea under Japanese occupation (turned over to U.S. occupation forces in 1945), 4.

3. Robert Whymant, *Stalin's Spy: Richard Sorge and the Tokyo Espionage Ring* (New York, 1998), 104–05.

4. Viktor Anfilov, *Doroga k Tragedii Sorok Pervogo Goda* (Moscow, 1997), 195; Ovidy Gorchakov, "Nakanune ili Tragedia Kassandry," *Gorizont*, no. 6, 1988, 31.

5. A. G. Fesiun, *Delo Rikharda Zorge: Neisvestnye Dokumenty* (Moscow, 2000). Unless otherwise indicated, the documents in this publication are declassified portions of the Sorge File (Delo Zorge) in the GRU archives.

6. Gorchakov, "Nakanune," 31.

7. Fesiun, *Delo Rikharda Zorge*, documents 136, p. 111; 140, p. 113; 143, pp. 114–15.

8. Ibid., documents 144, pp. 115–16; 146; 147, p. 117.

9. Ibid., document 145, p. 116. This document is reproduced in Aleksandr N. Yakovlev, ed., *1941 god* (Moscow, 1998), book 2, 175, along with an order from Golikov to send it to the usual recipients but to omit the section on the weakness of the Red Army.

10. Gorchakov, "Nakanune," 31, 43. In his book *Stalin i Razvedka* (Moscow, 2004), Igor A. Damaskin, a retired SVR colonel, claims that Sorge's report on the date of the

German attack was falsified during the Khrushchev period (263). However, a report on "The Sorge Spy Ring" by the headquarters of the Far East Command, U.S. Army, released on February 10, 1949, states that "Sorge predicted the attack would come on June 20th." According to Vladimir Malevanny, "Nezakrytoe Delo 'Ramzaia,'" *Nezavisimoe Obozrenie,* no. 40, 2000, the message read: "Approximately June 20 Germany will begin its attack on the USSR. The very latest date—around the twenty-third."

11. In Soviet military terminology an "army" consists of more than one corps.

12. Fesiun, *Delo Rikharda Zorge,* document 148, pp. 117–18; Yakovlev, *1941 god,* book 2, 252.

13. Gorchakov, "Nakanune," 57.

14. Fesiun, *Delo Rikharda Zorge,* document 153, pp. 120–21; Yakovlev, *1941 god,* book 2, 380.

15. Fesiun, *Delo Rikharda Zorge,* document 154, p. 121; Yakovlev, *1941 god,* book 2, 398–99.

16. Whymant, *Stalin's Spy,* 184.

17. Sergei Kondrashev, "Trudny Put Pravdy o Podvige Rikharda Zorge i ego Soratnikov" (speech presented at the Second International Symposium on Richard Sorge and His Comrades in Arms, sponsored by the Institute of Military History of the Russian Ministry of Defense and the Japanese-Russian Center for Historical Research, Moscow, September 25, 2000).

18. Fesiun, *Delo Rikharda Zorge,* document 38, pp. 55–56.

19. Ibid., p. 54.

20. Ibid., pp. 48–49. Proskurov's refusal to permit Sorge to return to Moscow at this time was twofold. First, he was afraid that Sorge would be arrested and imprisoned and, second, he knew how valuable an agent Sorge was and how great a loss to Soviet intelligence his return would create.

21. S. S. Smirnov, *Marshal Zhukov: Kakim My Ego Pomnin* (Moscow, 1988), 165–66.

22. Fesiun, *Delo Rikharda Zorge,* document 163, pp. 125–26.

23. Ibid., documents 176, 177, p. 132.

24. John Erickson, *The Road to Stalingrad: Stalin's War with Germany* (New Haven, 1999), 239.

25. Interview with Professor Shirai, *Moscow News,* October 11, 2000. Excerpt from "Richard Sorge: Hero of the Soviet Union," unclassified study by the CIA Counterintelligence and Security Program.

Chapter 9: NKVD Foreign Intelligence

1. The date December 20 is still commemorated by the Russian Intelligence Service with banquets and speeches to demonstrate the continuity between the present-day service and its predecessors.

2. E. M. Primakov and V. A. Kirpichenko, *Ocherki Istorii Rossyskoy Vneshnei Razvedki* (Moscow, 1997), vol. 3, 16–17.

3. A. Kolpakidi and D. Prokhorov, *Vneshnaia Razvedka Rossii* (Moscow, 2001), 112, 113. See also T. V. Samoilis, ed., *Veterani Vneshnei Razvedki Rossii: Kratky Biografichesky Spravochnik* (Moscow, 1995), 154, 155.

4. Aleksandr N. Yakovlev, ed. *1941 god* (Moscow, 1998), book 2, 391.

5. Interview with Sergei Kondrashev, Moscow, October 8, 2002.

6. A. I. Kokurina, N. V. Petrova, and R. G. Pikoia, eds., *Lubianka: VchK-OGPU-*

NKVD-NKGB-MGB-MVB-KGB, 1917–1960. Spravochnik (Moscow, 1997), 24–26. See also Kolpakidi and Prokhorov, *Vneshniaia*, 34.

7. Kolpakidi and Prokhorov, *Vneshnaia*, 34–35.

8. Data on reports signed by Bogdan Z. Kobulov for Merkulov in June 1941 taken from Yakovlev, *1941 god*, book 2, 335–37, 349.

9. Ibid., book 1, 134–35. See also *Novaia I Noveishaia Istoria*, no. 4, 1997, 95–96.

10. Yakovlev, *1941 god*, book 2, 250–51.

11. Ibid., 327–33.

12. Adam Ulam, *Stalin* (New York, 1973). Stalin was apparently so little affected by his April 1907 visit to London that he never mentioned it to Churchill during their several World War II meetings.

13. David Stafford, *Churchill and Secret Service* (New York, 1997), 222. Describing the pitfalls in Stalin's approach to intelligence analysis, David Stafford comments: "Paranoid about Western intentions, threatened by demons of his own creation, his hands still bloodied by his massive purges, Stalin sleepwalked his fatal path to the biggest intelligence disaster of the Second World War."

14. Kolpakidi and Prokhorov, *Vneshniaia*, 150–51.

15. Ibid., 342–44.

16. Primakov and Kirpichenko, *Ocherki*, 452.

Chapter 10: Fitin's Recruited Spies

1. E. M. Primakov and V. A. Kirpichenko, *Ocherki Istory Rossyskoy Vneshnei Razvedki* (Moscow, 1997), vol. 3, 414–43. See also Teodor Gladkov, *Korol Nelegalov* (Moscow, 2000), 178, 191, 199–202, 229, 327–28.

2. Aleksandr N. Yakovlev, ed., *1941 god* (Moscow, 1998), book 2, 400–01.

3. Ibid., 402.

4. Ibid., 403, 89, 130.

5. Ibid., 130–31, 405–06.

6. Ibid., 382, 383.

7. Ibid., 382–83.

8. A. Kolpakidi and D. Prokhorov, *Vneshniaia Razvedka Rossii* (Moscow, 2001), 454. For additional background on Lehmann and the circumstances surrounding the June 19, 1941, report, see ch. 20, below.

9. Yakovlev, *1941 god*, 403, 89, 130.

10. Donald Hiss, the brother of Alger Hiss, was reported by Whittaker Chambers to have been a member of the CPUSA. See Allen Weinstein, *Perjury: The Hiss-Chambers Case*, rev. ed. (New York, 1997).

11. Kolpakidi and Prokhorov, *Vneshniaia*, 130–31, 405–06.

12. Ibid., 406, 407.

13. Ibid., 382–83.

14. Nigel West and Oleg Tsarev, *The Crown Jewels: The British Secrets at the Heart of the KGB Archives* (New Haven, 1999), 174–77.

15. Yakovlev, *1941 god*, book 2, 200, 248–49. The shock felt in Fitin's directorate can be seen in the following note from the chief of the German Department, Pavel M. Zhuravliev to his assistant, Zoia Rybkina: "Telegraph Berlin, London, Stockholm, America, Rome. Try to clarify the details of the proposal." Perhaps the most accurate accounts of various aspects of the Hess affair can be found in David Stafford, ed., *Flight from Reality: Rudolf Hess and His Mission to Scotland, 1941* (London, 2002).

16. Yakovlev, *1941 god*, book 2, 120–21, 177, 186; A. P. Belozerov, ed., *Sekrety Gitlera Na Stole U Stalina Razvedka I Kontrrazvedka O Podgotovke Germanskoy Agressii Protiv SSSR. Mart-liun 1941* (Moscow, 1995), 140, 151–53, 156–57. See also Ye. Sinitsyn, *Rezident Svidetelstvuet* (Moscow, 1996).

17. Kolpakidi and Prokhorov, *Vneshniaia*, 216, 296–97.

18. It is ironic that after her Warsaw tour Modrzhinskaia returned to the center and by October 1942 had become the chief of the British Section of the Third Department. In this position she set out to prove that "the entire Cambridge ring was nothing but an exercise in disinformation." See West and Tsarev, *Crown Jewels*, 159.

19. Primakov and Kirpichenko, *Ocherki*, vol. 3, 293–94.

20. Yakovlev, *1941 god*, book 2, 154–55.

Chapter 11: Listening to the Enemy

1. Aleksandr N. Yakovlev, ed., *1941 god* (Moscow, 1998), book 1, 598. See also Viktor M. Chebrikov, ed., *Istoria Sovietskikh Organov Gosudarstvennoy Bezopastnosti* (Moscow, 1977), 313.

2. Oleg Matveyev and Vladimir Merzliakov, "Akademik Kontrrazvedki," *Nezavisimoe Voennoe Obozrenie*, no. 15, 2002, 7. Although in appearance a bespectacled academician, Fedotov was a very competent Chekist. He remained in counterintelligence until the arrival of Aleksandr N. Shelepin as KGB chairman in December 1958. Fedotov was fired and expelled from the party as part of Shelepin's purge of Stalin-era generals of state security.

3. Ibid.

4. Aleksandr Pronin, "Nevolnye Informatory Stalina," *Novoe Voennoe Obozrenie*, no. 45, 2001, 1–2.

5. A. P. Belozerov, ed., *Sekrety Gitlera Na Stole U Stalina. Razvedka i Kontrrazvedka O Podgotovke Germanskoy Agressy Protiv SSSR. Mart-liun 1941* (Moscow, 1995), 52–55. At the point at which the unidentified agent claims to have entertained Russian naval officers, a note is inserted, apparently by the German Department officers preparing the transcript: "Information from continuing surveillance of [the agent] shows that when speaking of his meeting with 'Russian officers' he lies; in reality no such meetings took place." Even counterintelligence officers had to protect themselves.

6. Matveyev and Merzliakov, "Akademik Kontrrazvedki," 7.

7. Belozerov, *Sekrety Gitlera*, 109–12.

8. Ibid., 144–47.

9. Ibid., 83–86.

10. Ibid., 150–51, 163–66, 168–69.

11. Ibid., 171–72.

12. Ibid., 178–79.

13. Ibid., 169–70.

14. Ovidy Gorchakov, "Nakanune, ili Tragedia Kassandry: Povest v dokumentakh," *Gorizont*, no. 6, 1988, 33–37. Gorchakov's contribution is puzzling. When Lieutenant General (retired) Aleksandr Aleksandrovich Zdanovich of the Federal Security Service (FSB) recently reviewed Gorchakov's articles, he told the author that Gorchakov had never served in Soviet counterintelligence nor was he ever given official access to FSB archives. Zdanovich does not know where Gorchakov got the ideas for the articles or who helped him write them. The code names were never in FSB archives and Zdanovich believes it would have

been difficult for counterintelligence to have handled this many sources, given losses suffered during the purges. In October 2002, when the author spoke with Zdanovich, he had not been able to find collateral information on Second Directorate prewar operations. However, the top-secret 1977 KGB history showed that in 1940–41 the directorate was very active indeed in working with human sources. On the other hand, there are strange errors in Gorchakov's report, of some of Vladimir Dekanozov's messages. In a June 21 radiogram to NKVD Moscow, for example, Dekanozov refers to Ismail Akhmedov as "NKVD" when he knew him as "GRU." Gorchakov himself refers to Akhmedov's chief as "B. Kobulov," but Dekanozov knew the NKVD resident was Amaiak Kobulov. Still, the entries reflecting reports from various agents working in embassies in Moscow are typical of reporting of this kind, and some are specifically supported by archival data.

15. Gorchakov, "Nakanune," 53–55, 56, 67.
16. Ibid., 57–58.
17. Ibid., 57.
18. Ibid., 58.
19. Ibid., 60.
20. Ibid., 58.
21. Ibid., 61. See also V. A. Zolotarev and G. N. Sevostianov, eds., *Velikaia Otechestennaia Voina, 1941–1945* (Moscow, 1998), book 1, 115.
22. Yakovlev, *1941 god*, book 2, 398.

Chapter 12: Working on the Railroad

1. S. V. Stepashin, ed., *Organy Gosudarstvennoy Bezopasnosti SSSR v Velikoy Otechestvennoy Voine* (Moscow, 1995), book 1, 55–56.
2. Aleksandr N. Yakovlev, ed., *1941 god* (Moscow, 1998), book 1, 93–94. S. R. Milshtein came to Moscow from the Tbilisi city party organization with Beria. He was shot in 1953.
3. Yakovlev, *1941 god*, book 1, 135–36, 157. The Belostokaia railroad was in the Bialystok district of Poland, which was placed on the Soviet side of the German-Soviet demarcation line. After 1945, the district was returned to Poland.
4. Ibid., 174–76. Although these reports were said to contain both marginal comments and listings of recipients, these were not included in the editorial commentary on the reports.
5. "Novye Dokumenty iz Arkhivov SVR I FSB Rossy o Podgotvke Germanei Voiny S SSSR, 1940–1941," *Novaia i Noveishaia Istoria*, no. 4, 1997, 94–104.
6. Yakovlev, *1941 god*, book 1, 268–69.
7. "Novye Dokumenty," 97–98.
8. Yakovlev, *1941 god*, book 1, 324–26, 426–27.
9. Ibid., 462–65.
10. Ibid., 545–58.
11. Ibid., 656–58, 681–83. It appears that when the NKVD was split into two commissariats in February 1941—the new NKGB and a rump NKVD—the Chief Transport Directorate was abolished. Its head, Milshtein, became chief of the Third (Secret-Political) Department of the NKGB. Although both reports bear the comment *"imeiutsia pomety"* ("includes notes"), none are in evidence. Had they been included, we might have learned more about what happened to these reporting sources when the organizational changes took place.

12. Ibid., 809–10, taken from the Central Archives of the SVR RF, d. 21616, t. 2, 36–41.

13. Yakovlev, *1941 god*, book 2, 352–55.

Chapter 13: The Border Troops Knew

1. Amy W. Knight, *The KGB: Police and Politics in the Soviet Union* (Boston, 1990), 227–32. See also Peter Deryabin and T. H. Bagley, *The KGB: Masters of the Soviet Union* (New York, 1990), 303–12. It may be reflective of a trend in today's Russia that the border troops have once more been placed under the Security Service (FSB).

2. S. V. Stepashin, ed., *Organy Gosudarstvennoy Bezopastnosti SSSR v Velikoy Otechestvennoy Voine* (Moscow, 1995), book 1, 52–54.

3. Georgy Sechkin, *Granitsa i Voina: Pogranichnye Voiska v Velikoy Otechestvennoy Voine Sovietskogo Naroda, 1941–1945* (Moscow, 1993), 75, 79.

4. TsA FSB RF, f. 540, op. 3, d. 3, 25–28.

5. Aleksandr N. Yakovlev, ed., *1941 god* (Moscow, 1998), book 1, 137–38.

6. Ibid., 119–29.

7. A. I. Chugunov, *Granitsa Nakanune Voiny, 1941–45* (Moscow, 1985), 115.

8. Sechkin, *Granitsa I Voina*, 54–55.

9. Chugunov, *Granitsa Nakanune Voiny*, 130–31. See also P. I. Zyrianov, ed., *Pogranichnye Voiska SSSR, 1939–1941: Sbornik Dokymentov i Materialov* (Moscow, 1970), 321.

10. Stepashin, *Organy*, book 1, 299.

11. Yakovlev, *1941 god*, book 1, 541–42.

12. Stepashin, *Organy*, book 1, 19–21.

13. Yakovlev, *1941 god*, book 1, 548–49.

14. David M. Glantz, ed., *The Initial Period of War on the Eastern Front, 22 June–August 1941* (London, 1993), 149.

15. Yakovlev, *1941 god*, book 1, 677–78.

16. Ibid., 800–03.

17. Stepashin, *Organy*, book 2, 82–85.

18. Ibid., 56–60.

19. Ibid., 62–64.

20. Ibid., 79–80, 96–97.

21. Ibid., 85–87.

22. Stepashin, *Organy*, book 2, 108–10.

23. Zyrianov, *Pogranichnye Voiska SSSR*, 383.

24. Ibid., 381–82.

25. Yakovlev, *1941 god*, book 2, 279–82.

26. Sechkin, *Granitsa i Voina*, 59.

27. Yakovlev, *1941 god*, book 2, 306–07. Although *napravlenie* (plural *napravlenia*) literally means "direction," in military usage it is translated "axis."

Chapter 14: Proskurov Is Fired

1. Vasily A. Novobranets, "Nakanune Voiny," *Znamia*, no. 6, 1990, 170.

2. A. Ostrovsky, "Sov. Sekretno. Osobo Interesno," *Sovietsky Voin*, September 1990, 70.

3. Boris Shaptalov, *Ispytanie Voiny* (Moscow, 2002), 54.

4. A. G. Pavlov, "Sovietskaia Voennaia Razvedka Nakanune Velikoy Otechestvennoy Voiny," *Novaia I Noveishaia Istoria*, no. 1, 1995, 51–52.

5. Ostrovsky, "Sovershenno Sekretno," 70.

6. Vitaly Nikolsky, *Akvarium-2* (Moscow, 1997), 37.

7. Mikhail Milshtein, *Skvoz Gody Voin i Nishchety* (Moscow, 2002), 57–58.

8. "Telegramma I. F. Dergacheva I. I. Proskurovu," *Izvestia TsK KPSS*, no. 3, 1990, 220. The RU residency in Sofia had developed excellent sources at the highest levels of the Bulgarian military establishment.

9. Aleksandr N. Yakovlev, ed., *1941 god* (Moscow, 1998), book 1, 13.

10. RGVA, Order of the NKVD USSR of July 27, 1940, f. 37837, op. 4, d. 381, 51.

11. Yakovlev, *1941 god*, book 1, 125.

12. This is taken from a historical novel by Igor Bunich, *Groza: Piatisotletniaia Voina v Rossy* (Moscow, 1997), 123–24. Much of this work is based on verifiable events and documents. Other elements are products of the author's vivid imagination.

13. Kenneth Campbell, "Admiral Erich Raeder: Reflections of His Strategic Thinking," *Intelligencer: Journal of U.S. Intelligence Studies*, vol. 14, no. 1, Winter–Spring 2004.

14. Ostrovsky, "Sov. Sekretno," 70.

15. Harold Shukman, ed., *Stalin's Generals* (New York, 1993), 77–78.

16. A. A. Grechko et al., eds., *Sovietskaia Voennaia Entsiklopedia* (Moscow, 1976), vol. 3, 585–86.

17. William J. Spahr, *Zhukov: The Rise and Fall of a Great Captain* (Novato, 1993), 22–23. See also O. F. Suvenirov, *Tragedia RKKA, 1937–1938* (Moscow, 1998), 109.

18. Grechko et al., *Entsiklopedia*, vol. 3, 585. The term *GRU*, the result of a reorganization, did not appear until February 1943.

19. Telephone interview with Vyacheslav M. Lure, coauthor of *GRU Dela i Liudi*, May 29, 2003.

20. Novobranets, "Nakanune Voiny," 172. See also Ismail Akhmedov, *In and Out of Stalin's GRU* (Frederick, 1984), 127–28. The idea that Golikov reported only to Stalin seems to have been generally accepted, but there are problems with this view. A study of the Kremlin visitors' lists from July 1940 to June 1941 shows that Golikov visited Stalin on November 22 and 25, 1940. On November 22 he arrived at 7:45 p.m. and left at 8:45, while other visitors that evening, such as Molotov, Voroshilov, Timoshenko, Mikoyan, Beria, Rychagov, and Meretskov stayed later. It would appear that Golikov was invited to give a report and that was all. On November 25 the time of his presence (from 7:30 to 8:35 p.m.) was the same as that of Timoshenko and Meretskov. There were no other military personnel there that evening. Golikov does not appear again on the visitors' list until April 11, 1941. He arrived at 11:15 p.m. and left at 11:45. This visit seems to be the sort one would expect if Golikov's only purpose was to give Stalin a private briefing. But only once in the entire prewar period? Probably not, assuming that the list gives an incomplete picture of Stalin's visitors and activities. On the other hand, to "report" directly to Stalin need not have meant (although Golikov might have implied to his subordinates that it did) a personal meeting with the Boss. Much simpler and more probable would have been for Golikov to turn in a report, together with his comments, to someone like A. N. Poskrebyshev, Stalin's personal secretary. A second reason for doubting that only Stalin saw certain reports and that the general staff was cut out is that a review of available declassified intelligence reports invariably shows that the distribution list included other recipients, such as the defense commissar and the general staff. The distribution lists were standardized as to the recipients and the number of copies sent to each.

Chapter 15: Golikov and Operation Sea Lion

1. Aleksandr M. Nekrich, *1941 22 Iiunia* (Moscow, 1965). See also "Kanun Voiny: Preduprezhdenia Diplomatov [On the Eve of War: Diplomats' Warnings]," *Vestnik MID*, no. 8, 1990, 76.

2. John H. Waller, *The Unseen War in Europe: Espionage and Conspiracy in the Second World War* (New York, 1996), 197–98; John Keegan, *The Second World War* (New York, 1989), 180; Read Anthony and David Fisher, *Deadly Embrace: Hitler, Stalin, and the Nazi-Soviet Pact* (New York, 1988), 606.

3. Aleksandr N. Yakovlev, ed., *1941 god* (Moscow, 1998), book 2, 80–81.

4. Ibid., 314–21.

5. Joshua Rubenstein and Vladimir P. Naumov, *Stalin's Secret Pogrom: The Postwar Inquisition of the Jewish Anti-Fascist Committee* (New Haven, 2001), 495.

6. Yakovlev, *1941 god*, book 2, 76–81.

7. Ibid., 45–47.

8. Ibid., 82–83.

9. Ibid., book 1, 459–61.

10. "Kanun Voiny," 71–72.

11. Ibid., 72.

12. Ibid., 74.

13. Petr I. Ivashutin, "Razvedka Bila Trevogu," *Krasnaia Zvezda*, February 2, 1991, 5. Ivashutin served in the KGB from 1956 to 1993 and was chief of GRU from 1963 to 1987.

14. Yakovlev, *1941 god*, book 1, 440–441.

15. "Kanun Voiny," 71.

16. Yakovlev, *1941 god*, book 1, 804.

17. V. V. Sokolov, "Novye Dannye o Podgotovke Germanskogo Vtorzheniia v SSSR v 1941," *Novaia I Noveishaia Istoria*, January–February 2000, 86–89.

18. Yakovlev, *1941 god*, book 2, 309–13.

19. "Kanun Voiny," 76.

20. Ibid., 76.

21. Ovidy Gorchakov, "Nakanune ili Tragedia Kassandry: Povest v Dokumentakh," *Gorizont*, no. 7, 1988, 61.

22. Vasily A. Novobranets, "Nakanune Voiny," *Znamia*, no. 6, 1990, 175.

23. Yakovlev, *1941 god*, book 1, 121–23; David Glantz, *The Initial Period of War on the Eastern Front: 22 June–August 1941* (London, 1993), 84. The size of Soviet and German divisions differed. Soviet rifle divisions were not up to strength, possessing on average from 8,000 to 12,000 men.

24. Ibid., 443–44, 450.

25. Ibid., 450.

26. Ibid., 746–47. See also 7, 288–90.

27. Ibid., 758–59.

28. Ibid., 776–78.

29. Ibid., 779–80.

30. Yakovlev, *1941 god*, book 2, 46–47.

31. Ibid., 87–89.

32. Ibid., 171–73.

33. Ibid., 213–14.

34. Ibid., 215. See also Keegan, *Second World War*, 164–71.

35. Yakolev, *1941 god*, book 2, 215–16, 296. See also V. A. Zolotarev and G. N. Sevostianov, eds., *Velikaia Otechesvennaia Voina, 1941–1945.* (Moscow, 1998), book 1, 114–15.

36. Yakovlev, *1941 god*, book 2, 289–90.

37. Ibid., 324–25, 333.

Chapter 16: "We Do Not Fire on German Aircraft in Peacetime"

1. Aleksandr N. Yakovlev, ed., *1941 god* (Moscow, 1998), book 2, 470–75.

2. V. A. Zolotarev, ed., *Nakanune Voiny: Materialy soveshchaniia vysshego rukovodia-shchego sostava RKKA, 23–31 Dekabria 1940* (Moscow, 1993), 144.

3. Ibid., 173–74.

4. Yakovlev, *1941 god*, book 2, 387.

5. Viktor Anfilov, *Doroga k Tragedii Sorok Pervogo Goda* (Moscow, 1997), 219, 200.

6. Zolotarev, *Nakanune Voiny*, 164–65.

7. P. I. Zyrianov, ed., *Pogranichnye Voiska SSSR, 1939–41: Sbrnok Dokymentov i Materialov* (Moscow, 1970), 292.

8. Ibid., 300, 303.

9. Georgy Sechkin, *Granitsa i Voina, 1941–45* (Moscow, 1993), 53. A similar order forbidding firing on German aircraft was issued to the covering troops of the Western Military Districts in April 1940 and to the Baltic Fleet in March 1941 (54).

10. Ibid., 54.

11. S. V. Stepashin, ed., *Organy Gosudarstvennoy Bezopastnosti SSSR v Velikoy Ote-chestvennoy Voine* (Moscow, 1995), book 1, 189.

12. Zyrianov, *Pogranichnye Voiska SSSR*, 302.

13. Sechkin, *Granitsa i Voina*, 54–55.

14. Zyrianov, *Pogranichnye Voiska SSSR*, 306–07.

15. Yakovlev, *1941 god*, book 1, 326–27.

16. Zyrianov, *Pogranichnye Voiska SSSR*, 364.

17. The material on Starshina's reporting in this section is taken from Yakovlev, *1941 god*, book 1, 550, 769–70, and book 2, 89–90, 180.

18. In the original report, Oranienburg was said to be "near Bremen." Actually, it is just north of Berlin, which makes sense for a photo reconnaissance unit whose product would be eagerly awaited by photo interpreters in the Air Ministry.

19. Paul Carell, *Hitler's War on Russia: The Story of the German Defeat in the East* (London, 1964), 60.

20. R. J. Sontag and J. S. Beddie, eds., *Nazi-Soviet Relations, 1939–1941*, 353–55; cited in "German Prehostilities Air Reconnaissance of Soviet Territory Prior to Invasion of June 22, 1941," Rand Memorandum RM-1349.

21. Zyrianov, *Pogranichnye Voiska SSSR*, 400–01.

22. A. G. Khorkov, *Grozovoi Iun* (Moscow, 1991), 131–35.

23. Matvie V. Zakharov, *Generalny Shatb v Predvoennye Gody* (Moscow, 1989). Zakharov died in 1972 but his memoirs were not published until 1989. Therefore, he must have written them during the period of "stagnation" under Leonid I. Brezhnev when efforts were made to rehabilitate Stalin. This may explain Zakharov's failure to cite the orders from Stalin not to interfere with German aerial reconnaissance.

24. John Erickson, *The Road to Stalingrad: Stalin's War with Germany* (New Haven, 1999), 101.

25. *Pravda*, 29 June 1941; cited in David J. Dallin, *Soviet Russia's Foreign Policy, 1939–1942* (New Haven, 1942), 365.

Chapter 17: German Deception

1. Barton Whaley, *Code Barbarossa* (Cambridge, 1974).

2. Aleksandr N. Yakovlev, ed., *1941 god* (Moscow, 1998), book 1, 661–64.

3. See the July 13, 1940, telegram from A. A. Shkvartsev, the Soviet ambassador in Berlin, reporting that Germany was preparing for a large-scale offensive against Britain (114). On September 10 Amaiak Z. Kobulov, counselor of the embassy (and NKVD foreign intelligence resident) in Berlin, met with Oskar von Niedermayer, one of Germany's long-time Russian specialists and then a consultant to the OKW, who insisted that England was Germany's main concern (222–24). A November 4 memorandum, "The Situation in Germany during the First Year of War," prepared by the Soviet embassy in Berlin described a meeting in Nürnberg devoted to colonial questions. Germany, confident of an early victory over England, expected to take over its colonies (339–40).

4. Yakovlev, *1941 god*, book 2, 195–96.

5. Oleg V. Vyshlev, *Nakanune: 22 Iiunia 1941 goda* (Moscow, 2001), 149.

6. John Keegan, *The Second World War* (New York, 1989), 171.

7. Vyshlev, *Nakanune*, 148.

8. VENONA, ref. no. 3/PPDT/T80, London to Moscow, no. 649, April 3, 1941. See also David Stafford, *Churchill and Secret Service* (Woodstock, 1997), 197–99. According to Vasily A. Novobranets, who was dismissed by Golikov and sent to a special RU rest home near Odessa, many of the officers staying there had been guilty of spreading tales of an impending German invasion. From time to time, such individuals would disappear, causing Novobranets to believe that the rest home was but a way station, with the ultimate destination the GULAG or worse.

9. German intentions were also signaled when Abwehr agents were sent into the USSR with instructions to bring back samples of Soviet fuel and lubricants to ensure they could be used in German vehicles (see ch. 13).

10. Yakovlev, *1941 god*, book 1, 181–93.

11. Ibid., 288–90.

12. See, for example, a report of January 15, 1941, in Yakovlev, *1941 god*, book 1, 538, and a May 30, 1941, report in A. P. Belozerov, ed., *Sekrety Gitlera Na Stole u Stalina* (Moscow, 1995), 135–36. These reports and others in the same period contained valid information (as most such deception did) to which the bit about Ukraine was added. The sources were often unaware that they were passing on deception.

13. Matvei V. Zakharov, *Generalny Shtab y Predvoennye Gody* (Moscow, 1989), 214–19.

14. Vyshlev, *Nakanune*, 153–60. The rumor illustrates how well the Germans coordinated their deception efforts; a visit by Stalin to Berlin was also a feature of Hitler's December 1940 and May 1941 letters to Stalin (see ch. 18).

15. Yakovlev, *1941 god*, book 2, 180–81.

16. Belozerov, *Sekrety Gitlera*, 148; Yakovlev, *1941 god*, book 2, 342–43, 382–83.

17. Whaley, *Code Barbarossa*, 171.

18. James Barros and Richard Gregor, *Double Deception: Stalin, Hitler, and the Invasion of Russia* (Dekalb, 1995), 52–57. According to Ponschab's assistant, Georg Korter, these materials were furnished by a Baltic journalist, Ivar Lissner (born Hirschfeld), who had been recruited by the Abwehr in return for its allowing his Jewish parents to leave Germany. Ostensibly, he obtained the documents from his contacts in the White Russian community, who in turn had sources in the Soviet consulate, then the largest in Harbin. There is no indication these documents were the result of code breaking by Ponschab or his staff, none of whom had the requisite expertise. When turned over to Ponschab, they were in German and appeared to be translations from Soviet diplomatic traffic in the Russian language.

19. Barros and Gregor, *Double Deception,* 171–73. In all, some twenty-four messages were found in the Weizsäcker file in German archives dating from March 6 to June 12, 1941. The contents were a mixture of truth, items invented out of whole cloth, and the occasional bit of apparently good information from Soviet intelligence sources—for example, a circular message from Moscow dated May 8 and forwarded by Ponschab on May 11 that spoke of British preparations to invade and occupy Syria, then under Vichy French control.

20. Barros and Gregor, *Double Deception,* 170–73. I asked Boris N. Labusov, head of the Public Affairs Bureau of the Russian Foreign Intelligence Service (SVR), about the details of the operation in October 2002. As of June 2003, when I again visited Moscow, no answers were forthcoming. I know from retired Lieutenant General Sergei A. Kondrashev, a former head of the KGB's disinformation service, that while the KGB (and its successor, the SVR) will speak in general terms about disinformation, it is extremely reluctant to discuss the success or failure of individual operations.

21. Barros and Gregor, *Double Deception,* 172–73. The "threat" to the Siberian railroad could have been related to the German practice of sending shipments of natural rubber to Germany from Far Eastern ports by rail. As the date for the invasion grew nearer, however, such shipments were halted.

22. William J. Spahr, *Zhukov: The Rise and Fall of a Great Captain* (Novato, 1993), 42, 47.

23. This examination is based primarily on pp. 586–813 of book 1 of *1941 god* and pp. 9–424 of book 2. This collection contains reports from NKGB and RU residencies abroad and from border troops, as well as RU Moscow periodical summaries. Timoshenko and Zhukov may have received more than are accounted for, but this could not be determined because many individual reports in *1941 god* are annotated *"Rassylka ne ukazana"* (Dissemination not indicated).

24. L. M. Chizhova, "Neslyshannye Signaly Voiny," *Istorichesky Arkhiv,* no. 2, 1995.

25. *1941 god,* book 1, 708.

26. Ibid., book 2, 175.

27. Ibid., 289–90.

28. Viktor Suvorov is the literary pseudonym of Vladimir B. Rezun, a GRU officer who defected in 1978. His book first appeared in Paris in 1988 and has since been published in a second Russian edition (Moscow, 1992) and in German and English editions.

29. The historical novelist Igor Bunich draws on the Suvorov thesis in a fictional account in which Stalin accepts Hitler's promise that he will attack England in mid-July 1941, withdrawing forces from the Soviet border for this purpose. Stalin, whose own attack would ostensibly have begun in early July, is deceived by Hitler, who invades the USSR on June 22nd (*Groza: Piatisotletniaia Voina v Rossy* [Moscow, 1997]).

30. Mikhail I. Meltiukhov, *Upushchenny Shans Stalina, Sovietski Soiuz I Borba za Evropu* (Moscow, 2002), 412; Boris Shaptalov, *Ispytanie Voinoy* (Moscow, 2002), 15, 20. Meltiukhov writes: "Political conditions for an attack against Germany by the USSR were sufficiently favorable. Unfortunately, Stalin, fearing an Anglo-German compromise, put off for at least a month the attack on Germany, which, as we now know, was the only chance to thwart the German invasion. This decision was probably Stalin's greatest historical miscalculation, forfeiting as it did the opportunity to destroy the strongest European power and, by reaching to the shores of the Atlantic Ocean, to eliminate the ancient Western threat to our country. As a result of it, the German leadership was able on June 22, 1941, to launch Operation Barbarossa, which, owing to the inability of the Red Army to defend itself, led to the tragedy of that year." Meltiukhov also criticizes Soviet intelligence for not having provided Stalin with precise information on Germany's intention to invade and the exact date of the invasion.

31. William J. Spahr, *Stalin's Lieutenants: A Study of Command under Duress* (Novato, 1997), 250.

32. E. M. Primakov and V. A. Kirpichenko, eds., *Ocherki Istory Rossyskoy Vneshnei Razvedki* (Moscow, 1997), vol. 3, 449–470.

33. Yakovlev, *1941 god*, book 1, 469–70.

Chapter 18: Secret Letters

1. Konstantin M. Simonov, "Zametki K. M. Simonova k Biografy G. K. Zhukova," *Voenno-Istorichesky Zhurnal*, no. 9, 1987, 50–51. Another reference to this correspondence is in William J. Spahr, *Zhukov: The Rise and Fall of a Great Captain* (Novato, 1993).

2. Aleksander N. Yakovlev, ed., *1941 god* (Moscow, 1998), book 2, 183–84.

3. Ibid., 193. In his *Grand Delusion: Stalin and the German Invasion of Russia* (New Haven, 1999), Gabriel Gorodetsky interprets the instructions given to Dekanozov by Stalin and Molotov (and written out in the latter's hand) as an indication of Stalin's desire to enter into correspondence with Hitler. In the event, von Schulenburg did not pursue the matter further, probably because he suspected Hitler had already made a firm decision to attack the Soviet Union and would have had little interest in a serious exchange of views with Stalin.

4. Lev Bezymensky, *Gitler i Stalin Pered Skhvatkoi* (Moscow, 2000), 470–73. Bezymensky's meeting took place at Zhukov's dacha. According to Bezymensky, Zhukov received him because he had served on Zhukov's staff in the spring of 1945 and was recommended by Zhukov's friend Konstantin Simonov.

5. Igor Bunich, *Groza: Piatisotletniaia Voina v Rossii* (Moscow, 1997), 356–58.

6. Marina Eliseeva, "Ofitsersky Korpus Politicheskoi v Politicheskoi Zhizni Rossy—Sbornik Dokumentov," *Krasnaia Zvezda*, November 26, 2003, 4. This is a review of volumes 5 and 6 of the document collection *Ofitsersky Korpus v Politicheskoi Zhizni Rossii* (Moscow, 2003), ed. Anatoli Pavlov. The Hitler letter appears in this work.

7. Bunich, *Groza*, 494–96.

8. Aleksandr Solzhenitsyn, *V Kruge Pervom* (New York, 1969), 96; cited in Spahr, *Zhukov*, 47.

9. This paragraph of the Hitler letter appears on p. 496 of Bunich's *Groza*.

10. Ibid., 492, 493.

11. Pavel Sudoplatov, *Special Tasks* (New York, 1994), 121.

12. L. G. Pavlov, "Ot 'Yunkersa' 1941 k Tsessne 1987" [From a Junkers in 1941 to a Cessna in 1987], *Voenno-Istorichesky Zhurnal*, no. 6, 1990, 43–46. This article contains the full text of Order No. 0035.

13. Ibid.

14. O. F. Suvenirov, *Tragedia RKKA, 1937–1938* (Moscow, 1998), 328, 376, 400.

15. See Dmitri Volkogonov, *Stalin: Triumph and Tragedy* (Rocklin, 1996), 277–79, for a description of Stalin's relations with others.

Chapter 19: The Purges Revived

1. RGVA, NKO Order of July 27, 1940, f. 37837, op. 4, d. 381, 51.

2. E-mail from Vyacheslav M. Lure, April 23, 2003.

3. RGVA, NKO Order of October 23, 1940, f. 37837, op. 4, d. 401, 381.

4. Alexandr N. Yakovlev, ed., *1941 god* (Moscow, 1998), book 1, 285.

5. Ibid., 342–47.

6. Alexander O. Chubaryan and Harold Shukman, *Stalin and the Soviet-Finnish War, 1939–1940* (London, 2002), 39–45, 122–27.

7. Smushkevich had been the senior Soviet air forces adviser in Spain and, despite Moscow's admonition that he was sent to Spain to lead not to fly, managed to shoot down a few German Messerschmidts. The name he used in Spain, "General Douglas," was well known to those from Göring's level down to kids in the streets of Madrid. When he returned from Spain, he was greeted as a hero. But Stalin and Voroshilov thought his patronymic, Vulfovich, was a bit too Jewish for a senior Soviet military leader. (Smushkevich was indeed Jewish, the son of a village tailor). The patronymic was accordingly changed to Vladimirovich. After performing to Zhukov's satisfaction at Khalkin Gol, he returned to Moscow to become head of the Red Army's air forces.

8. Rychagov distinguished himself as a fighter pilot in the Spanish civil war, then led a Soviet air unit in China against the Japanese. In the summer of 1938 he headed the air forces of the Far Eastern Front in their battles with the Japanese at Lake Khasan. In the Finnish war he commanded the air forces of the Ninth Army, after which he became chief of the Main Directorate of Aviation of the Red Army. Of course, his rapid rise to that position at the tender age of twenty-eight did not endear him to many of his contemporaries, but those who had served with him in Spain and China held him in special esteem.

9. Vyacheslav Rumiantsey, ed., *Khronos,* http://www.hrono.ru/biograf/rychagov.html (accessed October 13, 2004).

10. Chubaryan and Shukman, *Stalin,* 140, 144.

11. A. Ostrovsky, "Sov. Sekretno. Osobo Interesno," *Sovietsky Voin,* September 1990, 65–71.

12. Stanislav Gribanov, *Zalozhniki Vremeni* (Moscow, 1992), 159.

13. I. I. Basik et al., eds., *Glavny Voenny Soviet* (Moscow, 2004), 202–49, 423.

14. Yakovlev, *1941 god,* book 2, 54–56.

15. Dmitri Volkogonov, *Stalin: Triumph and Tragedy* (Rocklin, 1996), 375. The photocopy of the Timoshenko memorandum to Stalin between pp. 260–61 is unusually clear and sharp.

16. O. F. Suvenirov, *Tragedia RKKA, 1937–1938* (Moscow, 1998), 381.

17. A. A. Pechenkin, "Vozdushny As, Nachalnik Voennoi Razvedki, 'Zagovorshchik,'" *Voenno-Isorichesky Zhurnal,* no. 1, 2004, 32.

18. Aleksandr Bondarenko, "Aviatsia Prodolzhaet Otstavat'," *Krasnaia Zvezda,* February 19, 2002.

19. Pechenkin, "Vozdushny As," 32.

20. Suvenirov, *Tragedia RKKA,* 398.

21. AP RF, op. 24, d. 378, 203.

22. Ibid., 202.

23. Http://stalin.memo.ru/spiski/pg15202.htm.

24. AP RF, op. 24, d. 378, 199.

25. A. A. Pechenkin, "Cherny Den Krasnoy Army," *Novoe Voennoe Obozrenie,* February 21, 2003. Mikheev had served in the special departments of the NKVD before a military counterintelligence directorate was established within the Defense Commissariat. The arrangement lasted until July 1941, when military counterintelligence was returned to the NKVD. Mikheev was killed in action with the Southwest Front in September 1941. See S. V. Stepashin, *Organy Gosudarstvennoy Bezopastnost: SSSR V Velikoy Otechestvennoy Voine* (Moscow, 1995), book 1, 231.

26. Pechenkin, "Cherny." See also Suvenirov, *Tragedia RKKA,* 81.

27. AP RF, f. 3, op. 24, d. 378, 201, 199, 204, 203.

28. Ibid., 199.

29. Suvenirov, *Tragedia RKKA*, 376. See also Aleksandr Utkin, "Vse Nachalos s Avi-audarov," *Novoe Voennoe Obozrenie*, no. 2, 2001, 1, and Vyacheslav Rumiantsev, ed., *Khronos*, http://www.hrono.ru/biograf/shtern.html (accessed October 13, 2004).

30. Boris L. Vannikov, "Zapiski Narkoma," *Znamia*, 1988, nos. 1 and 2.

31. Suvenirov, *Tragedia RKKA*, 381. See also Nadezhda Shunevich, http://www.facts.Kiev.ua/April2002/1604/05.htm, and N. G. Kuznetsov, "Krutye Povoroty: Iz Zapisok Admirala," http://glavkom.narod.ru/kruto10.htm.

32. Basik et al., *Glavny*, 345–54.

33. AP RF, f. 3, op. 24, d. 378, 197; Suvenirov, *Tragedia RKKA*, 376.

34. A. Ostrovsky, "Sov. Sekretno. Osobo Interesno," *Sovietsky Voin*, September 1990, 71.

35. RGVA, f. 37976, op. 1, d. 523, 74.

36. Pechenkin, "Cherny."

Chapter 20: On the Eve

1. A. Ostrovsky, "Sov. Sekretno. Osobo Interesno," *Sovietsky Voin*, September 1990, 71.

2. Aleksandr N. Yakovlev, ed., *1941 god* (Moscow, 1998), book 2, 383.

3. Vladimir Petrov, *June 22, 1941* (Columbia, 1968), 204.

4. Harrison E. Salisbury, *The 900 Days: The Siege of Leningrad* (New York, 1969), 15.

5. F. Volkov, "The Coded Messages Sat in the Archives," *Krasnaia Zvezda*, December 23, 1989, 4.

6. S. V. Stepashin, ed., *Organy Gosudarstvennoy Bezopastnosti SSSR v Velikoy Otechestvennoy Voine* (Moscow, 1995), book 2, 252–53. See also V. A. Zolotarev and G. N. Sevostianov, eds., *Velikaia Otechestvennaia Voina, 1941–1945* (Moscow, 1998), book 1, 114.

7. A. N. Mertsalov and L. A. Mertsalova, *Stalinizm i Voina* (Moscow, 1994), 247.

8. Ostrovsky, "Sov. Sekretno," 71. As a result of Proskurov's order, none of the Seventh Army's aircraft were damaged when the Germans attacked.

9. Yakovlev, *1941 god*, book 2, 382–83.

10. Ibid., 298–301. See also Roy A. Medvedev, "I.V. Stalin v Pervye Dni Velikoy Otechestvennoy Voiny," *Novaia I Noveishaia Istoria*, March–April 2002, 118.

11. Stepashin, *Organy*, 249–50.

12. Eduard Sharapov, "One Hundred Hours until War," *Krasnaia Zvezda*, June 22, 1994. See also E. M. Primakov and V. A. Kirpichenko, *Ocherki Istory Rossyskoy Vneshnei Razvedki* (Moscow, 1997), vol. 3, 452.

13. Primakov and Kirpichenko, *Ocherki*, vol. 3, 452. It is doubtful that Yelena Modrzhinskaia was in this group. She was in Warsaw with her husband, Petr I. Gudimovich, NKGB resident under Soviet property official cover. They did not return to Moscow until after the war began.

14. Ibid.

15. Stepashin, *Organy*, 254–64. See Yakovlev, *1941 god*, book 2, 333, for Merkulov's instructions to Fitin for using a June 5, 1941, Belorussian NKGB report in a summary information report to the CC VKP(b).

16. Primakov and Kirpichenko, *Ocherki*, 338–54. Among the other advances by Germany's defense industries on which Lehmann reported were tank transporters, self-propelled artillery, production of all-metal fighters on conveyor belts, and large-scale production of submarines (Teodor Gladkov, http://www.avtoradio.ru/?an=arweek&uid=26016 [accessed June 15, 2004]).

17. Primakov and Kirpichenko, *Ocherki*, 348. The SVR history is silent on what hap-

pened to this report. The statement that Lehmann's report was considered "false and a provocation" appears p. 454 of A. Kolpakidi and D. Prokhorov's *Vneshniaia Razvedka Rossii* (Moscow, 2001). The Lehmann report does not appear in *1941 god*, which means that it was not among the documents Russian intelligence and security archivists gave the compilers. According to Igor A. Damaskin, a retired SVR colonel, because the report was sent via Ambassador Dekanozov's channel, it is not in SVR archives and either had been lost or was destroyed by Beria (*Stalin i Razvedka* [Moscow, 2004], 263, 264]).

18. Memorandum, Hqs Region XI CIC to Hqs 66th CIC Detachment, November 28, 1949. Declassified April 28, 2004, under Nazi War Crimes Disclosure Act, PL 105-246.

19. Aleksandr Chudodeev, "Chelovek iz 'Gruppy Ya,'" *Itogi*, July 5, 2001.

20. Primakov and Kirpichenko, *Ocherki*, 366. See also p. 423 for a June 22 NKGB report from London, the source of which was probably a member of the Cambridge Five with access to British intelligence. The report confirmed the Ostvald report and noted the presence of two German infantry divisions in the Rovaniemi area, with a third en route from Oslo.

21. Primakov and Kirpichenko, *Ocherki*, 380.

22. Ibid., 398–99.

23. Golikov's article appeared in *International Affairs*, October 10, 1969.

24. Primakov and Kirpichenko, *Ocherki*, 399.

25. David M. Glantz, *Stumbling Colossus: The Red Army on the Eve of World War* (Lawrence, 1998), 25, 26. See also Yakovlev, *1941 god*, book 2, 215–20, 280.

26. Glantz, *Stumbling Colossus*, 103.

27. Primakov and Kirpichenko, *Ocherki*, 341, 346.

28. Medvedev, "I. V. Stalin," 118.

29. Zolotarev and Sevostianov, *Velikaia*, 120.

30. Yakovlev, *1941 god*, book 2, 376–77.

31. Ibid., 387–88; 392–93.

32. Ibid., 413–14. See also William J. Spahr, *Zhukov: The Rise and Fall of a Great Captain* (Novato, 1993), 53–54.

33. Yakovlev, *1941 god*, book 2, 422.

34. Ibid., 495–96. Mikoyan's account offers another example of the problem of accepting the Kremlin visitor lists as wholly accurate. The log for June 21 does not include Mikoyan yet it is quite evident that he was present with other Politburo members that evening.

35. Yakovlev, *1941 god*, book 2, 604.

36. Zolotarev and Sevostianov, *Velikaia*, 129.

37. Yakovlev, *1941 god*, book 2, 423.

38. Ibid., 300.

Chapter 21: A Summer of Torture

1. "Moskve Krichali o Voine," *Voenno-Istorichesky Zhurnal*, June 1994, 24.

2. Aleksandr N. Yakovlev, ed., *1941 god* (Moscow, 1998), book 2, 432.

3. John Erickson, *The Road to Stalingrad: Stalin's War with Germany* (New Haven, 1999), 124. See also Yakovlev, *1941 god*, book 2, 431; for reasons unknown, this version of Directive No. 2 omits the sentence in the first paragraph ordering troops not to cross the frontier without special authorization.

4. Viktor Anfilov, *Doroga k Tragedii Sorok Pervogo Goda* (Moscow, 1997), 244–45.

5. Yakovlev, *1941 god*, book 2, 495–96.

6. P. N. Kryshevsky, ed., *Skrytaia Pravda Voiny: 1941 God* (Moscow, 1992), 51–58.

7. William J. Spahr, *Zhukov: The Rise and Fall of a Great Captain* (Novato, 1993), 53–56.

8. Kryshevsky, *Skrytaia Pravda Voiny,* 149.

9. Dmitri Volkogonov, *Stalin: Triumph and Tragedy* (Rocklin, 1996), 190. See also Mikhail Boltunov, "Komandarma Arestoval Ofitsera GRU," *Nezavisimoe Voennoe Obozrenie,* No. 43, 2003, 7. This article is based on notes made by the late Colonel General Khadzhi-Umar Dzh. Mamsurov, a GRU sabotage specialist who had served in Spain and was ordered by Voroshilov in July 1941 to arrest Pavlov. Boltunov suggests that Pavlov was not a "victim of circumstances" or "scapegoat" for "Stalin's shortsightedness with regard to the Fascist regime," that his fate was due to his own shortcomings. The article reflects the continuing controversy in Russia over Stalin's responsibility for Soviet losses in the war.

10. V. A. Zolotarev and G. N. Sevostianov, eds., *Velikaia Otechestvennaia Voina, 1941–1945* (Moscow, 1998), book 1, 137. See also Anfilov, *Doroga,* 226. As for the reasons for Kopets's suicide, it should be remembered that he was a Spanish civil war volunteer who appeared to be close to the leadership and on his way up. He was the head of the April 1940 discussion session on the Finnish campaign in which Ivan I. Proskurov and Stalin clashed. He must have been aware of the recent arrests of air force officers with Spanish civil war service, and he may well have feared retribution by Stalin and Beria. His replacement, A. I. Taiursky, is reported to have been arrested along with other air force officers. See L. L. Batekhin, *Vozdushnaia Moshch Rodiny* (Moscow, 1988), 204.

11. Anfilov, *Doroga,* 225–26. Chernykh was also a Spanish civil war volunteer pilot.

12. See Volkogonov, *Stalin,* 193.

13. Spahr, *Zhukov,* 54. See also Zolotarev and Sevostianov, *Velikaia,* 146.

14. Zolotarev and Sevostianov, *Velikaia,* 149.

15. O. F. Suvenirov, *Tragedia RKKA, 1937–1938* (Moscow, 1998), 376.

16. F. Ia. Tutushkin, Assistant Chief of the Third Directorate, NKO, to State Defense Committee, Attention: Comrade Stalin, July 8, 1941.

17. Yakovlev, *1941 god,* book 2, 467.

18. Kryshevsky, *Skrytaia Pravda Voiny,* 132–33, 265–67.

19. Harrison E. Salisbury, *The 900 Days: The Siege of Leningrad* (New York, 1969), 116–17; Yakovlev, *1941 god,* book 2, 441. See also http://wwii-soldat.narod.ru/merets.htm (accessed May 11, 2003).

20. "Pismo iz Lefortovo," *Trud,* December 14, 2001.

21. Suvenirov, *Tragedia RKKA,* 381, 460.

22. A. I. Gribkov, ed., *Istoria Ordena Lenina Leningradskogo Voennogo Okruga* (Moscow, 1974), 189–90; Yu. Nevakivi, "Finliandia i Plan 'Barbarossa,'" *Voina i Politika 1939–1941,* ed. A. O. Chubarian and G. Gorodetsky (Moscow, 2000), 454.

23. A. Ostrovsky, "Sov. Sekretno. Osobo Interesno," *Sovietsky Voin,* September 1990, 70.

24. Yakovlev, *1941 god,* book 2, 428–30.

25. AP RF, f. 3, op. 24, d. 377, 116–36; d. 420, 1–68. Cited in the "Stalinskie Spiski" (Stalin lists) of the Russian Society Memorial.

26. Suvenirov, *Tragedia RKKA,* 200–11; *Izvestia TsK KPSS,* no. 3, 1989, 140; cited in Suvenirov, 200.

27. S. V. Stepashin, ed., *Organy Gosudarstvennoy Bezopasnosti SSSR v Velikoy Otechestvennoy Voine* (Moscow, 1995), book 1, 3–8.

28. Ibid., 9.

29. *Izvestia TsK KPSS,* no. 3, 1989, 145; cited in Suvenirov, *Tragedia RKKA,* 214.

30. TsA MO, f. 32, op. 701 323, d. 38, 14–16; cited in Dmitri Volkogonov, *Stalin: Triumph and Tragedy* (Rocklin, 1996), 339.

31. "Vykhod Iz Labirinta: Yevgeny A. Gnedin i O Nem," http://www.memo.ru/history/diss/books/gnedin/memorial (accessed July 5, 2004). Gnedin was the son of Lenin's contemporary Aleksandr Lazarevich Helphand (Parvus). He was sentenced to ten years in the GULAG, served from 1941 to 1949, then spent until 1955 in exile in central Kazakhstan, after which he was rehabilitated. Until his death in 1983, he was an active human rights dissident. See also AP RF, f. 3, op. 23, d. 421.

32. "Kratkie Biografii i Posluzhnye Spiski Rukovodyashchikh Rabotnikov NKVD," http://www.memo.ru/nkvd/kto/biogr/gb79.htm (accessed November 11, 2003). Vlodzimirsky ended his service as head of the Investigative Unit for Especially Important Cases of the MVD (the former NKVD). He was arrested on July 17, 1953, and shot on December 23 of that year.

33. Http://ibooks.h1.ru/books/Antonov/001/010.html (accessed February 24, 2004).

34. Http://lib.bigmir.net/read.php?e=6375 (accessed November 11, 2003).

35. Igor Bunich, *Groza: Piatisotletniaia Voina v Rossii* (Moscow, 1997), 541–42. For a vivid description of the Sukhanovka prison, see Aleksandr Solzhenitsyn, *The Gulag Archipelago* (London, 1974), 181–84.

36. Yu. B. Rubtsov, *Marshaly Stalina* (Rostov-Na-Donu, 2000), 301.

37. Ibid. My description of investigative techniques does not do justice to the full repertoire available to the interrogators. For this, see Solzhenitsyn's *Gulag Archipelago*, which describes thirty-one different methods of torture, from the psychological to the physical, used by NKVD interrogators (103–17)

38. Aleksandr N. Yakovlev et al., eds., *Reabilitatsia: Kak Ehto Bylo. Dokumenty Presidiuma KPSS i Drugiie Materialy* (Moscow, 2000), 164–66.

39. Http://www.samara.ru/paper/41/3713/61137/. After her father's arrest, Smushkevich's daughter, Rosa, wrote to Stalin asking for his help. Stalin sent her letter to Beria, who saw her in his Liubianka office. There he told her not to worry: "You know your father's not guilty." Three days later Beria ordered the arrest of the fourteen-year-old as "the daughter of an enemy of the people." She and her mother were exiled to Kazakhstan where they spent the next thirteen years.

40. Rubtsov, *Marshaly Stalina*, 301.

41. Aleksandr Bondarenko, "Aviatsiya Prodolzhaet Otstavat'," *Krasnaia Zvezda*, February 19, 2002.

Chapter 22: The Final Reckoning

1. Paul Carell, *Hitler's War on Russia: The Story of the German Defeat in the East* (London, 1964), 102; http://www.facts.kiev.ua/April2002/1604/05.htm.

2. Alan Bullock, *Hitler and Stalin: Parallel Lives* (New York, 1993), 687. Stalin's "scorched earth" policy, announced by him in a radio address on July 3, 1941, called on the inhabitants of areas occupied by the Germans to remove or destroy anything that could be of use to the occupiers, such as railroad rolling stock, stores of grain or petroleum products, cattle, etc.

3. John Keegan, *The Second World War* (New York, 1989), 196; John Erickson, *The Road to Stalingrad: Stalin's War with Germany* (New Haven, 1999), 207–10.

4. A. Ostrovsky, "Sov. Sekretno. Osobo Interesno," *Sovietsky Voin*, September 1990, 71.

5. P. N. Kryshevsky, ed., *Skrytaia Pravda Voiny: 1941 God* (Moscow, 1992), 168–73.

6. Ibid.

7. A. Kopeikin, "Salud, Piloto Russo," *Aviatsia i Kosmonavtika*, no. 12, 1989, 31.

8. Erickson, *Road to Stalingrad*, 220–22.

9. Ostrovsky, "Sov. Sekretno," 71. See also Arkady Vaksberg, *Neraskrytye Tainy* (Moscow, 1993), 61.

10. Vaksberg, *Neraskrytye Tainy*, 61. See also A. A. Pechenkin, "Cherny Den Krasnoy Army," *Novoe Voennoe Obozrenie*, February 21, 2003, and http://memo.ru/intro1.htm (accessed September 16, 2003).

11. Vaksberg, *Neraskrytye Tainy*, 63.

12. Sergei Kononov, "Kto rasstrelival v NKVD," http://www.agentura.ru/dossier/russia/people/kononov/rasstrel/print (accessed February 24, 2004).

13. Vaksberg, *Neraskrytye Tainy*, 65; http://litcatalog.al.ru/slovar/k.html (accessed May 12, 2004). As of this writing, neither the RF Ministry of Defense nor the FSB has made available an official list of all those who were shot without trial on October 28, 1941. Vaksberg's list has been checked against the attachment "Martirolog RKKA, 1936–1941" to O. F. Suvenirov's *Tragedia RKKA* and is believed to be the most accurate available.

14. Http://www.facts.kiev.ua/April2002/1604/05.htm. See also http://ng.netroad.ru/archive226/news10.htm (accessed March 2, 2004). There are no archival references to support the claim that Rodos made this telephone call.

15. Statement by Galina Ivanovna Proskurov, RGVA, f. 37976, op. 1, d. 523, 159; telephone interviews with Lidia Ivanovna, October 2002, February 2003. See also Viktor Bochkarev, *60 Let v GRU* (Moscow, 2003), 32–34.

16. Pechenkin, "Cherny." The names of all those who were tried on February 13, 1941, and executed on February 23 are contained in Memorial's Stalin lists.

17. David Holloway, *Stalin and the Bomb* (New Haven, 1994), 105, 107, 116.

18. Interview with Sergei A. Kondrashev, August 11, 2003.

19. "Znai Nashhikh-Tsentralny Evreisky Resurs," http://www.sem40.ru/cgi-bin/fammopus.pl?action=print&id=792&mode=mat (accessed November 3, 2003). Fitin rented a room near the Palashevsky market and had to unload his own coal for heating.

20. A. Kolpakidi and D. Prokhorov, *Imperia GRU* (Moscow, 1999), book 1, 112–13. The assignment may have had to do with the Soviet discovery that the best source of badly needed uranium for Stalin's bomb was in the Soviet zone of Germany, but that is conjecture.

21. Ibid. See also T. V. Samolis, ed., *Veterany Vneshnei Razedki (Kratky Biografichesky Spavochnik)* (Moscow, 1995), 153–55.

22. Gabriel Gorodetsky, "Filipp Ivanovich Golikov," *Stalin's Generals*, ed. Harold Shukman (New York, 1993), 77–88.

23. Ibid., 118–19, 84–86. See also the excerpts from Khrushchev's memoirs in *Voprosy Istory*, no. 12, 1990, 84–92.

24. VENONA, Moscow to London, nos. 1630, 1618, January 1, 1947 ("Golikov Comments on Anglo-Soviet Repatriation Discussions and Gives Guidance to Soviet Officials in Germany"). As one who observed Soviet repatriation officers at work in Germany in the summer of 1945, I agree that it was indeed difficult to persuade Soviet displaced persons to return once their minds were made up to stay in the West.

25. William J. Spahr, *Stalin's Lieutenants: A Study of Command under Duress* (Novato, 1997), 200–02.

26. Ibid., 259.

27. Gorodetsky, "Golikov," 87.

28. Interview with Lidia Ivanovna, Moscow, May 11, 2004.

Conclusion

1. For the best picture of Soviet espionage in Great Britain in this period, see Nigel West and Oleg Tsarev, *The Crown Jewels: The British Secrets at the Heart of the KGB Archives* (New Haven, 1999). In *Stalin i Razvedka* (Moscow, 2004), Igor A. Damaskin presents various reports from American, British, German, French, Polish, and Japanese sources on the anti-Soviet machinations of various European states in the same time frame. For example, Stalin was shown a report in February 1937 claiming that France and England would pressure the Soviet Union to agree to a liberal-conservative coalition in Spain as a means of ending the civil war lest it spread to other states in Europe. Otherwise, they would seek an agreement with Germany and Italy (171–72).

2. Konstantin Umansky, the Soviet ambassador to the United States, outdid himself in this regard when, after a meeting with Undersecretary of State Sumner Welles in late May 1941, he told the press: "Information presented to the Soviet Union in London and Washington is directed toward the goal of provoking a conflict between Germany and the USSR" (Damaskin 262–63).

3. Viktor Anfilov, *Doroga k Tragedii Sorok Pervogo Goda* (Moscow, 1997), 193.

4. Ibid., 190. See also Konstantin M. Simonov, "Zametki K. M. Simonov k Biografii G. K. Zhukov," *Voenno-Istorichesky Zhurnal*, no. 9, 1987, 54.

5. Martin Amis, *Koba the Dread* (London, 2002), and Miklos Kun, *Stalin: An Unknown Portrait* (Budapest, 2003).

Appendix 1: Organization and Functions of Soviet Military Intelligence

1. At this time Soviet missions abroad were called "political representations" (*polpredstva*) rather than "embassies" to distinguish them from the diplomatic missions of capitalist nations.

2. Robert Whymant, *Stalin's Spy: Richard Sorge and the Tokyo Espionage Ring* (New York, 1998), 105–06.

3. See Aleksandr N. Yakovlev, ed., *1941 god* (Moscow, 1998), book 1, 219. See also no. 227.

4. Mikhail I. Meltiukhov, "Sovietskaia Razvedka i Problema Vnezapnogo Napadenia," *Otechestvennaia Istoria*, no. 3, 1998, 3–20.

5. V. P. Pavlov, "Moskve Krichali o Voice," *Voenno-Istorichesky Zhurnal*, no. 6, 1994, 21–26.

6. V. Novobranets, "Nakanune Voiny," *Znamia*, no. 6, 1990, 165–92.

7. Yakovlev, *1941 god*, book 1, 42–43.

8. S. L. Savin, ed., *Armia i Politika* (Kaluga, 2002), book 5, 521–22.

9. Vladimir Lota, "Sekretny Front Generalnogo Shtaba" *Krasnaia Zvezda*, November 2, 2002, 1, 4, 5.

Index